MEMORY DEVELOPMENT:
Universal Changes and Individual Differences

MEMORY DEVELOPMENT:
Universal Changes and Individual Differences

Edited by

FRANZ E. WEINERT
Max Planck Institute for
Psychological Research
Munich, West Germany

MARION PERLMUTTER
University of Michigan

LEA LAWRENCE ERLBAUM ASSOCIATES, PUBLISHERS
1988   Hillsdale, New Jersey   Hove and London

Lawrence Erlbaum Associates, Inc., Publishers
365 Broadway
Hillsdale, New Jersey 07642

Library of Congress Cataloging in Publication Data

Memory development : universal changes and individual differences /
edited by Franz E. Weinert, Marion Perlmutter.
p.   cm.
Bibliography: p.
Includes index.
ISBN 0-8058-0148-0
1. Memory.   I. Weinert, Franz E., 1930–   . II. Perlmutter,
Marion.
BF371.M454   1988
153.1--dc19   88-11143
                                                           CIP

Printed in the United States of America
10 9 8 7 6 5 4 3 2 1

Contents

Contributors

BAKER, J. G., Cornell University
BAKER-WARD, Lynne, North Carolina State University
BORKOWSKI, John G., University of Notre Dame
BRONFENBRENNER, Uri, Cornell University
BÜCHEL, Fredi P., Université de Genève, Switzerland
CECI, Stephen John, Cornell University
CHI, Michelene T. H., University of Pittsburgh
DENHIÈRE, Guy, Université de Paris-Sud, France
DIXON, Roger, University of Victoria
ELLIOTT-FAUST, Darlene J., University of Western Ontario
VON EYE, Alexander, The Penn State University
FLAMMER, August, Universität Bern, Switzerland
FORREST-PRESSLEY, Donna, University of Western Ontario
HALE, Catherine, University of Notre Dame
HERTZOG, Christopher, Georgia Institute of Technology, Atlanta
HUDSON, Judith, State University of New York at Albany
HUSSY, Walter, University of Trier, Germany
KNOPF, Monika, MPI für psychologische Forschung, München, Germany
KÖRKEL, Joachim, Fachklinik Hillersbach, Germany
LÜTHI, Ruth, University of Bern, Switzerland
MILSTEAD, Matt, University of Notre Dame
NAUS, Mary J., University of Houston
NELSON, Katherine J., City University of New York
ORNSTEIN, Peter A., University of North Carolina
PARIS, Scott G., University of Michigan
PERLMUTTER, Marion, University of Michigan
PRESSLEY, Michael, University of Western Ontario

SCHNEIDER, Wolfgang, MPI für psychologische Forschung, München, Germany
VERDONIK, Frederick, University of Michigan
WELLMAN, Henry M., University of Michigan
WEINERT, Franz E., MPI für psychologische Forschung, München, Germany

Preface

As several books on the development of memory have been published during the last few years, one may ask why it is necessary to present just another volume on this topic. In our view, there are at least three different reasons justifying our decision to publish this book. First, we consider it practical to jointly present different methodological and theoretical approaches in a single book. Second, we think it useful to not only emphasize the merits of current research but also identify its specific shortcomings, and deficiencies. Critical evaluations of this sort can be found in several chapters of this book. Finally, we think it particularly necessary to treat a topic that has been typically neglected in the field. That is, we believe that more emphasis should be given to the analysis of universal changes and individual differences in memory development. In this book, we try to describe important recent research trends and to evaluate their major outcomes, thus providing a picture of the state-of-the-art that may stimulate and regulate future research.

Undoubtedly, there are still many problems to solve in the field of memory development. As memory is of central significance for human development, it is particularly important to find valid scientific answers to open questions. Memory is a prerequisite for the development of thinking, and is in turn affected by advances in intelligent information processing. The development of memory is not only the result of universal changes in cognitive competencies but also depends on cultural, social, and personal experiences. Conversely, memory development can be seen as a necessary prerequisite for the emergence of collective knowledge and the acquisition of shared meanings within a cultural group. Although studies into the development of memory predominantly represent basic research, there are various possibilities to apply their results. What is needed now is not only more research, but also a good memory of what has been investigated in the past and new, fresh ideas about what should be studied next. This is exactly what this book offers to the reader.

All chapters of this volume are based on papers that were presented at a conference sponsored by the Max-Planck-Society and held at Castle Ringberg (West Germany). We wish to thank the authors for thoroughly revising their presentations, and also all those who assisted in preparing and completing the manuscript.

Franz E. Weinert
Marion Perlmutter

THE DEVELOPMENT OF MEMORY STRATEGIES

1 The Early Development of Memory Strategies

Henry M. Wellman
University of Michigan

> *Mnemonic activities necessary for proficient recall are not yet under planful or effective control by age 4 (Perlmutter & Myers, 1979, p. 83).*
>
> *The memory processing of young preschool children has been described as nonstrategic, nonplanful and nondeliberate and the results of this study have shown that these earlier descriptions seem largely accurate (Ratner, 1980, p. 64).*
>
> *Preschoolers rarely use mnemonic strategies to aid remembering and instead rely on their natural activities of understanding of object-event relations to mediate recall (Paris & Lindauer, 1983, p. 335).*

Memory strategies figure prominently in research into, and explanations for, memory development in older children and adults. However, the acquisition and development of such strategies are seldom invoked to account for memory developments in younger children, before the age of 6 or 7 years.

In the 1970s the generally accepted view of memory development was that increases in memory performance from about age six on were largely due to the older child's increasing propensity to employ deliberate memory strategies to aid both storage and retrieval. Conversely, children younger than this were thought to be nonstrategic in memory endeavors. This characterization of the young child received direct and indirect support from four sources. Soviet theory and research described the memory activities of young children as involuntary, not voluntary (Smirnov & Zinchenko, 1969). In North America young children were similarly described as generally production deficient (Flavell, 1970). Direct data on the presence of memory strategies were abundant for older children but were absent for preschoolers (e.g., Appell, Cooper, McCarrel, Sims-Knight, Yussen,

& Flavell, 1972). And finally, that memory strategies first appeared at around school age fit well with cross-cultural research on schooling itself. In this research (e.g., Wagner, 1978) it seemed that the increased memory demands placed on Western children entering into formal educational arrangements provoked strategic attempts to remember.

Starting in the mid 1970s, however, demonstrations of the employment of certain memory-like strategies by quite young children began to appear (see Wellman, 1977a). Yet, such demonstrations have had little impact on our basic views of memory development. At best, descriptions of memory development now make passing note of some early, limited strategic attempts to remember. Why do strategy accounts of memory development loom large for school age children but not for preschoolers? I believe this is because the strategic-looking memory activities of young children are seen as suspect on four grounds. Specifically, young children's putative memory strategies are (1) thought to be not really strategic, but instead manifestations of nondeliberate, involuntary response repertoires. Or, if strategic, they are (2) thought to be not mnemonic; they might be deliberate attempts to do something, but not specifically to remember. Or, if strategic and mnemonic, they are (3) thought to be limited and infrequent—limited to only quite helpful situations and thus occurring in the natural life of a child quite rarely. Finally, as a consequence of these limitations, memory strategies in young children are (4) thought to be insignificant in any explanatory sense: that is, the observed changes in memory performance over this age range are not seen as resulting from changes in strategy employment and effectiveness.

I argue that young children's memory activites *are* strategic, *are* mnemonic, *are* frequent, and that changes in memory performance in the preschool years *are* dependent on strategy developments. Thus, accounts of strategy development are no less (and no more) important for understanding early memory developments, past infancy, than for understanding later memory developments, past kindergarten.

ARE PRESCHOOLERS STRATEGIC IN MEMORY TASKS?

An answer to this question requires some definition of the construct strategic. This is a concept that is widely and variously employed. I begin my discussion with a strict specification of what constitutes a strategy as well as what evidence is required to attribute such strategies to children (see Wellman, 1977a), and examine whether preschoolers' memory activities are ever of that sort. Then I relax this definition and criteria, in hopes of capturing more fully the character and breadth of young children's strategic enterprises.

Sometimes the term strategy is used to refer to any procedures, or rule, or regularity that an organism might evidence in processing information. In this usage the term strategy is simply identical with systematic information processing. In common parlance, however, the term strategy more narrowly denotes some routine or procedure *deliberately* employed to achieve some end. This makes the term strategy distinctive, and this perspective on strategies is the most common one in the developmental literature (Flavell, 1970; Wellman, 1977a; Naus & Ornstein, 1983). In my usage, therefore, strategies include only deliberate or intentional attempts to help oneself, e.g., to help oneself remember. As such, defining and diagnosing memory strategies is based on defining and diagnosing deliberate or intentional behavior. This in turn is based on a means-ends analysis of behavior. A memory strategy invokes one behavior or activity—a means—to influence remembering—the end. The means include anything one might do that aids memory—like rehearsal. The ends include various acts of remembering–storing items for future use, retrieving items now, both storage for or current attempts at recognition, reconstruction, or recall. Does demonstrating that young children engage in the relevant means-end activity provide sufficient evidence to conclude that they behave strategically? That is, is it sufficient to demonstrate that the child produced an appropriate means and it resulted in the end? No, because the means, while appropriate and effective, could have been produced accidentally or incidentally, i.e., produced *not* as a result of an intention to achieve the goal, but as a byproduct of some other goal or some habitual response to the situation. To be a strategy, the means must be employed deliberately, with some awareness, in order to produce or influence the goal.

How can we tell whether a strategic-seeming behavior is indeed strategic? An important diagnostic method here is the "differentiation" experiment.

In studies of memory development to date one part of the procedures has always been to instruct the subject to remember. With this type of approach, the assessment of [proper intention] requires that the subject be instructed in a memory goal and that he (or a control group) be given a number of alternative instructions in similar situations to control for habitual production, production due to misunderstanding of the instructions and other nonintentional productions. If the child engages in strategic-looking behaviors only (or especially) in the memory condition that seems good evidence that the behavior was not just incidental to the goal of remembering (Wellman, 1977a, pp. 91-92).

A full fledged differentiation experiment requires (a) contrasting conditions where subjects are instructed to remember versus are presented the same materials but given control instructions, (b) direct observation of potential strategic activities showing such activities to occur only or especially in the memory condition, and (c) evidence that the observed activities, when engaged in, appropriately aid remembering.

Are full differentiation results available for young children? Yes. For example, Wellman, Ritter, and Flavell (1975) had 3-year-olds witness a toy being hidden in one of many containers by an adult who then left the room. Upon leaving the room the adult told half of the children to "wait with the dog" and half to "remember where the dog is." During the delay period 3-year-olds engaged in more looking at and touching of the actual hiding place (target container) when instructed to remember than when instructed to wait. Perhaps more importantly, children in the remember condition at times engaged in quite dramatic strategic displays, such as the girl who pointed repeatedly to the target container shaking her head yes, while pointing to incorrect containers and shaking her head no. Or the boy who moved the target container out of position, deliberately making it distinctive for later retrieval. Children given memory instructions remember more than subjects instructed to wait, and those engaging in higher levels of strategic activity had higher levels of recall.

As another case, consider a series of studies by DeLoache and Brown with 1½- and 2-year-olds. These studies are particularly interesting because of the very young age of the children. In the prototypic DeLoache and Brown study (1979, 1983), a toy is hidden in one of several natural locations in the child's own home (e.g., a big bird doll is hidden under a chair cushion or behind a book shelf), the child is engaged in other activities for a delay of 1 to 4 minutes or so, and then has to find the toy. If children are carefully observed during the delay interval, they manifest several potentially strategic behaviors similar to those observed by Wellman et al. (1975) with somewhat older children. Some children say the name of the toy aloud ("Big bird")—often together with its location ("Big bird chair") or their future task ("find Big bird"); others look at or point to or otherwise maintain attention on the hiding place during the delay; at times they even peek at the object while it is hidden (DeLoache, Cassidy, & Brown, 1985).

Now, of course such behaviors might not be strategic. The toy, while hidden, is still salient and attractive. Specifically, these behaviors might represent only (a) partly inhibited desires to play with the toy or (b) anticipatory goal responses. The observed behaviors might only be coincidentally related to remembering, and thus might still be apparent even if children were not involved in a memory task. Fortunately, DeLoache et al. (1985) tested same-age children in two other conditions. In one, the toy was *not* hidden but placed in a visible position; yet the child's task was still to retrieve it after a delay ("get big bird after he's taken a nap"). In the other condition, the toy *was* hidden, but the experimenter rather than the child was given the task of getting the toy after a delay ("I'll get big bird after he's taken his nap"). If the previous behaviors were simply manifesting desires to play with the toy, they should occur in all three situations. If they represented anticipatory goal responses, they should occur at least in the two situations where the *child's* goal was still to get the toy. However, only when the child's task was to remember the (hidden) object did such behaviors appear with any frequency. The same behaviors were significantly rarer in the other two conditions.

Several other studies also provide complete differentiation evidence for young children. For example, Yussen (1974) showed that 4- and 5-year-olds will deliberately inspect and attend to the to-be-remembered stimuli if instructed to remember them. Children instructed to remember a model's picture selections deliberately attended to the model (and avoided watching an attractive distraction) while children given alternate nonmemory instructions rarely did so. In some recent observations, I had 3-year-olds bury a toy in a sandbox in a small room. Then they and the adult left the room "to get some more toys" down the hall. Some of the children were told they would have to remember where the toy was when they came back; some were asked if they wanted to do anything before leaving but were not told to remember. When no mention was made of remembering, children simply departed; when remembering was mentioned, they often marked the hidden toy's location by making a mark on the smooth sand, building a mound over the toy, or placing another toy directly over it. Fifty percent of the children in the remember condition marked the hidden object; only 20% in the non-remember condition did so. In addition, Heisel and Ritter (1981) gave 3- and 5-year-olds a memory for location task where the child had to hide an object in one of 196 containers arranged in a 14 x 14 container grid, and then later had to remember where the object was. In this task some locations but not others are good hiding places because they are distinctive and thus provide clear spatial cues to the object's location—for example, the corners. Five-year-olds (but not 3-year-olds) deliberately hid the objects in these corner locations—this was a deliberate memory strategy because it occurred only in a memory condition (when instructed to remember), not in a contrasting no-memory condition. In a second study, Heisel and Ritter showed that 4-year-olds also used this strategy under some conditions.

These studies demonstrate, I believe, clear strategic competence in young children. Granting the presence of early strategic activity for the moment, based on full-fledged differentiation studies, it is also informative to consider young children's strategies if our criteria for the diagnosis of strategic activity are relaxed in certain ways. There are two issues here. One is simply methodological. Studies which do not employ the full differentiation method can still present convincing evidence as to the presence of strategic memory in young children. Specifically, the presence of some sort of deliberate memory activity can be inferred even if no specific activities are directly observed. For example, Acredolo, Pick, and Olson (1975) showed improved performance when 3-, 4-, and 5-year-olds were given intentional remember instructions versus when they were not. The researchers did not, however, attempt to observe or determine what sorts of strategies may have accounted for this effect. Similarly, incidental approaches to the task can be ruled out in ways other than using contrasting instructional groups. For example, we posed 2-, 3-, and 4-year-olds the problem of reminding their parents to do something (Somerville, Wellman, & Cultice, 1983). The child was instructed, on single occasions, to remind his or her parents to do something in the future. In general, even 2-year-olds were quite successful. Of course this success might be only incidental—if instructed to remind mother to get milk at the store, for example, the child might simply incidentally "remind" mother because of his or her own interest in the item. That is, without regard to any previous instructions, when seeing milk at the store the child might instruct mother to get some because of his or her desire for milk. However, incidental successes such as this could be ruled out as accounting for our data on two grounds. First, with shorter delays (1 to 4 hours) children were substantially better than chance at reminding, *even* if instructed to remind their parent about uninteresting, undesirable items or tasks (e.g., getting the wash out of the washer, etc.). Second, children at all three ages were significantly more likely to remind their parent about an item (whether of interest to them or not) after a short delay than after a long delay (approximately 12–24 hours). If the children were not trying to remind their parent, but were instead only requesting the item because something in the immediate environment provoked or cued them to do so *at the time of retrieval,* then the amount of delay since the original request should not matter. If they were remembering to remind their parent, then of course, delay interval should influence performance. And it did.

The second issue is more substantive. There were two critical features in the definition of memory strategies advanced earlier. The first was the requirement that strategies be deliberately employed, that is engaged specifically in order to accomplish the end. The second was the requirement that to be a memory strategy, the strategy should indeed aid remembering (that is, be a means to the end). The first feature is essential: if X is not deliberately employed in order to accomplish the hoped-for end, it is not a strategy. The second requirement, however, that the strategies undertaken work, while often useful diagnostically (i.e., in assessing whether a young child is acting strategically) is not definitionally essential. Strategic endeavors that are ineffective are nevertheless strategic if appropriately intended. If we relax this second requirement, it allows consideration of *faulty strategies*—activities undertaken to influence the end but which do not. Not surprisingly, examination of faulty strategies is especially informative when considering the early, often imperfect strategy use of very young children. Let me emphasize, however, that consideration of faulty strategies is legitimized because young children's strategies are also demonstrably effective, at least some of the time. That such children sometimes deliberately use effective memory strategies, as demonstrated in full-fledged differentiation experiments, opens the door for a wider consideration of early strategies and strategy development.

It should come as no surprise that there is also considerable evidence of faulty strategy use in young children—strategic behaviors in situations where they are not useful, or strategic behaviors that don't help. This should come as no surprise because young children are quite likely (a) to be mistaken as to whether some mnemonic activity is needed or what is needed, or if not mistaken, (b) to be incapable of carrying out the activity effectively. Somewhat surprisingly, the most typical mistake children reveal is over-use of a strategy, employing a strategy even when it is not necessary. For example, in one of the Wellman et al. (1975) studies, where 3-year-olds engaged in strategic behaviors, some did so more and some less. However, in that study *all* recalled almost perfectly, even those who did very little or nothing strategic. In a later study in that series, however, the problem was made more difficult and in this case those who were more strategic indeed recalled more. Similarly in the DeLoache et al. (1985) data, in the first studies, when only one object was hidden, most children performed at ceiling whether they engaged in strategic delay behavior or not. Only when the task was made more difficult by hiding three objects simultaneously was the presence or absence of strategies clearly related to success. Faulty *over-use* of strategies strongly speaks to the young child's strategic, though not necessarily effective, approach to memory tasks.

The Heisel and Ritter (1981) research shows a different sort of faulty strategy—employing a strategy where it is needed but choosing one that is ineffective. In that study where children had to store and then to find an object in a 14 × 14 location array, 3-year-olds did not use the effective spatial strategy of storing items in the salient corner locations. However, many of the 3-year-olds did engage in a deliberate but mistaken strategy. Almost half of the 3-year-olds in the remember condition attempted to hide the item in the exact same location on each and every trial. None of the 3-year-olds in the *no*-memory condition did this. However, since 3-year-old children used the nondistinctive middle locations of the array in executing this strategy, then in spite of their efforts they typically chose wrongly at retrieval.

Early faulty strategies are also apparent in a series of studies from Peter Ornstein's lab, first reported by Newman (1980). Newman had 4- and 5-year-olds interact with a set of toys (e.g., ball, car, doll) under two conditions—either (1) when instructed "to play with them," or (2) when instructed "to remember them." First of all, the children did quite different and logical things given these instructions. In essence, when told to remember, the children studied the toys, and when told to play, they played. Specifically, more manipulating of single toys or putting two toys together into a play scene occurred when children were told to play; and more scanning all of the toys and more naming them occurred when the chijdren were told to remember. This confirms that these 4- and 5-year-olds were deliberately trying to remember; trying to change their typical approach to the toys in some deliberate and reasonable fashion, when told to remember. However, their performance on a later memory test was no better in the one condition than the other. Thus the strategies they applied were faulty— e.g., simple naming was not sufficient to really aid memory for the names (Hagen & Kingsley, 1968), although grouping and rehearsal might have been.

These conclusions were corroborated in a careful extension of this same paradigm by Baker-Ward, Ornstein, and Holden (1984). Here 4-, 5-, and 6-year-olds were shown a set of toys and instructed in three different conditions: (a) Target-Remember (told to do anything to remember a specified subset of the object names), (b) Target-Play (told to be certain to play with a specified subset of the objects), and (c) Free-Play (simply told to play with the objects). Again, naming the stimuli and visual inspection were more frequent in the Target-Remember condition at all ages, and manipulating and playing with the stimuli were more frequent in both of the play conditions. For the younger children, various strategies were once again ineffective, or faulty; recall differed across the instruction conditions only for the 6-year-olds, not for the 4- and 5-year-olds.

In order to truly understand the early development of memory strategies, considerable further research is needed into the faulty strategies of young children. What deliberate but unsuccessful attempts to help themselves do young children employ? Fortunately, a natural extension of the differentiation experiment is available to help answer this question, as evidenced in the work by Baker-Ward et al. My point for now, however, is simply that young children can and do adopt a strategic approach to memory tasks—current evidence as to both their effective and faulty strategies is sufficient to certify that they do.

ARE EARLY STRATEGIES MEMORY STRATEGIES?

Granted that young children are demonstrably strategic in memory tasks, are they engaging in *memory* strategies? There are two interwoven suspicions underlying this question.

The First Suspicion

The first suspicion concerns the proper characterization of the child's deliberate activity. For example, in the Yussen (1974) study, children did nothing more than simply look at the items. Are such very general activities really memory strategies? Instructions to remember may heighten the child's activity in certain appropriate and specific ways (that indeed differentiate between memory and nonmemory conditions), but are children really evidencing *memory* strategies? Addressing this suspicion depends, in part, on what one considers a memory strategy. Certainly to most experimental psychologists the prototypic memory strategies are those of verbal rehearsal, categorical clustering and organization, imaginal and verbal elaboration. Insisting, to begin with, on my strict definition of strategies as deliberate, minimally effective attempts to remember, then there is still very little evidence of the use by preschoolers of strategies to verbally rehearse, cluster, or elaborate.

Suppose that young children do not use rehearsal, clustering, and elaboration, are there other activites that qualify as memory strategies? I appeal here to the advice of writers of how-to-do-it memory books. In addition to discussions of peg words, coding, method of loci, and imaginal elaboration, how-to-do-it books on memory consistently advocate that their readers engage in the following mnemonic behaviors: (1) *Try;* (2) *Attend;* and (3) *Use external reminders.* For most of us this sort of advice is eminently mnemonic—these are memory strategies, things to do which will specifically enhance remembering, even if they also seem simple and obvious.

Try:

You probably do not need to be told that remembering is hard work, it takes effort to learn and remember (p. 3). One way to reduce the problem of forgetting is to make a special effort (Higbee, 1977 p. 50).

The intention to remember—simply trying to remember—does not increase recall (e.g., Hyde & Jenkins, 1969); it only influences the rememberer to do other things that increase recall. However, since one is likely to do something extra when deliberately trying to remember, then trying to recall often does increase remembering. Notice that the rememberer need not think he or she is doing anything other than trying. An effective strategy, *from his or her point of view,* can simply be one of trying harder. Quite young children will deliberately try to remember things, as the previous review of differentiation studies showed. Indeed in some studies (e.g., Somerville et al., 1983) the child may be doing little more than adopting a deliberate set to remember. Further, preschoolers state, if queried about it, that simply trying or trying harder is one of the most efficacious things one can do to remember (Wellman, Collins, & Glieberman, 1981). This may qualify as a particularly potent but partly faulty strategy of young children—something they do that works but which is much less effective than a host of more specific things to do.

Attend:

One of the fundamentals of a trained memory is what I call Original Awareness. (Lorayne & Lucas, 1974, p. 6)
If you want to remember something you must pay attention to it . . . in the first place. (Higbee, 1977, p. 50).

Young children also deliberately attend in order to remember materials. Recall the study by Yussen (1974) cited earlier. As it turns out, considerable knowledge about attention and its role in learning supports this early use of deliberate attending in order to remember. Three-year-olds know that auditory and visual distractions make remembering harder (Wellman, 1977b). Such young children know that inattention retards or defeats learning and that both external factors (noise) and internal factors (interest level) can cause this result (e.g., Miller & Zalenski, 1982).

Intentionally reattending to to-be-remembered items is also an effective mnemonic strategy. Visually reattending to stimuli was termed visual rehearsal by Wellman et al. (1975) because like verbal rehearsal it pays two dividends. It increases the possibilities for storing the items and it shortens the delay interval; one now need remember only from the new encounter until recall. Young children employ reattention as a strategy to maintain memory over a delay. In the Wellman et al. (1975) work and the DeLoache et al. (1985) studies, children periodically named the task ("find Big Bird"), looked at the hiding container, or even peeked under it to see the item. In doing so they were re-presenting the to-be-remembered information to themselves throughout the delay. Some children in the Wellman et al. study were amazingly proficient at this, such as the girl who looked and pointed repeatedly at the target container nodding yes, while also looking and pointing at nontarget containers and shaking her head no.

External Memory Strategies:

It is easy to understand why the organized person is less likely to forget things. He has unwittingly acquired the habit of applying principles of memory. For example, the organized person makes a list of things that must be done (Kellet, 1983, p. 116).

Cues.   Perhaps the premier example of an external memory strategy is the use of external retrieval cues—e.g., notes to oneself, a string around the finger, putting the mail by the door to remember to mail it. Prototypically, one sets up such cues beforehand, so that when retrieval is required encountering or inspecting the cue elicits recall. Recall that in Wellman et al. (1975) 3-year-olds at times spontaneously set up spatial cues to remember—e.g., placing their hands on the baited container, or moving it to a distinct spatial location—and did so much more often when instructed to remember than when instructed otherwise. Similarly, 3-year-olds in the sand box study mentioned previously marked the sand to remember the location of a hidden object and rarely did this if not instructed to remember. And 4- and 5-year-olds in Heisel and Ritter (1981) strategically used distinctive corner hiding locations to aid future retrieval. Further, preschoolers know quite a lot about this strategy: 3-, 4-, and 5-year-olds know, if queried, that use of such cues makes a memory task easier (Ritter, 1978; Wellman, 1977b).

It is also clear that preschoolers have certain uninformed or faulty ideas about cues as well. For example, many young children in the Ritter (1978) study agreed that having two cues at different locations when only one item was hidden was okay, as long as the correct choice was indeed marked. Similarly in a study by Gordon and Flavell (1977) in a task using multiple hidden objects each of which was to be assigned a cue, 3-year-olds judged that highly associated cues would help retrieval but also that completely unrelated cues would as well (5-year-olds discriminated between these conditions). Further, there are several later steps in the acquisition of a full understanding of retrieval cue usage that continue to develop in elementary school children (Beal, 1985; Fabricius & Wellman, 1983). Thus, use of retrieval cue strategies develops over a long age range and mistaken notions and faulty strategies are apparent early in development. Specifically, young children seem to think any cue is useful, if it rules its locale or item *into* consideration. Consequently, they fail to notice that ambiguous cues are useless, because such cues do not rule other locales or items *out*. Nonetheless, the deliberate and at times effective employment of external cues is clearly demonstrable in 3-, 4-, and 5-year-olds.

Spatial Organization.   An external memory strategy of equal importance is spatially organizing an array of items in order to keep track of them. For example, in counting a large array of items (say coins on a table) one must count each one only once. The memory task is thus one of avoiding redundancy. An effective strategy is to arrange the items spatially, e.g., in a line and simply count them in order. Like many memory strategies, this one functions to reduce the amount of remembering required, i.e., it allows one to avoid having to specifically remember each and every previously considered item.

In counting items, children as young as 2 and 3 years enumerate them in systematic, spatially adjacent fashions (Gelman & Gallistel, 1978; Potter & Levy, 1968), or even move them as they count (Gelman & Meck, 1983). Similarly, when having to search comprehensively through many locations to find an item, they search systematically, in order, and thus avoid redundant search (Wellman, Somerville, Revelle, Haake, & Sophian, 1984). An obvious question about these performances, however, concerns whether they are incidental activities—perhaps just part of automatic processes of counting and searching—or whether they are deliberate strategies employed to aid remembering. We have addressed this question with 2-, 3-, and 4-year-olds (Wellman, Fabricius & Wan, 1987). Children were given two different keeping track tasks—one where they had to put an item into each of an array of containers and one where they had to take an item out. In both tasks children indeed typically proceeded in order (e.g., going from start to finish along a spatial sequence), and doing so was highly correlated with success—that is, avoiding redundant acts. However, the take-out task, like counting adjacent items, allowed incidental use of the strategy. One could proceed in order simply on the basis of a tendency to move the hand from one container to the next via an ''adjacent neighbor'' response tendency. The put-in task, however, was designed so that incidental activities of such a sort were obstructed. In the put-in task the child was required to pick up an item from a remote bowl, put it into a container and return to the bowl for a new item. In this situation, the adjacent location to the previous one is not adjacent to the child's hand when he or she is ready to do the next act (instead his or her hand is at the bowl). Thus, an adjacent neighbor response tendency could not produce patterns of ordered spatial adjacency. Yet even for the put-in task, 3- and 4-year-olds maintained their spatial strategy (going from first to last in order) more than expected by chance. Further, evidence on children's self-corrections while executing the task confirmed that they were deliberately attempting to avoid redundancies.

In summary, denial of mnemonic strategies to young children because they do not engage in the prototypic strategies of rehearsal, elaboration, and clustering confuses strategic memory behavior *in general* with performance of a set of *specific* memory strategies. It may be true that young children do not engage in the specific strategies of verbal rehearsal, categorical clustering, or imaginal elaboration. However, they do engage in other, clear-cut memory strategies including, at the least, trying, attending, and use of external memory cues and procedures. Use of external memory cues is a specially compelling sort of mnemonic competence because it is so obviously tailored to the goal of remembering in the future. Nonetheless it is just one of several sorts of strategies attempted by young children.

The Second Suspicion

A second and related suspicion about young children's putative *memory* strategies concerns whether young children know enough about the nature of memory goals, states and processes for their strategic behaviors to qualify as mnemonic. The argument here is that since strategic behaviors require intent on the subject's part, this in turn implies some appropriate knowledge of the intended goal and the intended means. The intended goal in this case is an internal cognitive one (storing and retrieving information), so mnemonic strategy use implies some knowledge of memory—some appropriate metamemory. Let me be clear that I do *not* believe the issue in this case is whether one can show a specific and direct causal link between a specific independently assessed piece of memory knowledge and the employment of a specific related strategy (for discussion of this related issue see Wellman, 1983). Instead, the problem is simply that a child who is completely without knowledge about memory—who knows nothing about memory tasks, goals, and strategies, nothing about the distinctive features of memory as a mental endeavor as contrasted with nonmental endeavors such as looking, or contrasted with other mental endeavors such as dreaming or guessing—such a child could not be mnemonically strategic. I take this suspicion seriously; a child who is completely ignorant about memory, could not truly be employing *memory* strategies.

It is now clear, however, that even young children are reasonably knowledgable about memory and about memory processes. Certainly they are sufficiently knowledgable to discount this suspicion. One important source of information on this point concerns the young child's understanding of the term remember. Several studies are now available on preschoolers' understanding of mental verbs—for example, *remember, think, know, pretend* (Johnson & Wellman, 1980; Macnamara, Baker, & Olson, 1976; Misciones, Marvin, O'Brien, & Greenberg, 1978; Shatz, Wellman, & Silber, 1983; Wellman & Johnson, 1979). It is clear that even 2-year-olds know that these verbs refer specifically to mental activities as opposed to simply looking at or physically manipulating objects (Shatz, Wellman, & Silber, 1983; Wellman & Estes, 1987). Somewhat older children, certainly by 4-years-of-age, understand many of the distinctive features of these various mental activities.

In addition, young children's knowledge of memory processes, strategies, and variables have been studied specifically (e.g., Wellman, 1977b; Yussen & Bird, 1979), and these studies show that 3-, 4-, and 5-year-old children know a reasonable amount about memory and memory strategies. Besides just factual information, young children also evidence a capacity to monitor their own memory. Four- and 5-year-olds evidence tip of the tongue states and are demonstrably accurate at feeling of knowing judgments (Cultice, Somerville, & Wellman, 1983). Even 2-year-olds can assess the certainty of their recall (DeLoache & Brown, 1984) in some circumstances.

In short, the argument that young children are without knowledge about memory and therefore could not be engaging in explicitly knowledge-driven memory strategies, fails, because the premise is demonstrably false. Young children possess a rich store of explicit knowledge about memory.

ARE YOUNG CHILDREN'S MEMORY STRATEGIES RARE?

There are at least two ways in which children's strategies possibly could be considered rare. First, they might be limited in number—e.g., young children might only evidence a single deliberate approach to a wide variety of memory endeavors instead of being able to generate a tailored variety of strategies in numerous different situations. Second, they might be limited in accessibility—deliberate strategies might appear only in quite helpful or compelling or instructive situations. A common and strong claim in the literature has been that these differing limitations co-occur; the young child possesses an extremely limited sample of strategies and even these are only used if strongly evoked, in helpful task situations.

The first possible limitation—that young children possess only one or two deliberate strategies—has been addressed in the previous sections. There it was shown that, as a group, young children are *not* limited to a single memory strategy. Instead: they deliberately try, they spend increased study time originally, they make efforts to overcome distractions, and they use reattending throughout a delay to deliberately remember things; they also use external retrieval cues and do so in a variety of ways; and they purposefully sequence items spatially in order to remember to do all, skipping none and doing none twice. Examination of young children's mistaken strategies also corroborates the extensive rather than limited nature of children's deliberate attempts to remember. Take for example their deliberate naming of to-be-remembered stimuli (Baker-Ward et al., 1984) even though naming without rehearsal is unlikely to effect their recall (Hagen & Kingsley, 1968).

There is an important limitation to this research, of course. That is, it examines groups of children. We do not know whether single children at these ages use all or most of these techniques. However, strategy use is so ubiquitous in some of the studies reviewed that it is very unlikely that the different studies simply tap different small subgroups of children, all with a single preferred strategy. Although more research is needed, the group data is consistent with characterizations of young children as possessing a rich, generative variety of memory strategies and is inconsistent with picturing them as using single stereotyped strategies.

Perhaps, however, while extensive in variety, young children's strategies are limited to atypical, specially compelling circumstances. As a result of this sort of doubt concerning young children's competence, the procedures in several of the first studies of preschoolers' strategy use were often extremely evocative (Ritter, Kaprove, Fitch, & Flavell, 1973; Ryan, Hegion, & Flavell, 1970). For example, in the Ryan et al. study, children were first told that they would have to remember several items later and shown some picture cues which could be used to aid recall. The "cues" were, in fact, polaroid snapshots of the items themselves. It was suggested to the children that "you can use these (the potential picture cues) to help you." Then the children were given a series of increasingly explicit prompts to elicit a strategic display.

For some specific strategies such prompting *is* needed with young children but it is by no means always needed. For example, in many studies simply an unadorned instruction that the child should remember the items is all that is required (Baker-Ward et al., 1984; DeLoache et al., 1985; Somerville et al., 1983; Wellman et al., 1975; Yussen, 1974). In other cases only the slightly more directive instruction that he or she can do anything to help him- or herself remember is added. In short, little more is often needed than the simple statement that the task is a memory one, in order to inform the child of the need to be strategic. In fact, in some studies the terms memory, or remember, or remind, are not mentioned at all and the child *infers* that memory demands are present. For example, in our keeping track studies (Wellman et al., 1987), children were told simply to put an item in every container. That children employ strategies to aid remembering in such implicit memory situations argues that quite a few everyday, noncontrived circumstances evoke strategic memory efforts on their part.

It is true that many studies exist where young children do not appear strategic. I would now argue, however, that in these studies young children were strategic, but that their strategic activities were unobserved or unobservable. Thus, in a situation requiring, say, memory of a string of items over a short delay, where rehearsal is appropriate, the fact that the young child is trying harder or looking strategically is unobservable. At least it is unobservable in the absence of special measures to observe it. In short, although the young child's strategic activities are often faulty, and are sometimes less obtrusive and less specialized than older children's, nonetheless it is typical, not atypical, of children in this age range to approach the task of learning and remembering something with some sort of deliberate strategy.

In correcting past underestimations of young children's strategic prowess, I do not wish to err in the other direction by ascribing too much strategic competence to them. Young children are at times nonstrategic or at least faulty in their approach where older children and adults are more effective—witness again the young child's failure to use rehearsal, elaboration, and clustering. It would, therefore, be satisfying to end this section with a taxonomy of tasks, strategies, and situations distinguishing where and how young children are likely to be strategic and where they are not. Indeed, previously (Wellman, 1977a), I suggested a simple taxonomy of this sort; I claimed that early strategic memory was only or especially apparent in tasks requiring external memory—e.g., memory for an object's location—or external strategies—e.g., use of external retrieval cues—and not in internal tasks—e.g., memory for a string of names—or tasks requiring internal strategies—e.g., rehearsal. However, this internal–external distinction now appears to have numerous exceptions. Young children have been shown to be knowledgable and strategic in tasks which are not obviously external ones—e.g., remembering persons' names (Cultice et al., 1983) or verballing reminding others (Somerville et al., 1983). They also use some nonexternal strategies like naming (e.g., Baker-Ward et al., 1984), though the ones they use are not necessarily effective. Indeed, the paucity of information on children's faulty strategy use means, I believe, that we have too little information to proprose a reasonably sensitive taxonomic scheme.

Still, some generalizations are possible and may prove useful in the interim (see also Ornstein et al., this volume). First, the internal–external distinction still makes some sense. At the least, more success is reported with young children with these sorts of tasks than any other in the literature. However, because of this success much less attention has been directed to studying other sorts of memory tasks with young children. Second, young children's strategic remembering is particularly apparent in tasks where remembering itself is obviously instrumental—remembering in order to get a toy and play with it or remembering in order to help mom—rather than as an end in itself—remembering a list of items. If this is true, it suggests that general strategic failures when they occur (i.e., the absence of any deliberate approach to the task) may often be motivational failures, the memory test used simply did not engage the child's strategic problem solving. But it also suggests that the young child faces a special difficulty in conceiving of remembering as an end in itself rather than a subgoal of some immediately obvious larger goal (see Istomina, 1975). Finally, in terms of evoking strategy use, young children are increasingly likely to utilize a specific, effective strategy if given increasingly strong prompts (e.g., Ritter et al., 1973; Ryan et al., 1970). But the same is demonstrably true of older children and adults as well (see Brown, Bransford, Ferrara, & Campione, 1983).

Remembering—storing and retrieving information for current or future use— is a complex, multifaceted job. Young children have only some not all of the job-related skills and understanding that they need and will eventually develop in order to do this job. The current evidence is as yet insufficient to adequately characterize the exact limits of their early skills and attempts. It is sufficient, however, to claim that even preschoolers possess a relatively rich and reasonably accessible repertoire of memory strategies, rather than a severely limited one.

ARE EARLY STRATEGY DEVELOPMENTS POWERFUL?

As the previous discussion points out, I have focused primarily on what young children in general *can* do. However, striking differences occur in memory performance across the preschool years as well. Traditional verbal memory span as measured on the Stanford-Binet goes from about two items at age $2\frac{1}{2}$ to about five items at age 7 (Woodworth & Schlosberg, 1954). Although 2-year-olds are essentially perfect at recalling the location of a single item hidden in a room of their own house (DeLoache & Brown, 1983), if multiple objects are hidden, memory performance increases over the preschool years. Thus, if three objects are hidden in their homes, 2-year-olds performance (which was at ceiling with one object) falls to about 50%. And when five items were hidden on an outside playground, 3-, 4-, and 5-year-olds remembered the locations 75, 85, and 95% of the time, respectively (Wellman et al., 1984). Similarly, if 2- and 3-year-olds must remember the location of a single item hidden in one of three or four identical locations on a table top, they are essentially perfect (Wellman et al., 1975). But if given eight identical locations, 3-year-olds remember the hiding place correctly only 70% of the time (Wellman et al., 1975). And if given 144 locations, 3- and 5-year-olds are correct only about 40 and 60% of the time, respectively (Heisel & Ritter, 1982). Finally, when recalling the items in a previously presented 9-item list, $2\frac{1}{2}$-year-olds recall only about 20%, while 4-year-olds recall 40% of the names (Perlmutter & Myers, 1979). In short, very young children are far from perfect rememberers and large changes in the accuracy and strength of their memories occur in the years 2 to 6. Do strategy developments—acquisition and refinement of strategies for remembering—account for these changes in performance, at least in part?

It is sometimes said that any method of determining if factor X accounts for observed difference Y requires experimental manipulation of X, as is done in training studies. Actually the empirical process of coming to such conclusions is more complex than just conducting training studies, depending in large part on an accumulating series of plausibility demonstrations and arguments. With older children, for example, claims that increasing strategy use account for observed developmental differences in memory performance proceed as follows.

1. Subjects at two ages—younger and older—are observed to differ in some memory performance.

2. Children across the same ages are shown—by direct observation or by experimental inference—to correspondingly differ in the employment of some strategy.

3. Differences in strategy use are found to correlate directly with differences in memory performance across and within ages.

4. Finally, if younger children or nonstrategic children are induced to produce the relevant strategies, their performance improves to be similar to that of older or strategic children. Conversely if older or strategic children are inhibited from using "their" strategy, performance worsens.

With elementary school age children several different research programs have demonstrated results of exactly this cumulative sort (e.g., Chi, 1977; Flavell, 1970; Naus & Ornstein, 1983). On this basis strategy developments have seemed a powerful, though not necessarily complete, account of memory changes in older children. Unfortunately, with younger children, probably because strategies have been presumed to be rare or severely limited, much less research of this sort exists and no programmatic efforts have been undertaken to provide all steps of the argument.

However, we possess more of the needed information for young children than is generally appreciated. Across several studies much of the needed evidence in steps 1, 2, and 3 exists. First, the initial paragraph of this section summarizes some of the changes in memory performance occurring over the preschool years (step 1). Second, while above-chance strategy use exists in even young preschoolers, the same studies often show age changes in strategy use during the preschool years as well. Some examples of this sort are presented in the first part of Table 1.1. Third (step 3), both within and across age groups, strategy use is appropriately correlated with increased performance in the preschool years.

Older preschool children who are more strategic remember more than younger ones, and within a single age children who are more strategic remember more than those who do not. Again, examples of this sort are presented in Table 1.1.

Still step 4 in this chain of logic—training studies—is often missing. While unfortunate, this is also understandable; training studies are the trickiest and costliest to conduct. In addition, since the feasibility of such studies depends on steps 1, 2, and 3 above, then demonstrations of these sorts typically precede and motivate training studies. The evidence presented in this chapter thus far makes a compelling case that the argument is alive and well through step 3, and this ought to spur further research.

Moreover, where available, the results of training studies are also as expected and thus promising. For example, in the first of their two studies Heisel & Ritter (1981) found that 5-year-olds, but not 3-year-olds, deliberately and consistently hid items in distinctive spatial locations to enhance remembering those locations later. Concomitantly, 5-year-olds remembered better than 3-year-olds in such tasks; and use of the strategy at that age was correlated with enhanced remembering. In a second study, they thus trained the focal strategy in younger children. They found that when induced to use the focal strategy, $2\frac{1}{2}$- and 4-year olds' memory was equal to that of the uninstructed 5-year-olds in the first study. A complementary example of strategy disruption is provided by Wellman et al. (1987). Recall in that study focused on children's use of a spatial ordering strategy to avoid redundancy. One of the two tasks was designed to obstruct strategy use and one not. As expected, the task designed to inhibit strategy use did inhibit it and memory performance (redundancy errors) was worse on that task in comparison to the control task.

Training studies themselves are, of course, only fallible indicators of naturally occurring developmental mechanisms (e.g., Kuhn, 1972); conclusions about developmental mechanisms are seldom completely definitive. Partly because of this, the role of strategy developments in accounting for memory changes in older children is currently contested (e.g., Bjorklund, 1985) in spite of the rich empirical evidence from training studies with older children. The contention here is that we have not taken seriously enough increases in children's knowledge base as an account of changes in memory performances (e.g., Chi, 1978). An argument that developmental changes in the knowledge base can completely account for memory changes, if true, would seem exceedingly applicable to preschoolers as well, since obvious changes in knowledge are even more apparent in these early years than in later ones—e.g., vocabulary acquisition alone builds from close to zero to several thousand words in these early years.

However, strategies and knowledge are not so easily dichotomized. One thing that increased knowledge in a domain must mean for the learner is increased knowledge of effective information handling procedures, at least within that domain. That is, strategies for representing, retrieving, and utilizing information of a particular sort are part of the knowledge acquired in knowledge acquisition.

TABLE 1.1

Strategy Use in Different Age Groups: Examples from Different Studies

STUDIES WITH MULTIPLE AGES

Heisel & Ritter (1983):

Task: Remember location of an object placed in 1 of a matrix of 144 locations

Strategy: Place object in a corner (salient) location

Findings

	3-years	5-years
Memory performance: (% correct at finding object on first trial)	43%	63%
Strategy: (% of corner placements)	28%	56%
Relation of performance to strategy: (% correct performance given strategy use)	82%	85%

Wellman et al. (1987)

Task: Considering each one of a number of objects once; memory performance is thus in terms of errors, specifically redundancies

Strategy: Considering objects in a spatial sequence, so that each is considered systematically, in turn

	2-years	3-years	4-years
Memory performance: (% of redundant acts)	29%	18%	8%
Strategy: (% of spatial sequencing)	54%	66%	90%
Relation of performance to strategy: (Correlation of strategy and performance)	-.55	-.78	-.64

Yussen (1974):

Task: Child is to remember model's choices as a model views a series of 15 picture triads and picks favorite from each triad

Strategy: Attention to model and not to distracting slide display on other wall

	4- and 5-years	7-years
Memory performance: (% of "favorite" items chosen correctly)	65%	82%
Strategy: (frequency of attention to model; % of total trials where model was observed)[a]	73%	90%
Relation between performance and strategy: (Correlations of performance measures and strategy measures)	significant[b]	

(Table 1.1 continued...)

(table 1.1 continued...)

STUDIES WITH SINGLE AGES

DeLoache et al. (1985):

Task: 3 objects hidden in room, child must find objects after 3 min delay

Strategy: Production of target behaviors such as looking at hiding locations, naming the object

22-months

Memory performance = % correct findings

Strategy = target behaviors produced

Relation of performance to strategy: (target behaviors directed to toys successfully versus unsuccessfully retrieved)   .86 vs. .36

Wellman et al. (1975):

Task: 1 object hidden in 1 of 8 identical containers, child must find after 45 sec delay

Strategy: Target behaviors such as looking at target location, touching it, making it distinctive, etc., during delay

3-years

Memory performance = % correct findings

Strategy = frequency and duration of target behaviors

Relation of performance to strategy (correlations of performance and strategy; all such correlations were significant and averaged the figure given)   .65

---

[a] Frequencies and durations were recorded. Results are similar for both measures; frequencies are presented here.
[b] The overall correlation of frequency of attention and recall was .79; for duration of attention and recall it was .55. Yussen states that significant correlations of strategy and performance are obtained within each age group, but he does not report these values.

"Knowledge effects" studies are thus often, in part, studies of strategy effects as well; "knowledge base" explanations of memory development are complements rather than contrasts to strategy acquisition explanations (see Naus & Ornstein, 1983; Ornstein & Naus, in press). My contention here is simply that the same complex interaction between strategies and knowledge holds in the preschool years as well. If it does, then strategy developments must be a significant, though not unique, determinant of developmental changes in memory performance during this period. The available data is quite consistent with this claim.

There is a last suspicion concerning the role that strategy developments play in the story of memory development which needs to be considered. This suspicion is also typically presented in relation to older children and adults, but, again, it seems specially applicable to the young child. This suspicion is that an overwhelming portion of the learning and retrieval of information in children or adults is *never* deliberate. This doubt as to the importance of strategy accounts of memory, regardless of age, rests on a thought experiment of the following sort. Imagine how limited our knowledge and cognition would be if our only store of information was that which we had deliberately stored in previous mnemonic attempts. Adopting this perspective it is obvious how much of our knowledge is not deliberately acquired: our native language, most of its grammar and vocabulary, most of our autobiographical personal histories and episodic memories, etc., were never deliberately stored and are often only automatically accessed or retrieved.

I submit, however, that attempts to pit deliberate versus incidental learning in our theoretic esteem are somewhat like attempts to pit nature versus nurture. On close inspection both are undeniably important. In this regard consider a second thought experiment—the exact complement of the first. Imagine that all our cognition and memory was of the incidental, involuntary sort. Human organisms, in this scenario, were designed such that nothing was deliberately stored or deliberately retrieved; these operations went on solely in automatic and incidentally organized fashions. To my mind, an organism limited in this fashion would seem more like an intelligent bumble bee than a conspecific human. That is, regardless of the fact that our knowledge is for the most part nondeliberately stored and retrieved, the deliberate strategic storage and retrieval of information remains a dramatic and fundamentally important feature of human cognition. Its development is equally dramatic. That such strategic memory endeavors have an early and rich inception is a significant and striking, albeit relatively ignored, part of the story of human memory development.

CONCLUSIONS

The main conclusions of this review are straightforward. Memory activities in young children are strategic and mnemonic, memory strategies are varied and frequently employed, and they exert an important influence on relevant age-related improvements in memory performance. The data supporting these claims are modest and in part promissory but, I believe, trustworthy and convincing. I have concentrated on marshalling the evidence to arrive at these conclusions. This seems an important task because the evidence has been previously overlooked, leading to a false story of early memory development. I think it particularly necessary to get this story correct; if we begin our developmental descriptions of memory skills in error, then the succeeding chapters of the story will be in error too.

Having arrived at these conclusions, however, it is also important to exploit them to shed light on larger questions about the development of memory strategies. Of special interest here is the question of where do effective strategies come from, how are they developed? To set the stage for this discussion consider once again the two important features of the definition of a memory strategy: that it indeed aid remembering (be a means to the end) and that it be deliberately employed with just that end in mind. Relaxing the first feature led to a consideration of faulty strategies. Relaxing the second leads to a consideration of incidental mnemonics. Incidental mnemonics are *not* strategic, since they are not deliberately employed, but they function like effective strategies because the activities incidentally engaged in do aid remembering.

Consideration of incidental mnemonics represents something of a return to the Russians' insistence on the importance of involuntary memory activities (e.g., Smirnov & Zinchenko, 1969). Incidental mnemonics are an important cognitive tool for us all. After we've telephoned the same number six times in a row we're likely to remember it for a while, since we've incidentally rehearsed and stored it. Moreover, incidental mnemonics seem likely to be an especially significant cognitive tool for preschoolers. Preschoolers are faced with enormous tasks for remembering—e.g., vocabulary and name memory—and they perform impressively on these tasks. Perhaps it is no coincidence that at this same age the developmental psychologist finds a child that comes to many of his or her experimental tasks with a set of nondeliberate response tendencies or biases. We tend to ignore these biases or carefully control them away in our research. For example, in the work described in this paper great investment of energy and ingenuity has been required to establish that attending in various ways or manipulating the items in various ways are not just incidental response tendencies masquerading as deliberate memory strategies. They are not, but there is a need to demonstrate this just because these behaviors are part of the automatic task tendencies of young children. While such behaviors are noise in our experiments on deliberate remembering, they are by no means noise for the young child. The things we call response biases are incidental mnemonics for the child. They ensure the pick-up and retention of a great deal of information in an organism whose deliberate devices for information acquisition are still in the process of development.

Several qualifications and elaborations are needed at this point if the above claim is not to be misunderstood. First, it still seems accurate *in one respect* to describe young children's "memory" as largely involuntary and older children's as more strategic, as in the Russian account. This is reasonably accurate with respect to the actual impact of memory activities on remembering. Since faulty strategies do not impact memory performance very much, the impact of the child's strategic endeavors will be felt more and more as the number of *effective* strategies increase. And these do increase substantially in the elementary school years. Nonetheless, strategy development begins much earlier and effective strategies evolve directly out of earlier faulty strategies. Second, the developmental course of acquisition of any single effective strategy still remains an open and interesting empirical question. That is, for example, even if this general account is true it is still an open question whether verbal rehearsal develops out of an earlier incidental naming mnemonic or an intentional visual rehearsal strategy or both. Finally, while this account depicts the young child as planful and strategic, needing only to acquire the right strategies, there is no presumption that this is the entire story. Surely the child must in the course of development become sensitive to the need to approach some memory tasks strategically where he or she had not done so before (Flavell & Wellman, 1977). However, this sort of development is probably a less common and important occurrence than previously thought, at least during the preschool years.

Along these lines, it is important to note that the data on memory strategies in toddlers and preschoolers reviewed here contribute to an array of converging current evidence that 2-, 3-, and 4-year-old children are strategic, planful, and deliberate in very many problem-solving endeavors. Specifically, they are obviously strategic and planful in their approaches to searching for objects even when memory is not an issue (Wellman, Fabricius, & Sophian, 1985), in their solution to certain problematic games (Klahr & Robinson, 1981), in counting and enumeration (Gelman & Gallistel, 1978), in other measurement activities (Miller, 1984), and in communicating to others (Shatz, 1983). In short, young children of this age can be generally characterized as planful and strategic, albeit not always successful. Strategic memory is only one part of a general early strategic prowess.

The account of the development of memory strategies outlined here—faulty strategies evolving into effective ones—carries two intriguing implications, one methodological and one theoretical. Methodologically, it further underscores the need for investigation of children's faulty strategies. The presence of such faulty strategies should be particularly revealing, according to this account, and the course of their refinement into effective strategies would be particularly important to investigate. Faulty strategies are by no means evidenced only by young children, but study of their early development is particularly needed. Research into children's faulty strategy use and strategy refinement could model itself on microdevelopmental studies of other problem solving strategies (e.g., Karmiloff-Smith, 1979; Karmiloff-Smith & Inhelder, 1975).

The theoretical implication is this. The current account contends that there is an extended period in strategy development that is characterized by faulty strategies. It is commonly assumed that improvements in remembering drive strategy acquisition. For example, it is thought that we see a burst of strategy acquisition soon after school entrance because school tasks place increased demands for accurate and voluminous remembering and that strategies are acquired in response to feedback from success and failure with these demands. Such an outcome-feedback mechanism may indeed account for this particular transition, but the same type of mechanism can not straightforwardly account for the acquisition of early *faulty* strategies. The development of faulty strategies is not straightforwardly tied to memory successes or efficiencies because faulty strategies are strategic endeavors with no payoffs in improved remembering.

Of course, seemingly faulty strategies may only be faulty in some situations but helpful in many others, and the child's problem may be only to learn where which strategies are appropriate. If this were true, and outcome feedback was the driving force, then even young children's strategies should be more often effective than faulty. However, I think we are likely to find that young children's strategies are more often faulty than effective. If so, this would support an alternate kind of account for the acquisition of (truly faulty) strategies. That is, very generally young children may simply come to prefer a strategic or intelligent approach to problem solving tasks, regardless of the immediate payoffs (Sophian & Wellman, 1987). Indeed I believe that the early appearance of numerous faulty strategies means we should bet our research resources on two other sorts of theoretical efforts to explain strategy developments: (a) attempts to form social accounts of strategy development, where, for example, other people encourage deliberate attempts at problem solving by the child (Wertsch, 1978; Laboratory of Human Cognition, in press) *even faulty ones,* and (b) attempts to appeal to the child's larger understanding of or theories about memory and memory tasks (Wellman, 1983, 1985) such that faulty approaches are generated by coherent but mistaken notions of what will work.

As these speculations suggest, much remains to be known about the early development of memory strategies. But as the body of this paper demonstrates, correct appraisal of what is already known yields several important conclusions. These conclusions, as to the strategic though often faulty nature of the memory activities of young children, should cause consideration of the early development of memory strategies to figure much more prominently into our description and theories of memory development.

ACKNOWLEDGMENT

Partial support for writing this chapter came from a Research Career Development Award and from research grant HD-13317 from NICHHD. Reprint requests should be sent to: H. M. Wellman, University of Michigan, Center for

Human Growth and Development, 300 North Ingalls Building, Ann Arbor, MI 48109.

REFERENCES

Acredolo, L. P., Pick, H. L., & Olson, M. L. (1975). Environmental differentiation and familiarity as determinants of children's memory for spatial location. *Developmental Psychology, 11*, 495–501.

Appell, L. F., Cooper, R. G., McCarrel, N., Sims-Knight, J., Yussen, S. R., & Flavell, J. H. (1972). The development of the distinction between perceiving and memorizing. *Child Development, 43*, 1365–1381.

Baker-Ward, L., Ornstein, P. A., & Holden, D. J. (1984). The expression of memorization in early childhood. *Journal of Experimental Child Psychology, 3*, 558–575.

Beal, C. R. (1985). Development of knowledge about the use of cues to aid prospective retrieval. *Child Development, 56*, 631–642.

Bjorklund, D. F. (1985). The role of conceptual knowledge in the development of organization in children's memory. In C. Brainerd & M. Pressley (Eds.), *Basic processes in memory development*. New York: Springer-Verlag.

Brown, A. L., Bransford, J. D., Ferrara, R. A., & Campione, J. C. (1983). Learning, remembering, and understanding. In J. H. Flavell & E. M. Markman (Eds.), *Cognitive development*. Vol. 3 of the *Handbook of Child Psychology*. New York: Wiley.

Chi, M. T. H. (1977). Age differences in memory span. *Journal of Experimental Child Psychology, 23*, 266–281.

Chi, M. T. H. (1978). Knowledge structures and memory development. In R. Siegler (Ed.), *Children's thinking: What develops?* Hillsdale NJ: Lawrence Erlbaum Associates.

Cultice, J. C., Somerville, S. C., & Wellman, H. M. (1983). Preschoolers' memory monitoring: Feeling of knowing judgments. *Child Development, 54*, 1480–1486.

DeLoache, J. S., & Brown, A. L. (1979). Looking for big bird: Studies of memory in very young children. *The Quarterly Newsletter of The Laboratory of Comparative Human Cognition, 1*, 53–57.

DeLoache, J. S., & Brown, A. L. (1983). Very young children's memory for the location of objects in a large-scale environment. *Child Development, 54*, 888–891.

DeLoache, J. S., & Brown, A. L. (1984). Where do I go next? Intelligent searching by very young children. *Developmental Psychology, 20*, 37–44.

DeLoache, J. S., Cassidy, D. J., & Brown, A. L. (1985). Precursors of mnemonic strategies in very young children's memory for the location of hidden objects. *Child Development, 56*, 125–137.

Fabricius, W. V., & Wellman, H. M. (1983). Children's understanding of retrieval cue utilization. *Developmental Psychology, 19*, 15–21.

Flavell, J. H. (1970). Developmental studies of mediated memory. In H. Reese & L. Lipsett (Eds.), *Advances in child development and behavior*. New York: Academic Press.

Flavell, J. H. (1985). *Cognitive development*. Englewood Cliffs, NJ: Prentice-Hall.

Flavell, J. H., & Wellman, H. M. (1977). Metamemory. In R. Kail & J. Hagen (Eds.), *Perspectives on the development of memory and cognition*. Hillsdale, NJ: Lawrence Erlbaum Associates.

Gelman, R., & Gallistel, C. R. (1978). *The child's understanding of number*. Cambridge MA: Harvard University Press.

Gelman, R., & Meck, E. (1983). Preschoolers' counting: Principles before skill. *Cognition, 13*, 343–359.

Gordon, F. R., & Flavell, J. H. (1977). The development of intuitions about cognitive cueing. *Child Development, 48,* 1027–1033.

Hagen, J. W., & Kingsley, P. R. (1968). Labeling effects in short-term memory. *Child Development, 39,* 113–121.

Heisel, B. E., & Ritter, K. (1981). Young children's storage behavior in a memory for location task. *Journal of Experimental Child Psychology, 31,* 250–364.

Higbee, K. L. (1977). *Your memory: How it works and how to improve it.* Englewood Cliffs NJ: Prentice-Hall.

Hyde, T. S., & Jenkins, J. J. (1969). The differential effects of incidental tasks on the organization of a list of highly associated words. *Journal of Experimental Psychology, 82,* 472–481.

Istomina, Z. M. (1975). The development of voluntary memory in preschool-age children. *Soviet Psychology, 13,* 5–64.

Johnson, C. N., & Wellman, H. M. (1980). Children's developing understanding of mental verbs: Remember, know, and guess. *Child Development, 51,* 1095–1102.

Karmiloff-Smith, A. (1979). Micro- and macro-developmental changes in language acquisition and other representational systems. *Cognitive Science, 3,* 91–118.

Karmiloff-Smith, A., & Inhelder, B. (1975). If you want to get ahead get a theory. *Cognition, 3,* 195–212.

Kellet, M. C. (1983). *How to improve your memory and concentration.* New York: Monarch Press.

Klahr, D., & Robinson, M. (1981). Formal assessment of problem-solving and planning processes in children. *Cognition, 13,* 113–148.

Kuhn, D. (1972). Mechanisms of change in the development of cognitive structures. *Child Development, 43,* 833–844.

Laboratory of Human Cognition. (in press). The zone of proximal development. In J. Wertsch (Ed.), *Culture, communication, and cognition: Vygotskian perspectives.* New York: Cambridge University Press.

Lorayne, H., & Lucas, J. (1974). *The memory book.* New York: Ballantine Books.

Mcnamara, J., Baker, E., & Olson, C. L. (1976). Four-year-olds' understanding of pretend, forget, and know: Evidence for propositional operations. *Child Development, 47,* 62–70.

Miller, K. (1984). Child as measurer of all things: Measurement procedures and the development of quantitative concepts. In C. Sophian (Ed.), *Origins of cognitive skills.* Hillsdale NJ: Lawrence Erlbaum Associates.

Miller, P. H., & Zalenski, R. (1982). Preschoolers' knowledge about attention. *Developmental Psychology, 18,* 871–875.

Misciones, J. L., Marvin, R. S., O'Brien, R. G., & Greenberg, M. T. (1978). A developmental study of preschool children's understanding of the words "know" and "guess". *Child Development, 49,* 1107–1113.

Naus, M. J., & Ornstein, P. A. (1983). The development of memory strategies: Analysis, questions, and issues. In M. T. H. Chi (Ed.), *Trends in memory development.* Basel: Karger.

Newman, L. S. (1980, August). Intentional and unintentional memory in young children: Remembering versus playing. Paper presented at the meetings of the American Psychological Association, Montreal.

Ornstein, P. A., & Naus, M. J. (in press). Effects of the knowledge base on children's memory. In H. Reese (Ed.), *Advances in child development and behavior* (Vol. 19). New York: Academic Press.

Paris, S. G., & Lindauer, B. K. (1983). The development of cognitive skills during childhood. In B. B. Wolman (Ed.), *Handbook of Developmental Psychology.* Englewood Cliffs NJ: Prentice-Hall.

Perlmutter, M., & Myers, N. A. (1979). Development of recall in two- and four-year-old children. *Developmental Psychology, 15,* 73–83.

Potter, M. C., & Levy, E. I. (1968). Spatial enumeration without counting. *Child Development, 39,* 265–273.

Ratner, H. H. (1980). The role of social context in memory development. In M. Permutter (Ed.), *Children's memory.* San Francisco: Jossey-Bass.

Ritter, K. (1978). The development of knowledge of an external retrieval cue strategy. *Child Development, 49,* 1227–1230.

Ritter, K., Kaprove, B. H., Fitch, J. P., & Flavell, J. H. (1973). The development of retrieval strategies in young children. *Cognitive Psychology, 5,* 310–321.

Ryan, S. M., Hegion, A. G., & Flavell, J. H. (1970). Nonverbal mnemonic mediation in preschool children. *Child Development, 41,* 539–550.

Shatz, M. (1983). Communication. In J. Flavell & E. Markman (Eds.), *Handbook of child psychology: Cognitive development* (Vol. 3). New York: Wiley.

Shatz, M. Wellman, H. M., & Silber, S. (1983). The acquisition of mental verbs: A systematic investigation of the first reference to mental state. *Cognition, 14,* 301–321.

Smirnov, A. A., & Zinchenko, P. I. (1969). Problems in the psychology of memory. In M. Cole & I. Maltzman (Eds.), *A handbook of contemporary soviet psychology.* New York: Basic Books.

Somerville, S. C., Wellman, H. M., & Cultice, J. C. (1983). Young children's deliberate reminding. *Journal of Genetic Psychology, 143,* 87–96.

Sophian, C., & Wellman, H. M. (1987). The development of indirect search strategies. *British Journal of Developmental Psychology, 5,* 9–18.

Wagner, D. A. (1978). Memories of Morocco: The influence of age, schooling, and environment on memory. *Cognitive Psychology, 10,* 1–28.

Wellman, H. M. (1977a). The early development of intentional memory behavior. *Human Development, 22,* 86–101.

Wellman, H. M. (1977b). Preschoolers' understanding of memory relevant variables. *Child Development, 48,* 1720–1723.

Wellman, H. M. (1983). Metamemory revisited. In M. T. H. Chi (Ed.), *Trends in memory development.* Basel, Switzerland: S. Karger.

Wellman, H. M. (1985). A child's theory of mind. In S. Yussen (Ed.), *The growth of reflection.* New York: Academic Press.

Wellman, H. M., Collins, J., & Glieberman, J. (1981). Understanding the combination of memory variables: Developing conceptions of memory limitations. *Child Development, 52,* 1313–1317.

Wellman, H. M., & Estes, D. (1987). Children's early use of mental terms and what they mean. *Discourse Processes, 10,* 141–156.

Wellman, H. M., Fabricius, W. V., & Sophian, C. (1985). The early development of planning. In H. M. Wellman (Ed.), *Children's searching: The development of search skill and spatial representation.* Hillsdale NJ: Lawrence Erlbaum Associates.

Wellman, H. M., Fabricius, W. V., & Wan, C. (1987). *Considering every available instance:* The early development of a fundamental problem solving skill. *International Journal of Behavioral Development, 10,* 485–500

Wellman, H. M., & Johnson, C. N. (1979). Understanding mental processes: A developmental study of *remember* and *forget. Child Development, 50,* 79–88.

Wellman, H. M., Ritter, K., & Flavell, J. H. (1975). Deliberate memory behavior in the delayed reactions of very young children. *Developmental Psychology, 11,* 780–787.

Wellman, H. M., Somerville, S. C., Revelle, G. L., Haake, R. J., & Sophian, C. (1984). The development of comprehensive search skills. *Child Development, 55,* 472–481.

Wertsch, J. V. (1978). Adult-child interaction and the roots of metacognition. *Quarterly Newsletter of the Laboratory of Comparative Human Cognition, 1,* 15–18.

Woodworth, R. S., & Schlosberg, H. (1954). *Experimental psychology.* New York: Holt.

Yussen, S. R. (1974). Determinants of visual attention and recall in observational learning by preschoolers and second graders. *Developmental Psychology, 10,* 93–100.

Yussen, S. R., & Bird, J. E. (1979). The development of metacognitive awareness in memory, communication and attention. *Journal of Experimental Child Psychology, 28,* 300–313.

2 The Development of Mnemonic Skill

Peter A. Ornstein
University of North Carolina at Chapel Hill

Lynne Baker-Ward
North Carolina State University

Mary J. Naus
University of Houston

INTRODUCTION

Over the past 20 years, a rich data base regarding age-related changes in the operation of memory strategies has been amassed (see Chi, 1983; Kail & Hagen, 1977; Ornstein, 1978). This research has shown convincingly that with increases in age, children become more proficient in spontaneously generating strategies or plans for the storage and retrieval of information. Despite the wealth of information regarding age-related changes in the operation of memory strategies, however, critical issues concerning the *development* of such mnemonics remain largely unaddressed. For example, little is known about the factors associated with the emergence of strategies, the processes by which these techniques are refined and "honed," and the manner in which they come to be applied effectively in multiple task settings (see Naus & Ornstein, 1983).

In this chapter, we advocate the examination of these critical issues in the development of memory strategies, and propose a conceptual framework that can be used to integrate and support research on children's memory. By analogy with the well-documented domain of motor-skill acquisition (e.g., Fitts, 1964), we contend that it is important to study the development of mnemonic skill as the use of strategies becomes increasingly effective, efficient, and routinized. Within this framework, strategy development is viewed as proceeding along a continuum of mnemonic effectiveness that ranges from the first tentative applications of mnemonic efforts in various highly salient and supportive contexts to the routine and efficient application of procedures in a broad array of situations.

To explore the utility of this approach, this chapter begins with a general overview of research on memory strategies, culminating with the articulation of a series of critical issues in the field. Next, the application of the skills perspective and its potential for addressing these unresolved issues is illustrated by research carried out in our laboratory. We examine the performance of children along the mnemonic continuum as they progress toward skilled memorization abilities. The implications of these findings for future research in memory development are considered throughout the chapter.

CURRENT RESEARCH ON THE DEVELOPMENT OF MEMORY STRATEGIES

Overview of Research Findings

Influences from a number of distinct areas of developmental psychology, cognitive psychology, and special education (see Ellis, 1970; Flavell, 1970; Ornstein, 1978) have contributed to an explosion of interest in the development of memory strategies. A variety of task settings involving memory for lists (including words, pictures, and objects), texts, stories, etc., have been used in research in this area. The developmental course of a number of different strategies such as rehearsal (Ornstein & Naus, 1978), organization (Ornstein & Corsale, 1979), and elaborative procedures, both verbal and visual (e.g., Levin, 1981; Pressley, 1982; Rohwer, 1973), has been carefully charted. In addition to numerous investigations carried out with normal children of school age, considerable research has been executed with special populations, particularly mentally retarded and learning disabled children (e.g., Belmont & Butterfield, 1977; Borkowski & Büchel, 1983; Borkowski & Cavanaugh, 1979; Campione & Brown, 1977; Worden, 1983). Further, much of this effort has been directed toward the development of training procedures to foster the memory performance of inefficient learners. In addition, there has been a growth of interest in lifespan memory development. Recent research has examined the mnemonic efforts of preschoolers (see Perlmutter, 1980; Wellman, this volume), adolescents (e.g., Pressley, Levin, & Bryant, 1983), adults (e.g., Bellezza, 1983) and the elderly (e.g., Roberts, 1983).

This great volume of research suggests a transition from relatively passive to more active techniques of memorization. For example, in free recall tasks (e.g., Ornstein, Naus, & Liberty, 1975), children in the early elementary school years tend to rehearse each to-be-remembered item as it is presented, whereas older subjects rehearse each item with several previously presented stimuli. These differences in rehearsal style are clearly related to corresponding differences in recall success, especially at the beginning and middle serial positions. Corresponding findings have been obtained in studies of children's organizational techniques (see Ornstein & Corsale, 1979). For example, when asked to sort a set of relatively unrelated words into groups that would facilitate remembering,

3rd graders tend to group in a more-or-less random fashion, even though it can be demonstrated that they can sort in a more organized manner, whereas 7th graders search among the items for semantically constrained organized groupings. Again, corresponding differences are obtained in recall performance.

With both rehearsal and organizational strategies, training studies have been employed to demonstrate direct links between strategy utilization and recall. Thus, for example, instructing younger children to rehearse more actively improves their recall (Naus, Ornstein, & Aivano, 1977; Ornstein, Naus, & Stone, 1977), and providing passive rehearsal instructions to older children interferes with their recall. In addition, young children's recall is facilitated by providing them with instructions to sort on the basis of meaning (Bjorklund, Ornstein, & Haig, 1977; Corsale & Ornstein, 1980), by yoking them to the sorting patterns of older children (Bjorklund et al., 1977; Liberty & Ornstein, 1973), or simply by providing experience with highly organized materials (Best & Ornstein, 1986). Overviews of the literature on rehearsal and organization can be obtained in reviews by Ornstein and Naus (1978) and Ornstein and Corsale (1979).

Unresolved Issues

Despite this concensus view concerning the operation of children's memory strategies, recent research has provided some qualifications to the picture presented above. Although space constraints will not permit a complete treatment of the recent literature, several current issues are examined briefly (see also Naus & Ornstein, 1983; Ornstein & Naus, 1985).

Origins of Strategies.   Relatively little is known about the origins of the strategies observed during the elementary school years, but, as suggested above, there is growing interest in the memory capabilities of preschoolers. Young children's tendencies to prepare intentionally for a memory goal have been documented; evidence is accumulating that even 4-year-old children behave strategically when asked to remember (see Wellman, this volume). Nonetheless, despite findings that indicate the mnemonic prowess of preschoolers, no work has been reported in which these capabilities are directly related to the strategic repertoire that is observed during the elementary school years. Further, although the work with preschoolers has contributed significantly to the understanding of their capacities to prepare intentionally for a memory demand, factors responsible for the emergence of memory strategies in early childhood remain unidentified.

Transitions in Skill Use.   Although memory strategies are present in early childhood, significant changes must transpire during the elementary school years before children's use of mnemonic mediation resembles that of mature subjects.

Adults and older children use strategies in a flexible fashion in a great variety of situations, whereas younger subjects—to the extent to which they behave strategically—tend to use mnemonic techniques in salient and supportive task environments (see Ornstein & Naus, 1985). Moreover, the strategies of older subjects seem to be executed in a manner that requires less effort than is the case with young subjects. Although there has been some attention paid to the issue of the generalization of strategies across situations (e.g., Best & Ornstein, 1986; Borkowski, Cavanaugh, & Reichhart, 1978), little work has been concerned with the changing effort requirements associated with the routinization of mnemonic skill. Recent research by Guttentag (1984) indicates that the attentional demands of an active rehearsal strategy may vary at different points in development. A possible implication of this finding is that age-related reductions in the effort requirements of memory strategies may be associated with their generalized deployment across situations.

The Role of Knowledge.   Recent theoretical statements have suggested a relationship between developmental changes in children's knowledge and their increasingly sophisticated use of memory strategies (Bjorklund, 1985; Ornstein & Naus, 1985). Age-related changes in both the contents of the knowledge base and the ease of access to stored information have significant implications for the deployment of strategies. Thus, what a child knows about the materials to be remembered may dramatically determine just what can be done strategically with those materials. In fact, a child may appear "strategic" when trying to remember some items and non-strategic with others, possibly leading to the first expressions of deliberate memorization with highly meaningful materials (Ornstein & Naus, 1985). Further in development, the increasing articulation of the knowledge system may facilitate the retrieval of stored information and thus diminish the effort required to execute various subcomponents of memory strategies. In addition to these concurrent influences of the knowledge system upon memory performance, it has recently been suggested that there are long-term effects of changes in the knowledge base on the development of strategies (see Bjorklund, 1985; Ornstein & Naus, 1985).

The Role of Metamemory.   With increases in age, there are corresponding changes in the child's understanding of the operation of the memory system and of the demands of various tasks that require remembering (Flavell & Wellman, 1977; Wellman, 1983). The role of this "metamemory" in actual memory performance is at present not completely clear (Cavanaugh & Borkowski, 1980; Salatas & Flavell, 1976). The absence of a direct correspondance between metamemory and recall may reflect inadequate techniques for the measurement of the metamemory judgments of children, insufficient theoretical attention as to just what the relationship between metamemory and memory should be at different points in development, or both (Best & Ornstein, 1986; Cavanaugh & Perlmutter, 1982; Schneider, 1985). Nonetheless, it seems clear that most successful efforts in training children in the use of mnemonic techniques that they would not spontaneously deploy involve supplementing the provision of strategy information with metamemory information (e.g., Borkowski et al., 1978; Paris, Newman, & McVey, 1982; Pressley et al., 1983). These findings support the conclusion that although metamemory may not orchestrate the expression of strategies, its role in the development of mnemonic skill must be understood.

Automatic Contributions.   Although it is clear that the operation of mnemonic strategies involves the deliberate deployment of specific techniques in the presence of a memory goal, this process may involve automatic contributions of two specific kinds (see Ornstein & Naus, 1985). First, recent evidence suggests that certain highly organized or salient sets of stimulus materials may actually serve to elicit strategies at a time during which they might not otherwise be observed (Bjorklund, 1985; Lange, 1973, 1978; Ornstein & Naus, 1985). For example, the use of highly associated stimulus items may facilitate the early execution of active sorting and rehearsal strategies (see Ornstein & Naus, 1985). Second, with practice and experience in executing particular strategies, as well as with the development of certain underlying information-handling capabilities, procedures that were at one time somewhat difficult to perform may later be executed with relative ease because they come to be less demanding of effort (see Guttentag, 1984). It would clearly seem essential to examine the attentional demands of strategies at different times in development.

Situational Specificities.   Analyses of children's differential performances in divergent contexts can serve to illuminate factors that serve to support the early development of mnemonic mediation. As indicated above, children's knowledge of the stimulus materials may influence to some extent the degree of "sophistication" that is expressed in their memorization efforts (Bjorklund, 1985; Lange, 1978; Ornstein & Naus, 1985). More generally, depending upon instructions, task demands, information processing supports, and motivation (Ornstein & Corsale, 1979; Ornstein, Medlin, Stone, & Naus, 1985; Paris, 1978; Paris & Cross, 1983), the degree of strategic involvement in the task may differ. Rather than dismissing these aspects of children's memory performance as examples of the ubiquitous production deficiency concept (Flavell, 1970), they can serve to provide a great deal of information concerning children's capabilities. Analyses of children's differential performances in divergent contexts can serve to illuminate factors that serve to support the early development of mnemonic mediation.

DIRECTIONS FOR FUTURE RESEARCH

The brief overview presented here suggests that despite the progress that has been made in understanding children's memory, much remains to be learned about the natural course of the development of strategies. In fact, it can be argued that the field has not progressed significantly beyond demonstrations of effective techniques in the memory performance of older children and their absence in the memory performance of younger children, at least in some contexts. It is clear, for example, that rehearsal and organization represent important strategies (Ornstein & Corsale, 1979; Ornstein & Naus, 1978), and that a considerable amount is known about their application. But it is also clear that relatively little is known about the ontogeny of skilled memorizing.

From our perspective, the gaps in our understanding of strategy development arise from three features of the developmental literature. First, research on children's memory has been characterized by cross-sectional investigations that do not provide long-term, within-subject assessments of skill development. Second, research has not explored systematically the variations in performance in individual children that may be associated with different task demands. Third, little emphasis has been placed on the effort requirements of various mnemonic strategies at different points in development.

Longitudinal research is necessary to permit a resolution of many of the issues discussed here (see Baltes & Nesselroade, 1979, for a discussion of the appropriate uses of longitudinal methodologies). The examination of the relationships between the first tentative applications of mnemonic mediation and the memory strategies characteristic of more mature subjects requires longitudinal analyses of the development of the behaviors applied in deliberate remembering. For example, are the children who spontaneously label stimuli at age five (e.g., see Baker-Ward, Ornstein, & Holden, 1984; Flavell, Friedrichs, & Hoyt, 1970) typically the children who first acquire verbal rehearsal? In addition, longitudinal research is necessary to document, the small, cumulative, and highly variable changes in the skill with which mnemonic mediators are applied. These changes can only be identified in longitudinal designs because the developmental function, rather than the absolute difference in magnitude between levels of performance at two points in time, must be examined.

Longitudinal methodologies can productively be integrated with research that focuses on performance in tasks that vary with regard to instructions, information processing supports, and the child's knowledge of materials. Research on such contextual specificities, typically interpreted in terms of production deficiencies (e.g., Brown & DeLoache, 1978), has not been used to systematically examine the determinants of effective strategy utilization. By analyzing the extent to which different contexts support strategy implementation, the dimensions of mnemonic performance that change with development can be delineated. For example, an 8-year-old's knowledge of interstimulus relationships may not routinely be translated into an organized sorting strategy, unless specific organizational prompting is provided or the materials to be remembered are themselves highly structured (compare, e.g., Corsale, 1978, and Corsale & Ornstein, 1980). A systematic delineation of such situational effects could facilitate the identification of changing information processing requirements in the execution of strategies. Given a longitudinal examination of the nature of tasks that involve remembering, it thus should be possible to predict the likelihood that children of different ages will utilize particular strategies in particular contexts. In this way, factors that underlie the origins and development of strategies can be determined.

Further, analyses of the characteristics of the contexts in which memorization attempts are observed could be used to define the changing effort requirements imposed by particular mnemonic strategies. For example, recent work by Guttentag (1984) indicates that the attentional demands of the "same" strategy may vary at different points in development. Using a dual-task paradigm, Guttentag found that young children's execution of a secondary finger-tapping task was more disrupted by their performance of a primary cumulative rehearsal task than was older children's. The possibility that effort requirements for strategy use may vary differentially with age across task settings may contribute to developmental changes in the efficiency with which mnemonic techniques are broadly applied. Thus, older children may be more active in their memorization attempts because the techniques that they use actually require less effort than those employed by younger children.

It is interesting to note that the emphases missing from the current study of memory development seem to characterize research in the area of skill learning and perceptual-motor coordination. In these areas of investigation (see, e.g., Anderson, 1981, 1982; Fitts, 1964), there is a tradition of tracing the refinement and development of skill—be it following a moving target, solving a mathematical problem, learning a code, learning to assemble a product, etc.—until it is efficiently executed and routinized. Students of skill learning have repeatedly demonstrated that performance improves as a function of extended practice, long after high criteria of accuracy have been obtained. Analyses of this improvement have focused on the growing integration and automatization of skill components, and the resulting reduction of the memory and effort requirements of the task (see, e.g., Anderson, 1982; Fitts, 1964).

To appreciate the perspective of those who analyze skill acquisition, consider the informal example provided by Chase (1966) of learning to drive a car. In the early stages of learning, the coordination of the clutch, accelerator, and brake pedals is not particularly smooth. Further, a great degree of concentration is required, as driving seems to exhaust available capacity, and sometimes requires verbal mediation as well, as one literally tells oneself what to do with the various pedals. During the early stages of skill learning, this job of coordination requires so much attention that it is difficult to drive while simultaneously listening to the radio, carrying on a conversation, etc. Later the various driving operations are integrated somewhat, and subjectively it appears as if driving is a less effortful task. There is a continued reduction in the effort requirements of driving, and the driver becomes able to divide attention between driving and a simultaneous conversation or other activity. However, even when driving seems to require little conscious attention, changes in road or traffic conditions may again require the investment of most of the driver's resources in the demands of driving the car.

It is our contention that much can be gained by viewing the development of children's memory strategies as a process analagous to the development of skill. With increases in age and experience, the various cognitive operations that are involved in strategy production and execution may become increasingly routinized and thus less demanding of attentional capacity (see Guttentag, 1984). The orientation of those who study skilled performance thus encourages a much broader perspective for the acquisition of mnemonic skill than that which has typically been employed. This point of view has led to the generation of a framework that can be used to characterize the growth of memory strategies from their first tentative applications in certain contexts that may be highly supportive to their eventual efficient use in a broad array of settings. This informal model posits a continuum of mnemonic effectiveness along which at least five different levels of mnemonic performance can be identified:

1. At early points along this continuum, the young child does not utilize strategies in the context of deliberate memory tasks.

2. Somewhat later, in the preschool years, a child may behave strategically in some situations that require remembering, but the effects of these mnemonic efforts may not be realized in actual memory "dividends."

3. Further along, in the early elementary-school years, the child's mnemonic efforts may be somewhat effective, but the deployment of strategies may be in part determined by the salience of the stimulus materials.

4. Later still, strategies may be used in a variety of settings, with stimuli of varying degrees of saliency, and these strategies are effective.

5. Finally, strategy implementation becomes increasingly effective, reflecting the routinization and automatization that comes from both practice and the development of certain underlying information handling skills (such as retrieval and the ability to make interconnections in the knowledge base).

Complete evidence for this projected continuum of mnemonic effectiveness is not yet available. Nonetheless, this perspective may help to organize the extant literature and to suggest directions for further research. In addition, this point of view, which focuses on automatic aspects of strategy deployment and the effort requirements of mnemonic skills, clearly has much in common with other views of cognitive development that have stressed automatization. Thus, for example, in Case's (1978; Case, Kurland, & Goldberg, 1982) account, automatization of elementary cognitive functions occurs as a result of practice and experience, leading to a functional enlargement of the space available in working memory for the handling of information processing operations. Similarly, Brainerd's (1981, 1983) working memory account of performance in various probability judgment tasks attributes increases with age in judgment performance to increases in working memory space that have come available as a result of the fundamental memory operations of encoding and retrieving. Although Brainerd has attempted to account for reasoning in terms of more fundamental changes in memory, it seems clear that the same mode of analysis can be used to deal with the development of strategies and the memory system itself. In addition, while not dealing with the automatization of mnemonic techniques as a result of practice and experience, Lange (1973, 1978), Bjorklund (1985), Frankel and Rollins (1985), and Schneider (1986) have argued that early strategy usage may be automatically determined by the associative structure of the knowledge base. (See Ornstein & Naus, 1985, for a review of these positions.)

PROGRESSION TOWARD SKILLED MEMORIZATION

To illustrate the usefulness of this view of a continuum of mnemonic effectiveness, we discuss several recent experiments on strategy deployment. Although longitudinal data are clearly necessary for tracing the progress of individual children, the studies presented briefly here nonetheless serve to illustrate the performance of children at different points on the continuum, as they move toward skilled memorization. The research discussed here identifies three points in the development of mnemonic skill. The first point corresponds to a position on the hypothetical continuum at which children understand that certain special behaviors are required when memorization is called for, but do not use mediation in a manner that results in recall facilitation (see level 2 on p. 38). At the second point, the strategies observed vary as a function of the organizational salience of the stimulus materials (see level 3 on p. 38). The third position illustrates a point at which children routinely apply strategies, but do so only with a greater degree of effort than is the case with older subjects (see level 5 on p. 38).

Early Expressions of Memorization

Baker-Ward et al. (1984) report findings that suggest that preschoolers have a rather substantial understanding of memorizing but that they may be less able than older children to exploit this understanding effectively for mnemonic advantage. Their 4-, 5-, and 6-year-old subjects were placed in a simple setting in which they could interact with a set of common objects and toys (e.g., frog, airplane, bandaid). The children's interactions with these objects were videotaped under different sets of instructions. Children in a Target Remember condition were told that they could play with all of the items, but that we would be particularly interested in their trying to remember a subset of the objects, i.e., the target objects. Children in a Target Play condition were given instructions that did not mention remembering but stressed playing with a subset of target objects. In contrast, children assigned to a Free Play condition were given general play instructions. Each subject had a 2 minute activity period in which to interact with the materials prior to a single recall trial. The plan was to infer the mnemonic behaviors of the Target Remember subjects by contrasting their approach to the task with that of the children in the two control groups who were given play instructions.

The use of a coding scheme revealed that even at age 4, children told to remember behaved differently from those told simply to play. Figures 2.1 and 2.2 document the extent to which selected behaviors were observed among children in each instructional condition at each age. As shown in Fig. 2.1, spontaneous verbal labeling or naming occurred in the Target Remember groups, and there was less play among the subjects in the Target Remember groups than in the two play control conditions. In addition, as shown in Fig. 2.2, the Target Remember groups also evidenced more visual inspection of the stimuli and more of what was called "unfilled time." "Unfilled time" was scored when a child was not paying direct attention to the objects, but did not seem to be off task,

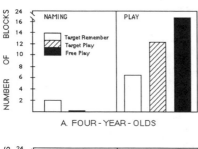

A. FOUR - YEAR - OLDS

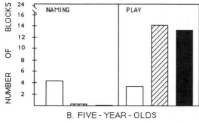

B. FIVE - YEAR - OLDS

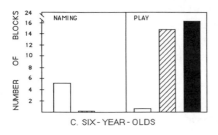

C. SIX - YEAR - OLDS

FIG. 2.1. Mean number of 5-second blocks of the activity period in which naming and play occurred for the 4-year-olds (Panel A), 5-year-olds (Panel B), and 6-year-olds (Panel C) in each instructional condition (adapted from Baker-Ward et al., 1984). Reproduced by permission of Academic Press

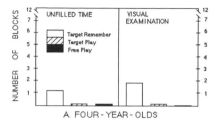

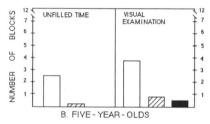

FIG. 2.2. Mean number of 10-second blocks of the activity period characterized by "unfilled time" and "visual examination" for the 4-year-olds (Panel A), 5-year-olds (Panel B), and 6-year-olds (Panel C) in each instructional condition (adapted from Baker-Ward et al., 1984). Reproduced by permission of Academic Press

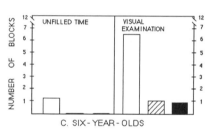

either. Informally, it seemed as if the children were using this "unfilled time" for reflection about the items and self testing. Given that the subjects asked to remember approached the task differently, with what might even be called a studious demeanor, would there by positive mnemonic consequences of their behavior? As shown in Fig. 2.3, the results indicated that clear facilitation in recall was associated with the memory instructions only at age 6. Whatever facilitation was present at the younger ages reflected the direction of the children's attention to a subset of the materials and not the effects of the memory instructions.

These findings imply that successful memorization requires more than the simple intent to remember. Even the 4-year-olds studied here demonstrated by their differential behaviors in the various instructional contexts some understanding of the deliberate nature of remembering. Although children at the different ages approached the memory task with similar behaviors, only the mnemonic efforts of the 6-year-olds resulted in significant enhancement of recall. These findings suggest that mnemonic mediators that appear to be similar in form may be employed with varying degrees of effectiveness at different points in develop-

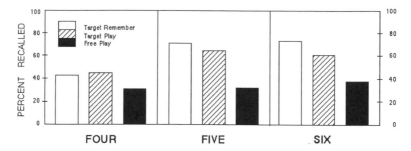

FIG. 2.3.   Percentage of the target objects recalled by the 4-, 5-, and 6-year-olds in each instructional condition (adapted from Baker-Ward et al., 1984). Reproduced by permission of Academic Press

ment. At one level, this may reflect age-related changes in the manner by which the mediators are deployed; similar external behaviors may correspond to different types of internal mediation at varying points in development. Yet, at another level, it is possible that the similarity in strategic efforts may be illusory; children of different ages may differentially combine the various mnemonic behaviors into qualitatively different strategies. That this may be the case is suggested by Baker-Ward et al.'s observation that verbal labeling or naming occurred in tandem with object manipulation among the younger subjects, whereas it was accompanied by visual examination among the 6-year-olds. Clearly, additional efforts need to be devoted to the development of higher-order coding schemes that may effectively capture these developmental changes in the coordination of mnemonic behaviors.

Situational Specificity of Early Strategies

A few examples will be presented to illustrate the fact that the characteristics of the stimulus materials to be remembered can strongly affect the types of strategies spontaneously employed by children. First, consider the performance of children in a sort/recall task in which subjects are asked to group sets of items prior to an attempt at recall. In situations such as this, the particular instructions that are provided can have a most dramatic effect on young children's performance (Bjorklund et al., 1977; Corsale & Ornstein, 1980). If 3rd and 7th graders are asked to sort relatively unrelated items so that the groups formed will help them to remember, the sorting of the older children is rather semantically constrained, whereas that of the younger children seems to be essentially random. The 7th graders search for meaningful relations among the stimuli (even these relatively unstructured items), whereas the 3rd graders do not appear to do this. However, it can be demonstrated that the young children do in fact have the knowledge that would permit them to sort in a manner similar to that of the older children. Further, by telling 3rd graders to form groups of items that ''go together'' or are ''similar in some way,'' as opposed to groups that will ''help you remember,'' we can observe a major change in sorting style and recall performance.

Interestingly, without changing the basic instruction to form groups that will facilitate remembering, 3rd graders do sort in an organized fashion with some sets of materials. For example, Corsale (1978), in dissertation work carried out in our laboratory, has shown that when sets of categorically related items are substituted for the more-or-less unrelated materials that were used previously, 3rd graders will spontaneously sort in a meaning-based fashion when told to form groups that will aid in remembering. Thus, with highly salient stimulus materials, young children will behave in a ''strategic'' fashion, interpreting instructions to form groups that will facilitate remembering as a prompt to sort in an organized fashion. In contrast, with unrelated materials, they do not seem to exploit this underlying knowledge in the service of a memory goal. Comparable findings have been obtained by Best and Ornstein (1986), who also showed that exposure to highly salient stimulus materials permits 3rd graders to induce an organizational strategy that they can transfer to sets of unstructured materials.

A second demonstration of the dependence of memory strategies on the stimulus properties of the to-be-remembered materials was obtained in a study of 3rd graders' rehearsal carried out by Tarkin (1981). Third graders rehearsed aloud while being presented with one of two lists. All words were known to the children, but the lists differed in meaningfulness, in the verbal learning sense of the term. Thus, some children rehearsed and recalled high meaningful items, that is, words that elicited many associations, whereas others were given words that were low in meaningfulness. As presented in Fig. 2.4, the data indicated marked differences in spontaneous rehearsal. The low meaningfulness group rehearsed fewer than two different items at each opportunity for rehearsal, whereas the high meaningfulness group typically rehearsed more than three items together. This value is characteristic of that of 6th graders who have been studied in our laboratory (see Ornstein & Naus, 1978). Corresponding differences were observed in recall performance.

We now have several demonstrations of this kind, all suggesting that children's attempts at strategies for memorization may vary as a function of the characteristics of the to-be-remembered material. In each instance, more ''sophisticated'' efforts are observed with stimuli whose organizational properties are rather salient. These outcomes suggest to us that observed strategies are to some extent stimulus-driven. Thus, in the sort/recall studies, there may be a type of obligatory semantic encoding at work, an encoding that is forced to a degree by the strong associative links among the items. These interconnections must be so salient that young children can do little to prevent organized sorting according to meaning when presented with the stimuli. And, with the rehearsal data, it seems quite likely that the more active strategies that are observed with the high meaningful items reflect an associative activation of the knowledge base. A type

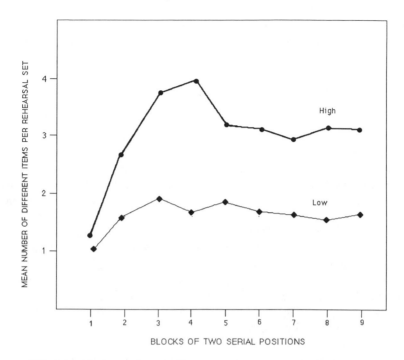

FIG. 2.4.   Mean number of different items per rehearsal set as a function of blocks of two serial positions for 3rd-grade children given high and low meaningfulness items (adapted from Tarkin, 1981).

of associative priming may make it easier for subjects to retrieve highly meaningful items from early list positions to include in an active fashion with later list items. Further, if it is assumed that the words typically used in experiments on memory may be functionally more meaningful for older children than for younger children, a view that is supported by the available normative data (see, e.g., Emmerich, 1979), a potential mechanism underlying the developing tendency for active rehearsal may be identified.

These demonstrations and the tentative interpretations that we have placed on them suggest that it may be difficult indeed to distinguish between automatic and deliberate aspects of strategy deployment. In both the rehearsal and organizational strategies, we observe what would seem to be automatic mediation by the child's pre-existing knowledge system. This claim, of course, is reminiscent of Lange's (1973, 1978) arguments concerning category clustering. Lange (see also Bjorklund, 1985; Frankel & Rollins, 1985) suggested that early demonstrations of clustering in the recall of preadolescent children may be more an automatic consequence of strong stimulus interconnections than the deliberate deployment of a strategy in the service of a memory goal. Our demonstrations differ from

Lange's in that our rehearsal and organizational effects are by definition observed at the input as opposed to the output side of the study/recall sequence. They thus seem to us to involve clear efforts at deliberate involvement in the task of remembering, but these deliberate efforts certainly seem to be influenced by automatic activation of the knowledge system.

The knowledge base effects that we have presented appear to be part of a broader picture of memory development. As suggested here, it seems likely that children's first successful attempts at deliberate remembering come about in salient, supportive contexts. When the task is that of committing highly associated stimuli to memory, children would seem to be supported in their efforts by certain characteristics of the items, more so than would be the case when they are given stimuli that lack strong interitem connections. Although firm data are lacking, we would suspect that after some success in remembering highly structured materials, children are able to transfer their strategic approach to other types of materials that are less supportive. The study of the transfer of organized sorting from highly organized to unrelated materials (Best & Ornstein, 1986) that was mentioned above suggests such a sequence in children's acquisition of deliberate memory skills. Longitudinal data are clearly necessary to support this claim.

Changes in Effort

Moving beyond the progression from highly salient to less supportive contexts, we find that there are other changes in mnemonic skill implementation that have not been studied extensively by developmental psychologists (see Ornstein & Naus, 1985). It seems likely that there are age-related changes in some fundamental information processing skills that influence the efficiency with which active memory strategies can be utilized. With increases in age—or with the provision of appropriate supports to younger children when they are lacking—the application of mnemonic strategies seems to require less effort and to become increasingly routinized. Thus, with increases in age, children clearly become more effective in strategy deployment, in part because they become more facile in the execution of some of the component parts of the strategies.

As an example, consider an active rehearsal strategy and the fact that success with this technique demands being able to retrieve previously presented items to include in current rehearsal. Clearly, as suggested here, this process may be facilitated by age-related associative changes in the knowledge base. But, more generally, there may be a developmental progression in retrieval ability that brings about increasingly active efforts at remembering. Indeed, our data (Ornstein et al., 1985) indicate that when the retrieval demands of the task are minimized, 2nd graders can execute an active rehearsal strategy quite effectively. In this experiment, 2nd graders rehearsed aloud under a variety of different rehearsal conditions. The numbers of different items in each rehearsal set are indicated in Fig. 2.5. Compared with a baseline condition, the children benefitted from an instruction to actively rehearse the items. However, the effectiveness of the instruction was enhanced markedly when the subjects were provided with either visual access to previously presented items or given additional processing time. Performance was maximized if both increased time and visual access were provided. As expected, recall was facilitated by the children's more efficient deployment of the rehearsal strategy. These data suggest that children in the early elementary school years may be aware of the importance of active mnemonic techniques, but less skilled than older children in using some of the component processes involved in implementing effective strategies.

These data suggest that with developmental advances in component skills such as retrieval, the application of mnemonic strategies requires less effort and becomes increasingly routinized or automatic. In fact, as discussed earlier, Guttentag (1984) demonstrated that the effort requirements of an active rehearsal technique are much greater for younger children than for older children. Thus, the execution of the strategy requires less allocation of attention for older than for younger children. Clearly these findings are consistent with those accounts of cognitive development (e.g., Case, 1978) in which the routinization of skill is stressed.

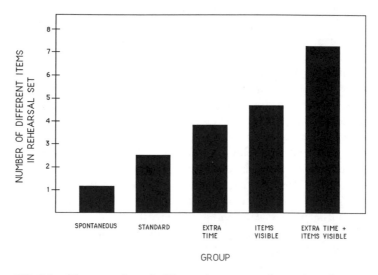

FIG. 2.5.   Mean number of different items per rehearsal set for 2nd grade children given active rehearsal instructions and other information processing supports. Adapted from Ornstein et al., 1985. Copyright (1985) by the American Psychological Association. Adapted by permission.

SUMMARY

We propose that memory skill progresses along a broad continuum. Our view is that the child moves from success in highly salient situations to the efficient use of a variety of memory skills in many different settings in which memorization is required. With practice in tasks that require remembering, with the articulation of the knowledge system, and with the development of supporting cognitive skills, children become increasingly efficient in the implementation of mnemonic skills. It is clear that this perspective implies that a complete understanding of the development of memory requires a longitudinal analysis of children at all stages of mnemonic competence. We need to move away from traditional cross-sectional research designs in which the focus is on particular mnemonic skills (such as the rehearsal and organizational techniques discussed here) to longitudinal designs that involve the assessment of children on a wide range of memory skills in a variety of different contexts. Only in this manner will we be able to truly hope to understand the emergence and development of skilled remembering.

ACKNOWLEDGMENTS

This chapter had its origins in papers presented at the meetings of the North American Society for the Psychology of Sport and Physical Activity (Ornstein, 1982), the Society for Research in Child Development (Ornstein & Baker-Ward, 1983) and the American Educational Research Association (Ornstein & Naus, 1984). Preparation of this paper was supported by the University Research Council of the University of North Carolina at Chapel Hill.

REFERENCES

Anderson, J. (1981). (Ed.). *Cognitive skills and their acquisition.* Hillsdale, NJ: Lawrence Erlbaum Associates.

Anderson, J. (1982). Acquisition of cognitive skill. *Psychological Review, 89,* 369–406.

Baker-Ward, L., Ornstein, P. A., & Holden, D. J. (1984). The expression of memorization in early childhood. *Journal of Experimental Child Psychology, 37,* 555–575.

Baltes, P. B., & Nesselroade, J. R. (1979). History and rationale of longitudinal research. In J. R. Nesselroade & P. B. Baltes (Eds.), *Longitudinal research in the study of behavior and development.* New York: Academic Press.

Bellezza, F. S. (1983). Mnemonic-device instruction with adults. In M. Pressley & J. R. Levin (Eds.), *Cognitive strategy research: Psychological foundations.* New York: Springer-Verlag.

Belmont, J. M., & Butterfield, E. D. (1977). The instructional approach to developmental cognitive research. In R. V. Kail & J. W. Hagen (Eds.), *Perspectives on the development of memory and cognition.* Hillsdale, NJ: Lawrence Erlbaum Associates.

Best, D. L., & Ornstein, P. A. (1986). Children's generation and communication of mnemonic organizational strategies. *Developmental Psychology, 22,* 845–853.

Bjorklund, D. F. (1985). The role of conceptual knowledge in the development of organization in children's memory. In C. J. Brainerd & M. Pressley (Eds.), *Basic processes in memory development: Progress in cognitive development research.* New York: Springer-Verlag.

Bjorklund, D. F., Ornstein, P. A., & Haig, J. R. (1977). Developmental differences in organization and recall: Training in the use of organizational techniques. *Developmental Psychology, 13,* 175–183.

Borkowski, J. G., & Büchel, F. P. (1983). Learning and memory strategies in the mentally retarded. In M. Pressley & J. R. Levin (Eds.), *Cognitive strategy research: Psychological foundations.* New York: Springer-Verlag.

Borkowski, J. G., & Cavanaugh, J. C. (1979). Maintenance and generalization of skills and strategies by the retarded. In N. R. Ellis (Ed.), *Handbook of mental deficiency.* Hillsdale, NJ: Lawrence Erlbaum Associates.

Borkowski, J. G., Cavanaugh, J. C., & Reichhart, G. J. (1978). Maintenance of children's rehearsal strategies: Effects of amount of training and strategy form. *Journal of Experimental Child Psychology, 26,* 288–298.

Brainerd, C. J. (1981). Working memory and the developmental analysis of probability judgment. *Psychological Review, 6,* 463–502.

Brainerd, C. J. (1983). Working-memory systems and cognitive development. In C. J. Brainerd (Ed.), *Recent advances in cognitive-developmental theory: Progress in cognitive development research.* New York: Springer-Verlag.

Brown, A. L., & DeLoache, J. S. (1978). Skills, plans, and self-regulation. In R. Siegler (Ed.), *Children's thinking: What develops?* Hillsdale, NJ: Lawrence Erlbaum Associates.

Campione, J. C., & Brown, A. L. (1977). Memory and metamemory development in educable retarded children. In R. V. Kail & J. W. Hagen (Eds.), *Perspectives on the development of memory and cognition.* Hillsdale, NJ: Lawrence Erlbaum Associates.

Case, R. (1978). Intellectual development from birth to adolescence: A neo-Piagetian interpretation. In R. Siegler (Ed.), *Children's thinking: What develops?* Hillsdale, NJ: Lawrence Erlbaum Associates.

Case, R., Kurland, D. M., & Goldberg, J. (1982). Operational efficiency and growth of short term memory span. *Journal of Experimental Child Psychology, 33,* 386–404.

Cavanaugh, J. C., & Borkowski, J. G. (1980). Searching for metamemory-memory connections: A developmental study. *Developmental Psychology, 16,* 441–453.

Cavanaugh, J. C., & Perlmutter, M. (1982). Metamemory: A critical examination. *Child Development, 53,* 11–28.

Chase, W. C. (1966). *A sound approach to reading.* Unpublished manuscript, University of Wisconsin.

Chi, M. T. H. (1983). (Ed.). *Trends in memory development research (Contributions to Human Development),* Vol. 9. Basel: S. Karger.

Corsale, K. (1978). *Factors affecting children's use of organization in recall.* Unpublished doctoral dissertation, University of North Carolina at Chapel Hill.

Corsale, K., & Ornstein, P. A. (1980). Developmental changes in children's use of semantic information in recall. *Journal of Experimental Child Psychology, 30,* 231–245.

Ellis, N. R. (1970). Memory processes in retardates and normals. In N. R. Ellis (Ed.). *International review of research in mental retardation* (Vol. 4). New York: Academic Press.

Emmerich, H. J. (1979). Developmental differences in ratings of meaningfulness, concreteness, and picturability. *Developmental Psychology, 15,* 464–466.

Fitts, P. M. (1964). Perceptual-motor skill learning. In A. W. Melton (Ed.), *Categories of human learning.* New York: Academic Press.

Flavell, J. H. (1970). Developmental studies of mediated memory. In H. W. Reese & L. P. Lipsitt (Eds.), *Advances in child development and behavior* (Vol. 5). New York: Academic Press.

Flavell, J. H., Friedrichs, A. G., & Hoyt, J. D. (1970). Developmental changes in memorization processes. *Cognitive Psychology, 1,* 324–340.

Flavell, J. H., & Wellman, H. M. (1977). Metamemory. In R. W. Kail & J. W. Hagen (Eds.),

Perspectives on the development of memory and cognition. Hillsdale, NJ: Lawrence Erlbaum Associates.

Frankel, M. T., & Rollins, H. A. (1985). Associative and categorical hypotheses in the free recall of adults and children. *Journal of Experimental Child Psychology, 40,* 304–318.

Guttentag, R. E. (1984). The mental effort requirement of cumulative rehearsal: A developmental study. *Journal of Experimental Child Psychology, 37,* 92–106.

Kail, R. V., & Hagen, J. W. (1977). (Eds.). *Perspectives on the development of memory and cognition.* Hillsdale, NJ: Lawrence Erlbaum Associates.

Lange, G. (1973). The development of conceptual and rote recall skills among school age children. *Journal of Experimental Child Psychology, 15,* 394–407.

Lange, G. (1978). Organization-related processes in children's recall. In P. A. Ornstein (Ed.), *Memory development in children.* Hillsdale, NJ: Lawrence Erlbaum Associates.

Levin, J. R. (1981). On functions of pictures in prose. In F. J. Pirozzolo & M. C. Wittrock (Eds.), *Neuropsychological and cognitive processes in reading.* New York: Academic Press.

Liberty, C., & Ornstein, P. A. (1973). Age differences in organization and recall: The effects of training in categorization. *Journal of Experimental Child Psychology, 15,* 169–186.

Naus, M. J., & Ornstein, P. A. (1983). The development of memory strategies: Analysis, questions, and issues. In M. T. H. Chi (Ed.), *Trends in memory development research (Contributions to Human Development),* (Vol. 9). Basel: S. Karger.

Naus, M. J., Ornstein, P. A., & Aivano, S. (1977). Developmental changes in memory: The effects of processing time and rehearsal instructions. *Journal of Experimental Child Psychology, 23,* 237–251.

Ornstein, P. A. (Ed.). (1978). *Memory development in children.* Hillsdale, NJ: Lawrence Erlbaum Associates.

Ornstein, P. A. (1982, May). *The development of mnemonic skill.* Paper presented at the meetings of the North American Society for the Psychology of Sport and Physical Activity, College Park, Maryland.

Ornstein, P. A., & Baker-Ward, L. (1983, April). *The development of mnemonic skill.* Paper presented at the meetings of the Society for Research in Child Development, Detroit.

Ornstein, P. A., & Corsale, K. (1979). Organizational factors in children's memory. In C. R. Puff (Ed.), *Memory organization and structure.* New York: Academic Press.

Ornstein, P. A., Medlin, R. G., Stone, B. P., & Naus, M. J. (1985). Retrieving for rehearsal: An analysis of active rehearsal in children's memory. *Developmental Psychology, 21,* 633–641.

Ornstein, P. A., & Naus, M. J. (1978). Rehearsal processes in children's memory. In P. A. Ornstein (Ed.), *Memory development in children.* Hillsdale, NJ: Lawrence Erlbaum Associates.

Ornstein, P. A., & Naus, M. J. (1984, April). *The influence of the knowledge base on the development of mnemonic strategies.* Paper presented at the meetings of the American educational Research Association, New Orleans.

Ornstein, P. A., & Naus, M. J. (1985). Effects of the knowledge base on children's memory strategies. In H. Reese (Ed.), *Advances in child development and behavior* (Vol. 19). New York: Academic Press.

Ornstein, P. A., Naus, M. J., & Liberty, C. (1975). Rehearsal and organizational processes in children's memory. *Child Development, 26,* 818–830.

Ornstein, P. A., Naus, M. J., & Stone, B. P. (1977). Rehearsal training and developmental differences in memory. *Child Development, 13,* 15–24.

Paris, S. G. (1978). Coordination of means and goals in the development of mnemonic skills. In P. A. Ornstein (Ed.), *Memory development in children.* Hillsdale, NJ: Lawrence Erlbaum Associates.

Paris, S. G., & Cross, D. R. (1983). Ordinary learning: Pragmatic connections among children's beliefs, motives, and actions. In J. Bisanz, G. L. Bisanz, & R. Kail (Eds.), *Learning in children: Progress in cognitive development research.* New York: Springer-Verlag.

Paris, S. G., Newman, R. S., & McVey, K. A. (1982). Learning the functional significance of mnemonic actions: A microgenetic study of strategy acquisition. *Journal of Experimental Child Psychology, 34,* 490–509.

Perlmutter, M. (Ed.). (1980). *New directions for child development* (Vol. 10: Children's memory). San Francisco: Jossey-Bass.

Pressley, M. (1982). Elaboration and memory development. *Child Development, 53,* 296–309.

Pressley, M., Levin, J. R., & Bryant, S. L. (1983). Memory strategy instruction during adolescence: When is explicit instruction needed? In M. Pressley & J. R. Levin (Eds.), *Cognitive strategy research: Psychological foundations.* New York: Springer-Verlag.

Roberts, P. (1983). Memory on strategy instruction with the elderly: What should memory training be the training of? In M. Pressley & J. R. Levin (Eds.), *Cognitive strategy research: Psychological foundations.* New York: Springer-Verlag.

Rohwer, W. D., Jr. (1973). Elaboration and learning in childhood and adolescence. In H. W. Reese (Ed.), *Advances in child development and behavior* (Vol. 8). New York: Academic Press.

Salatas, H., & Flavell, J. H. (1976). Behavioral and metamnemonic indicators of strategic study behavior under remember instructions in first grade. *Child Development, 47,* 80–89.

Schneider, W. (1985). Developmental trends in the metamemory-memory behavior relationship: An integrative review. In D. L. Forrest-Pressley, G. E. MacKinnon, & T. G. Waller (Eds.), *Cognition, metacognition, and human performance* (Vol. 1). Orlando, FL: Academic Press.

Schneider, W. (1986). The role of conceptual knowledge, strategy knowledge, and specific mnemonic context in the development of organizational processes in memory. *Journal of Experimental Child Psychology, 42,* 218–236.

Tarkin, B. (1981). *The effects of stimulus meaningfulness on children's spontaneous rehearsal strategies.* Unpublished senior honors thesis, University of Massachusetts.

Wellman, H. M. (1983). Metamemory revisited. In M. T. H. Chi (Ed.), *Trends in memory development research (Contributions to Human Development),* (Vol. 9). Basel: S. Karger.

Worden, P. E. (1983). Memory strategy instruction with the learning disabled. In M. Pressley & J. R. Levin (Eds.), *Cognitive strategy research: Psychological foundations.* New York: Springer-Verlag.

3 Strategies in Selective Recall

August Flammer
Ruth Lüthi
University of Berne—Switzerland

Recall of stored information is not only a constituent part of every information processing activity but is fundamental to all human thought and action. So it comes as no surprise that recall from memory has long been a central topic of research. Yet it is surprising that most of this research has followed a paradigm which is quite atypical of everyday life. This paradigm consists of presenting some to-be-memorized information, which is later to be recalled as accurately and as completely as possible.

Certainly, this does resemble some real life situations, e.g., encoding and recalling a telephone number, processing a piece of information in school, and recalling it in a test at a later time. More common in real life information processing, however, is the recalling of only some selected pieces of information from a previously encoded set of information. The situation of selective recall is very common, e.g., finding out whether Mark had been among the participants at a meeting the day before, answering to the question whether your grandmother wore glasses or not.

People apparently are quite efficient in recalling selectively. What is more noteworthy is that they typically get *directly* to the knowledge searched for and do not have to first put aside a lot of information which is also stored but not relevant to the task at hand. The reader may verify this with a simple thought experiment, for example, with the grandmother question mentioned above. This is especially striking in the case of selected recall from stored discourse-based information, e.g., information encoded from a read text.

Certainly, selective recall is not always successful. It is therefore important to find ways to improve it. This is the goal of an ongoing project of the authors. They proceeded by first looking at how people recall selectively. This led to a description of a small set of recall strategies. The next step was the determination of which strategy is best under what conditions. In part these conditions are assumed to be tied to the level of cognitive development.

This paper is organized as follows: after (1) a short review of the literature on the losses of recall through the changing of the "perspective" between encoding and recall, (2) two main strategies are described, and (3) their possible operationalization in experimental research presented. (4/5) An overview of own research on adults, and (6) on children follows. In conclusion, (7) first indications of ways to educate the optimizing selective recall is given.

RECALL FROM SELECTIVE PERSPECTIVES

The influence of subjective "perspectives", anticipations and cultural schemata on selective encoding and recall has often been studied within cognitive psychology (e.g., Bartlett, 1932; Bruner & Postman, 1949/50; Kintsch & Greene, 1978; Pichert & Anderson, 1977). But it was only in 1978 that a study was published in which the subjective perspective was experimentally changed during the interval between encoding and recall (Anderson & Pichert, 1978). These authors presented a story of two boys playing truant from school. Some of the subjects were told to read the text from the perspective of a potential homebuyer, others were told to read it from the perspective of a potential burglar. It seems clear that for each case a partly different set of items should be of interest, with an associated different likelihood of being encoded in long-term memory. This was experimentally confirmed by Pichert & Anderson (1977). The big question was whether a change in perspective *before* recalling, but *after* learning, would change these probabilities in favor of the items relevant to the new perspective. It did, as Anderson & Pichert (1978) have shown. This comes as a surprise since no item can be recalled which was not encoded in the first place (disregarding reconstruction of information, a danger which was reasonably well avoided in the experiments reported in this section). Material must be encoded which, under certain perspectives, is not recalled.

In the meantime it seems apparent that many factors contribute to the selection of recall from a new perspective, e.g., encoding preferences, retrieval bias, and editing bias (see Anderson, Pichert, & Shirey, 1983). The encoding bias is clearly present and can not be overcome after a certain and not too long time interval after encoding (Flammer, 1985). It has also been shown that the encoding bias is still reflected in the recognition performance (Borland & Flammer, 1985).

The confounding effect of any selectivity while editing the required recall information can be avoided by using appropriate methods, i.e., by explicitly asking that nothing but the selected items be recalled ("partial recall" vs. "full recall", see Flammer & Tauber, 1982).

There remains the influence of selective retrieval from (available) memory. There are reasons to believe that the available traces are not all accessible with the same ease and that a changed perspective can yield access to otherwise unimportant information. Clearly, information unimportant to the reading perspective and learned only incidentally, if at all, can at times be retrieved if it becomes important to the new perspective. This holds, even if it is virtually inaccessible to retrieval from the original perspective (cf. Lüthi, 1983). What are these different possible strategies?

Before attacking this question the reader's attention is drawn to the fact that— in sum—recall from a given perspective is less efficient usually if the encoding perspective was different. Leaving the perspective the same is better than to change it. But in real-life situations, the changing of the perspective is the normal case! Rarely do we anticipate all future use of a set of information when we encode it.

The outlook gets even worse when we take into account the delay between encoding and retrieval. Fass and Schumacher (1981) have been able to show that the loss due to a different perspective while reading was significantly larger in recall after 2 weeks than in immediate recall. Again, it should be noted that delays of weeks, months, and even years, constitute the normal recall situation in real life. Hence the importance of any hint that points to better strategies for improving delayed recall from a new perspective.

TRACE AND CALL-UP STRATEGIES

According to our understanding recall consists of two phases, the retrieval phase and the editing phase. Our interest focuses on the retrieval phase. Among several possible strategies of selective retrieval we chose the trace strategy and the call-up strategy for investigation. According to the *trace strategy* the subject searches his memory traces, checking every item to see whether it fulfills the conditions for selection. If it does, this item is edited. Then the search of the memory trace continues. According to the *call-up strategy,* however, the subject does not follow along the entire encoded trace network, but instead "calls" for any candidate meeting the conditions set by the selective perspective. This strategy allows a direct access to the criterion items.

An example of the trace strategy is the following: Assume that you are asked to list everything that you ate the previous day. According to the trace strategy you might start by searching your experiences from the beginning to the end of the day. You might first discover that you ate scrambled eggs for breakfast, then perhaps a snack during a meeting in the morning, etc. To answer the same question, the call-up strategy would not check seriatim the encoding of the morning, then lunch-time etc., but would try to access all items which have both a episodic encoding relating to yesterday and an encoding of being edible. It might then be that spaghetti comes up first, because spaghetti is one of your favorite dishes and you ate it with friends last night. It might also be that a cordon bleu dish comes up for a fraction of a second but is not further processed because there is no cordon bleu episode encoded for yesterday.

OPERATIONALIZATIONS

As our examples suggest, a simple way to distinguish empirically between the two strategies is to analyze the sequence of the report of the selectively recalled items. Provided reasonable assumptions can be made about the mental organization of the encoded items, then, according to the trace strategy, the sequence of selectively recalled items should mirror this organization. We believe this conclusion eminently reasonable when we present stories with a sequence of events which logically are more or less bound to a given order. Examples would be the story of an accident and its consequences, or the story of a trip to several cities that follows a more or less straight line.

So far, this only guarantees the identification of the trace strategy; any other sequence of recalled items would not automatically indicate the presence of the call-up strategy. In our own research we chose exemplars of a given category to be recalled. If, for example, a story about a trip were read, the recall task could be to write down all flowers that were mentioned in the text. The flowers as mentioned in the text may be chosen to vary heavily in their typicality, i.e., there should be some very typical (roses), some reasonably typical (lily) and some rather or very untypical flowers (hyacinth). According to research on the recall of examples from a category we can assume that there is a tendency to recall highly typical exemplars more readily than less typical exemplars (Mervis & Rosch, 1981). With regard to the call-up strategy we would then assume that highly typical items among the to-be-recalled items should come up earlier. For the call-up strategy to be identified we would therefore need to find a sequencing of the recalled items according to decreasing typicality.

STRATEGIES OF ADULT SUBJECTS

The proposed approach has led to two experiments so far. The general result is that the typical repertoire of adults contains both strategies. Both seem to be optimal under different conditions. However, subjects do not spontaneously use the optimal strategy in all conditions.

In the first experiment (Flammer, Grob, Jann, & Reisbeck, 1985) 187 College students were presented with three different texts, but without a specific perspective from which to read the text. They were simply told to remember as much as they could. Afterwards they were asked to write down all the exemplars of a given concept, e.g., food items, furniture items, or cloth items. Each text was $1\frac{1}{2}$ pages long and contained nine exemplars of one of the mentioned concepts, scattered through the whole text. The distribution of these exemplars followed either a steady decrease of typicality, a steady increase of typicality, or an increase followed by a decrease of typicality, according to the norm tables by Flammer, Reisbeck, & Stadler (1985).

Recall showed a clear recency effect for the last two exemplars presented. After having removed these two exemplars from consideration the results favored clearly the trace strategy. In the decreasing typicality text condition there were 104 positive correlations between the presentation (and typicality) order and the recall order against 55 negative correlations (binomial comparison: $p < .01$). In the increasing typicality text condition there were 90 positive correlations against 44 negative correlations between the recall order and the presentation order ($p < .01$), which means that at the same time there were 90 negative correlations against 44 positive correlations between the recall order and the typicality order. In the text condition with typicality first increasing and then decreasing, there were 99 positive correlations with the presentation order against 44 negative correlations ($p < .01$). We take these effects to be reasonably strong given the small number of recalled items (around four after removal of the last two ''recency items''). Because of this the reliability of the correlations could not be high, and proportional differences of the order of $\frac{2}{3}$ vs. $\frac{1}{3}$ are noteworthy.

Apparently, adult subjects use the trace strategy spontaneously, although it seems that there are many cases in everyday life where we use something like the call-up strategy. Assume you realize that you have misplaced your wallet. You may spontaneously create a mental image of your wallet in order to follow the associations leading from it, then eventually pointing to the place where in the past you have typically found it. You might go to two or three favorite places in your apartment where you often put your wallet. If this does not help, you might then try the more cumbersome but more promising trace strategy, i.e., think back to the time when you definitively had your wallet and work step by step through all your actions since then.

It seems that the call-up strategy is easier to operate and also faster, but that the trace strategy leads with more certainty to results, although it takes more energy. Especially when the search area is rather extended, the trace strategy is very laborious. In the case of our experiment the search area was rather small ($1\frac{1}{2}$ pages of reading), and the motivation to succeed rather high, since people mostly try to give of their best in psychological experiments. This could mean that our subjects spontaneously used the trace strategy which was really the better one under the given constraints, but which would not be the mostly chosen in ordinary-life situations.

There is another condition to consider in favor of the trace strategy. The selective recall had to be done only a few minutes after the text was read. This means that encoding of the text was still fairly complete and accurate—certainly a condition which facilitates the subject's adoption of the trace strategy.

To investigate whether these interpretations are empirically valid, one should extend the search base (text length) and the time interval between the encoding phase and the recall phase. That is what we did in the following experiment (Flammer & Grob, 1985). The text length was extended to 4 pages and time interval was used as an independent variable, being either 20 minutes (T0) or 3 weeks (T1). There was another independent variable included, viz., the instruction to either use the trace strategy (by mentally going the text through again; INS-TEXT), or the call-up strategy (by mentally going through all possible concept exemplars, from the most typical to the less typical; INS-TYP), or no instruction (control: INS-SPON). This was done for the following reason: If our predictions had been incorrect, i.e., if the trace strategy was not spontaneously used for immediate recall, and the call-up strategy was not spontaneously used for delayed recall, the strategy instruction should obtain the information about whether the subjects have both strategies in their repertoire and are able to use them if told to do so.

In the second experiment we used a text which was 4 pages long. In this text we included 16 exemplars of each of two concepts (furniture and clothes). We removed the first and the two last exemplars of each concept from the analysis to avoid any primacy and recency effects. The remaining 13 exemplars were arranged so that the typicality was increasing over the first half of the exemplars and decreasing over the second half. Thus the correlation of the recall sequence with the typicality rating could be measured independently of the correlation with the presentation order. By this, the design allowed for the detection of the adoption of a mixture of both strategies as well. Two hundred and fifty four college students served in this experiment.

The results which are related to the strategies are presented in Table 3.1. Let us first consider the correlations of the recall order with the presentation, the presence of which reflects the trace strategy. One part of this data is a replication

TABLE 3.1
Number of Positive and Negative Correlations Between
Text Order and Recall Order, Resp. Typicality Order and
Recall Order (r = 0 Excluded; Binomial Comparison)

		INS-SPON		INS-TEXT		INS-TYP	
		r(Te)	r(Ty)	r(Te)	r(Ty)	r(Te)	r(Ty)
T0	+	39	31	46	21	46	25
	−	33	40	22	45	31	53
T1	+	28	21	18	15	27	33
	−	17	22	15	19	22	17

of the first experiment, i.e., immediate recall (T0) in the condition without strategy instruction (INS-SPON). The pattern of these results correponds to those from the first experiment: there are more positive than negative correlations with the text sequence, although this time the difference is not significant. Is it because with the longer text (4 pages instead of 1½) and the slightly longer interval between encoding and recall (20 minutes instead of 5), the traces were less available for retrieval so that the subjects did not use this trace strategy to the same extent? The picture changes as predicted in INS-TEXT where the subjects clearly adopted the trace strategy as recommended. They tended to do so even under INS-TYP, although not significantly.

So far it seems that the trace strategy is preferred under condition T0; under T1 the positive correlations with the text sequence outweighed the negative correlations only very marginally. Even under the instruction to use the trace strategy the subjects did not do so in T1. This seems reasonable when we assume that the trace strategy is not effective after a delay, and that the subjects were aware of it and acted correspondingly.

Table 3.1 also contains correlations related to the call-up strategy. It was predicted and found that under T1 the call-up strategy would be adopted, at least if the subjects are instructed to do so. What is surprising with the call-up strategy are: first, that it was not favored in delayed recall when the subjects were not instructed to use it; second, that in immediate recall there is a clear tendency for negative correlations to occur with the typicality rating. This is even and especially clearly the case under INS-TYP, T0, i.e., when the subjects were instructed to first remember any instances of the concept and then to see whether those concepts would appear.

This result is puzzling. Clearly when the task is to relate instances to concepts, the less typical instances get more or deeper processing (see Flammer & Morger, 1985; Rosch et al., 1976). But this was not the task while reading the text. The preference for the atypical instances must have come about in the retrieval processes, and this only in immediate recall and not in delayed recall.

If it is true that in immediate recall the trace strategy is more appropriate, whereas with increasing delay the call-up strategy becomes more and more appropriate then the data related to the amount of recall could be used as a test. Figure 3.1 shows that in both texts the instruction for the call-up strategy brought about significantly more recalled items than the other conditions in T1; the reverse is true for immediate recall. While the first finding can be explained by an adoption of the call-up strategy, the second looks more complicated. The reader might remember that the instruction to use the call-up strategy in immediate recall led to a superiority of the atypical instances. Maybe there was some interference between strategy instruction and actual strategy use.

The trace strategy clearly was not only generally preferred in immediate recall but was also clearly more effective in immediate recall than in delayed recall.

And in both texts the conditions with no instructions (INS-SPON) led to slightly but consistently higher recall scores than the trace instruction in T0. It might really be better not to instruct people to do what they do in any given case. This corresponds to the general rule that more or less automated procedures are hindered by conscious control. Even if there is some efficiency to be gained, controling nevertheless needs resources which are no longer available for the main processes.

The fact that after a delay of 3 weeks the call-up strategy brought about the highest correct recall is a challenge for two reasons. First, it seems apparent the subjects do not (unless instructed) use this strategy in delayed recall, with a resulting less than optimal recall. Second, the intrusions (Fig. 3.1) were also highest with the call-up strategy in delayed recall. Maybe this strategy is very productive but bears the risk of too many errors. In terms of signal detection theory, although the sensitivity has not been altered, the response threshold has been lowered. We have a study in progress in which the subjects get a second instruction to go over their written recall again and delete responses that they feel might have been too readily accepted.

So far, it seems that the two proposed strategies speak to the reality of recall tasks, that each has its advantages, that each can be used by adult subjects although not always most advantageously. Both strategies have benefits and costs.

It should be added that neither our theory nor our data exclude the possibility that some subjects use both strategies. After having stressed the ecological validity of the research paradigm we should also add that there is at least one artificiality in our experimental design, which is the artificial delimitation of the memory search area. Clearly, when subjects are asked to remember all fruit, which were mentioned in a *just read* text, then the narrowing down of the searchable memory area is unambiguously defined by instruction. Yet, when we try to remember whether we have ever eaten snails the searchable memory area is at first glance very big. So far in our second example, the adoption of the trace strategy could never make sense. But it might be that there are clear criteria available to restrict the search to very few and small areas. This might even be done by something like the call-up strategy. For our example, the following stages can be imagined: (1) Are there typical situations in which the likelihood of having eaten snails is at least bigger than zero (call-up strategy)? The answer might be something like: maybe with friends, but certainly not at home. (2) Next question: Do I have friends who like to eat special dishes (call-up strategy)? (3) I might then go through my remaining memories point by point and find or not find an incidence of snail eating (trace strategy). Thus it seems that the trace strategy always presupposes a narrowing or determination of the search area. This is easily done in experiments, when the searchable memory entries are provided in the same experimental session. But it may be a more complicated process if the task is to remember something out of one's past.

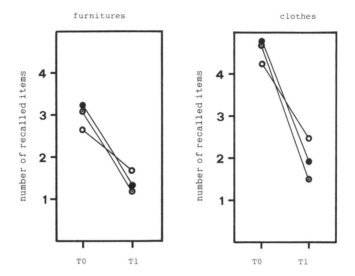

FIG. 3.1.   Correct recalled items of furnitures and clothes in immediate (T0) and delayed (T1) recall for trace strategy instruction (⊙——⊙), call-up strategy instruction (◯——◯) and no instruction (●——●). From Flammer and Grob (1985). Republished with permission of Hogrefe-Verlag.

PRIMED RECOGNITION

How can we explain this process of selective recall? What are the basic mechanisms underlying the two strategies? In our model, three basic assumptions about retrieval processes are made:

1. Basic to all retrieval are processes of activation. Memory items have first to be activated in order to be retrievable. The activation originates in a stimulated memory location (e.g., a presented word which contacts its representation), spreads out over a limited area of the representation network and thus makes more items accessible. These items are then retrieved and, if relevant, recalled. The activation level diminishes with the length of the spreading activation path (Collins & Loftus, 1975). The more strongly a memory item is activated the faster will it come to mind.

2. A further question is: In what directions will this activation spread? Or, more concretely, after stimulation of the original items, which items will be the next to be activated? We assume that the answer to this question depends on the structure of the memory network. The closer a related item, the stronger and

faster will be the activation (Collins & Loftus, 1975). The activation path can follow a categorical or an episodic link. The closeness of the categorical relations may depend on the typicality or the similarity of the related items. Episodic relations depend on the interdependence of the concerned items within a shared context. But the closeness is not the only important factor for activation. Another factor is the strength of the memory link. We can imagine that each part of the memory network has its own energy. A strong trace does not need as much activation as a weak trace in order to be retrievable. Thus, we assume that an interaction of the strength of the trace and the activation level will define the priority of the to-be-retrieved items.

3. The third assumption in our model concerns the decay of the activation. How can we be sure that the activation continues over a larger area of our memory network? We assume that when attentional activity is focused on a particular location, it becomes a source of new automatic spreading activation (see De Groot, 1983). If the subject finds an item corresponding or related to the parameters given by the selection criterion, he or she focuses attention on it. This process activates the new memory location and a new wave of activation will spread out in this area. A similar process goes on in a recognition task. A presented word activates its representation in the memory network. From this stimulated location the activation will spread out. If the next presented word is already activated, then it will be recognized faster than the first one. Each newly presented word will give a new *injection* of activation to its memory trace and so raise its activation level.

Using these three assumptions we can describe in more detail the functioning of the two retrieval strategies described in this paper. This allows us also to elaborate the conditions necessary for a strategy to be efficient in a selective recall task.

To apply a strategy means to proceed according to a plan. This plan should resolve the task at hand. In a series of experiments we asked our subjects to recall all the examples of furniture which were read in the preceding text. We assume that the word *furniture* finds its representation in the memory network which it activates. This activation spreads out, both along the categorical links to instances of this concept as well as along the episodic links to other text representations, because the task had referred also to *text*. However, we suppose that a person can control the direction of the spreading activation. According to the strategy adopted the subject's attention follows the links within the category structure or the episodic links due to the text structure.

Which strategy of the two is adopted depends on the subject's decision. And this decision depends among other things on the suitability of the network structure, i.e., on the actual strength and activation level of the relevant traces within the first stimulated area. If the categorical traces are stronger than the episodic ones (maybe because the subject, while reading, had especially focused on the furniture rather than on episodic events in the text), he or she might further direct his or her search along the categorical paths. On the other hand, if the subject retrieves important episodic items, he might come to prefer the trace strategy.

Thus, the choice of one of the two retrieval strategies is supposed to depend, among other things, on the spreading patterns of activation. The trace strategy may be an efficient strategy to remember information if the episodic links in the memory network are strong and complete. The call-up strategy may be chosen when the episodic links and other episodic information are rather weak or if through encoding strategies the categorical organization has been favored. Thus, we suppose that efficient selective recall according to one of the two strategies depends on both the strategy choice and the organization of the memory traces. The strategy must fit the memory organization in order to be effective. This holds for selective recall processes. Recognition processes, in contrast, are not *strategical* in this sense. Yet, recognition times also depend on memory organization because they depend on activation, and the spread of activation is assumed to follow the memory organization.

One method for examining the activation spreading processes in a recognition task is the primed recognition paradigm. We conducted two experiments with this method. In the first experiment (Flammer, Lüthi, & Morger, 1985) we primed the target items with categorical instances of different typicality ratings. These primes as well as the targets were concepts that had already been read in the text. The primes in this experiment varied according to their distance from the target items within the text. Thus, the manipulation of text distance (episodic relations) and typicality (categorical relations) should influence the activation spread and therefore the reaction time.

This first experiment did not yield coherent results, probably due to inappropriate SOAs (= stimulus onset asynchronies). We had a significant main effect of the test condition (specific set and order of the to-be-recognized items), independently of their position in the reading text. Thus, neither the episodic distance effect nor the typicality effect emerged. We even had an effect which was the inverse of our hypothesis: Less typical items were recognized faster than more typical test items.

In a second experiment (Flammer & Lüthi, 1988) we activated the to-be-recognized items with primes of varying categorical relations (category factor) and varying episodic relations (distance factor). The category factor had two levels: A prime either belonged to the same category or was from another category. The distance factor had three levels: Either (1) the prime was from the same sentence as the target item and had a direct episodic relation to it (example: if there was a sentence in the text like "He had much fun making money," "money" used as prime was expected to activate the memory representation of "fun" over a direct episodic link); or (2) the prime was from the same reading text as the target item, but not from the same sentence; or (3) the prime was not from the same text. In the last case there was no episodic relation available.

TABLE 3.2
Mean Reaction Times as a Function of the
Different Priming Conditions

	Same Category	Other Category
Close distance	1.84	1.36
Wide distance	1.87	1.98
not out of text	1.38	1.66

The results of the data from this last experiment are shown in Table 3.2. The analysis of variance confirmed a significant main effect of the 'distance factor' ($F = 3.08$; df $= 2,510$; $p < .05$). No significant main effect appeared for the *category effect*. However, there was a highly significant interaction ($F = 4.75$; df $= 2,510$; $p < .01$). The analyses within each category level showed that the *distance effect* was significant, if the prime was from the same category as the target item ($F = 3.16$; df $= 2,238$; $p < .05$). The group comparison by the Tukey test showed no significant differences between two groups. However, the contrast between the two groups with primes out of the text and the group with a prime that was not from the text was significant ($F = 6.28$; df $= 1$; $p < .05$). The distance effect was significant as well, if the prime was from another category ($F = 4.98$; df $= 2,272$; $p < .01$). The group comparison between the close and larger distance group was significant by the Tukey test ($p < .05$). Also significant was the contrast between the first group (close relation) and the two other groups ($F = 8.06$; df $= 1$; $p < .01$). If the prime and target were from the same category the verification latency was shortest after a prime not belonging to the text; if the prime and target belonged to different semantic categories, latency was shortest for close text distance. The analysis within each distance-level showed that the category effect was significant only for the close distance level ($F = 9.05$; df $= 1,172$; $p < .01$). However, it was an inverse category effect. The reaction time was shorter if the prime was from another category rather than the same category.

These data suggest an interference of the two factors. The shortest verification times were obtained if there was only one (experimentally intended) relation between prime and target. Perhaps when too many items are activated, the subject's task becomes more complicated and thus more time consuming.

EFFECTS OF PERSPECTIVES AND USE OF STRATEGIES IN RETRIEVAL TASKS: EXPERIMENTS WITH CHILDREN

A further question in our research is whether or not children use the same retrieval strategies as adults. Until recently, it had been believed that the inferior memory performance of children was the result of either the unavailability or the nonuse of strategies (see Hudson & Fivush, 1983). Today a broadly accepted view is that age-related improvement of memory performance could be due to changes in mental procedures (Pressley, 1982) and to higher degrees of knowledge in the domain of the to-be-remembered material (Chi, 1978). Children use strategies as well, but these may differ in their efficiency from the strategies used by adults (see Ford & Keating, 1981). The study of the age-related use of encoding strategies as well as of the development of the retrieval strategies has become an important area of study within the research of memory development (cf. Bray, Justice, & Zahm, 1983; Dempster & Rohwer, 1983; Kobasigawa, 1977; Rohwer & Litrownik, 1983).

In a selective recall task we examined whether the children used the same two strategies as adults (the trace strategy and the call-up strategy). To use the call-up strategy following the typicality order of the instances of a concept presumes that the children can classify the exemplars of the concept. The ability to classify depends on the knowledge of a certain concept and the characteristics of the relevant instances (Chi, 1983). Therefore in our experiments we used concepts which were very familiar to children such as clothes, fruits, flowers, etc. The children know many instances of these concepts. However, not all instances are equal in typicality. We assumed an organization similar to that of the adults. Normally, children first learn the names of those instances which are typical for the adults. Parents teach them first to identify apples (as example of fruit), roses (as example of flowers), and so on, which makes these instances very familiar. A child starts to build up a new concept by means of instances out of its immediate environment, which is generally the same as that of their parents. The child probably learns concepts through prototypes, not by definition. This results in instances being of more or less similarity and frequency which in turn determine their typicality. The extent to which an exemplar of a concept is more or less typical should influence its accessibility. Thus, the most typical instances come to mind first and will be recalled first, if the categorical traces are activated and the children use the call-up strategy.

However, the children may also have the possibility of conducting their search following the (episodic) text structure. The use of the trace strategy according to the texts used here, i.e., stories, presumes that children are able to order events chronologically and to encode this order in memory.

The first experiment was conducted by Zimmermann (1984). One hundred and four 4th-grade children with a mean age of 10 years participated in this experiment. They had to read a narrative of 2 pages in length (half of the subjects were presented with a fairy tale, the other half with a detective story). In each story there was a hero who had to remember certain things. The children were instructed to identify with the main character (the hero) of the story in the following manner; they were told that they should help the story hero in remembering his items. Each story could be read from two perspectives. In the fairy tale the hero had to focus either on the fruits or on the flowers, in the detective story he had to focus either on the furniture or on the clothes. Each text contained nine instances of each of the two concepts. As in the experiments with adults, typicality was crossed with temporal order by ensuring that the temporal distribution of these instances i.e., their sequential distribution through the passage, first increased and then decreased in typicality.

After reading the children played an arithmetic game which lasted 5 minutes. Then the children proceeded to the recall phase. Half of them in each group were instructed to write down all the items the story hero had to remember. The other half of the children were instructed to write down all items from the alternative perspective, on which their attention was drawn only then.

First, we examined whether or not the reading perspective had influenced the number of the recalled instances of the target concept. The results showed a highly significant difference in recall performance between the two different recall conditions (F = 7.73; df = 1,96; $p < .01$). The subjects of the group who had to recall the instances relevant to the reading perspective (nonshift condition) recalled an average of 4.07 items. The subjects who had to recall instances of the alternative concept (perspective shift condition) recalled an average of only 3.22 items. Thus, the perspective shift resulted in a deterioration of the recall performance. This result corroborates the findings with adults (see above).

As in the experiment with adults Zimmermann computed (1) the correlations between the individual recall order and the typicality in order to test the call-up strategy, and (2) the correlations between the individual recall order and the order of text position in order to test the trace strategy. With the two groups combined, the binomial test for the positive versus negative correlations between text order and recall order (to test the trace strategy) showed no significance (84 positive correlations versus 85 negative). The results related to the call-up strategy tended to indicate that the children had some preference for this strategy, although the binomial test was not significant (99 positive versus 74 negative correlations between typicality order and recall order).

These are the results obtained from all subjects, independently of the recall condition. In the analyses for each recall condition (shift versus nonshift) neither group yielded significant differences between positive and negative correlations (Table 3.3). However, there was a stronger tendency to use a positive call-up strategy in the shift condition than in the nonshift condition.

Why did the children not use the trace strategy? There are at least two possible reasons. First, as a consequence of the task instruction to remember the instances of a given concept the episodic information may have been encoded very incompletely. Second, on looking at the texts again one could surmise that the text structure did not help to find the required instances, because there was no functional or logical relation between the instances and the specific text positions. To follow the text sequence may be a helpful strategy only if the episodic information provides significant cues to point to specific instances. This was evidently not the case in these stories.

In order to examine the last explanation we wrote new stories. In these stories the instances of the given concepts were meaningfully linked to a certain text

TABLE 3.3
Number of Positive and Negative Correlations Between Text
Order and Recall Order (Trace Strategy) and Between
Typicality Order and Recall Order (Call-up Strategy)
as a Function of the Recall Condition; Both Texts Pooled

Recall Condition	Trace Strategy		Call-up Strategy	
	+	−	+	−
nonshift	42	41	45	39
shift	42	44	54	35
total	84	85	99	74

position. Example: In the description of a trip to the top of a mountain there are many flowers which can be found by a hiker. These flowers have a more or less fixed position in the real world: Roses can be found in villages, but edelweiss grow only on the rocks on top of the mountains, and not in the forest nor in the alps. Thus, if the subject in his or her mind goes from the village to the mountains, he or she may find useful cues to the related items.

Thirty-two 2nd-grade and 32 4th-grade children from the city of Berne participated in this second experiment. Because the second-grade children were not advanced enough in writing and reading, the texts were played back from the tape recorder and the items were recalled orally.

The results of this experiment show that the age effect on the amount of recalled items was only significant for the nonshift condition. The fourth-graders recalled more instances than the second-graders of the concept on which they had focused during reading. For the incidentally learned material no differences could found between 2nd- and 4th-graders (Table 3.4).

The age differences in the nonshift condition can be explained by the more efficient application of the encoding strategy. For the material which had to be recalled in the shift condition no encoding strategy had been indicated. This explanation is supported by the comparison of the different recall condition groups within each age group. There is a significant recall condition effect only for 4th-grade children, not for 2nd-graders. The 2nd-graders did not recall more instances in the nonshift condition than in the shift condition group.

This explanation puts all the burden of the differences on the encoding. This is justified if sensible recall strategies can be found in both conditions. Indeed,

TABLE 3.4
Number of Recalled Items in the Two
Recall Condition Groups as a
Function of Age; Two Texts Pooled

	Nonshift	Shift
second-grade	3.81	3.38
fourth-grade	5.53	3.81
P	< .05	n.s.

Kobasigawa (1977) and Hudson and Fivush (1983) have shown that retrieval strategies develop even earlier than encoding strategies. To compare our two age groups in their use of the trace and call-up strategy we calculated the correlations between their recall order of the retrieved items and the typicality order and between the recall order and the text order as we did in the former experiment. Over all subjects the binomial test significantly favored the trace strategy ($p < .01$), but was also just significant for the call-up strategy ($p = .05$).

In the further analysis we examined the use of the two strategies for the two age groups and the two conditions separately. The results are shown in Table 3.5. For the 4th-grade children in the nonshift condition there were significant binomial test results in favor both of the trace strategy ($p < .01$) and of the call-up strategy ($p < .05$). All other tests were nonsignificant. Obviously, as far as our two strategies are concerned, they could be detected only in the one condition which also yielded the best recall.

What might be surprising is the fact that both strategies were applied. We first speculated that this could be an artifact of our experimental condition of the items distribution. Remember that the distribution of the items followed first an increase in typicality, and in the second half, a decrease in typicality. Now, assume that the subjects recalled the items according to the trace strategy and assume that they concentrated especially on the first half of the text. This would have produced an inverse call-up effect. We examined this possibility and found an equal number of recalled items from the first and from the second part in the text. Thus, the artifact hypothesis could be dismissed.

Although the correlations indicate the presence of both strategies, the indica-

TABLE 3.5
Text and Typicality Correlations as a Function of
Recall Condition and Age

	Trace Strategy	Call-up Strategy
total	80 − 32 $p<.01$	39 − 61 $p=.05$
fourth-grade, nonshift	30 − 2 $p<.01$	7 − 22 $p<.01$
fourth-grade, shift	16 − 11 $p>.05$	9 − 13 $p>.05$
second-grade, nonshift	19 − 10 $p>.05$	12 − 13 $p>.05$
second-grade shift	15 − 10 $p>.05$	11 − 13 $p>.05$

tions for the trace strategy are somewhat stronger, albeit not significant. This holds for the binomial quotients ($\frac{80}{32}$ vs. $\frac{61}{39}$) as well as for the means of the correlations (not reported here).

The trace strategy really only appeared in the second children's experiment. We attribute this difference to the kind of story we used. The meaningful links between the instances and their text position might have been helpful in the application of the trace strategy.

A further question to examine was whether or not the recall condition would influence the use of strategy. Table 3.5 shows the different results for the two recall condition groups: the recall strategies are highly significant for the recall in the non-shift condition, but not for the shift condition group.

As already mentioned, both shifted recall groups did not show strong indication of any particular strategy. This is somewhat surprising in the case of the 4th-graders as the nonshift subjects had the text structure available for the trace strategy. Were the shift subjects too disturbed by the surprising recall instruction? If so, it seems reasonable to assume that they tried to use the call-up strategy. There is evidence that they tried hard to do so: There were 60 wrongly recalled items remembered by the children in the shift condition (as opposed to zero in the nonshift condition). And of those 60 items 28 were the second most typical items of the typicality norm list (like tulip for flowers, pear for fruits or closet for furniture). Taken together with the small number of correctly recalled items, this may have resulted in a poor reliability of the correlation which should indicate the use of the call-up strategy.

CONCLUSION

The two selective recall strategies that are proposed here may not be the only ones used. Nevertheless, there now is quite strong evidence that under appropriate conditions subjects do indeed employ them. Among these conditions is the requirement that the episodic knowledge is complete and coherent enough to allow a *complete* search according to the trace strategy. Our results indicate that with an increasing interval between encoding and recall this is less and less warranted. Our results also indicate that the subjects are aware of this problem, since mostly they do not apply the trace strategy after a longer interval.

Following longer retention intervals the call-up strategy seems to be more appropriate than the trace strategy. However, our results show that this strategy becomes unreliable as the interval increases (i.e., more and more intrusions occur). Maybe the subjects are also aware of this, as when given no instructions, they apply this strategy less frequently. Nevertheless, they can apply it when instructed to do so. Should such instructions be generally recommended? Certainly they would have to be adapted to different selective recall conditions. The general form could be: "Think of things that are possible 'there' and watch to see whether they really are!" Clearly this is a problematic recall procedure when the encoding traces are no longer very strong. The mental rehearsal of items may easily overlay the original long-term trace or lead to the conviction that the items was in the long-term memory already before.

On the other hand it is still true that the call-up strategy is not dependent on the episodic trace and is therefore more effective after long intervals and in cases where the episodic traces are very extended, e.g., searching in a large part of one's own biography. There must be ways to overcome the problem of false intrusions. We suppose that there are adequate testing procedures, like searching the episodic encodings around the candidate item to find out whether there are sufficiently plausible links from the item to appropriate episodes.

Our research has thrown new light on why the Ebbinghaus retention curve moves downward over time. In the case of selective recall this decay seems to be due to the more potent strategy becoming obsolete and to the error proneness of the remaining strategy. We believe that future research should try to overcome the barriers to successful selective recall. On the other hand we believe that the search for additional strategies should be continued.

If the two strategies proposed here are valid in the sense that they are anchored in the structure of the encodings, then we remain puzzled by our results (or nonresults) in the priming experiments. Certainly, the priming methodology is delicate, and further attempts should be made to verify the general activation model underlying the working of the strategies.

Another reason to distrust the generality of our two strategies is the failure to find them in 8-year-old children. While the 10-year-olds' findings corresponded quite nicely to what we found with adults, the 8-year-olds' findings were not. Was it a problem of reliability? The experiments should be repeated. In any case, what were the strategies that they used? Was it that their retrieval was random, and that it was only through the editing or output decisions that the open recall was not chaotic? This is a possibility, but should not readily be accepted in order not to miss the chance to find out the retrieval strategies they possibly use.

ACKNOWLEDGMENT

Part of the research reported in this paper was funded by the Swiss National Science Foundation, project no. 1.629-0.82. The authors acknowledge the valuable help of Ursula Zimmermann. They are deeply indepted for the editorial help of Alex Wearing, University of Melbourne.

REFERENCES

Anderson, R. C., & Pichert, J. W. (1978). Recall of previously unrecallable information following a shift in perspective. *Journal of Verbal Learning and Verbal Behavior, 17,* 1–12.
Anderson, R. C., Pichert, J. W., & Shirey, L. L. (1983). Effect of the readers schema at different points in time. *Journal of Educational Psychology, 75,* 271–279.

Bartlett, F. C. (1932). *Remembering. A study in experimental and social psychology.* Cambridge, England: Cambridge University Press.

Borland, R., & Flammer, A. (1985). Encoding and retrieval processes in memory for prose. *Discourse Processes, 8,* 305–317.

Bray, N. W., Justice, E. M., & Zahm, D. N. (1983). Two developmental transitions in selective remembering strategies. *Journal of Experimental Child Psychology, 36,* 43–55.

Bruner, J., & Postman, L. (1949–50). On the perception of incongruity: A paradigm. *Journal of Personality, 18,* 206–228.

Chi, M. T. H. (1978). Knowledge structures and memory development. In S. R. Siegler (Ed.), *Children's thinking: What develops?* Hillsdale, NJ: Lawrence Erlbaum Associates.

Chi, M. T. H. (1983). Knowledge-derived categorization in young children. In D. R. Rogers & J. A. Sloboda (Eds.). *Acquisition of symbolic skills.* New York: Plenum.

Collins, A. M., & Loftus, E. F. (1975). A spreading activation theory of semantic processing. *Psychological Review, 82,* 407–428.

De Groot, A. M. B. (1983). The range of automatic spreading activation in word priming. *Journal of Verbal Learning and Verbal Behavior, 22,* 417–436.

Dempster, F. N., & Rohwer, W. D. (1983). Age differences and modality effects in immediate and final free recall. *Child Psychology, 54,* 30–41.

Fass, W., & Schumacher, G. M. (1981). Schema theory and prose retention: Boundary conditions for encoding and retrieval effects. *Discourse Processes, 4,* 17–26.

Flammer, A. (1985). L'influence de titres sur la comprehension et le rappel de textes. In B. W. Biancho (Ed.), *Lettura e ricezione del testo* (293–306). Lecce: Adriatica Editrice Salentina.

Flammer, A., & Grob, A. (1985). Behaltensdauer und selektive Wiedergabe. *Zeitschrift für Entwicklungspsychologie und Pädagogische Psychologie, 4,* 287–298.

Flammer, A., Grob, A., Jann, M., & Reisbeck, C. (1985). Mentale Repräsentation und selektive Wiedergabe. *Zeitschrift für experimentelle und angewandte Psychologie, 32,* 21–32.

Flammer, A., & Lüthi, R. (1988). *Episodische und kategorielle Aktivierungseffekte in Wiedererkennungsaufgaben. Archiv für Psychologie* (in press).

Flammer, A., Lüthi, R., & Morger, V. (1985). Strategies des selektiven Erinnerns: Ein Experiment mit gesteuertem Wiedererkennen. *Archiv für Psychologie, 137,* 255–271.

Flammer, A., & Morger, V. (1985). Die Wirkungen von Voraktivierung und Typikalität auf die Verifikation von Begriffsexemplaren. *Schweizerische Zeitschrift für Psychologie, 44,* 1–16.

Flammer, A., Reisbeck, C., & Stadler, S. (1985). Typikalitätsnormen für dreizehn Begriffe für eine deutschschweizerische Studentenpopulation. *Sprache und Kognition, 4,* 49–63.

Flammer, A., & Tauber, M. (1982). Changing the readers perspective. In A. Flammer & W. Kintsch (Eds.), *Discourse processing.* Amsterdam: North-Holland.

Ford, M. E., & Keating, D. P. (1981). Developmental and individual differences in long-term memory retrieval: Process and organization. *Child Development, 52,* 234–241.

Hudson, J., & Fivush, R. (1983). Categorical and schematic organisation and the development of retrieval strategies. *Journal of Experimental Child Psychology, 36,* 32–42.

Kintsch, W., & Greene, E. (1978). The role of culture-specific schemata in the comprehension and recall of stories. *Discourse Processes, 1,* 1–13.

Kobasigawa, A. (1977). Retrieval strategies in the development of memory. In R. V. Kail & J. W. Hagen (Eds.), *Perspectives on the development of memory and cognition.* Hillsdale, NJ: Lawrence Erlbaum Associates.

Lüthi, R. (1983). *Der Einfluss von Lese- und Abrufperspektiven auf das Erinnern von Textmaterial.* Lizentiatsarbeit. Universität Freiburg.

Mervis, C. B., & Rosch, E. (1981). Categorization of natural objects. In N. R. Rosenzweig & L. W. Porter (Eds.), *Annual Review of Psychology, 32,* 89–115.

Pichert, W. P., & Anderson, R. C. (1977). Taking different perspectives on a story. *Journal of Educational Psychology, 69,* 309–315.

Pressley, M. (1982). Elaboration and memory development. *Child Development, 53,* 296–309.

Rohwer, W. D., & Litrownik, J. (1983). Age and individual differences in the learning of a memorization procedure. *Journal of Educational Psychology, 75,* 799–810.

Rosch, E., Mervis, C. B., Gray, W. D., Johnson, D. M., & Boyes-Bream, P. (1976). Basic objects in natural categories. *Cognitive Psychology, 8,* 382–439.

Zimmermann, U. (1984). *Perspektive und Gedächtnisstrategien bei Kindern.* Lizentiatsarbeit. Universität Freiburg.

II

METAMEMORY: PROBLEMS OF STRATEGY GENERALIZATION AND STRATEGY TRAINING

4

Components of Children's Metamemory: Implications for Strategy Generalization

John G. Borkowski
Matt Milstead
University of Notre Dame

Catherine Hale
St. Mary's College

> *What, then is memory development the development of? It seems in large part to be the development of intelligent structuring and storage of input, of intelligent search and retrieval operations, and of intelligent monitoring and knowledge of these storage and retrieval operations—a kind of "metamemory", perhaps. (Flavell, 1971, p. 277)*

From its sketchy beginning in 1971 to its more elaborate contemporary formulations (Pressley, Borkowski, & O'Sullivan, 1985), metamemory theory has steadfastly maintained a key assumption that has proved difficult to verify: Components of metamemory are the precursors, and perhaps determinants, of a wide variety of strategic-based performance. This chapter reviews the 15-year search for the elusive connections between memory behavior and memory knowledge that are necessary to give plausibility to metamemory theory. First, we summarize research from the decade of the 1970s, suggesting reasons why early research on metamemory failed to produce theoretical advancements. Next, recent models of metamemory, developed by Pressley et al. (1985) and revised by Borkowski, Johnston, and Reid (1987), are used to integrate extant data on metamemory and to point the way toward new research issues. Finally, reflections on the origins and dynamics of various components of metamemory are offered as a way of integrating metamemory theory with various attributional and contextual theories of cognition.

EARLY PERSPECTIVES ABOUT METAMEMORY: FIRST WAVE RESEARCH

The initial enthusiasm that greeted Flavell's (1971) early insights about meta-memory was translated into two distinct research directions. One approach was to examine directly the relationship between metamemory and memory. This approach was based on the assumption that children's memory performance was influenced, and possibly determined, by their knowledge of what actions were appropriate and beneficial in solving memory problems. Children were assumed likely to use a strategy if they knew when and in what situations that use was appropriate. The second approach was to examine developmental differences in the contents of metamemory. Most of the studies generated by the second approach revealed much about what children know and don't know about memory, but revealed little about how children use that knowledge in memory situations (e.g., Kreutzer, Leonard, & Flavell, 1975). Because these two approaches characterize the first wave of research on metamemory, we examine them in more detail, searching for issues and obstacles in the emergence of metamemory theory.

Direct-Link Approach

Interest in discovering linkages between metamemory and memory was stimulated by metamemory's potential for explaining various anomalies in the memory literature, notably production deficiencies in young children (Brown, 1975). That is, young children often fail to spontaneously produce strategies which they could use with some facility if directed to do so. Metamemory provides a potential explanation: Children might use strategies provided they knew when and in what situations those strategies were appropriate. Developmental differences in memory could then be explained in terms of children's knowledge about when and where strategic behavior was useful or necessary (Borkowski & Cavanaugh, 1979). This line of reasoning led to two major outlets for research—correlational studies and training studies.

The method used in the correlational studies was typically to ask several questions about memory knowledge, then to present a memory task and observe if good performance was related to metamemorial awareness of the task. Few of these correlational studies revealed a significant relationship between metamemory and memory performance. For example, Kelly, Scholnick, Travers, and Johnson (1976) examined the relationship of prediction (and postdiction) of recall with measures of recall readiness, recall accuracy, and strategy use. No significant correlations were found for kindergarteners, 1st graders, 4th graders, or college students. Furthermore, awareness of the beneficial effects of a strategy was not always found to lead to the use of the strategy in memory situations (e.g., Salatas & Flavell, 1976).

The second method—intervention or training studies—was based on the assumption that training in the use of mnemonics would lead to greater understanding of memory, and in turn, to improved performance in relevant memory situations. Brown and her colleagues (e.g., Brown & Barclay, 1976; Brown & Campione, 1977; Brown & DeLoache, 1978; Campione & Brown, 1977) conducted a series of intervention studies to improve children's awareness of factors influencing memory performance, such as memory span, the need to monitor performance, and the effectiveness of mnemonic strategies. Although training was sometimes found to improve immediate performance, maintenance over time and its transfer to new tasks was seldom evidenced (see Borkowski & Cavanaugh, 1979, and Brown, Bransford, Ferrara, & Campione, 1983, for reviews).

When training and correlational studies failed to find support for a direct relationship between metamemory and memory, it was concluded that the initial ideas about the concept of metamemory may have been too simplistic and deterministic (Flavell & Wellman, 1977). Theorists began to realize that understanding the relation between metamemory and memory would require more than the computation of a simple correlation between a memory behavior and a seemingly relevant aspect of metamemory.

Developmental Differences

The other major research approach to the analysis of metamemory was to make no explicit assumptions about specific relationships between metamemory and memory, but instead to examine developmental changes in the contents of memory knowledge. Most of these early studies asked children to report what they knew about the effects of a number of variables on remembering. The classic example of this genre was Kreutzer, Leonard, and Flavell's (1975) extensive interview study of children (in kindergarten, and grades 1, 3, and 5) who were asked to respond to questions about hypothetical memory situations. Whereas younger children thought of some appropriate memory behaviors, older children were generally more strategic and planful, often suggesting rather sophisticated mnemonics.

A framework for classifying studies focusing on developmental differences was provided by Flavell and Wellman (1977) who presented a taxonomy or classification scheme of memory knowledge in which two domains of meta-memorial knowledge were delineated—sensitivity and variables. *Sensitivity* refers to an awareness of the need to employ deliberate mnemonics in a particular task. In general, *variables* refer to knowledge of what factors influence performance in a memory problem. This latter classification can be subdivided into three categories: (1) person variables include knowledge about one's own and others' characteristics, limitations, and abilities as memorizers; (2) strategy variables include knowledge about the usefulness of storage and retrieval strategies in one's repertoire; and (3) task variables include knowledge of all the characteristics of materials and task demands that influence memory performance. Lastly, Flavell and Wellman proposed that metamemory also included knowledge about interactions between sensitivity, task, strategy, and person variables. As we shall shortly see, these reflections on the interaction of variables was perhaps the most important insight for the subsequent development of metamemory theory.

The net result from the Kreutzer's et al. developmental classification of memory knowledge and Flavell and Wellman's taxonomy for categories of metamemory was a host of demonstration studies that revealed much about what particular groups of children (e.g., kindergarteners versus 3rd graders or mentally retarded versus normal children) know and don't know about memory, but revealed little about how children acquire that knowledge or how they use it to improve performance in a range of memory situations.

First Wave Research and Metamemory Theory

Although developmental differences in metamemory were amply documented by the late 1970s, the nagging question remained as to whether metamemory was a viable construct for more general cognitive theories—viable in the sense that it would prove useful in accounting for individual differences in memory performance. Recent reviews suggested contrasting perspectives. On the one hand, Cavanaugh and Perlmutter (1982) concluded that, though not all was lost, empirical verification of metamemory was problematic at best. These authors cited the general lack of clarity in theoretical conceptions of metamemory, problems with assessment of metamemory, and failure to account for children's understanding of task variables. In contrast, Wellman (1983) provided a more optimistic picture of the current state of our understanding of metamemory, concluding that explorations of the relationship between metamnemonic knowledge and strategic memory behavior had provided, at least in some instances, preliminary empirical support for the construct. Wellman was critical, however, of overly simplistic views evidenced in the literature regarding the direct influence of metamemory on memory behavior.

Methodological Issues in Metamemory Research: The Cavanaugh–Perlmutter Critique. Cavanaugh and Perlmutter (1982) argued against relying solely on verbal reports as sources for metamemorial information since this method assumes verbal accessibility of metamnemonic knowledge (see Brown et al., 1983). Furthermore, they contended that the existing low level correlations between metamemory and memory behavior could not easily be explained because of poor internal validity in most research efforts. That is, factors associated with verbal accessibility were often confounded with hypotheses about the meta-memory–memory relationship. Additionally, they cited undesirable demand effects that contaminated research using "feeling of knowing" (e.g., Markman, 1973; Yussen & Levy, 1975) and recall readiness (e.g., Flavell, Friedrichs, & Hoyt, 1970; Masur, McIntyre, & Flavell, 1973) as measures of metamemory. Finally, they criticized the use of a single index of metamemory and, in the case of verbal self-reports, the lack of a rationale for the use of probes to enhance the quality of introspective reports.

Cavanaugh and Perlmutter (1982) concluded their critique by arguing for a reconceptualization of metamemory. They urged that reliability and validity of assessment procedures needed additional research attention. In order to accomplish that goal, it was suggested that theoretical work was needed in order to specify more intricate interrelationships among different areas and types of memory knowledge. They cogently argued that investigators should use multiple assessments of metamemory to improve their chances of tapping into these interrelationships. Finally, and perhaps more germane to the interest of this chapter, they insisted upon more precise predictions concerning the nature and locus of metamemory-memory relationships.

Wellman's Interactionist Perspective. Wellman (1983), as noted earlier, was somewhat more optimistic about the status of metamemory research. He too however, was critical of past research which often relied on single indices of metamemory. Moreover, Wellman (1983) argued that metamemory should be viewed as the individual's "theory of mind," which is ". . . likely to be a highly integrated set of notions, propositions and concepts." Research should focus more on the child's integration and synthesis of information about memory tasks and processes. Further, the use of manipulative studies rather than correlational techniques alone was advocated since they might be expected to result in more sophisticated theories of metamemory. Finally, Wellman suggested that concurrent metamemory assessments are preferable to retrospective, verbal reports. In support of these suggestions, he cited work on effort allocation (Gruneberg & Monks, 1974; Wellman, 1979) and study time allocation (Brown & Smilcly, 1978), utilizing manipulative designs with concurrent measures of metamemory. In these projects, the relationship between metamemory and memory performance was found to be reliable under highly specific conditions which included an integration of task demands and available control processes.

Alternative Perspectives on First Wave Research. Schneider (1985), in a review of the metamemory literature, suggested that the discrepant conclusions of the two earlier reviews resulted from considerations of different areas of metamemory research. Cavanaugh and Perlmutter (1982) were primarily concerned with research on task variables, whereas Wellman (1983) focused more on evidence in line with a broader conception of metamemory in which person variables interacted with strategy variables. After performing a more extensive and inclusive review, Schneider (1985) concluded that the findings of both reviews were valid for the particular sample of metamemory studies considered. That is, when only studies examining task variables (as reviewed by Cavanaugh & Perlmutter, 1982) were analyzed, little support was found for the link between metamemory and memory. On the other hand, when Schneider examined the research focusing on the dynamic aspects of person variables (as reviewed by Wellman, 1983), he found strong support for the metamemory–memory behavior relationship. Moreover, when Schneider considered both types of research as well as training studies with paired associate and free-recall learning tasks (which were not extensively considered in the previous reviews), he found a significant and substantial relationship between metamemory and memory behavior; his meta-analysis of the existing data set yielded an overall correlation of .42.

Schneider also presented evidence that supported earlier arguments (cf. Borkowski, Reid, & Kurtz, 1984) that training and intervention studies may be especially appropriate for substantiating the metamemory–memory behavior relationship. Training studies using paired associate (e.g., Kendall, Borkowski, & Cavanaugh, 1980) and free-recall learning (e.g., Paris, Newman, & McVey, 1982) have found significant correlations between metamemory and memory behavior. For example, Kendall et al. (1980) trained mentally retarded children in the use of elaborative strategies for deployment on paired associate tasks. Significant correlations were found between metamemory scores and recall, and between metamemory and the quality of strategic behavior (i.e., verbal elaborations). In a similar study with normal children, Kurtz, Reid, Borkowski, and Cavanaugh (1982) also found sizable correlations between pretest assessments of metamemory and strategy use on transfer tests.

Results from several training studies involving free-recall learning tasks have also documented significant relationships between metamemory and memory (Borkowski, Peck, Reid, & Kurtz, 1983; Paris et al., 1982). Furthermore, Borkowski et al. (1983) found metamemory to be a better predictor of memory performance than cognitive tempo, a factor which previously was found to be related to performance on a variety of cognitive tasks. Similarly, Paris et al. (1982) investigated metamemory–memory relationships using a causal modeling procedure and found that metamemory had a significant effect on memory performance. Additionally, the effects of training on memory performance were mediated by metamnemonic knowledge about the ''value'' of trained strategies. Finally, both studies provided preliminary support for the contention that the causal links between metamemory and memory performance and behavior are bidirectional (cf. Borkowski, 1985; Brown, 1975). Metamemory is both a potential cause and a consequence of memory behavior. The question that remains to be addressed, and the subject of our discussion of second generation research, is how various aspects or components of metamemory influence specific cognitions and memory behaviors.

In sum, metamemory research conducted during the last decade has provided important information about the links between metamemory and memory behavior, as well as insightful suggestions about the direction of research that is surely to follow. Perhaps most important was the recommendation that metamemory needs to be conceived as a multifaceted phenomenon and that theoretical work must move beyond the simplistic assumptions of the direct-link approach, and instead describe metamemory as an integrated and interactive system of knowledge. It has become apparent that manipulative studies that involved training and multiple assessments of metamemory provide the clearest support for the causal effects of metamemory on memory performance (Paris et al., 1982). Strategy training, combined with assessment of its generalization to new tasks, appears to be the most sensitive context in which to understand how individual differences in preexisting levels of metamemory influence performance (Borkowski, 1985). Finally, in contrast to conclusions reached by some earlier reviews, the recent review by Schneider (1985) concludes that metamemory is a viable construct in cognitive development theories, with potentially important explanatory power.

METAMEMORY: THEORETICAL AND EMPIRICAL ADVANCES

The second wave of research on metamemory can be characterized by increased theoretical complexity, manipulative rather than correlational methods, use of multiple tasks and strategies, and mini-longitudinal designs. In this section, we describe these shifts in research orientation within the framework of a model of metamemory first developed by Pressley et al. (1985) and extended by Borkowski et al. (1987). After describing the model, we interpret the outcomes of several recent studies from new perspectives derived from the model.

COMPONENTS OF METAMEMORY

We conceptualize metamemory in terms of a number of interactive, mutually related components. At this stage of model building, several major components seem to deserve independent theoretical specification because they appear to have unique developmental histories, are differentially influenced by experience and instruction, and fill distinctive roles in explaining differences in learning and memory performance among normal, gifted, mentally retarded, and learning disabled children, and even among children with seemingly similar learning abilities (i.e., equivalent IQ's). The major components of metamemory, listed in order of their developmental emergence, are the following: Specific Strategy Knowledge, Relational Strategy Knowledge, General Strategy Knowledge, and Metamemory Acquisition Procedures (Pressley et al., 1985). In the following sections, we outline the function of each metamemory component, describe a series of studies that suggest the importance of Specific Strategy Knowledge in acquiring new skills, expand the function of General Strategy Knowledge to include motivational properties that seem useful in explaining strategy generalization phenomena, and point out the integrative role within the system played by Metamemory Acquisition Procedures.

Specific Strategy Knowledge.   Knowledge about particular strategies, such as rehearsal, organization, and elaboration, and their application are aspects of metamemory called Specific Strategy Knowledge. For instance a child may know that organizing a 24-item list into units will make it easier to learn or that cumulative rehearsal within small groups of interrelated items is more efficient than rote, repetitive rehearsal. These types of Specific Strategy Knowledge accumulate slowly as a child matures, their development being paralleled by the hierarchical emergence of complex strategies that require mental transformations (cf. Neimark, 1976). Specific Strategy Knowledge likely involves understanding (a) a strategy's goals and objectives, (b) the tasks for which the strategy is appropriate, (c) its range of applicability, (d) the learning gains expected from consistent use of the strategy, (e) the amount of effort associated with its deployment, and (f) whether the strategy is enjoyable or burdensome to use (e.g., elaborative imagery has inherent interest value whereas cumulative rehearsal requires considerable efforts). These are some of the possible attributes of a strategy that the child might acquire after guided prolonged instruction in its use or after more independent extensions of the strategy—both successful and unsuccessful—to new tasks. After several strategies are acquired, we hypothesize that *general attributes* or features common to all strategies become apparent to the child. In turn, a knowledge about key attributes should make new strategy acquisition more rapid and durable. The child has an understanding about the reasons why specific attributes were included in an instructional package or gives evidence of the fact the essential information is missing if the instructional message is incomplete.

When a child possesses a number of strategies together with knowledge about their various uses, he or she is able to make an *informed* judgment about strategy deployment on novel, transfer tasks. Sophisticated learners—both children and adults—are in command of strategy knowledge to varying degrees and their intelligent use of strategies cannot occur without it. Figure 4.1 shows the relationship between Specific Strategy Knowledge about three strategies that develop sequentially (repetition, organization, and verbal elaboration) as they might influence strategy use depending on the nature of the to-be-learned task. The three strategies share common attributes (e.g., when to use and not use each

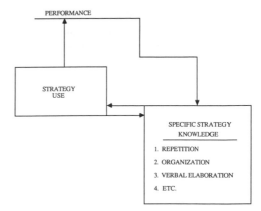

FIG. 4.1. A model of early metamemory development: The relationship between strategy use and Specific Strategy Knowledge.

strategy) and likely possess unique strategy-specific attributes (e.g., realizing that verbal elaborations must draw upon other information in memory in order to be executed).

In terms of the emergence of metamemory, we assume that there is a dynamic, causal bidirectionality between actual strategy use and Specific Strategy Knowledge. Not only does Specific Strategy Knowledge guide the deployment of individual strategies, but the continued use of a strategy results in an expansion and refinement of Specific Strategy Knowledge about it. In turn, enhanced knowledge increases the likelihood that the strategy will be put to good future use, being especially relevant on far generalization tasks (Brown, 1975).

Relational and General Strategy Knowledge. As Specific Strategy Knowledge about multiple strategies is acquired, two other components of metamemory emerge: Relational Strategy Knowledge and General Strategy Knowledge. Relational Strategy Knowledge is that aspect of metamemory which helps the child to understand the comparative merits associated with a number of specific strategies. The aim of relational knowledge is to enable a classification system to be formed for contrasting the strengths and weaknesses of specific strategies. Relational strategy knowledge helps to highlight the attributes of a number of competing strategies in the face of different task demands, providing useful comparative information for strategy selection and revision decisions that are part of the domain of a more advanced metamemory component (Metamemory Acquisition Procedures). Because we know little about the development of Relational Knowledge, this component is not considered in the remainder of this paper.

In terms of patterns of metamemory development, General Strategy Knowledge follows the accumulation of Specific and Relational Knowledge. General Strategy Knowledge reflects the child's understanding that effort is required to apply strategies and that an effortful, strategic approach often results in more successful performance than a nonstrategic approach. Feedback about a strategy's effectiveness enhances more general understanding about the value of being planful and strategic. Figure 4.2 adds Relational and General Strategy Knowledge to Specific Knowledge, showing their interdependent development as the child begins to face more challenging learning tasks.

We believe that a unique property of General Strategy Knowledge—one not found in other components of metamemory—is its motivational character (Borkowski et al., 1987). General knowledge about the value of behaving strategically results in expectations about self-efficacy which, in turn, motivate children to confront challenging learning tasks. In a sense, this gives energizing properties to the General Strategy Knowledge component of metamemory. Of course, the energizing properties of General Strategy Knowledge facilitate only performance for those children who believe that they have the capacity and skills to take on learning challenges without undue fear of failure.

Metamemory Acquisition Procedures (MAPs). Because instructors (or teachers) usually are not sufficiently explicit or detailed in providing strategy instructions, children are often left to their own devices in deciding how and when to use a strategy. Metamemory Acquisition Procedures are those aspects of metamemory which provide, from a theoretical perspective, the mechanisms necessary for children to make such decisions. First of all, they help children learn more about lower-level strategies; they detect insufficient strategy information and fill-in-gaps in instructions so that a strategy can be formated to the

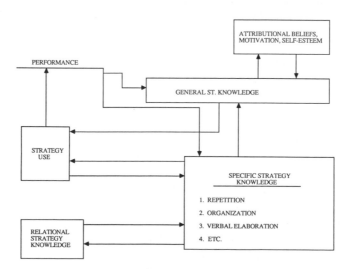

FIG. 4.2. A model of emerging metamemorial knowledge: The interface of Relational and General Knowledge with Specific Strategy Knowledge.

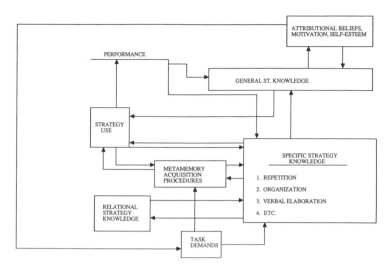

FIG. 4.3.   A model of mature metamemory: Specific, Relational, and General Knowledge as guided by Metamemory Acquisition Procedures.

unique requirements of a task and so that missing information about strategy attributes can be acquired. This aspect of metamemory leads to the development of more detailed representations about Specific Strategy Knowledge, resulting in an increased likelihood of strategy generalization.

The second function of Metamemory Acquisition Procedures is to supply regulating processes useful in implementing and modifying specific strategies. Chi (1987) refers to these higher-order processes as meta-strategies, or rules that govern the use of other rules. These higher-order rules are useful in making decisions about how and when to use a strategy or to switch to a new strategy when an earlier one proves ineffective.

Figure 4.3 presents the entire model, including higher-level Metamemory Acquisition Procedures. To reiterate, the dual function of MAPs is to enhance the development of lower-level Specific Strategy Knowledge as well as to provide implementation and monitoring routines for strategy use given the unique demands of the task at hand. Metamemory Acquisition Procedures are particularly important in the development of self-control behavior in young or developmentally delayed children (Campione, Brown, & Ferrara, 1982). Repeated checking and monitoring of a strategy's effectiveness lead to knowledge about its benefits and about the relative difficulty involved in its implementation. Independence in problem solving, task perseverence in the face of errors, and trial and error behaviors are signs of the operation of Metamemory Acquisition Procedures.

Metamemory Components and the Problem of Strategy Generalization

One of the more perplexing problems in cognitive development centers on strategy generalization. Children who have acquired a potentially useful strategy often fail to utilize that strategy on transfer tests. Our theory holds that two interrelated concepts, memory knowledge and attributional beliefs, help explain individual differences in strategy generalization (Borkowski et al., 1987). As children learn more about how their own minds operate (i.e., as Specific, Relational, and General Strategy Knowledge accumulate), they come to realize the importance of an interrelated causal sequence: that strategy use generally produces good performance and that success is often due to effort expended in strategy deployment and failure to its absence. This process is aided by higher-level processes (MAPs) that fill-in-the-gaps in Specific Strategy Knowledge and implement, monitor, and revise strategies appropriate for generalization tasks. In short, knowledge about the effects of strategic behavior—at both subordinate and superordinate levels—in concert with the energizing influence of effort-related attributional beliefs appear to be important conditions for successful strategy generalization on difficult transfer tasks. The interaction represents the essence of our componential theory of metamemory (Borkowski et al., 1987; Pressley et al., 1985).

Individual Differences in Specific Strategy Knowledge. In a series of studies, we have assessed the importance of prior metamemorial knowledge about a wide variety of Specific Strategies for understanding the deployment of acquired strategies on transfer tests. In these studies we have focused on children who have been given strategy training and assessed in terms of their metamemorial knowledge about *other strategies*. The interesting, common feature of the resulting data is that knowledge about a variety of *irrelevant* strategies predicts the acquisition and transfer of a new, task-relevant strategy. We interpret these results to reflect the importance of understanding about general strategy attributes.

Kurtz et al. (1982) taught an elaboration strategy to 2nd graders using self-instructional procedures; the strategy was totally new to all subjects. On a subsequent test for strategy maintenance, prior knowledge about other Specific Strategies (e.g., organization and rehearsal) correlated significantly with strategy use ($r = .50$). In another study, children were selected on the basis of cognitive tempo scores so as to form impulsive and reflective subgroups (Borkowski et al., 1983). Not only were differences in metamemory found between subgroups but, more importantly, knowledge about other subordinate processes predicted long-term use of a newly-acquired reading strategy independent of cognitive tempo and general intelligence (Kurtz & Borkowski, 1987). Finally, Borkowski and Peck (1986) discovered that metamemory was among several variables that distinguished gifted from average children (the other general factors being perceptual efficiency and general knowledge). Prior memory knowledge about *irrelevant* Specific Strategies was the best predictor of strategy use when gifted children were given minimal strategy training and tested on both near and far transfer tasks.

Taken together, these data suggest that Specific Strategy Knowledge about a wide range of strategies provides a framework useful for acquiring and understanding a new strategy. Old knowledge provides the context in which a newly acquired strategy receives its interpretation and meaning. Based on the model, we hypothesize that a rich metamemorial knowledge base about irrelevant strategies supplies information about a range of essential attributes necessary for understanding the utility of a newly presented strategy. In the absence of a rich knowledge base, a strategy can become *welded* to the training task (Brown, 1975). This would occur because information about some attributes of the strategy are known incompletely or are missing altogether. For instance, a child might fail to understand the range of tasks to which the strategy is and is not applicable. Problems in strategy generalization are the likely consequence of insufficient strategy information. Viewed from this perspective, prior metamemorial knowledge about Specific Strategies acts in concert with other variables that influence strategy acquisition such as the quality and amount of instruction, determining the probability of transfering old strategies to new tasks or inventing new ones.

General Strategy Knowledge, Attributional Beliefs, and Generalization. Another correlate of broadly based Specific Strategy Knowledge is General Strategy Knowledge: children who have frequently engaged in strategy-based learning are likely to understand the general utility of behaving strategically, especially on unfamilar or complex tasks. They not only come to know about the efficacy of being strategic, they come to believe in themselves as effective and efficient learners. We have collected three sets of data that support, in a very general way, the theoretical ties that we postulate relate General Strategy Knowledge, attributional beliefs, and strategy transfer:

1. Following thorough, extensive strategy training, children who attributed their successes on individual items to effort (and their failures to lack of effort) were found to be both more strategic and higher in metamemorial knowledge than those children who attributed learning outcomes to noncontrollable factors such as ability or task characteristics (Kurtz & Borkowski, 1984).

2. Children who held established beliefs about the role of effort in producing success on academic tasks were higher in metamemory and showed greater strategy transfer than children who tended to attribute performance outcomes to non-controllable factors (Borkowski & Krause, 1985).

3. Hyperactive children who received self-control training in combination with attributional training showed less hyperactivity, were more strategic on

transfer tests, and displayed altered attributional styles in comparison with hyperactive children given only self-control training (Reid & Borkowski, in press).

These sets of data establish a basis for linking motivation and General Strategy Knowledge. From this perspective, beliefs about strategy efficacy and Specific Strategy Knowledge conjointly influence strategy transfer, with the former providing orienting and sustaining properties.

Given its theoretical and applied significance, the final study in the series described above deserves further explication. Many learning disabled (LD) and hyperactive children do not understand the connection between effortful, strategic behavior and successful performance. As a consequence, they often fail on transfer tests. It appeared that theoretically based interventions designed to improve cognitive, metacognitive, and motivational processes were needed to enhance strategy transfer in LD and hyperactive children. To test the construct validity of this interactive hypothesis, Reid and Borkowski (in press) designed a study that compared the effectiveness of three training conditions: an Executive condition, an Executive plus Attributional condition, and a control condition. The Executive condition taught general self-control procedures as well as specific strategies appropriate for selected learning tasks (paired-associates and sort-recall). Children in the Executive plus Attribution condition were also given training designed to enhance both antecedent and program-generated attributions.

In antecedent attributional training, the child reflected on the causes of past successes and failures in and out of the classroom. The training included three aspects: (a) a discussion regarding beliefs about the causes of failure, (b) an opportunity to successfully perform a previously failed item in the training package using previously learned self-control steps, and (c) a reflection on beliefs about the causes of success. The thrust of antecedent attributional retraining was on remote classroom behaviors (e.g., why success or failure in math occurred last week). Program-generated attributions were trained by providing feedback to the child about the reasons for correct and incorrect answers to specific items on both the paired-associate and sort-recall readiness tasks.

Measures of strategy generalization at a 3-week posttest showed broad changes in performance, especially for children in the combined Executive plus Attributional condition. Strategy scores on the transfer tests were strikingly higher for children receiving the complex package than for children in the other two groups. Furthermore, attributional responses, reflecting beliefs about the reasons for success and failure on the transfer tests as well as more enduring beliefs about the causes of past performance on academic tasks, were dramatically altered in the Executive plus Attribution condition as was impulsivity as shown on the MFF20. Self-control training, without a focus on attributional beliefs, produced changes in attributional beliefs similar to those found in the control condition.

Results from a long-term assessment showed that changes in attributional beliefs persisted over a 10-month period following training. Additionally, children receiving the attributional boost scored significantly higher than children in the Executive-only condition on a test of general strategic knowledge. These findings highlight the importance of including attributional retraining in cognitive (i.e., strategy use) and metacognitive (i.e., self-control) training programs, especially when treating children who have experienced extensive academic failures. We believe attributional training is an essential step in producing independent learners. Apparently, attributional beliefs are tied tightly to metacognitive knowledge and serve an energizing function as LD and hyperactive children encounter complex, challenging tasks.

Metamemory Acquisition Procedures and Strategy Transfer. Several recent studies have included the training of higher-order, executive processes (one of the dual functions of MAPs) as part of large-scale instructional packages. Palincsar and Brown (1984) recently developed a training procedure called reciprocal teaching in which the unique feature is the gradual transfer of comprehension monitoring skills from teacher to student. Reciprocal teaching provides the child a system for understanding and implementing four specific comprehension strategies: summarizing, questioning, clarifying, and predicting. Higher-level skills are an integral part of their training package (Brown & Palincsar, 1967). Similarly, Borkowski and Varnhagen (1984) found that a self-instructional routine assisted retarded children in the eventual generalization of anticipation and paraphrasing strategies to a gist recall task. Finally Pressley, Forrest-Pressley, and Elliot-Faust (this volume), in a complex componential analysis of variables responsible for the development of comprehension monitoring skills, showed that a self-instructional routine, adapted from Meichenbaum and Goodman's (1971) procedures, augmented performance on a delayed maintenance test. In short, data are accumulating suggesting the important role of MAPs in guiding the implementation and monitoring of lower-level strategies during generalization.

Methodological Issues in Metamemory Research. Instructional research using strategy training and transfer paradigms has generally assumed that children in an experimental group who are about to receive an identical training routine are equivalent in terms of their susceptibility to cognitive intervention. We argue that this assumption ignores striking variability in metamemory about Specific Strategies and in attributional beliefs, thus ignoring several of the critical contributors to durable and general strategy transfer. This variability needs to be taken into account, either experimentally or statistically, if strategy training studies are to be maximally predictive of strategy generalization. It should be emphasized that historical differences in metamemory have generally been ignored in past instructional research.

Elsewhere in this volume, Pressley and colleagues have argued for more detailed analyses of strategy training effects, designed to partial out the causal components in training packages. Although we support the call for more sophisticated componential analysis in instructional research, it should be noted that many learning experiences facilitate the development of multiple aspects of metamemory. If this observation is correct, future research will need to ensure that specific experimental manipulations influence metamemory components individually rather than collectively. This is necessary if the decoupling of the effective elements in instructional packages is to be successful.

Finally, it will be important for future research on metamemory to take into account the relationship between domain-specific knowledge and individual metamemory components. Chi (1987) has identified the important role played by domain-specific knowledge in determining performance on a wide range of memory and cognitive tasks. In most of the research cited in the present review, the effects of domain-specific knowledge have been minimized by adapting highly familiar pictures or words as stimulus materials. The importance of metamemory is less clear in situations where large individual differences exist in *both* domain-knowledge and memory-knowledge. In general, we would expect an interaction between these two factors: given a task with large individual differences in the domain of information being learned, children high in domain-specific knowledge should profit little from instructions on metamemory components. In contrast, children low in domain-specific knowledge should realize sizable improvements following metamemory training.

Conclusions About Metamemory and Strategy Generalization.   Recent studies on strategy transfer lead us to the following general conclusions about the major components of metamemory. (1) Metamemory about a wide range of subordinate processes is a causal factor that helps explain strategy activation and use on new tasks. Specific Strategy Knowledge, higher-level executive routines, and general beliefs about self-directed learning are major components of metamemory that help explain strategy transfer. (2) "Welding" of a strategy to a single task occurs for children who are deficient in their knowledge of the essential attributes that define most strategies. (3) Within-group individual differences in strategy transfer among a *homogeneous* group of children are explained, in part, by prior differences in metamemory about other strategies, especially when strategy instruction is minimal or incomplete. An understanding of or essential strategy attributes is hypothesized to be one mechanism responsible for new strategy acquisition. (4) Between-group performance differences, such as is commonly found in studies of giftedness, impulsivity-reflectivity, retardation, and race, are generally paralleled by differences in metamemorial knowledge about Specific Strategies and, perhaps, by differences in other aspects of metamemory. Although the actual causes of group differences that we attribute to metamemory are varied, their consequence is the same—the ineffective or immature execution of strategic behaviors on challenging, novel problem-solving tasks. (5) Attributional beliefs, associated with general memory knowledge, play a distinctive role in orienting and sustaining attention especially on difficult strategy generalization tasks. (6) Strategy transfer will occur only if Metamemory Acquisition Procedures are in place prior to strategy training or are taught as part of the overall instructional package. Without MAPs, the child is without essential strategy selection, formating, monitoring and revision routines.

For a newly acquired strategy to be transferred, and for strategy invention to eventually become commonplace, young children must first possess mature, low-level knowledge about a wide range of specific strategies. Then, they must come to appreciate the general importance of strategies in leading to successful performance and must believe in their own capacity to control learning outcomes. Finally, they need executive routines to carry out decisions about strategy selection and monitoring. To understand the transferability of a newly acquired strategy, we need a detailed history of the child's past experiences with other seemingly *irrelevant* subordinate strategies (Specific Knowledge), an assessment of the child's ability to employ relevant superordinate processes (MAPs), and information concerning the child's beliefs about the role of strategies in producing learning successes. It is this individual history that gives shape to each child's metamemorial knowledge states and corresponding cognitive processing abilities.

SOCIAL DETERMINANTS AND CORRELATES OF METAMEMORY

Throughout this chapter, the issue of strategy generalization has been a primary concern. In this section, the topic of generalization is considered from the perspective of how social-motivational factors influence the development of metamemorial knowledge. Concepts drawn from attribution theories (Covington, 1987; Weiner, 1979) as well as from cross-cultural research based on Vygotsky's (1962) cultural-contextualistic framework are especially relevant. Potential contact points between these two frameworks and the current model are discussed.

Attribution Theory and Metamemory

Recent theories about generalization have emphasized the importance of both external and internal factors (Brown et al., 1983; Laboratory of Comparative Human Cognition, 1982). For example, the process of generalization, when viewed from the framework of attribution theorists (e.g., Covington, 1987; Weiner, 1979) may be affected by external and internal components which are used in setting criteria used to judge success and failure. External components are exemplified by teachers setting performance standards for their students, or parents for their children. Internal components consist of children's comprehension of feedback based on established criteria, or their incorporation of externally determined performance standards for themselves on generalization tasks (Covington & Beery, 1976). Furthermore, motivation for future performance is, in large part, determined by internalized causal attributions about success and failure based on past experiences (Paris & Cross, 1983).

In the literature on attribution theory, children's performance and the processes involved in setting criteria are viewed as part of a larger framework of motivation based on causal attributions concerning successes and failures. Two dimensions of causal attributions have been identified: (1) internal/external; and (2) stable/unstable. Individuals may attribute success or failure to one of the four pairwise combinations. For instance, success may be attributed to ability (internal/stable), effort (internal/unstable), task difficulty (external/stable), or luck (external/unstable). In terms of development, children are at first unable to differentiate between the effects of effort (unstable) and ability (stable) on outcomes (Covington, 1987). As development progresses, children become increasingly capable of integrating a more differentiated understanding of these variables (i.e., stable/unstable, internal/external) into their causal attributional system.

When developmental issues are considered, parallels between causal attributions and metamemory emerge. For example, Wellman (1983) cited studies demonstrating that with increasing age, children exhibit a more differentiated and integrated understanding of the effects of effort on memory performance (Bisanz, Visonder, & Voss, 1978; Brown & Smilely, 1978; Masur, McIntyre, & Flavell, 1973). Furthermore, he argued that processes investigated by attribution researchers are closely related to those in metamemory research, and that ". . . this research (attribution research) is itself a demonstration of the influence of metacognition on performance."

Other researchers have demonstrated that metamemorial and attributive processes are related. Fabricius and Hagen (1983) found attributions about strategy efficacy to be predictive of subsequent strategy use. Similarly, Kurtz and Borkowski (1984) reported that children who demonstrated successful strategy transfer and higher levels of metamemory tended to attribute their successful learning to effort expended during the study period. Finally, in the Reid and Borkowski (in press) training study discussed above, learning disabled and hyperactive children who received both metacognitive (self-control) and attributional training demonstrated more substantial and prolonged strategy generalization than children who received only self-control training.

Although we believe a reliable relationship between attributive and metamemorial states has been demonstrated, the dynamics of the underlying developmental processes have not been specified. Borkowski et al. (1987) suggested that attributive and metacognitive processes are bidirectionally linked. They argued that the acquisition of metamnemonic knowledge is influenced by causal attributions regarding past performance. Further, attributions appear to play an important role in future application of metamnemonic knowledge in transfer situations. The questions of how, and under what circumstances, these processes are related remain largely unanswered and unexplored. As attribution research has indicated (e.g., Covington & Beery, 1976), social factors such as the attributional and metacognitive impact of adult guidance on children's performance may provide clues about how the processes are related. Thus, research within a cultural-contextualistic framework, which emphasizes social-cultural factors, may prove to be an important guide in this theoretical and empirical search.

Interactions Between Metacognition and the Social Context

In recent years, the intricate linkages between culture and cognition have been the focus of increased theoretical attention (e.g., Laboratory of Comparative Human Cognition, 1982; Wertsch, 1979). Cross-cultural research has demonstrated the impact that cultural factors have on mnemonic (Sharp, Cole, & Lave, 1979) and metamnemonic processes (Schneider, 1985). For example, Schneider, Borkowski, Kurtz and Kerwin (1986) reported greater spontaneous use of categorization strategies by children in Germany than by children in the United States even when matched on grade placement, SES, IQ, and age. Cross-cultural differences in cognitive processes such as those noted by Schneider have been explained in terms of differences in the learning contexts and learning opportunities in the home and school (cf. Rogoff & Lave, 1984). Vygotsky's (1962) work on culture and cognition has provided the broadest theoretical framework for contextual explanations.

In Vygotsky's theory, cognitive development is the intra- and inter-personal process of acquiring culturally relevant information which can be useful for interpreting events, stimulating production of goals, and providing means to reach those goals. These processes assist the learner in acquiring *specific strategy knowledge*. Vygotsky contended that cognitive development is culture-specific, involving an internalization of learning processes and the products of those processes. Investigations of cognitive development based on Vygotsky's theory have typically examined cultural influences at two levels: the level of socio-cultural history and the immediate social context (Rogoff & Lave, 1984). Findings from both types of investigations provide important clues about how components of metacognition develop.

Socio-Cultural History.   An example of an investigation aimed primarily at the first level is Scribner and Cole's (1981) study of the Vai peoples of Africa. Scribner and Cole compared the cognitive abilities of individuals with different cultural experiences within the Vai culture. More specifically, they examined the effects of different kinds of literacy practice on other cognitive skills. In a series of studies, the skills of individuals were contrasted from different backgrounds in which experience with one of the following literacies was dominant: English, Koranic, Arabic, or Vai. The literacy experiences could be distinguished by the following factors: (1) use of literacy for letter writing; (2) experience with literacy emphasizing syllables versus whole words; and (3) extent of practice in rote recall. Scribner and Cole identified these experiential factors as potential determinants of performance in parallel cognitive skills. For example, they predicted letter writing would provide experience with adopting other perspectives; hence, benefits from this experience should be demonstrated on measures of egocentrism. Specifically, it was predicted that experience with letter writing (a characteristic of the English literacy experience) would result in less egocentric communications. The results supported their predictions: individuals with English literacy experience evidenced the least egocentric communications.

A second experiential factor was assessed by communication tasks which incorporated syllables as the central unit of analysis. Results indicated that Vai literates (those whose literacy system was based on syllables) demonstrated superior performance. Concerning the third experiential factor, Koranic literates (whose experience included frequent practice with rote recall) evidenced superior performance on serial recall tasks. These findings demonstrated that specific literacy experiences differentially influenced performance on various cognitive tasks. Further, the results suggested the importance of context-specific factors, such as the cultural relevance of the task, as determinants of cognitive development.

Immediate Social Context. In Vygotsky's theory, culturally prescribed learning situations play central roles in development. The relevance of particular strategies is identified and made explicit, thus contributing to the growth of metamnemonic knowledge. It is the learning that takes place in social interactions which serves as the foundation for cognitive development. Further, the requirements of learning tasks, and the child's understanding of those requirements, act in concert to define a major construct in Vygotsky's theory: the zone of proximal development. The zone of proximal development refers to the psychological interval between the child's current and potential levels of understanding. Learning requirements that fall within the zone are gradually mastered as information about relevant aspects of task solutions accumulates, such as knowledge about essential strategy attributes. With repeated opportunities, the child is able to successfully complete a task within the zone, utilizing lower-level strategies more successfully. It is at the second level of analysis, the immediate social context, that the process of cultural transmission can be investigated in more detail.

Recent ethnographic studies of socialization processes have documented a wide-spread practice among adults of arranging and orchestrating learning situations so as to be sensitive to the child's zone of proximal development (Greenfield, 1984; Laboratory of Comparative Human Cognition, 1982; Rogoff & Gardner, 1984). For example, Rogoff and Gardner (1984) described interactions between mothers and their children in a naturalistic learning situation. Requirements of the tasks included learning about memory and organizational strategies involving classification of familiar objects (kitchen items). In the task, mothers taught their children about organizing the kitchen items, and how that would help their memory for location of the items. Mothers were observed beginning the task by framing it or describing it to their children in interesting and understandable terms, for instance as a "fun problem" that was like "just coming home from the store."

Following the initial description, mothers modeled strategic approaches, giving both a rationale (e.g., to improve memory) and specific examples of organization. Next, the mothers attempted to transfer the responsibility of solving the memory problem by engaging the child in strategic organization of the kitchen items. Finally, they monitored the children's level of skills and encouraged self-monitoring by asking about the accuracy of their classifications, often comparing them to the organization of the kitchen at home, as well as questioning and/or informing them about the usefulness of the strategy. In sum the mothers: (1) framed the task in an intelligible, interesting way; (2) modeled solutions; (3) attempted to transfer responsibility for the task to the child; and (4) monitored children's performances as well as encouraged self-monitoring by the children themselves. These observations show how the development of metacognitive components, such as self-monitoring or specific strategy knowledge, is supported and encouraged by the environment.

However, as Rogoff and Gardner (1984) noted, it would be simplistic to think that children are merely passive recipients of information. Instead, children actively participate in learning by providing hints about their willingness to accept more responsibility for problem solution. Although the adults often provide their children with the necessary structure, children are active participants in the learning process.

As active participants, children must call upon their metacognitive skills to benefit from teaching. For example, Liberian apprentice tailors were gradually introduced to basic sewing skills in a manner similar to other interactions within the zone framework (Lave, 1977). Interestingly, when the apprentices began making entire garments, they were not guided gradually into the process, but received brief, intensive training and were then left to their own devices. Although many learning situations are structured so as to be sensitive to the growing abilities of children, learners are not always guided in a step-by-step piecemeal fashion. Transfer of responsibility is sometimes gradual and sometimes abrupt. Successful learners are those who are capable of dealing with both types of transitions.

Children in other cultures are also exposed to variations in teaching style, and can learn in a variety of teaching situations. For instance, Wertsch, Minick, and

Arns (1984) reported differences in teaching styles for middle class U.S. mothers versus school teachers in a puzzle task. In general, mothers used more physical, direct regulation than teachers (e.g., placement and replacement of puzzle pieces), with children looking at the model twice as often for the mothers than for the teachers. Kantos (1983) demonstrated that children learn from their fathers as effectively when given only general encouragement with no strategic advice or feedback as they do when given both. These findings suggest that, while adults' sensitivity to the zone of proximal development is a significant factor in directing the acquisition of strategic knowledge, children's active participation in communication and their independent learning activities, such as filling-in-gaps in instructions, are also of importance.

Relationship to Metacognition. In terms of our model of metacognition, three observations about social contexts are relevant: (1) Knowledge about strategies (general, specific and relational) is influenced by the socio-historical environment, which provides the context necessary for applying strategies for learning and remembering (e.g., cloth for tailors' apprentices or history books for middle school students in the United States). In a general way, the environment provides the organization of the physical (e.g., clothing shops versus middle schools) and social (e.g., interactions with tailors versus teachers) learning context. Finally, the relevance of specific strategies is determined by the culture: some strategic knowledge is emphasized while other knowledge is not, as in the case of different Vai literacy experiences; (2) The immediate social context provides support for children's internalization of strategies. As the need for and use of strategies is laid out by the adult, the child adds to their knowledge base by engaging MAP's. As the knowledge base grows, the child calls on his or her own executive routines (such as self-monitoring) more frequently. Responsibility for problem resolution is thereby transferred from the adult to the child as MAPs become operative. (3) The child, through the development of general strategy knowledge and the use of MAPs becomes increasingly sensitive to variations in immediate learning contexts, both in terms of task demands and the quality of social interactions. These variations stimulate self-monitoring processes in the child, such as filling-in-gaps in instruction when comprehension is incomplete and augment the continued development of MAPs so that future experiences with both guided and independent learning activities yield a greater store of specific strategy knowledge, with an attendant increase in general strategy knowledge.

Assessment of Metacognitive and Attributional Processes

In a brief summary of zone assessment, Day (1983) identified seven potential dependent measures: (1) degree to which a child benefits from specific training procedures; (2) degree of specific explicit instruction required to raise performance to a specified criteria; (3) maintenance of training; (4) quantity of additional training needed for maintenance; (5) spontaneous transfer; (6) response to transfer with assistance; and, (7) speed of learning. In terms of our model, these measures could be adapted or combined with existing measures of metacognition to build on previous investigations. For example, Kurtz and Borkowski (1984) found that causal attributions about performance were positively related to the transfer of trained strategies. In extending that study, assessment of such factors as speed of learning could provide important instructional information concerning the relationship between speed of learning and attributional beliefs. Additionally, instructional packages based on Vygotsky's framework (e.g., Palincsar & Brown, 1984) provide a more comprehensive assessment of the degree of specificity required for individual children to reach age-appropriate criteria, maintain that level of performance, and transfer learning to new tasks. The use of continuous assessment during training might provide a more precise examination of how and when children exercise MAPs such as filling in gaps in instruction. Finally, the process of acquiring knowledge about essential strategy attributes could be monitored continuously using the zone framework.

An interesting extension of assessment is suggested by the findings regarding variations in task demands and quality of social interactions in teaching situations. It is likely that teacher and learner variables interact to influence strategy acquisition, maintenance, and transfer. Children's exposure to variation in both task demands and the quality of social interactions may enhance performance for some children (e.g., those with positive attributions) while restricting performance for others (e.g., those with negative attributions). Clarification of the interaction between internal variables (such as causal attributions or prior general strategy knowledge) and external variables (such as the quality of social interactions) may provide important clues as to how social contexts stimulate or inhibit acquisition, maintenance, and transfer of strategies.

An Integration of Social Contexts, Attributions, and Metamemory

When children are engaged in socially guided learning activities which fall within the zone of proximal development several important factors can be identified: (1) The task has been defined and understood, learning criteria have been established, and supportive guides and cues to strategy utilization have been provided or initiated. (2) A child's strategy-oriented efforts are likely to result in success, thus providing the opportunity for enhancing positive attributions about both effort and ability. It is in this context that Specific Strategy Knowledge is enriched and information about general attributes common to most strategies acquired. As strategies are used, the child usually receives various types of feedback and guided instruction about the match between the task and the strategy. An understanding of this match is what we have previously referred to as formating (Borkowski & Varnhagen, 1984). It is also helpful if the child projects the use of a particular strategy into future contexts, visualizing and describing appropriate matches (and mismatches) with other tasks that lie among the generalization continuum.

A recent study being carried out in our laboratory is useful in clarifying how young children are guided into richer insights about the attributes essential for complete Specific Knowledge about a strategy. Second- and 3rd-grade children were trained in the use of a categorization strategy appropriate for free-recall learning and an elaborative strategy for paired-associate learning. The intent was to enhance the generalizability of these strategies by providing enriching instructions about important strategy attributes that focused the child's attention on when to use and when not to use each strategy. Some children were given future-oriented (prospective) feedback about the general usefulness and applicability of these strategies to other tasks and about essential attributes of each strategy (such as grouping and rehearsing objects during encoding) that would improve recall on other tasks. Instances that defined inappropriate strategy use were also included. Other children received specific feedback about the reasons for past learning successes and failures (retrospective feedback). For instance, the experimenter stressed success in remembering individual items that had been recalled correctly. If some items had not been sorted or rehearsed appropriately and not recalled, the result was attributed to a failure to use a relevant strategy. Finally, other children received a combination of these two types of feedback. It was expected that children who received both prospective and retrospective feedback, would demonstrate higher levels of strategy generalization and understand more about the importance of strategy attributes. It remains to be seen whether more precise hypotheses can be formulated about essential attributes of all (or most) strategies and whether their subsequent manipulation will result in generalization gains.

As situational demands change, as task performances become routinized, and as other cognitive skills and world knowledge are obtained, children will, with increasing frequency, independently add to their knowledge about essential strategy attributes. In this way, they gain internal control over the development of metacognitive skills and knowledge. Additionally, as their fund of specific strategy knowledge is expanded and enriched, more positive attributions about their performance should develop. Finally, as children are provided less and less contextual support, reliance on higher-level knowledge and processes (MAPs) increases. A child without higher-level, executive processes would have an incomplete understanding about a newly presented strategy because of the inability to fill-in-the-gaps in Specific Strategy attributes. In contrast, the metacognitively advanced child becomes increasingly aware of his or her own zone of proximal development as each experience activates multiple components of metamemory.

As children develop a richer, more complete base of Specific and General

Strategy Knowledge, and as they become better able to reflect upon the requirements of new learning tasks, they develop the basic competencies required for
teaching themselves, and others as well, about strategy implementation and
monitoring (see Brown & Palincsar, 1987). As higher level skills are exercised
and utilized, the Specific and Relational Strategy Knowledge bases become fine-
tuned. These changes allow for more accurate and comprehensive abstractions in
General Strategy Knowledge and corresponding positive beliefs about the importance of self-initiated and self-directed learning. All of these components, acting
in concert, provide clues about how to approach novel, challenging tasks. In this
sense, the interaction of learning contexts, attributional beliefs, and the quality of
metamemory components define each child's learning ability and learning
potential.

ACKNOWLEDGMENT

The writing of this chapter was supported, in part, by NIH grant HD-17648 and
HD-21218. Many of the theoretical ideas in this chapter were developed while
the first author was a visiting scholar at the Max Planck Institute for Psychological Research, Munich, FRG, during the summer of 1984.

REFERENCES

Bisanz, G. L., Visonder, G. T., & Voss, J. T. (1978). Knowledge of one's own responding and the
    relation of such knowledge to learning: A developmental study. *Journal of Experimental Child
    Psychology, 25*, 116–128.
Borkowski, J. G. (1985). Signs of intelligence: Strategy generalization and metacognition. In S.
    Yussen's (Ed.), *Development of reflection in children*. San Diego: Academic Press.
Borkowski, J. G., & Cavanaugh, J. C. (1979). Maintenance and generalization of skills and strat-
    egies by the retarded. In N. R. Ellis (Ed.), *Handbook of mental deficiency: Psychological theory
    and research*. Hillsdale, NJ: Lawrence Erlbaum Associates.
Borkowski, J. G., Johnston, M. B., & Reid, M. K. (1987). Metacognition, motivation, and the
    transfer of control processes. In S. J. Ceci (Ed.), *Handbook of cognitive, social, and neuro-
    psychological aspects of learning disabilities*. Hillsdale, NJ: Lawrence Erlbaum Associates.
Borkowski, J. G., & Krause, A. (1985). Metacognition and attributional beliefs. In *Proceedings of
    the XXIII International Congress of Psychology*. Amsterdam: Elsevier Science Publisher.
Borkowski, J. G., & Peck, V. (1986). Causes and consequences of metamemory in gifted children.
    In R. Sternberg & J. Davidson (Eds.), *Conceptions of giftedness*. Cambridge, England:
    Cambridge University Press.
Borkowski, J. G., Peck, V., Reid, M, K., & Kurtz, B. (1983). Impulsivity and strategy transfer:
    Metamemory as mediator. *Child Development, 53*, 459–473.
Borkowski, J. G., Reid, M. K., & Kurtz, B. E. (1984). Metacognition and retardation: Paradig-
    matic, theoretical, and applied perspectives. In R. Sperber, C. McCauley, & P. Brooks (Eds.),
    Learning and cognition in the mentally retarded. Baltimore, MD: University Park Press.
Borkowski, J. G., & Varnhagen, C. K. (1984). Transfer of learning strategies: A contrast of self-

instructional and traditional formats with EMR children. *American Journal of Mental Deficiency,* *88*, 369–379.

Brown, A. L. (1975). The development of memory: Knowing, knowing about knowing, and knowing how to know. In H. W. Reese (Ed.), *Advances in child development and behavior* (Vol. 10). New York: Academic Press.

Brown, A. L., & Barclay, C. R. (1976). The effects of training specific mnemonics on the metamnemonic efficiency of retarded children. *Child Development, 47*, 71–80.

Brown, A. L., Bransford, J. D., Ferrara, R. A., & Campione, J. C. (1983). Learning, remembering, and understanding. In P. H. Mussen (Ed.), *Handbook of child psychology,* New York: Wiley.

Brown, A. L., & Campione, J. C. (1977). Training strategic study time apportionment in educable retarded children. *Intelligence, 1*, 94–107.

Brown, A. L., & DeLoache, J. S. (1978). Skills, plans, and self-regulation. In R. S. Siegler (Ed.), *Children's thinking: What develops?* Hillsdale, NJ: Lawrence Erlbaum Associates.

Brown, A. L., & Palincsar, A. S. (1987). Reciprocal teaching of comprehension strategies: A natural history of one program for enhancing learning. In J. D. Day & J. G. Borkowski (Eds.), *Intelligence and exceptionality.* Norwood, NJ: Ablex.

Brown, A. L., & Smiley, S. S. (1978). The development of strategies for studying tests. *Child Development, 49*, 1076–1088.

Campione, J. C., & Brown, A. L. (1977). Memory and metamemory development in educable retarded children. In R. V. Kail & J. W. Hagen (Eds.), *Perspectives on the development of memory and cognition.* Hillsdale, NJ: Lawrence Erlbaum Associates.

Campione, J. C., Brown, A. L., & Ferrara, R. A. (1982). Mental retardation and intelligence. In R. J. Sternberg (Ed.), *Handbook of human intelligence.* Cambridge, England: Cambridge University Press.

Cavanaugh, J. C., & Perlmutter, M. (1982). Metamemory: A critical examination. *Child Development, 53*, 11–28.

Chi, M. T. H. (1987). Representing knowledge and meta-knowledge: Implications for interpreting metamemory research . In F.E. Weinert & R. H. Kluwe (Eds.), *Metacognition, motivation, and learning.* Hillsdale, NJ: Lawrence Erlbaum Associates.

Covington, M. V. (1987). Achievement motivation, self-attributions, and exceptionality. In J. D. Day & J. G. Borkowski (Eds.), *Intelligence and exceptionality.* Norwood, NJ: Ablex.

Covington, M. V., & Beery, R. (1976). *Self-worth and school learning.* New York: Holt, Rinehart and Winston.

Day, J. D. (1983). The zone of proximal development. In M. Pressley & J. Levin (Eds.), *Cognitive strategy research: Psychological foundations.* New York: Springer-Verlag.

Fabricius, W. V., & Hagen, J. W. (1983). The use of causal attributions about recall performance to assess metamemory and predict strategy memory behavior in young children. *Developmental Psychology, 19*, 15–21.

Flavell, J. H. (1971). First discussant's comments: What is memory development the development of? *Human Development, 14*, 272–278.

Flavell, J. H., Friedrichs, A. G., & Hoyt, J. D. (1970). Developmental changes in memorization processes. *Cognitive Psychology, 1*, 324–340.

Flavell, J. H., & Wellman, H. M. (1977). Metamemory. In R. V. Kail and J. W. Hagen (Eds.), *Perspectives on the development of memory and cognition.* Hillsdale, NJ: Lawrence Erlbaum Associates.

Greenfield, P. M. (1984). A theory of the teacher in the learning activities of everyday life. In B. Rogoff & J. Lave (Eds.), *Everyday cognition.* Cambridge, MA: Harvard University Press.

Gruneberg, M. M., & Monks, J. (1974). Feeling of knowing and cued recall. *Acta Psychologica, 38*, 251–265.

Kelly, M., Scholnick, E. K., Travers, S. H., & Johnson, J. W. (1976). Relations among memory, memory appraisal, and memory strategies. *Child Development, 47*, 648–659.

Kantos, S. (1983). Adult-child interaction and the origins of metacognition. *Journal of Education Research, 77*, 43–54.

Kendall, C. R., Borkowski, J. G., & Cavanaugh, J. C. (1980). Metamemory and the transfer of an interrogative strategy by EMR children. *Intelligence, 4*, 255–270.

Kreutzer, M. A., Leonard, C., & Flavell, J. H. (1975). An interview study of children's knowledge about memory. *Monographs of the Society for Research in Child Development, 40*, 1–58.

Kurtz, B. E., & Borkowski, J. G. (1984). Children's metacognition: Exploring relations among knowledge, process, and motivational variables. *Journal of Experimental Child Psychology, 37*, 335–354.

Kurtz, B. E., & Borkowski, J. G. (1985). Development of strategic skills in impulsive and reflective children: A longitudinal study of metacognition. *Journal of Experimental Child Psychology, 43*, 129–148.

Kurtz, B., Reid, M. K., Borkowski, J. G., & Cavanaugh, J. C. (1982). On the reliability and validity of children's metamemory. *Bulletin of the Psychonomic Society, 19*, 137–140.

Laboratory of Comparative Human Cognition. (1982). Culture and Intelligence. In R. Sternberg (Ed.), *Handbook of Human Intelligence*. Cambridge, MA: Cambridge University Press.

Lave, J. (1977). Tailor-made experiments and evaluating the intellectual consequences of apprenticeship training. *Quarterly Newsletter of the Laboratory of Comparative Human Cognition, 2*, 1–3.

Markman, E. (1973). Factors affecting the young child's ability to monitor his memory. Unpublished doctoral dissertation, University of Pennsylvania.

Masur, E. F., McIntyre, C. W., & Flavell, J. H. (1973). Developmental changes in apportionment of study time among items in a multitrial free recall task. *Journal of Experimental Child Psychology, 15*, 237–246.

Meichenbaum, D., & Goodman, J. (1971). Training impulsive children to talk to themselves: A means of developing self-control. *Journal of abnormal psychology, 77*, 115–126.5

Neimark, E. D. (1976). The natural history of spontaneous mnemonic activity under conditions of minimal experimental constraint. In A. D. Pick (Ed.), *Minnesota symposia on child psychology. Vol. 10*. Minneapolis: University of Minnesota Press.

Palincsar, A. S., & Brown, A. L. (1984). Reciprocal teaching of comprehension-fostering and monitoring activities. *Cognition and Instruction, 1*, 117–175.

Paris, S. G., & Cross, D. R. (1983). Ordinary learning: Pragmatic connections among children's beliefs, motives, and actions. In J. Bisanz, G. Bisanz, & R. Kail (Eds.), *Learning in children*. New York: Springer-Verlag.

Paris, S. G., Newman, R. S., & McVey, K. A. (1982). Learning the functional significance of mnemonic actions: A microgenetic study of strategy acquisition. *Journal of Experimental Child Psychology, 34*, 490–509.

Pressley, M., Borkowski, J. G., & O'Sullivan, J. T. (1985). Children's metamemory and the teaching of memory strategies. In D. L. Forrest-Pressley, G. E. MacKennon, & T. G. Waller (Eds.), *Metacognition, cognition, and human performance*. San Diego: Academic Press.

Reid, M. K., & Borkowski, J. G. (in press). Causal attributions of hyperactive children: Implications for teaching strategies and self-control. *Journal of Educational Psychology*.

Rogoff, B., & Lave, J. (1984). *Everyday cognition: Its development in social context*. Cambridge, MA: Harvard University Press.

Rogoff, B., & Gardner, W. (1984). Adult guidance of cognitive development. In B. Rogoff & J. Lave (Eds.), *Everyday cognition*. Cambridge, MA: Harvard University Press.

Salatas, H., & Flavell, J. H. (1976). Behavioral and metamnemonic indicators of strategic behaviors under remembered instructions in first grade. *Child Development, 47*, 81–89.

Schneider, W. (1985). Developmental trends in the metamemory-memory behavior relationship: An integrative review. In D. L. Forrest-Pressley, G. E. MacKinnon, & T. G. Waller (Eds.), *Metacognition, cognition, and human performance.* San Diego: Academic Press.

Schneider, W., Borkowski, J. G., Kurtz, B. E., & Kerwin, K. (1986). Metamemory and motivation: A comparison of strategy use in German and American children. *Journal of Cross-Cultural Psychology, 17,* 315–336.

Scribner, S., & Cole, M. (1981). *The psychology of literacy.* Cambridge, MA: Harvard University Press.

Sharp, D. W., Cole, M., & Lave, C. (1979). Education and development: The evidence from experimental research. *Monographs of the Society for Research in Child Development, 44,* Serial No. 178.

Vygotsky, L. S. (1962). *Thought and language.* Cambridge, MA: MIT Press.

Weiner, B. (1979). A theory of motivation for some classroom experiences. *Journal of Educational Psychology, 71,* 3–25.

Wellman, H. M. (1979). *The role of metamemory in memory behavior: A developmental demonstration.* Unpublished paper, University of Michigan.

Wellman, J. M. (1983). Metamemory revisited. In M. T. H. Chi (Ed.), *Trends in memory development research.* Basel, Switzerland: Karger.

Wertsch, J. V. (1979). From social interaction to higher psychological processes: A clarification and application of Vygotsky's theory. *Human Development, 22,* 1–22.

Wertsch, J., Minick, N., & Arns, F. (1984). The creation of context in joing problem-solving. In B. Rogoff & J. Lave (Eds.), *Everyday cognition.* Cambridge, MA: Harvard University Press.

Yussen, S. R., & Levy, V. M., Jr. (1975). Developmental changes in predicting one's own span of short term memory. *Journal of Experimental Child Psychology, 19,* 502–508.

5

What is Strategy Instructional Enrichment and How to Study It: Illustrations from Research on Children's Prose Memory and Comprehension

Michael Pressley
University of Western Ontario

Donna Forrest-Pressley
Children's Psychiatric Research Institute
London, Ontario

Darlene J. Elliott-Faust
University of Western Ontario

HOW TO STUDY STRATEGY INSTRUCTIONAL ENRICHMENT

The modern study of strategy instruction with children is now 20 years old, with Flavell's (1970) seminal research on rehearsal strategies (e.g., Flavell, Beach, & Chinsky, 1966) the starting point. There have been many studies in which children were trained to use various strategies for accomplishing a variety of goals, such as memorizing for recall and reading for comprehension (Pressley, Heisel, McCormick, & Nakamura, 1982). Despite extensive research, however, there still are definitional debates about what constitutes a strategy.

The Nature of Strategies

There is no disagreement that strategies involve more than just processes that are a simple consequence of doing the task (e.g., Waters & Andreassen, 1983). For instance, turning the pages of a book while reading is not strategic, nor does simply looking at words on a page qualify as a reading strategy. There is also no disagreement that effective strategies accomplish cognitive purposes. They enhance memory, comprehension, composing, self-control and many other goals (Pressley & Levin, 1983a, 1983b). A thornier issue is whether strategies necessarily are deliberately instigated (voluntary) as suggested in earlier commentaries (e.g., Brown, 1978; Flavell, 1977). Recent definitions retaining the intentionality attribute (e.g., Paris, Lipson, & Wixson, 1983; Paris, Newman, &

Jacobs, 1985) seem to exclude many behaviors considered strategic by cognitive psychologists. For instance, not all of what are considered perceptual strategies (e.g., Rayner & Pollatsek, 1981), language and communication strategies (e.g., Clark & Clark, 1977; Shatz, 1978), and mathematical computational strategies (e.g., Siegler & Shrager, 1984) are deliberate or voluntary. Children's use of memory strategies in particular is not always tied to understanding of the strategy's effects (e.g., Ghatala, Levin, Pressley, & Lodico, 1985; Pressley, Ross, Levin, & Ghatala, 1984). When learners lack such an understanding, they cannot be using strategies deliberately. Also, it is now recognized that strategy functioning at its best occurs without deliberation. It is more reflexive than voluntary (e.g., LaBerge & Samuels, 1974; Torgesen & Greenstein, 1982). On the other hand, although cognitive strategies are not always consciously deployed, they are almost always potentially controllable (cf. Brown, 1978, p. 79)—people can turn them on and off if they choose to do so. Strategies contrast with nonstrategic forms of processing that cannot be controlled easily, such as some types of inferencing (e.g., Bransford & Franks, 1972).

Given all of these considerations, Pressley, Forrest-Pressley, Elliott-Faust, and Miller (1985) defined strategies as *composed of cognitive operations over and above the processes that are a natural consequence of carrying out a task, ranging from one such operation to a sequence of interdependent operations. Strategies achieve cognitive purposes (e.g., comprehending, memorizing) and are potentially conscious and controllable activities.* See Pressley, Forrest-Pressley, Elliott-Faust, and Miller (1985) for additional commentary about important considerations in strategy definition, as well as commentary on the evaluation of the concept of strategy and its relationship to other constructs (e.g., Miller, Galanter, & Pribram's, 1960, plans). Notably, all of the strategic interventions considered in this chapter met the requirements of the definition developed by Pressley, Forrest-Pressley, Elliott-Faust, and Miller (1985).

The Nature of Strategy Instructional Research

Strategy instruction in most research efforts consisted of specifying to children the processing that they were to carry out, with the criterion task following closely after training and structurally identical to the training situation. Children were usually under strict instructional control to carry out the strategic processing of interest (Pressley, Heisel, McCormick, & Nakamura, 1982). An example concretizes this approach.

Pressley (1976) trained 8-year-old children to create internal images representing the meaning of text that they read. Children practiced with sentences and worked up to longer passages. The subjects received feedback in the form of slides depicting acceptable imaginal depictions. Controls were instructed only to try very hard to remember the practice materials (i.e., they were provided no explicit processing instruction). Immediately after training the children were presented another concrete story to read. Imagery subjects were reminded by the experimenter to use the imagery strategy and controls were urged again to try very hard. Story recall was assessed immediately after the children read the passage. Imagery subjects remembered more than control learners. Thus, Pressley (1976) showed that 8-year-olds benefit from an instruction to carry out imaginal processing of text. The lower performance of control subjects suggests that children probably do not spontaneously process prose imaginally, or at least not to the extent that they could do so.

The basic design of many strategy instruction experiments is similar to the one used by Pressley (1976). Some specific set of processing operations is taught to experimental subjects but not to control learners. Assessments are limited to the specific training task and situation. There is no concern about materials, temporal, or setting generalization. This design generates information about whether a particular type of instruction can produce processing that affects a particular performance of interest. Only by conducting experiments of this type is it possible to conclude unambiguously that a particular variety of processing can influence performance. See Belmont and Butterfield (1977) for additional commentary on this instructional approach to memory process research, as well as Butterfield, Siladi, and Belmont (1980).

Given the enormous number of educationally relevant cognitive strategies that have been suggested, but never submitted to empirical evaluation (cf. Cook & Mayer, 1983; Tierney, Readence, & Dishner, 1985), there is an important role for this design in many studies to come. For instance, although summarizing, predicting, self-questioning, and inferring are all recommended in the reading instructional literature, the data base on these strategies is meagre, especially for child learners (e.g., Forrest-Pressley & Gilles, 1983; Levin & Pressley, 1981; Pressley, Heisel, McCormick, & Nakamura, 1982). Thus, even though these techniques are included in many training packages, some of which are reviewed later in this chapter, there is little empirical basis for the claim that these strategies increase children's reading comprehension, and thus, the need for research on each of them.

Still, more is required than study of unembellished training of single strategies (processes). (1) Many real-world educational tasks require several types of processing. For instance, prose comprehension instruction often includes modifying how readers preview an article, read it, and review it (Levin & Pressley, 1981). Reflecting this need, many contemporary interventions include multiple strategies. (2) Unembellished strategy instruction does not lead to durable strategy use (e.g., Borkowski, 1985; Pressley, Borkowski, & O'Sullivan, 1984, 1985; Pressley, Borkowski, & Schneider, 1987). That is, training subjects how to execute a strategic process is not sufficient to get them to use it when the experimenter/teacher is not around to provide prompting.

This second point has been addressed in both the cognitive-theoretical and educational applications literatures. For instance, Pressley, Forrest-Pressley,

Elliott-Faust, and Miller (1985) argue that efficient strategy use depends on substantial knowledge about the strategy such as goals for which it is appropriate, the materials to which it can be adapted, and the constraints on its use. Those authors offered a model of how strategic and metastrategic knowledge interweave in the able strategy user to produce strategy maintenance and generalization. Both strategic and metastrategic knowledge can be enhanced by richer and more elaborate strategy instruction, and thus, such instruction leads to more durable strategy use (also Pressley, Borkowski, & O'Sullivan, 1984, 1985). Learners are more likely to continue use of memorization strategies when instruction highlights strategy utility (e.g., Borkowski, Carr, & Pressley, 1987; Pressley, Levin, & Ghatala, 1984; Pressley, Ross, Levin, & Ghatala, 1985) and includes information about how, when, and where to use strategies (e.g., O'Sullivan & Pressley, 1984).

A similar hypothesis has been offered by Duffy and his associates at Michigan State (Duffy et al., 1984; Duffy et al., 1987; Roehler & Duffy, 1984). Duffy's group studied teachers' talk in real-world classrooms and obtained associations between students' awareness of processing and the quality of teachers' explanations about cognitive processing. Teaching behaviors that increase students' awareness include:

1. providing students with assistance by emphasizing and explaining skills;
2. providing linkages between past teaching and present teaching;
3. making references to situations when the skills can be applied;
4. modeling overtly the invisible mental processes that are part of cognitive abilities; and
5. presenting tasks as occasions for problem solving in the identification of relevant skills that can be applied.

Duffy and his reasearch team believed that increasing students' awareness of skills will increase their use of skills with concomitant increases in performance.

The Michigan State group have been successful in changing teachers' behaviors so that they provide more elaborate explanations of reading skills to their students. This teaching increased students' awareness as predicted and lead to the expected increases in reading achievement (see Duffy et al., 1987). The Michigan State researchers are continuing to study the link between explanations of cognitive skills and students' achievement and have developed a comprehensive model for teaching reading which has elaborated instruction of strategies at its core (e.g., Duffy & Roehler, 1986, 1987). Duffy's, Roehler's, and their associates' work make clear that investigators studying real-world instructional practices are producing hypotheses very similar to the metacognitive-performance linkage theories developed by cognitive developmental theorists. Both groups are proposing that strategy instruction should be more than simple teaching of single strategies.

ENRICHED STRATEGY INSTRUCTION

In response to the inadequacies of single-strategy training, a number of researchers and practitioners have developed enriched instructional packages. Before reviewing any specific studies, we first overview the components in such treatments and how these components enrich instruction. This list follows from examination of many packages designed to remedy a variety of problems, packages varying both in the number of components and the components that were emphasized (Pressley, 1979; Pressley, Cariglia-Bull, & Snyder, 1984; Pressley, Reynolds, Stark, & Gettinger, 1983)—that is, not all components were found in all packages.

Multiple Strategies

Many packages include several strategies. (1) Strategies differ as to when they can be applied. For instance, summarizing can occur only after reading, but prediction must take place before text is processed completely. (2) Different strategies are appropriate for different subgoals (e.g., Levin, 1986). Skimming aids initial comprehension of text; looking back is appropriate for filling in knowledge gaps necessary to understand subsequent text; reviewing promotes consolidation. (3) Applying several different strategies may lead to strategic persistence since it is more interesting to carry out a variety of procedures than continually executing one process. (4) Because all strategies in a package may not be effective for all learners (e.g., Cronbach & Snow, 1977), including several strategies increases the likelihood that there is something effective for everyone.

Experimenter-Provided Specific Strategy Knowledge

Instructional enrichment can include information about why, when, and where to use strategies. Learners who possess such information should be better prepared to make decisions about when to deploy a procedure. Also helpful is knowing the effort required to deploy a strategy, the payoff if it is deployed, and whether the strategy is fun or not. Pressley, Borkowski, and O'Sullivan (1984, 1985) and Pressley, Borkowski, and Schneider (1987) dubbed these types of information Specific Strategy Knowledge, since a specific set of knowledge is associated with each strategy a learner possesses. All researchers who have considered this type of information have hypothesized it to be critical to self-regulated strategy use (e.g., Armbruster & Brown, 1984; Paris et al., 1983; Pressley, Borkowski, & O'Sullivan, 1984, 1985).

With child learners it is especially important to provide such information as part of instruction. Children do not derive extremely accurate specific strategy knowledge from experiences with strategies (Pressley, Levin, & Ghatala, 1984). Also, specific strategy knowledge that is derived by children is not always employed when it could prove helpful (Pressley, Ross, Levin, & Ghatala, 1984). There is evidence, however, that adding specific strategy information (e.g., Duffy et al., 1987; O'Sullivan & Pressley, 1984) and that drawing children's attention to this type of information (Pressley, Ross, Levin, & Ghatala, 1984) increases use of strategies that children are taught.

Monitoring Strategies

Instructional packages often include procedures for monitoring strategy use and strategy effectiveness. Learners are taught to self-check if they are using the strategies and to note carefully how their performance is tied to processing. Monitoring plays two roles in strategy self-regulation. First, it assists on-line decision making about strategies—Is the present strategy working? If not, would another strategy be more appropriate? Second, monitoring produces information that can become permanent specific strategy knowledge. Thus, if a learner detects that summarizing is not working, but realizes that failure is due to poor initial comprehension of the passage, she or he might encode that summarization strategies should only be used once material is understood. That information could aid future regulation of the summarizing strategy. Training children to use monitoring strategies facilitates regulation of other strategies that they are taught (Ghatala, Levin, Pressley, & Lodico, 1985; Lodico, Ghatala, Levin, Pressley, & Bell, 1983).

Attributional and Motivational Components

People can interpret difficulties they experience in different ways. Failures may be due to bad luck, low effort, poor ability, or encountering too difficult a task (e.g., Weiner, 1979). The interpretation a person makes can play a critical role in determination of subsequent encounters with the task. If failure is attributed to low ability, task persistence is less likely than if failure is presumed due to low effort. Unfortunately, those who are candidates for strategic interventions (i.e., people having problems with tasks they face in the world) are often ones who make self-defeating attributions. For instance, learning disabled children often attribute their failures to lack of ability, and thus, are more likely to stop trying (e.g., Butkowsky & Willows, 1980; Cohen, 1983; Cullen & Boersma, 1982; Pearl, 1982). Thus, designers of packages include components aimed at changing attributions. Effort and technique are emphasized as determinants of behavior; participants are taught to interpret outcomes as within their control. As with other components cited here, there are some data on the effects produced by attribution retraining (e.g., Reid & Borkowski, 1985).

There are a variety of other motivational components in treatments, often self-statements that remind subjects of positive outcomes associated with carrying out the trained strategies or serve as self-reinforcers following execution of task-appropriate behaviors. Coping self-statements also occur prominently in many treatment packages. Thus, subjects are taught to make comments such as, "Hey, good job. I'm doing very well," after a correct response, or, "Well, if I make a mistake, I can remember to think more carefully next time, and then, I'll do better" (Kendall & Wilcox, 1980, p. 83). "Remember, don't worry about mistakes. Just try again. Keep cool, calm, and relaxed. Be proud of yourself when you succeed. Have a blast!" (Meichenbaum & Asarnow, 1979, p. 18). For an extensive discussion of the role of motivational variables in instruction, see Borkowski, Carr, Rellinger, & Pressley (in press).

Practice With Strategies

Strategy practice is often preceded by experimenter modeling of the processing, with subjects first executing the process with experimenter help faded gradually. Practice is hypothesized to increase strategy use and generalization after training, especially when distributed over settings, tasks, and time (e.g., Kirschenbaum & Tomarken, 1982; Stokes & Baer, 1977). Practice permits the learner to see that the strategy has general appropriateness—the strategy is not welded to a particular training task, situation, or time (e.g., Brown, 1978). A second benefit is that strategies are usually executed with greater facility after practice. As learners become more skillful with a technique, they may encode that the strategy is easy to use, and thus, be more likely to use it in the future. With practice some learners may discover that strategies can be modified, how the strategy relates to other strategies, and the utility of strategies (e.g., Pressley, Borkowski, & O'Sullivan, 1984, 1985; Pressley, Levin, & Ghatala, 1984). In short, specific strategy knowledge is enriched during practice. Pressley, Goodchild, Fleet, Zajchowski, and Evans (in press) make the case in detail that effective instruction of complex strategies always requires extensive practice.

Self-Instructional Training

Learners are taught to instruct themselves to use trained strategies in particular orders and in particular situations. The self-instructions often incorporate strategies, specific strategy knowledge, and monitoring procedures. Learners can be taught to self-instruct themselves to define the problem and to focus attention on relevant dimensions. Self-reinforcement and coping self-statements are sometimes included as well (Meichenbaum, 1977). In general, self-instructions are first modeled by a teacher, with use transferred gradually to the child, and overt self-instruction eventually supplanted by covert self-instruction (e.g., Meichenbaum & Asarnow, 1979).

Why should self-instruction training increase proficient strategy functioning? First of all, it makes prominent important specific strategy knowledge such as when to deploy which strategies—that is, the self-instruction sequences strategy execution and schedules monitoring at appropriate points. The reminders to stay on task and to focus on relevant aspects of the problem should increase appropriate task persistence, as should self-reinforcement and coping strategies.

Potent Styles of Teaching

It would be difficult to specify *typical* teaching behaviors, either as operationalized in research efforts or as occur in classrooms during strategy instruction. Although most investigators have given little thought to teaching style, some researchers consider particular instructional styles to be critical to their enrichment package. For instance, cognitive behavior modifiers almost always include substantial modeling of strategies, with learners' execution of the strategies closely guided at first, only gradually becoming autonomous (Meichenbaum, 1977). One recent emphasis in instructional packages has been interactive teaching with instruction adjusted "on-line" to the level of the child. There is ample theoretical speculation (e.g., Bruner, 1983; Day, 1983; Greenfield, 1984; Rogoff & Gardner, 1984) and a growing data base supporting the effectiveness of this approach to teaching (e.g., Hodapp, Goldfield, & Boyatzis, 1984; Greenfield, 1984; Manzo, 1968; Wood, Wood, & Middleton, 1978). Pressley, Snyder, and Cariglia-Bull (1987) provide extensive discussion of this issue, concluding that good teaching involves elaborated description of strategies and when to use them, modeling, and corrective interaction with students (e.g., the Duffy & Roehler approach; Duffy et al., 1987).

Summary of the Components

Including these components in instruction should increase what learners know about strategies—and the more one knows about a strategy, the more likely is generalized and appropriate use (e.g., Borkowski, in press). Enrichment increases learners' specific strategy knowledge in several ways:

1. Learners can derive specific strategy knowledge through practice with strategies.

2. "Practicing" several strategies that are part of a package may make apparent the unique advantages of each strategy than does learning and practicing them separately.

3. External agents such as teachers or experimenters can tell them information.

4. Monitoring can produce knowledge.

5. In providing motivational/attributional information, experimenters inform the participants that they are capable of executing strategies with benefits following strategy execution.

6. The self-instructional coordination of strategies is also largely metacognitive—self-instructional reminders of processing sequence make "when" information more salient and knowledge of strategy use-end state associations is increased by self-reminders to think of the goal and plan of attack at the beginning of processing.

7. Strategy knowledge enrichment is a by-product of some styles of teaching, such as modeling of a strategy which is often accompanied by commentary about when and where to use the strategy—presumably, many of the adjustments to the level of the child in interactive teaching involve addressing problems of strategy appropriateness and fitting strategies to particular situations.

RESEARCH ON ENRICHED INSTRUCTIONAL PACKAGES

Typical Studies

Although enriched treatment packages are more intricate than unembellished single-strategy training, the structure of most experiments evaluating these packages has not been very complex. Evaluation studies typically include two conditions, one the treatment package and the other a control condition. The control is often a pretest-posttest, no treatment condition. Alternatively, control subjects may be provided a presumably ineffective treatment during time corresponding to instruction in the experimental condition.

To illustrate this typical research approach, we discuss two recent (and typical) studies of enriched instruction that were designed to improve reading comprehension and prose processing. Studies of prose memory and comprehension are appropriate to highlight in a volume such as this since these problems have proven especially attractive to cognitive developmentalists interested in enriched instruction. The most educationally important issues addressed in this literature are how to increase children's memory and comprehension of text.

Paris and Oka (1986); Paris, Cross, and Lipson (1984); Paris and Jacobs (1984)[1]

Paris and his associates taught 3rd and 5th Grade children a variety of reading strategies (e.g., skimming, inferring, summarizing) over a 4-month period. The in-the-classroom lessons included specific strategy knowledge, such as how, when, and why to use the strategies. The lessons were provided by a teacher-experimenter. The content was illustrated using devices such as bulletin boards

---

[1]The same experiment was reported in both Paris, Cross, and Lipson (1984) and Paris and Jacobs (1984). The two articles differ in the dependent measures reported.

and elaborated through dialogues between students and the teacher that included modeling, feedback, and persuasion. The instructional points were reiterated with in-the-class exercises such as worksheets. Finally, the regular classroom teachers were encouraged to extend the principles taught in the experimental curriculum to other instructional arenas. The control subjects received the same pretests and posttests as experimental children, but no other special treatment.

A variety of pre- and posttests were administered in these studies including standardized measures of reading comprehension, cloze tests requiring memory for text read shortly before the measure was administered, and prose error detection tests (e.g., Markman, 1979). Measures of reading strategy knowledge were also included. These included interview questions tapping various aspects of knowledge about reading, including probes about particular strategies that were taught in the experimental curriculum. A multiple-choice questionnaire tapping knowledge of reading strategies that were trained as part of the experimental package was also administered.

After training, experimental subjects had greater knowledge of the trained strategies than did control learners. There was a small increase as well from pretest to posttest on reported use of strategies by experimental subjects, but no increases by control learners. Reading awareness (i.e., knowledge of reading tasks, understanding strategies, and knowledge of monitoring) increased from pretest to posttest for both experimental and control subjects, but more for children in the experimental condition. There were posttest differences in comprehension in favor of experimental subjects, but with the effects significant only for some measures, but never large in magnitude (Cohen, 1977; see Worden, 1987). Finally, there were significant correlations between the metacognitive awareness measure and reading comprehension, such that greater awareness was associated with better comprehension.

Paris' preferred interpretation of his data is that the treatment increased reading awareness, which in turn facilitated strategy acquisition and improved comprehension. The metacognitive aspects of their instruction were particularly critical to the success of the intervention according to the discussions offered in Paris & Oka (1986), Paris and Jacobs (1984), and Paris, Cross, and Lipson (1984).

Palincsar and Brown (1984)

Palincsar and Brown (1984) studied Grade 7 poor comprehenders. In the most complete instructional condition (*reciprocal training*) subjects were taught strategies to execute while reading—summarizing (self-review), questioning, and clarifying. The subjects were given extensive practice using these strategies and feedback about their performance. These strategies incorporated a monitoring component. For example, if the reader experienced difficulty summarizing, that would indicate reading comprehension was not occurring.

Instruction in strategy use in the reciprocal training condition followed the "reciprocal" teaching model (Manzo, 1968)—the teacher and the students took turns asking questions, constructing summaries, making predictions, etc. Subjects were exposed to much specific strategy knowledge during the 20–day course of the training. The tutor made a concerted and successful effort to pitch the instruction near the students' current level of understanding, consistent with models of teaching derived from Soviet ideas about development (e.g., Rogoff & Gardner, 1983).

There were three other conditions in the study. *Control* subjects took the same pretests and posttests as reciprocal training subjects, but received no other aspects of the intervention. The *test control* subjects received the same regimen of practice tests and feedback that the reciprocal training subjects received, and they took the pretests and posttests. Subjects in the *locating information* treatment group were taught how to find answers in passages, an intervention known to facilitate reading comprehension (e.g., Palincsar, 1982; Raphael, Wonnacat, & Pearson, 1981). They were also given the daily comprehension exercises, the pretests, and posttests.

The quality of summaries and questions improved over the course of instruction in the reciprocal training condition. Over time the students' questions became more like the tutor's, with the proportion of verbatim questions declining. Although asking for clarifications and making predictions did occur, they were not as frequent as questioning and summarizing. Improvement on the daily comprehension measures was greater in the reciprocal training condition than in the other two groups given the assessments. The reciprocal training subjects clearly performed better on the posttest than subjects in the other three conditions.

Generalization probes were taken for the students in the reciprocal training and untreated control groups. In general, after training, reciprocally trained subjects learned more from in-class social studies and science passages than did control learners. Reciprocal training subjects improved in their summarization skills over the course of instruction; pretest-posttest performance improvements in summarization did not occur for control subjects. Reciprocal training subjects produced better questions (e.g., better related to main ideas, paraphrased) for passages after training; there was not a reliable pretest–posttest improvement in self-questioning for control subjects. Reciprocal training subjects' detection of anomalous sentences in text improved reliably from pretest to posttest; controls' detections did not.

Palincsar and Brown (1984, Expt. 1) noted that for all students in the reciprocal training condition, improvements in reciprocal interactions were followed by improvements in objective comprehension. This correlation suggested that the processes shaped and improved during reciprocal training were producing the comprehension shifts.

In a second study, reciprocal training was carried out by classroom teachers in classroom settings. Although there was no control condition in the study, pretest-posttest improvements in reading comprehension were obtained. This study established that classroom teachers could implement the Palincsar and Brown training package. The teachers were enthusiastic about the intervention and the improvements it produced. Palincsar, Brown and their associates have continued research on reciprocal instruction with consistent success given population (e.g., grade 1) and instructor variations (e.g., peers) (Palincsar, 1986; Palincsar, Brown, & Martin, 1987).

Discussion of Palincsar and Brown (1984) and the Paris Experiments

The most fundamental requirement for an instructional package to be considered effective is that there be clear improvement in performance following the onset of treatment. Both Palincsar's and Brown's (1984) and Paris' packages are successful given this criterion. These outcomes will stimulate additional research. Careful study of these two experiments, however, suggests some important challenges for researchers doing this followup work.

Total Time Controls. Did trained learners acquire more from instructional input than subjects not receiving training, given the same amount of time with the input? No data about time spent on posttraining assessments were provided in the reports of these studies. Perhaps trained subjects took longer to process materials than nontrained children because of the complexity of the trained processing? Although confoundings of learning interventions and study time have occurred in many studies of naturalistic learning (Faw & Waller, 1976, provide a review), such confoundings make unambiguous interpretations of learning outcomes more difficult. Thus, those interested in enriching instruction need to provide explicit information about study times in the various conditions of their experiments.

Direct Assessment of Processing. Processing changes that result from instruction should be documented as directly as possible (Butterfield et al., 1980). Neither Palincsar and Brown (1984) nor the Paris experiment were rich in direct assessment of processing on criterion tasks, although Palincsar and Brown (1984) provided admirable documentation of ongoing processing during training. We point out, however, that "direct" process measures are often difficult to obtain with children, and always more difficult than with adults. For instance, verbal descriptions of processing obtained from adults are easier to interpret than children's verbal descriptions. Also, on-line direct measures of process require individual treatment and assessment of subjects—that is, a research approach incompatible with group-administered interventions, the principal focus of Palincsar's, Brown's, and Paris' work.

Statistical Problems.   There are many statistical-design issues that come to mind in reviewing the illustrative studies. One is that workers in this area need to think about what constitutes an important effect. This problem is salient in comparing the Paris' designs and Palincsar and Brown's study. The latter experiment included only six subjects per condition, resulting in low power for detecting anything but the most smashing effects. In contrast, because of very high ns per condition in the Paris experiment, power was great even for miniscule effects in these studies (especially Paris & Oka, 1986). Many of the outcomes that were interpreted as important were small indeed. Which approach is right? Some would say that improving comprehension, especially in poor readers, is a clinical problem, and thus, the appropriate criterion is clinical significance, that is, large, clear effects with functioning changed so dramatically that statistical analysis is unnecessary (e.g., Baer, 1977). Others argue that educational treatments producing positive effects as small as 0.4 standard deviation can be of practical value (e.g., Cronbach & Snow, 1977), especially if the small advantage is enjoyed by learners on many occasions. Although not offering an opinion as to which approach should be followed, we believe that investigators in this area should consider carefully the size of effects that they wish to detect and design experiments accordingly and explicitly inform the consuming public about the magnitude of effects that were produced.

A second statistical concern is that units of treatment and units of analysis were mismatched in the illustrative studies. Subjects were treated in groups, but analyses were carried out on the individual scores. Conventional parametric analyses of individual scores when subjects are treated in groups results in a Type I error rate that is inflated relative to the nominal error rate (Levin, 1985). There are nonparametric methods for analyzing research with as few as three to five groups per condition (e.g., Levin, Marascuilo, & Hubert, 1978), and these techniques can be applied easily to the types of data produced in studies of instructional enrichment. Such statistical methods are often very powerful. Investigators should employ alternative procedures when important assumptions of conventional analyses are not met.

Effects Produced by Specific Components.   A great challenge for investigators following up the two illustrative studies will be to determine the effects produced by the various components in these instructional enrichment packages. *For instance, although Paris concluded that the improvements obtained in his study were due to increased awareness produced by the enrichment components, this claim is unjustified.* Any one of the components in the package or any combination of them could be the *causal* factor (perhaps *both* for increased reading performance and awareness in the treated condition). It could have been the bulletin board. It could have been encouraging classroom teachers to use the method. It could have been the learning metaphors and/or the worksheets. The list goes on and on. In short, the metacognition components were completely confounded with many other instructional variables, making impossible convincing conclusions about metacognition and instruction.

Closing Comment on Palincsar and Brown (1984) and the Paris Studies

Our goal in providing the critiques presented in this section is to be constructive. The types of interventions studied in this research are very important, enough so to justify much additional study. In fact, we are extremely impressed by the comprehensive and integrated treatments offered both by Palincsar and Brown and by Paris and his associates. Future evaluations of these treatments promise gains for both applications and theory. We emphasize in closing this section that there are many instructional recommendations in the literature that are not effective by any criteria (Cook & Mayer, 1983; Pressley, Levin, & McDaniel, 1987). Thus, there is every reason for enthusiasm about the outcomes in studies such as the ones reviewed so far, even though the results are preliminary from our point of view. Some of our suggestions are cost free or almost so (e.g., collecting and reporting study time data on criterion tests, analyzing data with treatment unit means as the unit of analysis), and thus, these suggestions may be adopted more readily than others that were made. One recommendation, however, is particularly expensive. The basic two-group design in which a complex package is compared to a non-treatment control condition is usually inadequate for analytical investigations of complex instructional interventions. More sensitive and complicated designs are required. The focus now turns to studies and designs that permit conclusions about instructional components.

SEARCHING FOR POTENT COMPONENTS IN INSTRUCTIONAL PACKAGES

There are a number of reasons to want information about the effects of particular components in complex treatments. The most obvious to cognitive developmental theorists is that component analyses permit evaluation of theoretical perspectives. By manipulating the enrichment components outlined earlier, it should be possible to determine the role of metacognition in strategy instruction, whether causal attributions have an impact on strategy use, whether *higher-order* monitoring strategies and/or verbalized self-instructions serve a regulating role in cognition, whether teaching *matched* to the cognitive level of the child is more potent than other types of instruction, as well as information relevant to a number of other theoretical positions about cognition.

A second reason for research on components is that these complex treatments are expensive in terms of time and effort. There is high incentive to streamline by eliminating aspects of instruction that do not enhance the intervention. From a pragmatic perspective, the more expensive a component, the more urgent the need to evaluate it.

The best way to conduct research that is informative about components is to manipulate the components systematically in true experiments. To determine if strategy X promotes learning, compare learning with and without X. Does adding metacognitive component B affect use of strategies? Compare conditions with strategies X, Y, and Z, varying the presence of B. Experiments with as few as two conditions can be informative about particular components. Alternatively, experiments with a number of conditions can be conducted with elements "titrated" in and out. For example, consider an experiment with a no treatment control condition, a condition with just strategy X, one with just strategy Y, one with metacognitive component B added to X, one with B added to Y. Such a study would allow evaluation of the efficacy of strategies X and Y, as well as metacognitive component B.

The titration tactic has been used in investigations of metacognitive embellishment of memory strategy instruction, producing in-depth understanding of the effects of several different components on children's use of associative memory strategies. Because that work is reviewed in detail elsewhere (Pressley, Borkowski, & O'Sullivan, 1984, 1985; Pressley, Forrest-Pressley, Elliott-Faust, & Miller, 1985), and because of the focus in this chapter on prose processing, we do not cover the same ground here. The first analytical example is a smaller scale experiment (three conditions) that provided information about one aspect of enrichment; the second included four cells that addressed two components; the third was a more complex study that permitted resolution of several issues within the same study. All three experiments illustrate well that the many design considerations raised earlier can be incorporated into research without compromising the integrity of complex treatments.

Short and Ryan (1984)

Short's and Ryan's (1984) goal was to improve the reading comprehension of poor 4th-grade readers. Their most complete treatment condition included attribution training and a specific complex strategy. The "story-grammar" strategy included use of five "wh" questions about the settings and episodes of narratives:

1. Who is the main character?
2. Where and when did the story take place?
3. What did the main character do?
4. How did the story end?
5. How did the main character feel?

As subjects read training passages, they were instructed to take notes in the margins and make underlinings relevant to these questions continually asking themselves these questions to determine if they could answer them. Attribution training consisted of reminding subjects of the importance of effort in successful reading performance. Subjects were also taught to self-verbalize a set of attributional–motivational self-statements before processing each passage. These self-statements included:

> Enjoy the story; praise yourself for a job well done; try hard; just think about how happy you will be when it comes time for the test and you're doing well; and give yourself a pat on the back.

In the other two conditions of the experiment, subjects received only one of the two components (i.e., there was a story-grammar strategy condition and an attribution training condition). With this design it was possible to determine if adding attribution training to strategy instruction increases performance or if adding strategy training to the attributional intervention resulted in reading performance gains. Subjects in all conditions practiced with stories similar to the criterion task. Practice was spread over three sessions during the course of a week.

There were pretest to posttest gains on reading recall measures in the strategy + attribution and the strategy only conditions, but not in the attribution only condition. There were no reliable differences between the conditions on the pretest; strategy and strategy + attribution subjects outperformed attribution subjects on the posttest. Poor readers in the strategy and strategy + attribution conditions performed near the level of skilled 4th-grade readers on the posttest; attribution subjects performed well below the level of skilled readers. More posttest study behaviors (notes, underlining) were observed in the strategy + attribution and strategy conditions than in the attribution condition. Importantly, however, study times on the posttest did not differ between conditions.

By comparing conditions that differed in specific components, it was possible to determine an active ingredient in the strategy training-attribution training package. Of course, there could have been additional decomposition of the treatment package, for instance, by including a treatment with only some of the story-grammar questions. Investigating such a treatment would be justified if there were theoretical reasons to believe that one aspect of the treatment was principally responsible for the training effects, or if some part of the training were very expensive (e.g., children experienced great difficulty answering a particular type of question). Short and Ryan (1984) did not have such concerns. Most treatment packages, however, are more complex than the one studied by Short and Ryan (1984), and thus, require more complicated studies to establish which components contribute to the effects produced by the entire package.

Graves (1987)

Graves (1987) taught children in grades 5 through 8 who experienced comprehension difficulties to find the main ideas in text. The most complex intervention included direct instruction of ways to find the main idea and self-monitoring training. Two treatments were each based on one of the two components—a direct instruction condition and a self-monitoring condition. The fourth condition was a control condition that experienced neither component.

The direct instruction component included providing the definition that a main idea "tells what the whole story is about." The subjects practiced finding main ideas, with feedback provided as subjects produced main ideas. Self-monitoring training involved teaching subjects to ask themselves, "Do I understand what the whole story is about?" They were also instructed to reread if they did not understand. Control subjects were simply told the meaning of the main idea, with practice opportunities, but without the extensive feedback that was part of direct instruction.

The results were clearcut. The two-component treatment produced better detection of main ideas than direct instruction alone; direct instruction was better than self-monitoring training, which produced more detection of main ideas than control instruction.

Elliott-Faust and Pressley (1986)

The specific prose-processing problem studied by Elliott-Faust and Pressley (1986) was children's comprehension monitoring of prose passages that were read to them. Grade-school children often overlook ambiguities and inconsistencies in otherwise meaningful presentations (e.g., Beal & Flavell, 1982; Flavell, Speer, Green, & August, 1981; Markman, 1977, 1979, 1981; Patterson, O'Brien, Kister, Carter, & Kotsonis, 1981; Singer & Flavell, 1981), such as the blatantly contradictory information contained in the following passage:

> One of the things that children like to eat everywhere in the world is ice cream. Some ice cream stores sell many different flavors of ice cream, but the most popular flavors are chocolate and vanilla. Lots of different kinds of desserts can be made with ice cream. Some fancy restaurants serve a special dessert made out of ice cream called Baked Alaska. To make it they put ice cream in a very hot oven. The ice cream in Baked Alaska melts when it gets that hot. When they make Baked Alaska, the ice cream stays firm and does not melt. (Markman, 1979, p. 646).

Markman believes that children fail to detect inconsistencies because they do not process adequately whether they are understanding a message and whether the message makes sense. If that hypothesis is correct, teaching children to carry out

117

such processing should increase their detection of flawed text. This was one issue investigated by Elliott-Faust and Pressley (1986).

Elliott-Faust and Pressley's second concern was whether adding a self-instructional component to training would enhance durable use of the trained strategies, consistent with Meichenbaum's and Asarnow's (1979) speculations. Their position followed from observations of maintained and generalized strategy use in reading tasks after instructions in the use of reading techniques that include self-instruction (e.g., Bommarito & Meichenbaum, 1978; Egeland, 1974). Because self-instructional enrichment was one of several components in those treatment packages, it was not possible to conclude that self-instruction was the component that produced the benefits. In fact, with only a few exceptions (e.g., Asarnow & Meichenbaum, 1979; Graves, 1987; Kurtz & Borkowski, 1984; Miller, 1985), the self-instructional contributions have not been separated from the effects of other components (see Pressley, Reynolds, Stark, & Gettinger, 1983).

Elliott-Faust's and Pressley's most complete condition included complete self-controlled training of comparison processing. Complete self-controlled training subjects were told first the criterion for deciding something did not make sense, with the Elliott-Faust and Pressley (1986) explanation modeled after Markman and Gorin (1981):

> For example, suppose you heard, "Squirrels love lettuce." Then, later you heard, "Squirrels hate lettuce." Those two sentences don't go together. When sentences don't go together, then the story doesn't make sense. Suppose one part of the story said, "Bears are friendly animals," then another part said, "Bears are ferocious animals." It would be confusing to have two sentences that do not go together like that in a story. I want you to tell me if you find any parts in the story that do not go together, that do not make sense.

The comparison strategy taught in the complete self-controlled training condition was one used by adults who identified inconsistencies proficiently (Elliott-Faust, 1984). The children first were taught to compare sentences (i.e., make *local comparisons*) at input in the following fashion:

> OK, now we will do five practice stories together so that I can show you a good way to listen to a story to make sure it makes sense. After we do the five practice stories, there will be four stories for you to do by yourself. OK, this is how we are going to listen to the stories to see if they make sense. First, we will listen carefully to each part of the story. Then, when there is a pause we will compare the sentences to see if they make sense together. To compare the sentences, we will ask, "Do these sentences make sense together?" OK, let's go over what we are going to do when we listen to the stories to see if they make sense. First, we will listen carefully to the parts of the story that are read, then we will compare the sentences to see if they make sense together. We will ask, "Do these sentences make sense together?"

A second pass through the stories was required to introduce a second aspect of comparison, *wholistic comparison:*

> OK, now we will listen to those stories again and this time we will compare the sentences to see if they go together *and* we will check to see if the whole story makes sense. We will check to see if all parts of the story make sense together by asking, ''Does the whole story make sense?'' after we hear each part of the story. So we will listen carefully to each part of the story and then we will ask, (1), ''Do these sentences make sense together?'' and (2) ''Does the whole story make sense?''

Use of these two aspects of comparison was embedded in a self-instructional routine. Specifically, children were taught to pose the self-question, ''What am I supposed to do? when first presented the task and materials. They also learned that the appropriate response was to listen to the story and see if it made sense. The self-question, ''What is my plan?'' followed, with self-reminders, ''I must listen carefully to each part of the story,'' ''I must ask, 'Do these sentences make sense together?' '' and ''I must ask, 'Does the whole story make sense together?' '' While executing the strategies the subjects were taught to ask and answer, ''Am I using my plan? and after completing a passage, ''How did I do?'' In short, the complete training was very complex, including the five components summarized in Table 5.1.

There were seven other conditions in the experiment. Each of these was formed by eliminating components from the most complete treatment as detailed in Table 5.1. The main questions that can be answered given this setup are whether adding self-instruction improves training of the local + wholistic comparison strategies (condition 1 versus condition 2 in Table 5.1) and whether local + wholistic comparison training, local comparison training alone, or wholistic comparison training alone is effective (condition 2 versus condition 3 and condition 5, condition 3 versus condition 5). The only form of training evaluated in previous research was the provision of a standard of evaluation, which Markman and Gorin (1981) showed to be potent relative to no training. The Elliott-Faust and Pressley design permitted evaluation of Markman's and Gorin's (1981) training relative both to the various comparison training conditions and the complete training package. Several subsidiary hypotheses could also be studied using this design—such as whether simple exposure to training materials would be sufficient to increase performance (condition 7 versus condition 8) and whether simply providing subjects with the inconsistency information produced by comparison processing would improve error detection (condition 4 versus condition 5).

The criterion task for all subjects was evaluation of eight Markman-like passages, with four presented immediately after instruction and four presented six to eight days later. Three inconsistent passages and one consistent story were

TABLE 5.1

Components in Each of the Conditions of Elliott-Faust and Pressley (1986)

Condition	Appropriate Standard of Evaluation	5 Practice Stories in Training	Sentence Input Comparison Training	Wholistic Comparison Training	Self-Instructional Training
1. Complete self-Controlled training	X	X	X	X	X
2. Local comparison*					
Wholistic comparison training	X	X	X	X	
3. Local comparison training	X	X	X		
4. Passive training	X	X*			
5. Appropriate standard*					
Story exposure	X	X			
6. Appropriate standard for judgment	X				
7. Posttest only					
8. Story exposure control		X			

*Were told the inconsistency in each sample story.

presented at each testing. The children were not prompted or reminded to use trained strategy/strategies on these occasions, but only were told to judge the comprehensibility of the passages. Other measures were taken after subjects completed judging the four stories, including self-reports by the children of their processing of stories.

Measures associated with the inconsistency judgments (i.e., number of inconsistencies detected, quality of inconsistency explanations, and proportions of children who performed perfectly—detecting errors in the three inconsistent passages and only those passages) were generally consistent, with analyses of each of these variables yielding very similar patterns of results, with several of these reported in Elliott-Faust and Pressley (1986). Because of the consistency across dependent measures and because of space limitations, only the proportions of perfect performers are presented here. See Table 5.2.

On the immediate posttest, Elliott-Faust and Pressley (1986) replicated Markman and Gorin's (1981) finding that providing an appropriate standard of evaluation produces better performance than the control instruction. The other notable outcome on the immediate posttest was that best performances occurred in the local comparison + wholistic comparison training condition and the complete self-controlled training condition. The judgments made in these two conditions did not differ. Thus, it is possible to obtain even greater performance gains than Markman and Gorin (1981) did. The results on the delayed test differed from the immediate posttest outcomes in one important way. Complete self-controlled training produced better delayed detection than did local comparison + wholistic comparison training. Although not discussed until this point, some strategy

TABLE 5.2
Proportions of Perfect Monitorers

Condition	Immediate Posttest	Delayed Posttest
1. Complete self-controlled training	.667	.792
2. Local comparison*		
Wholistic comparison training	.667	.417
3. Local comparison training	.333	.458
4. Passive training	.500	.458
5. Appropriate standard*		
Story exposure	.458	.250
6. Appropriate standard for judgment	.333	.500
7. Posttest only	.042	.125
8. Story exposure control	.083	.250

*Were told the inconsistency in each sample story.

utilization measures were also taken. In brief, there were converging data that processing immediately after training was very proficient in both the local comparison + wholistic comparison training condition and in the complete self-controlled training condition relative to the other conditions of the study. The advantage was more durable in the complete self-controlled training condition. These results were consistent with two positions that are essential to our view of cognitively based instruction—(1) cognitive strategy training can improve children's performance (Pressley, Heisel, McCormick, & Nakamura, 1982), and (2) enrichment effects are more likely on maintenance and/or generalization measures than on performance immediately after training (Pressley, Forrest-Pressley, Elliott-Faust, & Miller, 1985).

Discussion of Short and Ryan (1984), Graves (1987), and Elliott-Faust and Pressley (1986)

The most striking advantage of these studies over those discussed earlier was that conclusions about individual components were possible. In extolling that virtue, we realize that all conclusions in these studies were generated in particular task/learning component environments, and thus, general conclusions about particular aspects of training are tentative. Such tentativeness is required until multiple replications across situations can be obtained. Perhaps attributional instruction would impact more forcefully on forms of strategy training besides the story-grammar training used by Short and Ryan (1984). Perhaps another form of story-grammar training would have greater effects. See Borkowski, Johnston, and Reid (1986) for comments on this point. Also, there is no guarantee that Elliott-Faust and Pressley's (1986) self-instructional regimen would be effective with other strategies. The only way to produce general conclusions about components is to do numerous studies with the components of interest varied systematically in a number of situations.

One possibility is that ANOVA-type manipulation of components might produce more systematic knowledge. Thus, perhaps the five component complete training package in Elliott-Faust and Pressley (1986) could be studied in a $2 \times 2 \times 2 \times 2 \times 2$ design with each of the five components systematically varied (i.e., either present or absent from the package). The assumption is that such a setup would generate information about interactions between components not possible from the experiment conducted by Elliott-Faust and Pressley (1986). There are two problems with this approach, however, that preclude its use. One is that it is cumbersome (e.g., 32 conditions in the above example). The other is that some components cannot be added to treatments unless particular other components are present. For instance, the self-instructional sequence by Elliott-Faust and Pressley could not be executed without other basic strategies (e.g., the comparison strategies) to self-instruct. In that same study, comparison training could not have occurred without the presence of practice stories or a standard of evaluation.

There were a number of positive aspects of the Short and Ryan (1984), Graves (1987), and Elliott-Faust and Pressley (1984) experiments. Training time was equivalent in all conditions of each study, so that between-condition effects could be interpreted as differences in learning efficiency. Even more critical, testing time was equated in Short and Ryan (1984) and Elliott-Faust (1986). Some "direct" assessments of process were taken in Short and Ryan (1984) and Elliott-Faust and Pressley (1986), and the patterns of differences on these process measures corresponded to the patterns of differences on the other performance measures. That is not to say, however, that direct assessment was exhaustive. For instance, there were no direct "attributional" behavior measures in Short and Ryan (1984), and Elliott-Faust and Pressley (1986) could have complemented their verbal self-reports with more behavioral measures.

The units of treatment and analysis were congruent in these three studies. We view the running of subjects individually, versus in groups, as especially praiseworthy. Work on process training should occur at the individual level before attempts are made to train processes in the classroom. Although there is some loss of correspondence with real-world teaching when subjects are treated individually, it is much more certain that learners are under instructional control (e.g., Levin, Pressley, McCormick, Miller, & Shriberg, 1979). Since process-based explanations of experimental outcomes are most convincing when the processing of learners' can be assessed directly, the classroom offers no advantage relative to individual treatment of subjects as far as fine-grained analysis of learners' processing is concerned. It is much easier to get on-line processing measures for individual learners than with children in a group. On the other hand, because of the differences between classroom and individual treatment situations, there is no guarantee that instruction that works with individuals will facilitate in-class learning. More naturalistic research must follow laboratory demonstrations to make convincing arguments that an instructional intervention can influence outcomes in actual schooling environments (e.g., Marx, Winne, & Walsh, 1985).

The three experiments discussed here are not the only analytical examinations of strategic processing during prose learning. Particularly relevant to research considered previously in this chapter, Palincsar (1984) reported an analysis of the reciprocal teaching component of her reciprocal training package. In general, reciprocal teaching (i.e., teaching with student-teacher exchanges and feedback) proved more potent than teaching by demonstration or teaching that emphasized student practice. Palincsar (1984) established that reciprocal interaction between students and teachers is a critically important contributing factor to the reciprocal training effects obtained by Palincsar and Brown (1984). Palincsar and her associates are continuing their work to identify other active ingredients in reciprocal training.

SUMMARY AND CLOSING COMMENTS

The bulk of strategy instructional research consists of tests of single strategies. One two-group comparison often is all that is needed to determine if strategy X is effective. This design is useful still because many strategy proposals have never been submitted to evaluation at all, let alone systematic evaluation.

Another related species of strategy instruction has evolved—the multiple-component, enriched strategy instruction. There is no way that single, two-group experiments can provide comprehensive analysis of the active versus inactive ingredients of these packages, although single components can be evaluated with single, two-group designs. Information about more than one component requires either larger experiments or a number of simple experiments with the presence of enrichment components varied systematically.

Decomposition of complex treatments is a long, expensive, and tedious process. For instance, consider Elliott-Faust and Pressley's (1986) most complete treatment. Although that investigation established that self-instruction produced benefits over and above strategy gains, the self-instruction was a complex entity that could be subdivided further into several parts, including motivational, strategy informational, and attentional components. We do not expect, however, that decomposition will be exhaustive either in this case or in most cases. Components will be studied if doing so informs theory. Some expensive components will be evaluated to determine if the benefits they produce are worth the costs.

There are many methodological traps that line the road to information about instructional enrichment. One of the most disturbing, perhaps because we have encountered it so frequently in reviewing the literature, is lack of attention to learners' time on task (and particularly, time on the criterion test task). Unless investigators provide this information, instructionally-produced differences are impossible to interpret unambiguously. In general, researchers in this area can benefit greatly by attention to traditional methodological concerns of researchers studying learning and cognition.

Refined work on enriched instruction is required for three reasons: (1) There is little strategy instruction in classrooms compared to what could occur (e.g., Beck, 1984; Durkin, 1984; Pearson, 1984; Pressley, Goodchild, Fleet, Zajchowski, & Evans, in press). Of the strategy instructional recommendations that do exist in the curriculum and instruction literatures, most have not been studied, or worse yet, studied, proven wrong, and yet remain in curriculum and instruction texts. See Levin and Pressley (1981) and Pressley and Levin (1986) for extensive commentaries. (2) The tasks children encounter in school are complicated and require instruction that matches these complications (e.g., Marx et al., 1985). It seems intuitive that training packages will be better suited to this task than training individual processes without instructional embellishment. (3) Research on instructional enrichment can advance theory—and in fact, is often essential to theory advancement (e.g., Underwood, 1975). For instance, theoretical claims about the potency of self-instruction (e.g., Meichenbaum, 1977) can only be established by experiments that demonstrate that self-instructional training is sufficient to provide the advantages enjoyed by learners who use self-instruction "spontaneously." In short, much follows from complex experimental analyses of complex treatments.

ACKNOWLEDGMENT

The writing of this chapter was supported by separate grants to the first two authors from the Natural Sciences and Engineering Research Council of Canada. Most of the ideas were developed while authors Pressley and Forrest-Pressley were visiting scholars at the Max Planck Institute for Psychological Research, Munich, FRG, during the summer of 1984. We are grateful to John Borkowski, August Flammer, Ruth Luthi, Annemarie Palinscar, and Elizabeth Short for their helpful comments on a previous version of this chapter.

REFERENCES

Armbruster, B. B., & Brown, A. L. (1984). Learning from reading: The role of metacognition. In R. C. Anderson, J. Osborn, & R. J. Tierney (Eds.), *Learning to read in American schools: Basal readers and content texts* (pp. 273–281). Hillsdale, NJ: Lawrence Erlbaum Associates.

Asarnow, J. R., & Meichenbaum, D. (1979). Verbal rehearsal and serial recall: The mediational training of kindergarten children. *Child Development, 50,* 1173–1177.

Baer, D. M. (1977). Reviewer's comment: Just because it's reliable doesn't mean that you can use it. *Journal of Applied Behavior Analysis, 10,* 117–119.

Beal, C. R., & Flavell, J. H. (1982). Effect of increasing the salience of message ambiguities on kindergartener's evaluations of communicative success and message adequacy. *Developmental Psychology, 18,* 43–48.

Beck, I. L. (1984). Developing comprehension: The impact of the directed reading lesson. In R. C. Anderson, J. Osborn, & R. J. Tierney (Eds.), *Learning to read in American schools: Basal readers and content texts.* (pp. 3–20). Hillsdale, NJ: Lawrence Erlbaum Associates.

Belmont, J. M., & Butterfield, E. C. (1977). The instructional approach to developmental cognitive research. In R. V. Kail, Jr. & J. W. Hagen (Eds.), *Perspectives on the development of memory and cognition.* (pp. 437–482). Hillsdale, NJ: Lawrence Erlbaum Associates.

Bommarito, J., & Meichenbaum, D. (1978). *Enhancing reading comprehension by means of self-instructional training.* Waterloo, Ontario: University of Waterloo, unpublished manuscript.

Borkowski, J. G. (1985). Signs of intelligence: Strategy generalization and metacognition. In S. Yussen (Ed.), *The development of reflection* (pp. 105–144). New York: Academic Press.

Borkowski, J. G., Carr, M., Rellinger, E. A., & Pressley, M. (in press). Self-regulated strategy use: Interdependence of metacognition, attributions, and self-esteem. In B. F. Jones & L. Idol (Eds.), *Dimensions of thinking: Review of research.* Hillsdale, NJ: Lawrence Erlbaum Associates.

Borkowski, J. G., Carr, M., & Pressley, M. (1987). "Spontaneous" strategy use: Perspectives from metacognitive theory. *Intelligence, 11,* 61–75.

Borkowski, J. G., Johnston, M. B., & Reid, M. K. (1986). In S. J. Ceci (Ed.), *Handbook of cognitive, social, and neuropsychological aspects of learning disabilities*. Hillsdale, NJ: Lawrence Erlbaum Associates.

Bransford, J. D., & Franks, J. J. (1972). The abstraction of linguistic ideas: A review. *Cognition: An International Review of Cognitive Psychology, 2*, 211–249.

Brown, A. L. (1978). Knowing when, where, and how to remember: A problem of metacognition. In R. Glaser (Ed.), *Advances in instructional psychology*. (pp. 77–165). Hillsdale, NJ: Lawrence Erlbaum Associates.

Bruner, J. (1983). *Child's talk*. Oxford, England: Oxford University Press.

Butkowski, I. S., & Willows, D. M. (1980). Cognitive-motivational characteristics of children varying in reading ability: Evidence for learned helplessness in poor readers. *Journal of Educational Psychology, 72*, 408–422.

Butterfield, E. C., Siladi, D., & Belmont, J. M. (1980). Validating theories of intelligence. In H. W. Reese & L. P. Lipsett (Eds.), *Advances in child development and behavior* (Vol. 15). New York: Academic Press.

Clark, H. H., & Clark, E. V. (1977). *Psychology and language*. New York: Harcourt, Brace & Jovanovich.

Cohen, J. (1977). *Statistical power analysis for the behavioral sciences*. New York, NY: Academic Press.

Cohen, R. L. (1983). Reading disabled children are aware of their cognitive deficits. *Journal of Learning Disabilities, 16*, 286–289.

Cook, L. K., & Mayer, R. E. (1983). Reading strategies training for meaningful learning from prose. In M. Pressley & J. R. Levin (Eds.), *Cognitive strategy research: Educational applications* (pp. 87–131). New York: Springer-Verlag.

Cronbach, L. J., & Snow, R. E. (1977). *Aptitudes and instructional methods: A handbook for research on interactions*. New York: Irvington.

Cullen, J. L., & Boersma, F. J. (1982). The influence of coping strategies on the manifestations of learned helplessness. *Contemporary Educational Psychology, 7*, 346–356.

Day, J. D. (1983). The zone of proximal development. In M. Pressley & J. R. Levin (Eds.), *Cognitive strategy research: Psychological foundations* (pp. 155–176). New York: Springer-Verlag.

Duffy, G. G., Roehler, L. R., Vavrus, L. G., Book, C. L., Meloth, M. S., Putnam, J., & Wesselman, R. (1984, April). *A study of the relationship between direct teacher explanation of reading strategies and student awareness and achievement outcomes*. Presented at the Annual Meeting of the American Educational research Association, New Orleans.

Duffy, G. G., & Roehler, L. R. (1986). *Improving classroom reading instruction: A decision-making approach*. New York: Random House.

Duffy, G. G., & Roehler, L. R. (1987). Improving reading instruction through the use of responsive elaboration. *The Reading Teacher, 40*, 514–520.

Duffy, G. G., Roehler, L. R., Sivan, E., Rackliffe, G., Book, C., Meloth, M., Vavrus, L., Wesselman, R., Putnam, J., & Bassiri, D. (1987). The effects of explaining the reasoning associated with using reading strategies. *Reading Research Quarterly, 22*, 347–368.

Durkin, D. (1984). Do basal manuals teach reading comprehension? In R. C. Anderson, J. Osborn, & R. J. Tierney (Eds.), *Learning to read in American schools: Basal readers and content texts* (pp. 29–38). Hillsdale, NJ: Lawrence Erlbaum Associates.

Egeland, B. (1974). Training impulsive children in the use of more efficient scanning strategies. *Child Development, 45*, 165–171.

Elliott-Faust, D. J. (1984). *An instructional approach to promoting listening comprehension monitoring capabilities in grade 3 children*. London, Ontario: University of Western Ontario, unpublished dissertation.

Elliott-Faust, D. J., & Pressley, M. (1986). How to teach comparison processing to increase children's short- and long-term comprehension monitoring. *Journal of Educational Psychology, 78*, 27–33.

Faw, H. D., & Waller, T. G. (1976). Mathemagenic behaviors and efficiency in learning from prose. *Review of Educational Research, 46,* 691–720.

Flavell, J. H. (1970). Developmental studies of mediated memory. In H. W. Reese & L. P. Lipsitt (Eds.), *Advances in child development and behavior* (Vol. 5). New York: Academic Press.

Flavell, J. H. (1977). *Cognitive development.* Englewood Cliffs, NJ: Prentice-Hall.

Flavell, J. H., Beach, D. R., & Chinsky, J. M. (1966). Spontaneous verbal rehearsal in a memory task as a function of age. *Child Development, 37,* 283–299.

Flavell, J. H., Speer, J. R., Green, F. L., & August, D. L. (1981). The development of comprehension monitoring and knowledge about communication. *Monographs of the Society for Research in Child Development, 46* (Serial No. 192).

Forrest-Pressley, D. L., & Gilles, L. A. (1983). Children's flexible use of strategies during reading. In M. Pressley & J. R. Levin (Eds.), *Cognitive strategy research: Educational applications* (pp. 133–156). New York: Springer-Verlag.

Ghatala, E. S., Levin, J. R., Pressley, M., & Lodico, M. (1985). Training cognitive strategy monitoring in children. *American Educational Research Journal, 22,* 199–216.

Graves, A. W. (1987, April). *Metacomprehension vs. direct insturction training in reading for learning disabled students.* Presented at the annual meeting of the American Educational Research Association, Washington DC.

Greenfield, P. M. (1984). A theory of the teacher in the learning activities of everyday life. In B. Rogoff & J. Lave (Eds.), *Everyday cognition: Its development in social context* (pp. 117–138). Cambridge, MA: Harvard University Press.

Hodapp, R. M., Goldfield, E. C., & Boyatzis, C. J. (1984). The use and effectiveness of maternal scaffolding in mother-infant games. *Child Development, 55,* 772–781.

Kendall, P. C., & Wilcox, L. E. (1980). Cognitive-behavioral treatment for impulsivity: Concrete versus conceptual training in non-self-controlled problem children. *Journal of Consulting and Clinical Psychology, 48,* 80–91.

Kirschenbaum, D. S., & Tomarken, A. J. (1982). On facing the generalization problem: The study of self-regulatory failure. In P. C. Kendall (Ed.), *Advances in cognitive-behavioral research and therapy* (pp. 119–200). New York: Academic Press.

Kurtz, B. E., & Borkowski, J. G. (1984). Children's metacognition: Exploring relations among knowledge, process, and motivational variables. *Journal of Experimental Child Psychology, 37,* 335–354.

LaBerge, D., & Samuels, S. J. (1974). Towards a theory of automatic information processing in reading. *Cognitive Psychology, 6,* 293–323.

Levin, J. R. (1985). Some methodological and statistical "bugs" in research on children's learning. In M. Pressley & C. J. Brainerd (Eds.), *Cognitive learning and memory in children* (pp. 205–233). New York: Springer-Verlag.

Levin, J. R. (1986). Four cognitive principles of learning-strategy instruction. *Educational Psychologist, 21,* 3–18.

Levin, J. R., Marascuilo, L., & Hubert, L. (1978). N = non-parametric randomization tests. In T. R. Kratochwill (Ed.), *Strategies to evaluate changes in the single subject.* New York: Academic Press.

Levin, J. R., & Pressley, M. (1981). Improving children's prose comprehension: Selected strategies that seem to succeed. In C. M. Santa & B. L. Hayes (Eds.), *Children's prose comprehension: Research and practice* (pp. 44–71). Newark, DE: International Reading Association.

Levin, J. R., Pressley, M., McCormick, C. B., Miller, G. E., & Shriberg, L. K. (1979). Assessing the classroom potential of the keyword method. *Journal of Educational Psychology, 71,* 583–594.

Lodico, M. G., Ghatala, E. S., Levin, J. R., Pressley, M., & Bell, J. A. (1983). The effects of strategy-monitoring on children's selection of effective memory strategies. *Journal of Experimental Child Psychology, 35,* 263–277.

Manzo, A. V. (1968). *Improving reading comprehension through reciprocal questioning*. Syracuse, NY: Syracuse University, unpublished doctoral dissertation.

Markman, E. M. (1977). Realizing that you don't understand: A preliminary investigation. *Child Development, 48,* 986–992.

Markman, E. M. (1979). Realizing that you don't understand: Elementary school children's awareness of inconsistencies. *Child Development, 50,* 643–655.

Markman, E. M. (1981). Comprehension monitoring. In W. P. Dickson (Ed.), *Children's oral communication skills* (pp. 61–84). New York: Academic Press.

Markman, E. M., & Gorin, L. (1981). Children's ability to adjust their standards for evaluating comprehension. *Journal of Educational Psychology, 73,* 320–325.

Marx, R. W., Winne, P. H., & Walsh, J. (1985). Studying student cognition during classroom learning. In M. Pressley & C. J. Brainerd (Eds.), *Cognitive learning and memory in children* (pp. 181–203). New York, NY & Berlin, FRG: Springer-Verlag.

Meichenbaum, D. H. (1977). *Cognitive behavior modification*. New York: Plenum.

Meichenbaum, D., & Asarnow, J. (1979). Cognitive-behavioral modification and metacognitive development: Implications for the classroom. In P. C. Kendall & S. D. Hollon (Eds.), *Cognitive-behavioral intervention: Theory, research, and procedures* (pp. 11–35). New York: Academic Press.

Miller, G. E. (1985). The effects of general and specific self-instructional training on children's comprehension monitoring performance during reading. *Reading Research Quarterly, 20,* 616–628.

Miller, G., Galanter, E., & Pribram, K. (1960). *Plans and the structure of behavior*. New York: Holt, Rinehart & Winston.

O'Sullivan, J. T., & Pressley, M. (1984). Completeness of instruction and strategy transfer. *Journal of Experimental Child Psychology, 38,* 275–288.

Palincsar, A. S. (1982). *Improving the reading comprehension of junior high students through the reciprocal teaching of comprehension monitoring strategies*. Champaign-Urbana, Ill: University of Illinois, unpublished doctoral dissertation.

Palincsar, A. S. (1984, April). *Reciprocal teaching: Working within the zone of proximal development*. Presented at the annual meeting of the American Educational Research Association, New Orleans.

Palincsar, A. S. (1986). The role of dialogue in scaffolded instruction. *Educational Psychologist, 21,* 73–98.

Palincsar, A. S., & Brown, A. L. (1984). Reciprocal teaching of comprehension-fostering and monitoring activities. *Cognition and instruction, 1,* 117–175.

Palincsar, A. S., Brown, A. L., & Martin, S. M. (1987). Peer interaction in reading comprehension instruction. *Educational Psychologist, 22,* 231–253.

Paris, S. G., Cross, D. R., & Lipson, M. Y. (1984). Informed strategies for learning: A program to improve children's reading awareness and comprehension. *Journal of Educational Psychology, 76,* 1239–1252.

Paris, S. G., & Jacobs, J. E. (1984). The benefits of informed instruction for children's reading awareness and comprehension skills. *Child Development, 55,* 2083–2093.

Paris, S. G., Lipson, M. Y., & Wixson, K. K. (1983). Becoming a strategic reader. *Contemporary Educational Psychology, 8,* 293–316.

Paris, S. G., Newman, R. S., & Jacobs, J. E. (1985). Social contexts and functions of children's remembering. In M. Pressley & C. J. Brainerd (Eds.), *Cognitive learning and memory in children* (pp. 81–115). New York, NY & Berlin, FRG: Springer-Verlag.

Patterson, C. J., O'Brien, C., Kister, M. C., Carter, D. B., & Kotsonis, M. E. (1981). Development of comprehension monitoring as a function of context. *Developmental Psychology, 17,* 379–389.

Pearl, R. (1982). LD children's attributions for success and failure: A replication with a labeled LD sample. *Learning Disability Quarterly, 5,* 173–176.

Pearson, P. D. (1984). Guided reading: A response to Isabel Beck. In R. C. Anderson, J. Osborn, & R. J. Tierney (Eds.), *Learning to read in American schools: Basal readers and content texts* (pp. 21–28). Hillsdale, NJ: Lawrence Erlbaum Associates.

Pressley, G. M. (1976). Mental imagery helps eight-year-olds remember what they read. *Journal of Educational Psychology, 68,* 355–359.

Pressley, M. (1979). Increasing children's self-control through cognitive interventions. *Review of Educational Research, 49,* 319–370.

Pressley, M., Borkowski, J. G., & O'Sullivan, J. T. (1984). Memory strategy instruction is made of this: Metamemory and durable strategy use. *Educational Psychologist, 19,* 84–107.

Pressley, M., Borkowski, J. G., & O'Sullivan, J. T. (1985). Children's metamemory and the teaching of memory strategies. In D. L. Forrest-Pressley, G. E. MacKinnon, & T. G. Waller (Eds.), *Metacognition, cognition, and human performance.* New York: Academic Press.

Pressley, M., Borkowski, J. G., & Schneider, W. (1987). Cognitive strategies: Good strategy users coordinate metacognition and knowledge. In R. Vasta & G. Whitehurst (Eds.), *Annals of Child Development,* Vol. 4 (pp. 89–129). Greenwich, CT: JAI Press.

Pressley, M., Snyder, B. L., & Cariglia-Bull, T. (1987). How can good strategy use be taught to children? Evaluation of six alternative approaches. In S. Cormier & J. Hagman (Eds.), *Transfer of learning: Contemporary research and applications.* Orlando, FL: Academic Press.

Pressley, M., Cariglia-Bull, T., & Snyder, B. (1984). Are there programs that can really teach thinking and learning skills? *Contemporary Education Review, 3,* 435–444.

Pressley, M., Forrest-Pressley, D. L., Elliott-Faust, D., & Miller, G. E. (1985). Children's use of cognitive strategies, How to teach strategies, and What to do if they can't be taught. In M. Pressley & C. J. Brainerd (Eds.), *Cognitive learning and memory in children* (pp. 1–47). New York: Springer-Verlag.

Pressley, M., Goodchild, F., Fleet, J., Zajchowski, R., & Evans, E. D. (in press). The challenge of classroom strategy instruction. *The Elementary School Journal.*

Pressley, M., Heisel, B. E., McCormick, C. B., & Nakamura, G. V. (1982). Memory strategy instruction. In C. J. Brainerd & M. Pressley (Eds.), *Progress in cognitive development research* (Vol. 2), *Verbal processes in children* (pp. 125–159). New York: Springer-Verlag.

Pressley, M., & Levin, J. R. (1983a). *Cognitive strategy research: Educational applications.* New York: Springer-Verlag.

Pressley, M., & Levin, J. R. (1983b). *Cognitive strategy research: Psychological foundations.* New York: Springer-Verlag

Pressley, M., & Levin, J. R. (1986). Elaborative learning strategies for the inefficient learner. In S. J. Ceci (Ed.), *Handbook of cognitive, social, and neuropsychological aspects of learning disabilities* (pp. 175–211). Hillsdale, NJ: Lawrence Erlbaum Associates.

Pressley, M., Levin, J. R., & Ghatala, E. S. (1984). Memory strategy monitoring in adults and children. *Journal of Verbal Learning and Verbal Behavior, 23,* 270–288.

Pressley, M., Levin, J. R., & McDaniel, M. (1987). The keyword method of vocabulary learning compared to alternative interventions. In M. McKeown & M. E. Curtis (Eds.), *The nature of vocabulary acquisition* (pp. 107–127). Hillsdale, NJ: Lawrence Erlbaum Associates.

Pressley, M., Reynolds, W. M., Stark, K. D., & Gettinger, M. (1983). Cognitive strategy training and children's self-control. In M. Pressley & J. R. Levin (Eds.), *Cognitive strategy training: Psychological foundations* (pp. 267–300). New York: Springer-Verlag.

Pressley, M., Ross, K. A., Levin, J. R., & Ghatala, E. S. (1984). The role of strategy utility knowledge in children's strategy decision making. *Journal of Experimental Child Psychology, 38,* 275–288.

Raphael, T. E., Wonnacott, C. A., & Pearson, P. D. (1981, December). *Heightening students' sensitivity to information sources: An instructional study in question-answer relationships.* Paper presented at the annual meeting of the National Reading Conference, Dallas.

Rayner, K., & Pollatsek, A. (1981). Eye movement control during reading: Evidence for direct control. *Quarterly Journal of Experimental Psychology, 33A,* 351–373.

Reid, M. K., & Borkowski, J. G. (1985, April). *A cognitive-motivational training program for hyperactive children*. Presented at the biennial meetings of the Society for Research in Child Development, Toronto.

Roehler, L. R., & Duffy, G. G. (Eds.). (1984). Direct explanation of comprehension processes. In G. C. Duffy, L. R. Roehler, & J. Mason (Eds.), *Comprehension instruction* (pp. 265–280). New York: Longman.

Rogoff, B., & Gardner, W. (1984). Adult guidance of cognitive development. In B. Rogoff & J. Lave (Eds.), *Everyday cognition: Its development in social context* (pp. 95–116). Cambridge, MA: Harvard University Press.

Shatz, M. (1978). On the development of communicative understandings: An early strategy for interpreting and responding to messages. *Cognitive Psychology, 10*, 271–301.

Short, E. J., & Ryan, E. B. (1984). Metacognitive differences between skilled and less skilled readers: Remediating deficits through story grammar and attribution training. *Journal of Educational Psychology, 76*, 225–235.

Siegler, R. S., & Shrager, J. (1984). Strategy choices in addition: How do children know what to do? In C. Sophian (Ed.), *Origins of cognitive skills* (pp. 229–294). Hillsdale, NJ: Lawrence Erlbaum Associates.

Singer, J. B., & Flavell, J. H. (1981). Development of knowledge about communication: Children's evaluations of explicitly ambiguous messages. *Child Development, 52*, 1211–1215.

Stokes, T. F., & Baer, D. M. (1977). An implicit technology of generalization. *Journal of Applied Behavior Analysis, 10*, 349–367.

Tierney, R. J., Readence, J. E., & Dishner, E. K. (1985). *Reading strategies and practices: Guide for improving instruction*, 2nd edition. Boston: Allyn & Bacon.

Torgesen, J. K., & Greenstein, J. J. (1982). Why do some learning disabled children have problems remembering? Does it make a difference? *Topics in Learning and Learning Disabilities, 2*, 54–61.

Underwood, B. J. (1975). Individual differences as a crucible in theory construction. *American Psychologist, 30*, 128–134.

Waters, H. S., & Andreassen, C. (1983). Children's use of memory strategies under instruction. In M. Pressley and J. R. Levin (Eds.), *Cognitive strategy research: Psychological foundations* (pp. 3–24). New York: Springer-Verlag.

Weiner, B. (1979). A theory of motivation for some classroom experiences. *Journal of Educational Psychology, 71*, 3–25.

Wood, D., Wood, H., & Middleton, D. (1978). An experimental evaluation of four face-to-face teaching strategies. *International Journal of Behavioral Development, 2*, 131–147.

Worden, P. E. (1987). The four M's—Memory strategies, metastrategies, monitoring, and motivation. In S. J. Ceci (Ed.), *Handbook of cognitive, social, and neuropsychological aspects of learning disabilities* (pp. 213–230). Hillsdale, NJ: Lawrence Erlbaum Associates.

6 Training of Memory Strategies with Adolescents and Adults in Vocational Schools

Fredi P. Büchel
University of Genève
Genève Switzerland

The starting point to our research was the observation that most of the adolescent and adult apprentices in vocational schools show a rather passive attitude in performing cognitive tasks. In a pilot study we interrogated some successful and some poor students in a 1 hour interview. From these interviews we learned that study skills and knowledge about strategies of most professional students are very modest. Students had some vague ideas about cribs and temporal distribution of learning, but in general they didn't know how to integrate this knowledge into their everyday learning. That is, they didn't know which strategy would be the most useful for a given task. From this pilot study and from studies conducted by others (Dansereau, 1978; Dansereau et al., 1979; Dobrovolny & McCombs, 1980; McCombs & Dobrovolny, 1980; Weinstein, 1978; Weinstein, Underwood, Wicker, & Cubberly, 1979) we concluded that learning efficiency of professional students could be increased by systematic strategy training.

Up to this point we have just a rather simple problem of applied psychology. In such a situation one can refer to strategy packages that others had used for similar purposes. For example, Dansereau and his collaborators (Dansereau, 1978; Dansereau et al., 1979) had taught professional students in military schools different strategies to increase learning from technical texts. Weinstein (Weinstein, 1978; Weinstein et al., 1979) trained other professional students with similar strategy packages. But there are at least three problems with these studies: (1) The training gains were not very dramatic in terms of pre/post mean-differences. (2) All these strategy packages were deduced from usual study skills and study habits questionnaires. It can be argued that with these questionnaires we ask just idiosyncratic theories about strategies, but not everyday learning behavior. They do not give us answers about which overt and covert activities students use in learning situations. And they do not tell us anything about the usefullness of the reported strategies. (3) If we take the idea of metacognitive regulation seriously, we have to start from an interactional definition of strategies. That means that the usefulness of a strategy is a function of the strategy itself, the learner and the task. Therefore the helpfulness of a strategy can be predicted only in very special cases. Most of the strategies can be defined only a posteriori. This leads to an empirical definition of strategies: A strategy is an overt or covert learning activity that turned out to be helpful for a special learner in a special learning situation. In order to find empirical strategies we can observe what learners do when they learn and then compare these activities with some performance measures. But how can we transform such observational protocols into data? We have to cut the flow of learner's activity into units of observation (punctuation), and we have to label these units, that means we have to put them into a priori categories. This has been our approach to defining strategies.

RESEARCH QUESTIONS AND HYPOTHESES

A first study with 35 adult chemical apprentices should furnish us with a general view of the strategic activities of the students before and after training. We were especially interested in the following questions:

1. Which overt and covert activities do professional students show when they are learning from a textbook? Thus we tried to get an inventory of all the activities that students undertake in a text learning situation, without being influenced by previous training.

2. Would it be possible to influence the strategical behavior of our students by means of a training package which contained mainly metacognitive and executive knowledge? We expected an increase of inferential activities and general reflective study behavior and a decrease of episodic perception of reality and of automatic reading through. Bransford, Stein, Shelton, and Owings (1980) demonstrated that successful readers ask more questions than poor readers in order to make meaningful what they read. Feuerstein (1980) observed what he calls an ''episodic grasp of reality'' as being responsible for a lot of deficiencies in cognitive functioning. ''Grasping an event episodically reduces it to vague and undefined dimensions with little relation to its most relevant characteristics to other events that have preceded and that may follow'' (Feuerstein, 1980, p. 102).

3. In which learning activities do successful students differ from poor students? Would it be possible to draw a profile of strategic behavior of successful students and another and different one of poor students?

4. From the literature we know that some strategies are said to be task-specific (e.g., mathematic procedures; see Shavelson, 1981) and others are said to be generally applicable (e.g., metacognitive and executive strategies; see Borkowski & Cavanaugh, 1979; Feuerstein, 1980; Kendall, Borkowski, & Cavanaugh, 1980). Would it be possible to identify different types of strategies on a specifity dimension?

METHOD

Thinking Aloud

In order to detect covert learning activities of the subjects, we used the method of thinking aloud. This method has a long tradition in psychological research (Ericsson & Simon 1979a). In the last decade it has been applied by Norman and his collaborators (Bott, 1979; Norman, Gentner, & Stevens, 1976) for studying how students learn a computer language and by Simon (Newell & Simon, 1972; Simon, 1979) and many others (see Ericsson & Simon, 1979b) for studying problem-solving tasks. In a theoretical paper Ericsson and Simon (1979b) postulate that thinking-aloud-statements pass only through short-term memory, but not through long-term memory, and would be therefore free of systematic adaptations, as attributed to long-term memory. We presented our students with instructional texts and invited them to read aloud and learn the text and, in addition, to report everything that went through their heads during reading and learning. We used two texts of about 1 page and one drawn schema of a personal computer (from Dwyer & Critchfield, 1980, p. 6) before the intervention and two texts and one list of meaningful words after the training. All sessions where taperecorded and transcribed afterwards.

Training Procedure

In the training sessions we taught a strategy package consisting of (1) formally defined strategies such as visualization of what we read, asking questions about the content and others. (2) Executive routines such as goal setting, planning behavior with the help of means-end analysis, time regulation and self-control. (3) Knowledge about how memory works, and stimulation and actualization of individual past memory experiences. For every strategy we explained why it would be helpful to use it, and we practiced on several tasks.

The 17 subjects of the training group were taught in 8 lessons of each about 90 minutes. The 18 control group subjects did not receive any training at all. They participated only in pre- and posttest measurements.

RESULTS

A Model for Protocol Analysis

In order to analyze the thinking-aloud protocols we were guided by a model of self-directed learning (Büchel & Borkowski, 1983).

The model (Fig. 6.1) contains as its main components: Metaknowledge about strategies, a program and response generator to compile and supervise plans, as well as strategies to execute the learning tasks. The central part of the model consists of a program generator. This is a highly structured and task-independent algorithm. It can be compared with a sketch for a main program in a structured computer language. It contains statements about what to do for selecting the best strategies for a given task type and how to compile these strategies to get a task- and subject- specific program. It also contains some checking and monitoring routines at the right places. These routines are found to be important for strategy generalization (e.g., Brown & Barclay, 1976; Brown, Campione, & Barclay, 1979; Büchel, 1983; Campione & Brown, 1977). The second important part of the model is a task matrix together with a strategy taxonomy related to the task matrix. This system is responsible for the subject specifity of the programs compiled by the program generator. The task matrix as well as the strategy taxonomy are connected with the program generator through specific metacognitions. That means, a concrete task will not be related directly to a concrete strategy; but knowledge about specific features of a task together with knowledge about specific abilities of the learner in different test situations will enable this learner to select appropriate strategies. Finally, the response generator is introduced into the model as a last overall control before outputing the response.

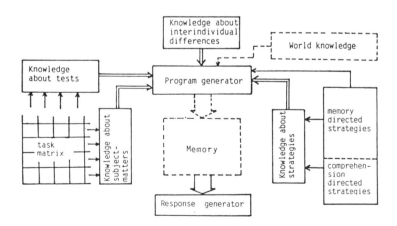

FIG. 6.1. A model of self-directed learning.

Description of Learning Strategies

From this model we derived a first set of expected categories of learning activities. We tested this category system with several samples of protocols from another pilot study (see Büchel, 1982, pp. 356–358). After some revisions we arrived at a system with good agreement between two raters (Table 6.1) and adequate retest-correspondence (Table 6.2). This last revised system contains the categories shown in Table 6.3.

If we compare the categories listed in Table 6.3 with the model of self-directed learning (Fig. 6.1), we miss some categories. For example, in the group of metacognitive knowledge we do not find any knowledge about strategies. We eliminated this kind of metaknowledge from the list, because we did not find any statements to fill out this category in the pilot study protocols. With the help of this category system we analyzed the protocols of 11 subjects of the experimental group and 6 control subjects. Table 6.4 presents the frequencies of pre- and posttest. In order to facilitate comparisons, row scores are transformed into percentages. Categories with very small frequencies are eliminated. Therefore the total of $\bar{X}\%$ pre and $\bar{X}\%$ post will be less than 100%.

Following, we describe and discuss the categories:

1. Knowledge about subject matters is described in Flavell and Wellman (1977). We did not expect the significant decrease of this category and will discuss this later.

2. Knowledge about test is also a category from the Flavell and Wellman (1977) paper. As expected, we find a disordinal interaction between group and trial (pre/post).

3. Identification of instruction is a category taken from Kluwe (1980). It

TABLE 6.1
Point-By-Point Correspondence With Two Raters

Raters	A–B	A–B	A–C	A–C	F–G	D–E	D–E	D–E	D–E
Analyzed Units	19	34	17	13	94	75	35	33	20
Correspondence (%)	79	62	77	92	88	95	86	58	75

TABLE 6.2
Point-By-Point Correspondence After One Week

Raters	A–B	A–B	A–C	A–C	F–G	D–E
Analyzed Units	92	78	75	98	122	123
Correspondence (%)	96	91	83	87	74.6	95.12

TABLE 6.3
Categories in Text Learning

Metacognitive Knowledge

  1. Knowledge about subject matters
  2. Knowledge about tests

Program Generator

  3. Identification of instruction
  4. Identification of idiosyncratic learning goals
  5. Regulation of working intensity
  6. Time regulation
  7. Checking

Response Evaluation

  8. Response evaluation

Memory- and Comprehension-Directed Strategies

  9. Paraphrasing
10. Mechanical reading repetition
11. Backward transition
12. Underlining
13. Extracting
14. Summarizing
15. Drawing schemata
16. Passive strategies
17. Story elaboration
18. Questioning
19. Activating knowledge
20. Inferential thinking

---

means that the subject searches for information which helps him to understand more clearly what he has to do.

4. Identification of idiosyncratic learning goals means that a subject compares the given instruction with his own expectations and with knowledge about himself as a learner.

5. Regulation of working intensity. The subject asks himself how completely and exactly he will do the work. This category is taken from Kluwe (1980).

6. Time regulation. Also taken from Kluwe (1980), this category is counted when the subject asks a question about learning time during the learning phase.

7. Checking is described in Brown (1978). The subject compares his memory and understanding of the text with a standard.

8. Response evaluation. Last checking of the whole task before final formulation.

9. Paraphrasing. Subjects repeated parts of the text, which were written in good German, in their own words, meaning in Swiss German.

10. Mechanical reading repetition. This category was counted when a subject repeated one or more sentences without interruption by another category.

11. Backward transition. Repetition of one or more words or sentences after a thinking or checking category. It is the category with the highest frequencies

TABLE 6.4
Pre- and Posttest Frequencies as Raw Scores ($\bar{X}$) and
Percentages ($\bar{X}$%) of Categories in Text Learning

Cat. Nb.	Category Name		$\bar{X}$ Pre	$\bar{X}$ % Pre	$\bar{X}$ Post	$\bar{X}$ % Post
1.	Knowledge about	EG	5.091	2.258	3.710	1.322
	subject matters	CG	9.166	3.921	2.833	1.098
2.	Knowledge about	EG	2.182	0.953	5.091	2.283
	tests	CG	4.333	1.695	1.167	0.539
3.	Identification	EG	5.000	2.274	6.727	2.711
	of instruction	CG	6.833	3.144	4.167	1.633
4.	Identification of	EG	2.182	0.956	2.091	1.176
	id. learning goals	CG	3.833	1.933	1.834	0.656
5.	Regulation of	EG	3.273	1.420	3.910	1.648
	working intensity	CG	3.333	1.551	3.499	1.401
6.	Time regulation	EG	6.363	2.552	3.088	1.220
		CG	5.667	2.466	4.001	1.430
7.	Checking	EG	1.273	0.680	1.909	0.811
		CG	2.500	1.132	2.000	0.792
8.	Response	EG	8.545	3.583	4.455	1.616
	evaluation	CG	4.500	1.850	6.000	2.179
9.	Paraphrasing	EG	28.899	13.255	28.546	10.688
		CG	40.833	18.535	17.667	6.703
10.	Mechanical	EG	10.545	5.681	6.727	3.043
	reading rep.	CG	3.333	1.416	33.166	10.698
11.	Backward	EG	48.227	21.954	58.000	23.918
	transition	CG	67.666	29.331	92.333	34.238
12.	Underlining	EG	2.273	1.231	7.182	3.505
		CG	1.167	0.552	14.330	5.979
13.	Extracting	EG	8.636	3.679	7.091	3.996
		CG	6.000	2.433	18.833	5.155
14.	Summarizing	EG	2.909	1.332	19.455	8.089
		CG	0.000	0.000	14.383	5.866
15.	Drawing schemata	EG	8.182	3.291	5.727	2.516
		CG	13.500	5.415	5.667	2.041
16.	Passive strategies	EG	1.455	0.589	0.455	0.166
		CG	0.833	0.393	0.000	0.000
17.	Story elaboration	EG	0.000	0.000	2.091	3.350
		CG	0.000	0.000	0.500	0.586
18.	Questioning	EG	10.273	4.870	6.546	2.687
		CG	8.334	3.819	3.166	1.414
19.	Activating	EG	3.637	1.741	2.731	1.163
	knowledge	CG	1.166	0.564	1.833	0.651
20.	Inferential	EG	8.000	3.839	10.910	5.302
	thinking	CG	7.334	3.615	3.834	1.901

and may be considered as an unassuming form of thinking and controlling activity.

12. Underlining could be observed overtly.

13. Extracting means that one or more words are copied verbally.

14. Summarizing is a category which increased significantly in the posttest, but this is true also for the control group. The effect seems to be task-specific.

15. Drawing schemata is also highly task-specific.

16. Passive strategies are counted when the subject makes statements like "I try to do something" or "I try to understand," but he does not do anything at all.

17. Story elaboration is also a rather task-specific strategy, as described by several authors (e.g., Bower, 1970; Lindsay & Norman, 1977).

18. Questioning others or himself is described in many papers of Flammer and his collaborators (e.g., Flammer, 1981; Flammer, Kaiser, and Müller-Bouquet, 1981) and by Norman (1973) and Miyake & Norman (1979). It turned out to be a very helpful strategy.

19. Activating knowledge. The subject enriches and compares the text information with knowledge from other texts and other situations.

20. Inferential thinking seems to be one of the most important thinking activities. As expected, EG increased significantly, and CG decreased. It is a fastidious activity, which is done only by motivated learners.

Changes in Strategic Behavior

We were interested if it would be possible to change the strategic behavior of experimental subjects in a desired direction. In order to answer this question we substracted the mean pre/post-differences of the control group from that of the experimental group. These empirical differences were compared with theoretically expected differences. Twenty-three of 32 differences fitted our expectations. This is significant on a binominal distribution.

High-Performer–Low-Performer Differences

In the experiment students were asked to recall after the learning/thinking aloud phase everything they remembered. These recall protocols were analyzed. We calculated a score for remembered key concepts and one for relations. In order to find out in which categories successful students differ from poor students, we compared the students with highest recall with students with lowest recall. For this comparison we analyzed the data of only one text, and we did not use exactly the same categories as described earlier. In our sample we detected one student with a recall score of 39, which is more than twice as high as the group mean of 16.7. This student (B24) was not included into the high-performer group, but we

TABLE 6.5
N, X̄, and S of the Compared Extreme Groups

Group Name	N	X̄	S
High-performers (concepts)	5	21.8	3.0
High-performers (relations)	3	14.0	1.4
Low-performers (concepts)	5	9.6	2.3
Low-performers (relations)	3	4.3	.5
B24 (concepts)	1	39.0	
B24 (relations)	1	25.0	
Sch (concepts)	17	16.7	7.5
Sch (relations)	17	9.9	4.9

compared him separately with the other groups. The extreme group and B24 were compared additionally with the whole sample (Sch). For all groups category frequencies are transformed into percentages. Group descriptors are resumed in Table 6.5.

Tables 6.6 and 6.7 present the category frequencies of high- and low-performers. (H%-L%) give the absolute %-difference between the two groups. Because raw scores between the categories differ significantly, we calculated additionally the ratio (H%-L%): (H%+L%) = D%. The highest positive D% is calculated for the category: hypotheses confirming. High performers not only make hypotheses about what they read, but they also try to confirm them. This is true for recall of key concepts and for recall of relations. But it must also be mentioned that the absolute frequencies of both groups are small.

The highest negative D% appears for the category: time regulation. Low performers are much more engaged in time control during learning. This fact seems to be in conflict with most metacognitive theories (e.g., Kluwe, 1980). These theories postulate time control as an important executive function. But it should be distinguished between control functions during the learning process

TABLE 6.6
Raw Scores and Percentage (%) of High (H) and Low (L) for Concepts

Category	H	H%	L	L%	H%-L%	D%
Paraphrasing	26.0	20.8	32.6	23.3	-2.5	5.7
Summarizing	25.2	20.2	23.4	16.7	3.5	9.5
Structural relations	11.4	9.1	8.2	5.9	3.2	21.3
Questioning	7.0	5.6	7.6	5.4	.2	1.8
Checking-Resp. evalu.	9.2	7.4	6.6	4.7	2.7	22.3
Mech. reading repet.	9.4	7.5	8.4	6.0	1.5	11.1
Inferential thinking	4.2	3.4	6.6	4.7	-1.3	-16.0
Functional relations	4.0	3.2	5.2	3.7	- .5	- 7.2
Knowledge subj. matter	8.8	7.0	7.2	5.2	1.8	14.8
Clarify concepts	3.2	2.6	10.2	7.3	-4.7	-47.5
Time regulation	2.4	1.9	15.8	11.3	-9.4	-71.2
Knowledge about test	6.0	4.8	1.8	1.3	3.5	57.4
Info enrichment	4.8	3.8	3.8	2.7	1.1	16.9
Hypotheses evaluation	1.6	1.3	2.0	1.4	- .1	- 3.4
Hypotheses confirming	1.6	1.3	.4	.3	1.0	62.5

TABLE 6.7
Raw Scores and Percentage (%) of High (H) and Low (L) for Relations

Category	H	H%	L	L%	H%-L%	D%
Paraphrasing	29.7	25.3	28.0	20.0	5.3	11.7
Summarizing	8.0	7.0	22.7	16.2	-9.2	-39.7
Structural relations	11.7	10.2	7.3	5.2	5.0	32.5
Questioning	8.3	7.2	6.3	4.5	2.7	23.1
Checking-Resp. evalu.	7.0	6.1	8.0	5.7	.4	3.4
Mech. reading repet.	13.0	11.3	10.0	7.1	4.2	22.8
Inferential thinking	8.5	9.7	8.0	5.7	.4	5.6
Functional relations	11.7	10.2	7.3	5.2	5.0	32.5
Knowledge subj. matter	2.3	2.1	8.0	5.7	-3.6	-46.2
Clarify concepts	1.3	1.1	11.3	8.1	-7.0	-76.1
Time regulation	1.7	1.5	17.7	12.7	-11.2	-78.9
Knowledge about test	3.3	2.9	3.0	2.1	.8	16.0
Info enrichment	4.3	3.8	4.7	3.4	.4	5.6
Hypotheses evaluation	1.0	.9	.3	.2	.7	63.6

and such before and after. There is no doubt that successful learning needs some control of the learning environment. Nevertheless, our data demonstrate rather clearly that such control is not done during the learning phase by successful students. Time regulation shows significantly negative correlations with a lot of performance measures. Thinking activities on a lexical level (clarifying concepts) are also highly prefered by low-performers. It is interesting, that this negative difference occurs also in concept recall. It seems that independent of the task type, expert learners never do invest much in the learning of single concepts. Therefore they are much more engaged in the finding of structural relations.

The differences between group means of single categories can not be tested statistically by the t-test, because sample sizes are too small. Therefore we tested by x^2 the hypothesis, that the extreme profiles differ significantly from the profile of the whole sample. The results are resumed in Table 6.8.

Task Specificity of Learning Activities

A learning activity can be said to be generally useful, if it facilitates the learning of a big set of different tasks and at the same time does not make more difficult

TABLE 6.8
x^2 of the Profile Differences Between Extreme Groups
and the Whole Sample

o - e	x^2	df	p = .5	
High - Sch (concepts)	10.1	10	18.31	ns
Low - Sch (concepts)	19.9	10		s
High - Sch (relations)	27.0	10		s
Low - Sch (relations)	30.6	10		s
B24 - Sch (concepts)	60.0	10		s

the learning of other tasks. Most learning activities seem to be more of a task-specific usefulness than of a general one. Nevertheless, most researchers expect that there would be at least some few general strategies, which would be responsible for transfer of strategies. For example, Sternberg (1979) and Butterfield (1979) proposed metacognitive activities as such general strategies.

In order to test this question we calculated correlations between categories of learning activity and different performance measures. We tested 20 different performance measures before and 20 after training. They consist of the recall of the thinking aloud texts, the subtests of a German learning test (LGT; Bäumler, 1974), and 5 subtests of a German intelligence test (IST-70; Amthauer, 1970). If a category correlates positively with many performance measures and negatively with none, and that before and after training, then it can be said to be a general or task-independent activity. We found only two learning activities that can be interpreted as general strategies: (1) searching for structural relations, and (2) asking questions. Additionally, we found one negative general strategy: This is time regulation, which showed only negative correlations.

DISCUSSION

We can now ask the question if the reported data fit our expectations as resumed in the model of self-directed learning (Fig. 6.1). The model is confirmed insofar as we found most of the predicted activities. But if we consider category frequencies, we must admit some surprises. For example, in the model (Fig. 6.1), metacognitive knowledge plays a crucial role, but we could not identify so many metacognitions. Perhaps this kind of knowledge is so highly overlearned that it does not appear in thinking aloud protocols. Perhaps our texts were not difficult enough for provoking metacognitive thinking. But it could also be that adult learners are very much concentrated on the text and on thinking activities directly related to it, and very few on metacognitive knowledge.

The data reveal an even more important lack of our model: Thinking activities, such as inferential thinking, explicit search for structural and functional relations, should take a central place in a model of self-directed learning. Levin (1982) makes a distinction between memory-directed and comprehension-directed cognitive activities. For text learning, Kintsch (1982) calls memory a "byproduct of processing" or a "consequence of processing; what is remembered is what has been processed." The most important implication from our data is the central role that processing activities have to play in a model of text learning. A positive effect of a good strategy training would be the replacement of more or less automatic reading activities, such as paraphrasing and especially mechanical reading repetitions, by processing activities. We consider our study as a beginning in this direction.

But there is another problem again. One would expect a close strategy-performance relation. Not only strategic behavior should change after training, but also performance in text recall, learning-test and IQ-test should increase. Over all, such increases could be demonstrated (Büchel, 1983), but they are inconsistent and often even not significant. This is not so surprising. The same has been found for metamemory-memory-connection (Cavanaugh & Perlmutter, 1982). It would be worthwhile to discuss some possible reasons for the modest performance increases in our study:

1. Thinking aloud protocols show that the training contained not only helpful strategies, but also such with negative correlations with performance. That confirms our conviction that a strategy training has to start from an empirical definition of strategies.
2. Together with performance tests we presented our students different motivational tests, and we found significant correlations

- between performance and locus of control (r between .33 and .54)
- between performance and the conviction that what was learned in the training lessons, would be helpful for further learning in other subject-matters (r between .46 and .66).

We conclude from these findings that a training model should be completed by the variables which control how much a learner is convinced of the usefulness of the strategies we teach him.

ACKNOWLEDGMENT

The reported research is supported by the Swiss National Science Foundation (Grant No. 4.323.0.79.10 and 4.651.0.83.10) The Author acknowledges the valuable editorial support by John Borkowski, University of Notre Dame, Indiana, Klaus Bischof, University of Basel and Stirling GB, and Sabine Hofer-Frackmann, University of Basel and Bochum.

REFERENCES

Amthauer, R. (1970). *Intelligenz-Struktur-Test 70*. Göttingen: Hogrefe.
Bäumler, G. (1974). *Lern- und Gedächtnistest. LGT 3*. Göttingen: Hogrefe.
Borkowski, J. G., & Cavanaugh, J. C. (1979). Maintenance and generalisation of skills and strategies by the retarded. In N. R. Ellis (Ed.), *Handbook of mental deficiency*. Hillsdale, NJ: Lawrence Erlbaum Associates.
Bott, R. A. (1979). *A study of complex learning: Theory and methodologies*. CHIP Report No.82. UCSD, La Jolla, CA.
Bower, G. H. (1970). Analysis of a mnemonic device. *American Scientist, 58*, 496–510.

Bransford, J. D., Stein, B. S., Shelton, T. S., & Owings, R. A. (1980). Cognition and adaptation: The importance of learning to learn. In J. Harvey (Ed.), *Cognition, social behavior and the environment*. Hillsdale, NJ: Lawrence Erlbaum Associates.

Brown, A. L. (1978). Knowing when, where, and how to remember: A problem of metacognition. In R. Glaser (Ed.), *Advances in instructional psychology* (Vol. 1). Hillsdale, NJ: Lawrence Erlbaum Associates.

Brown, A. L., & Barclay, C. R. (1976). The effects of training specific mnemonics on the meta-mnemonic efficiency of retarded children. *Child Development, 47*, 71–80.

Brown, A. L., Campione, J. C., & Barclay, C. (1979). Training self-checking routines for estimating test readiness: Generalisation from list learning to prose recall. *Child Development, 50*, 501–512.

Büchel, F. P. (1982). Metacognitive variables in the learning of written text. In A. Flammer & W. Kintsch (Eds.), *Discourse Processing*. Amsterdam: North-Holland.

Büchel, F. P. (1983). *Lernstrategien bei Jugendlichen und Erwachsenen in der beruflichen Ausbildung*. Basel. Habilitationsschrift.

Büchel, F. P., & Borkowski, J. G. (1983). *Prediction and explaining strategy generalisation: Task analysis and generalisation elements*. Berichte und Arbeiten aus dem Institut für Psychologie der Universität Basel, Nr. 17, Basel.

Butterfield, E. C. (1979). *Instructional techniques that produce generalized improvements in cognition*. Paper presented at the Congress of International Association for the Scientific Study of Mental Deficiency, Jerusalem.

Campione, J. C., & Brown, A. L. (1977). Memory and metamemory development in educable retarded children. In R. Kail & J. W. Hagen (Eds.), *Perspectives on the development of memory and cognition*. Hillsdale, NJ: Lawrence Erlbaum Associates.

Cavanaugh, J. C., & Perlmutter, M. (1982). Metamemory: A critical examination. *Child Development, 53*, 11–28.

Dansereau, D. (1978). The development of a learning strategies curriculum. In H. F. O'Neil (Ed.), *Learning strategies*. New York: Academic Press.

Dansereau, D. F., McDonald, B. A., Collins, K. W., Garland, J., Holley, C. D., Diekhof, G. M., & Evans, S. H. (1979). Evaluation of a learning strategy system. In H. F. O'Neil, Jr. & C. D. Spielberger (Eds.), *Cognitive and affective learning strategies*. New York: Academic Press.

Dobrovolny, L., & McCombs, B. L. (1980). *Study skills remediation: Beneficial effects of individualized skill training*. Paper presented at the AERA meeting at Boston. April 1980.

Dwyer, T. A., & Critchfield, M. (1980). *A bit of BASIC*. Reading, MA: Addison-Wesley.

Ericsson, K. A., & Simon, H. A. (1979a). *Sources of evidence on cognition: An historical overview*. C.I.P. Working Paper No.406. Carnegie-Mellon University.

Ericsson, K. A., & Simon, H. A. (1979b). *Thinking-aloud protocols as data*. Working Paper No.397. Carnegie-Mellon University.

Feuerstein, R. (1980). *Instrumental enrichment*. Baltimore: University Park Press.

Flammer, A. (1981). Toward a theory of question asking. *Psychological research, 43*, 407–420.

Flammer, A., Kaiser, H., & Müller-Bouquet, P. (1981). Predicting what people ask. *Psychological Research, 43*, 421–429.

Flavell, J. H., & Wellman, H. M. (1977). Metamemory. In R. V. Kail & J. W. Hagen (Eds.), *Perspectives on the development of memory and cognition*. Hillsdale, NJ: Lawrence Erlbaum Associates.

Kendall, C. R., Borkowski, J. G., & Cavanaugh, J. G. (1980). Metamemory and the transfer of an interrogative strategy by EMR children. *Intelligence, 4*, 255–270.

Kintsch, W. (1982). Memory for text. In A. Flammer & W. Kintsch (Eds.), *Discourse processing*. Amsterdam: North-Holland.

Kluwe, R. H. (1980). *Metakognition: Komponenten einer Theorie zur Kontrolle und Steuerung eigenen Denkens*. Habilitaitonsschrift. Universität München.

Levin, J. R. (1982). Pictures as prose-learning devices. In A. Flammer & W. Kintsch (Eds.), *Discourse processing*. Amsterdam: North-Holland.

Lindsay, P. H., & Norman, D. A. (1977). Human information processing. New York: Academic Press.

McCombs, B. L., & Dobrovolny, J. L. (1980, April). *The study skills questionnaire: Preliminary validation of a measure for assessing students perceived areas of study skills weakness*. Paper presented at the Annual Meeting of AERA, Boston.

Miyake, N., & Norman, D. A. (1979). To ask a question, one must know enough to know what is not known. *Journal of Verbal Learning and Verbal Behavior, 18,* 357–364.

Newell, A., & Simon, H. A. (1972). *Human problem solving*. Englewood Cliffs, NJ: Prentice-Hall.

Norman, D. A. (1973). Memory, knowledge, and the answering of questions. In R. Solso (Ed.), *The Loyola symposium on cognitive psychology*, Washington, D.C.: Winston.

Norman, D. A., Gentner, D. R., & Stevens, A. L. (1976). Comments on learning, schemata and memory representation. In D. Klahr (Ed.), *Cognition and instruction*. Hillsdale, NJ: Lawrence Erlbaum Associates.

Shavelson, R. J. (1981). Teaching mathematics: Contributions of cognitive research. *Educational Psychologist, 16,* 23–44.

Simon, H. A. (1979). *Models of thought*. New Haven: Yale University Press.

Sternberg, R. J. (1979). Components of human intelligence. *Technical Report No. 19*. Yale University.

Weinstein, C. E. (1978). Elaboration skills as a learning strategy. In H. F. O'Neil Jr. (Ed.), *Learning strategies*. New York: Academic Press.

Weinstein, C. E., Underwood, V. L., Wicker, F. W., & Cubberly, W. E. (1979). Cognitive learning strategies: Verbal and imaginal elaboration. In H. F. O'Neil, Jr. & C. D. Spielberger (Eds.), *Cognitive and affective learning strategies*. New York: Academic Press.

III KNOWLEDGE STRUCTURE AND MEMORY DEVELOPMENT

7 Scripts and Memory: Functional Relationships in Development

Katherine Nelson
City University of New York

Judith Hudson
State University of New York at Albany

A mother of two preschool boys recently said to one of us, in recounting a feat of memory by her 4-year-old: "I know that young children are supposed to have remarkable memory but Jonathan is really astounding in what he remembers." The contrast of this comment with the characterization by developmental psychologists of young children's memory as impoverished is ironic. Is the mother's impression misguided? Is the view of developmental psychologists wrong? Can the two views be reconciled somehow?

Our work on memory for everyday events by young children may provide a way of reconciling the casual lay impression that young children do remember their experiences remarkably well, and the view from the laboratory that their memory is deficient at best. This work proceeded from the assumption that the study of what children do well might give better clues to the development of skills and competencies than the study of what they do poorly. When we found that 3-year-old children were quite good at relating facts about the events they participated in, we explored the implications of this discovery for their memory performance in related tasks.

What children tell us about their knowledge of routine events can be termed their *scripts* for these events. We assume that these scripts bear a strong relation to their underlying *event representations,* also termed scripts, from which these reports are generated. We have found also that they are usually quite accurate representations of the actual *event structure* of the event in question. For example, children's scripts of what happens at the day care center are generally reported in correct casual-temporal sequence, and the details of participants and props are accurately reported. Of course, the script may be incomplete, indeed often skeletal, but its relational structure and content is rarely misrepresented.

Children's script reports appear to reflect the general characteristics of scripts as defined in cognitive psychology (Schank & Abelson, 1977) in terms of their part-whole sequential structure, causal relations, and general slots, that is, entries for variables that are filled in on particular instantiations of the script. For example, the script for eating dinner may contain slots for meat, vegetables, and dessert, which can be filled by different food items on different occasions. Scripts can also contain optional action slots such as having coffee after dinner, which may or may not occur at any particular meal. Scripts, like other schemas (see Mandler, 1979), organize information about the world and provide "top-down" structures that automatically guide comprehension and action within situations to which a schema representation applies.

Schemas in general, of which the script is one type, differ from categories, which have been used so extensively in the study of children's memory, in important ways (Mandler, 1979). Whereas categories are characterized by inclusion ("isa") relations, schemas are part-whole structures whose parts are related by a variety of relations within an overall configuration. Coordinate category members form a list of equal members, whereas schemas form more complex relational structures whose constituents may be embedded within each other. A great deal of research on young children's memory has been concerned with the degree to which the material to be learned is organized by the learner, and in particular whether young children can take advantage of the categorical structure built into a list of words to be learned. Although some studies have found categorical effects in preschool children's recall (e.g., Myers & Perlmutter, 1978), the bulk of the research has shown that children of this age are poor at using category knowledge in this way (for example, Lange, 1978; Moely, 1977). In contrast, research that has been carried out to investigate schematic organization in memory has shown that schemas may be employed to aid memory from a very early age (Hudson & Fivush, 1983; Mandler, 1979, 1983). In addition to scripts, the schemas used in this research have included scenes and stories.

Two general questions are raised by these observations: Why do schemas aid memory? and How do schemas aid memory? We address these questions here in the context of our research on scripts in relation to various types of memory and memory tasks.

To begin with, it is worth noting some ways in which memory contexts or tasks that employ schematically organized material, and specifically scripts, may differ from those that employ categorically organized material. First, schemas are organized wholes, where the whole implies its parts. As discussed earlier, script components (actors, actions, props, locations) are represented in terms of slots that can be filled by various slot fillers. Depending on the event, different slot fillers are more or less likely to occur and probability values for the occurrence of particular slot fillers are also included in the script. For example, at a 4-year-old's birthday party, the participants, games, presents, and type of cake may vary from party to party. However, certain types of games such as musical chairs or pin the tail on the donkey are more likely to be played than baseball or tag. Because scripts are wholistic structures, what occupies one slot will constrain the range of possibilities for filling other slots. So for a particular birthday party, expectations for what games will be played and what presents will be given will be different if the party is for a 4- or 12-year-old. Further, in the case of scripts, the whole is a sequentially organized event, so that each successive part bears a temporal, spatial, and often causal relation to the preceding and succeeding parts. In contrast, category members may be related to one another primarily in terms of their relation to the superordinate node. Dog and tiger, for example, are related in that both are animals, but relations of other kinds between the two are hard to identify.

The part–whole organization of the script is derived from one's experience with variations and contingent relations in real-world events. In contrast, categorical organization is abstracted from the culture and the language. In fact the relation between the script and the category is similar to the relation observed in language (Saussure, 1959) between syntagmatic and paradigmatic structure (Nelson, 1982, 1985). Syntagmatic structure is based on relations between unlike elements in a sequential configuration, as in a sentence. Paradigmatic structure, on the other hand, is based on relations between elements that can occupy the same position in a syntagmatic structure, and that are considered similar on these grounds; for example, verbs are those elements in a sentence that occupy the verb position, regardless of any other similarity relation. In the case of scripts, elements that can occupy the same slot may form a category on the basis of their substitutability; for example, the different things that can be eaten for lunch may form a good category for the child. As Saussure noted, syntagmatic relations are apparent in the experienced world, while paradigmatic relations are abstract constructions of the mind. Thus the two types of structures—schema and category—may be considered different in terms of their degree of abstraction from real world experience.

Another difference between the two structures is their relation to goals. It has been demonstrated (Istomina, 1975) that when young children have a clearly understood goal for remembering, their memory even for word lists is greatly improved. In the case of scripts, the goal of the event is incorporated into the structure itself; thus when a script can be used to aid memory it instantiates a goal which in itself may make the memory task more meaningful. The child may not always understand the goal; thus scripts may vary in the support they provide for the child's memory depending upon whether the goal is understood and shared by the child.

Scripts have been considered variously as knowledge structures (Schank & Abelson, 1977) or as general memory organizers (Schank, 1983). On the one hand, the study of the relation between scripts and episodic memory (in Tulving's 1972 sense) is that of the influence of knowledge on memory. On the other hand, the study is that of a particular type of memory organization on the memory for a specific episode or presentation. The present research combines these two approaches. On the one hand, scripts organize knowledge in a particular domain of events, for example, in the case of the young child, getting dressed, going to preschool, having lunch. Knowledge of the organization of these events in general can be expected to affect what is remembered of a particular episode of that event. Moreover, script-based knowledge of a more abstract type (for example, knowledge of the types of clothes that can be put on in the morning) can also be expected to affect memory in situations that are less directly connected with the script itself. On the other hand, script structures can be expected to affect how an episode is remembered, that is, providing the organization that enables the child to put its parts into the appropriate sequential relationships. Thus we expect to find both content and organizational effects of scripts on young children's memory.

It is important to note that schemas can have both positive and negative effects on the accuracy of memory. The existence of a relevant schema may provide the structure that enables an episode to be remembered. But, as Bartlett (1932) noted originally, the existence of a schema may distort the memory for a story or an episode in the direction of the pre-existing schema, dropping out details that do not fit the schema and substituting schematic constituents for those actually experienced. Neisser's (1981) report on John Dean's memory for meetings with President Nixon included several examples of these kinds of intrusions, confusions and fusions of elements from repeated episodes. Similar negative effects on the accuracy of memory have been noted by Linton (1975, 1982) in her study of her own episodic memories, and by the research on script-based story memory in adults (e.g., Bower, Black, & Turner, 1979). Some of the research we report below will also note negative as well as positive effects of schemas on memory in young children.

In the following sections we report on two lines of research that reveal the relation of scripts and specific memory, one concerned with memory for material (usually stories or lists) that the child is asked to learn, the other with undirected or spontaneous memory for "real-life" episodes. In the last section we outline a model that accounts for the interrelations between scripts and specific memory as observed in these studies.

RECALL OF LEARNED MATERIAL

Story Recall

One way of investigating the effect of scripts on memory is to present the child with a script-based story and to examine the properties of recall for characteristics of the script structure. This paradigm has been used with adults in such studies as Bower et al. (1979), and Graesser, Woll, Kowalski, and Smith (1980).

In the first study carried out with children for this purpose, McCartney and Nelson (1981) constructed stories that were based on a presumed common "having dinner and going to bed" script. Two types of stories, both 24 propositions in length, one emphasizing the dinner script, and the other emphasizing the bed script, were read to 5- and 7-year-old children, who were asked to recall the story after a brief delay. Children at both ages recalled the main and central acts, as previously identified, significantly more frequently than subsidiary filler acts. This was true independently of serial position. For example, eating dinner was remembered more often than the conversation that took place at dinner. Older children remembered more than younger children, but the additional material remembered consisted primarily of the details of the episodes; both ages remembered the main acts equally well. Both ages also sequenced their recall in the correct order almost perfectly, that is in the order presented, which was in the order of the real world event.

Thus this study provided a first demonstration that knowledge of a familiar script would guide recall of what was remembered of a story based on that script, as well as the sequence in which it was remembered. It was evident from this study that in script-based stories (as in stories constructed on the basis of story grammars, e.g., Mandler & Johnson, 1977) not all elements are remembered equally well, and that which ones are remembered is predictable on the basis of script analysis. However, this study also left open a number of questions to be pursued in subsequent research.

The influence of three factors on memory for stories was investigated in a study by Hudson and Nelson (1983). These were type of event, presence of an explicit goal, and canonical sequencing. Each of these factors was expected to affect the accuracy of story memory in specific ways. Real-world events can be seen to vary in terms of the degree to which they are structured in an invariant causally based sequence. Some events can only happen in a specific order because of the logical relationship between actions. For example, dinner must be served before it can be eaten. On the other hand, some events display a highly flexible order. For example, in the birthday party event games may be played before or after eating cake. Abelson (1981) labeled these different types strong and weak scripts. In addition, some generally invariant orders depend on conventional or pragmatic rather than logical relations, such as singing Happy Birthday before cutting the birthday cake. It might be expected that invariant order, whether logical or conventional, would provide more support for recall and correct sequencing than a variable order event. Moreover, when a story contains misordered sequences, the effect on recall should be greater for the logically structured event.

In addition, those events that are more familiar to children should be more strongly represented in scripts and thus the effect of the script structure on memory (both positive and negative) should be stronger. Finally, the presence or absence of an explicit goal statement should enhance or detract from story memory to the extent that children are aware of and affected by the organization of the script around a goal.

Preschool children (mean age 4:9 years) and 1st-grade children (mean age 6:8 years) heard two script-based stories of equal length: one about a birthday party (a familiar but loosely structured event) and the other about making cookies (a less-familiar but more logically structured event). In the control condition both stories were presented in canonical order and opened with a goal statement (e.g., "One day it was Sally's birthday and Sally had a birthday party"). In one experimental condition the stories contained setting statements but no goal statement. For example, the Birthday Party story opened with the main character sitting by the window looking for her friends and no mention was made of her birthday. In a second experimental condition some of the actions in the stories were misordered. For example, in the Making Cookies story the story characters put the pan in the oven before they mixed the dough. All children heard and recalled the stories twice and were seen a third time on the following day for delayed recall.

Level of recall of all stories was generally high and sequencing was generally accurate for both age groups. As expected in terms of the effects discussed above, children recalled more from the story about the presumably more familiar event (birthday party) but sequenced acts more accurately in the more logically structured event story (making cookies). However, contrary to expectations, both quantity of recall and sequencing of recall were relatively unaffected by the manipulations that deleted goal information and misordered causally related acts. Nonetheless, it appears that these manipulations did have more subtle effects on the content of children's recall. Although the goal was not explicitly stated in the goalless stories, children at both ages were able to infer the goals of both events. This was evident by the fact that they were able to provide goals when asked at the end of the study. However, preschoolers often intruded goal statements into their recall, and for the making cookies story only lack of a goal statement affected amount of recall for this group. Thus it appears that in most cases the appropriate event representations were available for comprehension and retrieval of script information, and as a result the disruptions in processing, which would be expected if event representations were not available, did not occur.

Although the misordered acts did not reduce recall, children tended to repair these temporal violations in several ways, primarily by omitting one or both of the acts presented out of sequence. In addition preschoolers more often than 1st graders reordered acts or transformed them, for example by stating that the "children took presents (i.e., favors) home" in place of the misordered act "children brought presents" which was placed toward the end of the story. Preschool children also often collapsed a number of acts into one, as in the making cookies story stating that the characters "baked cookies," thereby avoiding the logical contradiction of putting the pan in the oven before mixing the cookie dough.

These differential age effects add up to an interesting difference in the way the two age groups appeared to use scripts in processing stories. First-grade children were less affected than preschool children by story manipulations and differences between the two events. The level of older children's recall was high in all conditions in both stories, their sequencing of recall was generally accurate and consistent, and they were consistent in which parts of the stories they recalled over conditions and recall trials. The deletion of goal information from the beginning of the stories had no effect on 1st graders' recall. They were able to recall misordered acts in a nonlogical sequence, although they tended to selectively forget one of the acts in a misordered act pair.

In contrast, preschool children seemed to rely more on the activation of familiar scripts than did older children. Their recall was best for the story about the more familiar event (birthday party) and they had least difficulty sequencing the more logically structured event story (making cookies). Preschool children also added goal information to the goalless stories more often than did 1st graders, which suggest that they had trouble distinguishing inferred goals from the information actually presented in the stories. In addition, younger children were less able to recall information that did not match their event representations. For example, younger children were more likely to resolve logical inconsistencies in the misordered stories by simply eliminating *both* of the acts in the misordered act pairs, and were less able to order acts as they were presented in the stories.

In summary, these results indicate that while children's recall at both ages was influenced by their generalized event representations (that is, their scripts), flexibility in the use of script structures in recall appears to increase with age. First graders remembered discrepant or unexpected information better than preschool children. This trend is consistent with studies finding greater flexibility in recall of stories and scenes by adults and older children (Mandler, 1983). Although younger children are able to use schematic structures to guide retrieval automatically, older children seem also to be able to use these structures more deliberately and are not necessarily limited to only one automatic retrieval mechanism. Thus this study suggested that there may be a developmental progression from a schema-bound dependence on implicit and automatic use of familiar schemas to a more explicit and deliberate use of schemas in memory.

This conclusion was given additional weight in a study by Slackman and Nelson (1984) of memory for an unfamiliar script presented in story form. In this experiment three similar stories about visiting a friend were constructed and presented over 3 successive days. Although each story contained similar content and structure (i.e., in each the main character got ready, took a form of transportation to a friend's house, engaged in activities, had something to eat and left), each varied in terms of the main characters and the specifics of the subsequences, props, and so on. On the fourth day a novel story based on the restaurant script was presented, and delayed recall was obtained for all stories on the following day. This design enabled us to examine the increasing effects over time of the acquisition of a script on memory for instances.

In this study three age groups, 4, 6, and 8 years, participated. The expected formation of a general schema as more stories of the same type were presented was observed at all ages. This was evidenced in the fact that elements of the visit-a-friend story were confused with each other in later recall, and when intrusions were made they were of general items that were consistent with the stories. Intrusions from the novel story did not occur, nor did intrusions from the "friend" story into the novel story. Moreover, children at all ages demonstrated a high level of veridical sequencing, and sequencing was better for those parts of the stories that were constructed to have an invariant sequence than for those parts that were variable. In addition, repeated exposure to narrations about similar events led to more generic script-based recall, shown by the fact that with time, more general than specific items were recalled, more slot-fillers were confused or deleted, and for the older subjects, general rather than specific act items were intruded. This finding is consistent with Bartlett's proposal (1932) that memory for more specific details decreases over time, although the gist remains. It is also consistent with the finding by Martin, Harrod, and Siehl (1980) that more exposure to versions of an event narrative lead to more abstract summaries, as well as with that of Graesser et al. (1980), indicating initially better memory for atypical, and later, better memory for typical script actions. Thus this study provided evidence of schematization in memory over time for children as young as four similar to that previously observed for adults.

There were developmental differences as well as similarities in this study, however. Older children recalled more than younger, as usual, but there were no age differences in accuracy of sequencing. Children at all ages made meaningful paradigmatic substitutions, did not intrude idiosyncratic information, and tended to confuse similar stories with each other but not with the novel story. On the other hand, older children deleted more slot-fillers in delayed recall, intruded general rather than specific items, and added story-consistent information, all in contrast to the preschoolers' performance. The fact that preschoolers did not add story-consistent information, as did the older children, suggests that older children draw more on existing knowledge to guide recall.

Finally, consistent with the results from the Hudson and Nelson (1983) study, preschoolers and 1st-graders recalled more from the temporarily invariant part of the story than from the variable part, while 3rd-graders did not, thus suggesting that the younger children were more dependent upon the organization provided by the schema (built up from the invariant sequence) than were the older children.

List Recall

That scripts may have an effect on memory for lists of items that are script-related and not only on script-based stories has been demonstrated in two experiments by Lucariello and Nelson (1985). In the first of these studies two lists of items in three familiar categories were constructed and presented to preschool children for recall. The lists were based on the elicitation of items from children who were asked to tell "all the foods you eat for lunch" or dinner, or breakfast, for example. Similarly, animals and clothes appearing in three different script contexts each were elicited. One (slot-filler) list contained category items from one script context for each category, while the other (taxonomic) list contained the most frequently mentioned item from each context in each category. Categories were blocked in presentation, and recall was either free or constrained. In one constrained condition children were given category cues (e.g., tell me all the foods on the list) for both the script and taxonomic lists. Script cues were given in another condition (e.g., tell me all the things you can eat for lunch on the list) for the slot-filler list only. Thus there were 5 conditions altogether: taxonomic free recall, taxonomic constrained recall, slot-filler free recall, slot-filler category constrained recall, and slot-filler constrained recall.

Results showed that in terms of both amount recalled and organization of recall the slot-filler list was superior to the taxonomic list. Moreover, script cues for the slot-filler list produced higher recall than category cues did. Thus it appeared that the script organization was guiding children's memory for and organization of the material presented in the form of word lists. A second study replicated these results and demonstrated that the slot-filler effect was superior to the effect of the organization provided by a complementary list, composed of items present in script contexts but not in the same script slots. Thus the script-based slot-filler category appears to have a strong influence on young children's memory performance. We are currently investigating these effects further (Kyratzis, Lucariello, & Nelson, in preparation).

Story and List Recall Compared

The previous studies revealed the effects of schematic script organization on story recall and indicated that script structure improved the organization and recall of categorized word lists as well. In a study directly comparing the effects of organization of categorized lists and script based stories, Hudson and Fivush (1983) presented preschool and kindergarten children with either a birthday party story or a taxonomic word list. The story contained 9 central acts derived from previous research with preschool children and the list contained 3 items each from the animal, fruit, and funiture categories, based on the most frequent choices of preschool children (Rosner & Hayes, 1977). It should be noted that while this list was not script-derived, as was the Lucariello and Nelson (1985) list, the items represented were high associates and in the case of fruit were common slot-fillers. The material was presented and recalled twice in either a successive condition (two presentations followed by two recalls) or an alternative condition (each presentation followed by recall). Amount of recall generally improved over trials except in the successive presentation of the taxonomic list. It is notable that recall of the story improved on the second trial at both ages even when the story was first presented twice and the child was then asked to recall twice. This was not true for the list, where recall actually declined on the second trial for preschool children in the successive condition. Thus there seemed to be something in the story condition that was aiding children's recall over and above that of immediate memory. Total amount recalled did not vary by type of material, however. As usual, kindergartners recalled more than preschoolers.

The organization of story recall was measured by a sequencing index and the organization of list recall by a clustering index. Analyses showed that kindergarten children organized recall better on the second recall trial in both presentation conditions and this pattern was the same for both the list and the story. Preschool children, on the other hand, organized story recall better than list recall, and did not show the same increased organization over recall trials as the kindergarten children; organization of story recall was quite good on both recall trials and organization of list recall was relatively poor on both trials.

Overall then, both familiarity with the structure of the material and ability to use that structure strategically appeared to influence preschool and kindergarten children's performance in this study. There was no evidence of strategic organization in preschool children's recall of either the categorically organized list or the schematically organized story. They recalled essentially the same units and organized those units in the same way regardless of how many times they heard or recalled the material. However, their story recall was well organized across trials, suggesting that the schematic structure of the story automatically guided recall. In contrast, kindergarten children's recall of both the story and the list was better organized on the second recall trial, and this improvement was evident even when children did not hear the material again between trials. This suggests that kindergarten children are able to use both categorical and schematic structures strategically to organize recall and therefore may benefit from successive chances to reorganize their recall.

These results suggest that whereas preschool children seem to be unable to use either categorical or schematic structures deliberately to organize recall, kindergarten children are able to use both structures strategically. While categorical knowledge improves over the age studied, as prior research has shown, schematic knowledge does not appear to develop in the preschool years, but the ability to use this knowledge strategically does. Support for this interpretation is found in the story recall protocols. After kindergarten children recalled story units in the correct order, they were frequently able to recall additional units when probed. Since these were now out of order, their sequencing scores were lowered. However, they were then often able to integrate these additional units into the correct sequence on the next recall trial. Preschool children, however, seldom recalled additional units when probed. It appeared that preschool children simply "read off" the recalled story units from their internal representation, but were unable to reflect back upon the representation to fill in additional information. Kindergarten children seemed to be able to use the underlying structure intentionally to recall more material. While previous research has emphasized the intentional use of categorical structures for directing memory search, schematic structures are generally considered to organize recall automatically. These results suggest that schematic structures also come under deliberate control. An interesting sidelight on this issue is raised by Bjorklund's (in press) argument that categorical structure is also used initially in an automatic or unintentional mode before it comes under strategic control.

Summary

These studies have provided evidence that scripts provide an automatic organizational structure for memory in young (preschool) children. While scripts do not necessarily increase amount recalled, they do guide output, as shown by the finding that story recall is sequentially ordered, includes the main concepts, that children can infer absent goals and repair misordered sequences, and that scripts provide organization for list memory. Older children are more flexible in their use of scripts and other schemas, and their memory appears to be less schema bound. When a script is being learned and remembered, it becomes more schematized, that is, more generalized, containing fewer details, over time. When lists are composed of script-based categories in contrast to broader categorical structures, recall and organization of the material to be remembered by preschool children is improved. These studies have all involved the kind of artificial verbal materials typical of laboratory experiments with children and adults of all ages. But one of the interesting questions is whether these results can be generalized to more naturally occurring situations in which children remember events. As the introductory quote indicated, and as recent research (e.g., DeLoache, 1980) has demonstrated, children in their natural surroundings in everyday life appear to have very good memories, much better than our laboratory experiments usually reveal. In the next section we examine some of the effects of scripts on what children remember from their everyday experiences, that is effects on their autobiographical memories.

UNDIRECTED MEMORY

How is recall of your third birthday party similar to recalling a story about a birthday party? Suppose that you could actually remember this episode. It is very likely that your recall would include intrusions and distortions similar to those found in recall of script-based stories (Linton, 1975, 1982; Neisser, 1981). For example, if you recalled the birthday cake, it is quite possible that your recall would not be accurate with respect to the actual cake present at the party, but would be based on what a typical birthday cake should look like as represented in your birthday party script. If you remembered a gift you received, could you be certain that you received that gift on your third birthday and not your fourth? Perhaps you have no memory for this episode, but you could generate a plausible account of what such a party would be like given general knowledge about birthday parties and about people and places that were significant to you at that time. This can occur when specific episodes become fused into a general script and are no longer accessible as distinct individual episodes.

How might a 3-year-old's recall of her third birthday party differ from that of a 5-year-old or an adult? We might predict better recall for the younger child because it would be a more recent episode for her than for an older child or adult. However, if younger children's autobiographic recall is more schema bound, a 3-year-old's recall could include more distortions in the direction of a canonical birthday party script. In addition, because children's use of scripts in recall becomes more flexible and strategic with age, as indicated in the research reviewed here, a preschool child who cannot remember a particular birthday party may not be able to generate a plausible account on the basis of general event knowledge. In this case, a 3-year-old child may not be able to remember anything at all while a 5-year-old or an adult could generate some appropriate episodic information.

These issues were investigated in a study by Hudson and Nelson (1986) comparing scripts of 3- and 5-year-olds for two familiar events—snack at summer day camp and dinner at home—with their specific memories for recent episodes of the same events. Half the children were asked to report "What happens . . . ?" for both events in one interview and "What happened yesterday . . . ?" in an interview 1 week later. The remaining children were asked the same question in the reverse order. At the end of the second interview, children were asked to recall episodes of less familiar events, a field trip or birthday party at camp (e.g., "What happened at Hilary's birthday party?" and an episode of their own choice ("What happened one time when you did something really special?").

Children's scripts and episodic memories were analyzed in terms of length, content, level of generality, and tense use. Length of recall was measured as the number of propositions children reported in either a script or an episodic account. Because both accounts were about the same events, overlap in content as measured by the particular activities children reported was inevitable. The content of children's reports was analyzed in terms of four information categories: acts, descriptions, conditionals, and elaborations. An act is any action reported by a child in a script or episodic account ("I just come running to snack"). Descriptions include both physical and affective descriptions ("He's bigger than me," "Apple juice is one of my favorite drinks"). Conditionals specify acts or states which follow or co-occur in a temporal sequence as well as actions and states that must exist in order for another action to occur ("when it was rest time," "if people are eating ahead of people"). Elaborations are repetitions of act propositions that include additional details ("We had juice for snack. . . . We had orange juice''). Prior research has shown that children's scripts consist primarily of acts and act elaborations with some conditionals, but few descriptions (Fivush, 1984; Nelson & Gruendel, 1981). In contrast, episodic memories should include a higher proportion of descriptions that provide more specific information (Martin et al., 1980). Two measures of generality and specificity were also used. First, mention of optional qualifiers such as ''sometimes'' and ''usually'' were coded. These are used in reporting options and alternatives in script reports, but should not be necessary in describing a single episode. Particular qualifiers referring to specific people, times, and locations were also coded. These should be more apparent in episodic reports (Martin et al., 1980).

Results indicated that children's scripts and episodic reports were very similar in content and level of generality. Children tended to mention mostly acts (56%) and act elaborations (23%) in response to both questions and use of particular qualifiers did not vary across reports although optional qualifiers were used only in the script reports. However, scripts and episodic accounts varied in terms used (the scripts were reported in the timeless present tense and episodic reports used in the past tense) and length; scripts were longer than episodic memories (8.37 vs. 6.52 propositions). Older children reported more information in response to both questions, but no other age differences were found.

Thus routine occurrences of familiar events were difficult for children to recall in that children's episodic reports were shorter in length than their scripts and mention of rich episodic detail was strikingly absent from these memories. This effect could be a result of fusion processes in memory whereby routine occurrences of familiar events, that is, episodes in which nothing out of the ordinary happens, are fused into the general script. Memory should be better for atypical episodes because these may be tagged in memory in terms of distinctive event features. Because fusion and confusion effects become more evident with increasing experience, episodes of less familiar events (i.e., those that have only been experienced a few times) should be easier to represent in memory as separate episodes.

This interpretation was supported by the finding that when children were asked to recall episodes of less familiar events, their recall was longer and more detailed than their recall of yesterday's snack and dinner. However, effects of familiarity, typicality and cuing were confounded in these data. Some of the special episodes children recalled appeared to be very familiar events such as visiting a friend and going to the beach, and it was not always clear from children's reports that they were describing atypical episodes. In addition, if individual episodes are stored in memory in terms of features of the episode that distinguish it from the general script, the temporal cue ''yesterday,'' which was used to elicit children's memories of snack and dinner, would not provide a good retrieval mechanism while the cues ''one time'' and ''special'' might be more effective in evoking autobiographic memories.

A follow-up study compared scripts and episodic memories for 3-, 5-, and 7-

year-olds for events that varied systematically in terms of familiarity. Children were asked to report either "what happens" or "what happened one time" for three events: an event that had been experienced more than 5 times, an event that had been experienced 2–5 times and a one-time experience as designated by parental reports. Children were interviewed about a variety of enjoyable events such as birthday parties, trips to the circus, zoo, beach, and amusement parks. Although children differentiated scripts and episodic memories in terms of tense use, content, and level of generality, familiarity had a strong effect on both types of reports. With increased experience, children's reports included a higher proportion of act propositions, fewer episodic details, less use of the past tense, and script reports included more optional qualifiers. Thus, increased experience led to more general and less episodic memory reports. However, in contrast to the first study, there were no differences in the length of children's scripts and episodic memories, possibly because the "one time" cue was more effective than the "yesterday" cue used in the prior study.

With age, children reported more propositions in response to both questions, but there were no age differences for any other measures. Still, 3-year-olds were the only children to give script reports instead of specific memories when recalling an episode of a very familiar event. Older children included both general and episodic information in these reports, for example, "You play games. . . . We played pin the tail on the donkey." This difference suggests that older children may have used their scripts to generate episodic information while younger children simply "read off" their scripts instead of formulating episodic accounts.

The episodes of familiar events that children recalled appeared to stand out because they were very recent or they involved personally salient people and places. A few memories included violations in the standard event such as a thunderstorm at the beach, or a trip to the zoo when a favorite species was missing. These findings are consistent with the proposal that specific episodes are tagged in memory in terms of distinctive slot fillers and deviations from the routine.

A study by Fivush, Hudson, and Nelson (1984) further highlighted effects of novelty and cuing on children's autobiographic memory. This study compared kindergarten children's recall of an unusual class trip to an archeology exhibit to their scripts for what happens when you go to a museum. Some children were asked, "What happens when you go to the museum?" 2 weeks before the trip and some were asked 6 weeks after the trip. In addition, some children were asked, "What happened when you went to the Jewish Museum?" on the same day as the trip and some were asked 6 weeks after the trip. All children were asked to recall the field trip 1 year later. Although children had been to museums before, this visit was unique because children were allowed to handle archeologists' tools, they pretended to dig for artifacts, and they made clay models of artifacts.

After 6 weeks, children's memory for the episode was as accurate and detailed as their immediate recall. After 1 year, children's recall was equally accurate, but children required more specific cues to recall the same information that was so easily accessed before. Whereas only 7% of the children were able to recall the trip given the original question, "Can you tell me what happened when you went to the Jewish Museum?", an additional 53% responded when they were asked, "Do you remember you learned about archeology?" In addition, children's museum scripts did not vary from the pretrip to the posttrip interview. The finding of no change in children's scripts together with the finding that children were able to remember details of the episode 1 year later suggests that this atypical occurrence was not incorporated into the general script. Although children needed more specific cues to recall the episode after 1 year, because this was an unusual occurrence, specific cues were available that could effectively differentiate this trip from all others.

While these studies provide evidence that familiarity and cuing influence children's representation and retrieval of autobiographic memories, these effects are often confounded with other factors in recall of real-world episodes. For example, children go to the zoo more frequently than they go to Disneyland, but birthday parties are experienced more often than trips to the zoo. Thus familiarity is confounded with different types of events. In addition, some episodes are more likely to be rehearsed than others. Linton found that rehearsal influences the accessibility of autobiographic memory, but this factor could not be controlled in the studies reviewed thus far.

A study by Hudson (1984) examined preschool children's recall of specific episodes when familiarity, time delay, rehearsal, and cuing were all controlled. Nursery school (mean age 4:7) and kindergarten (mean age 5:8) children participated in either a single creative movement workshop (the episodic condition) or a series of workshops once a week for 4 weeks (the script condition). Four weeks after the first and last workshops in the series, children in the script condition were asked to recall those episodes. Children in two episodic conditions experienced workshops identical to either the first or last workshops children in the script condition experienced. They also recalled workshops 4 weeks later. In addition, half of the children in each age group and condition were asked to recall the workshops on the same day they were experienced which gave them additional verbal rehearsal of the workshops. In both the immediate and delayed sessions, children were given successively more specific cues for recall. For example, children were first asked, "Can you tell me what happened in the (first or last) workshop?" and later were asked, "Did you sing some songs?"

Results were consistent with the findings from studies of children's use of scripts in story recall that increased experience with an event results in more extensive, but less accurate recall. There were no effects of experience on children's immediate recall, but after 4 weeks, children in the script condition recalled more activities than children in the episodic condition. However, this also produced more intrusions in recall as they had difficulty distinguishing between particular workshops. Both rehearsal and more specific cues increased children's recall across conditions. However, rehearsal did not improve accuracy of recall. Even when they had rehearsed recall of particular workshops on the same day they had occurred, children in the script condition confused individual episodes in recall at 4 weeks. Older children recalled more activities than younger children and both age groups' recall improved with rehearsal. However, nursery-school children tended to rely more heavily on specific cues in recall than did kindergarten children, suggesting that the younger children were less efficient at directing their own memory search.

Summary

These studies showed that scripts also provide an organizational structure for children's recall of real-world events. In trying to remember a specific occurrence of a familiar event, a general event representation may be automatically activated to guide recall in much the same way that recall of event-based stories is schematically organized. Similar kinds of distortions in memory occur as recall of "what happened" becomes confused with "what should have happened" based on general knowledge about the event. Thus, effects of fusion and confusion found in children's memory for specific episodes of familiar events. In contrast, memories of single experiences included more episodic details and were more accurate because there were fewer sources of confusion for these events. Atypical episodes may also be linked in memory to general event representations, but because they include unusual or unexpected slot fillers, they can be tagged in memory in terms of their distinctive features. These studies suggest that in order for an episode to be remembered, it must be considered unusual or different for some reason. Very routine episodes, such as dinner or snack may be forgotton entirely and some single experiences, such as a creative movement workshop, may be atypical enough to be remembered very well. These studies also showed that cuing and rehearsal improve children's real-world memory. In the next section we integrate these findings with the research on children's recall in directed memory tasks into a functional model of early memory development.

A Model of Early Memory Development

We would like to be able to account within a single model for the effect of scripts both on children's undirected memory for episodes and on their ability to remember stories, lists, and other material presented to them for memorization. In order to do this we need to consider what the structure of a memory system designed to function adaptively in the young child's life might be. We consider in this regard that the memory demands for the young child might not be much different from that of any of the higher mammals. A relevant question then is "what is memory good for in terms of the life circumstances of children and other creatures?'' The essential characteristic would not seem to be reflecting on pleasant or unpleasant experiences, or that of learning abstract or arbitrary material. Rather, memory is functional to the extent that it guides action and interaction in the present and future. If the child can predict what will happen in the future on the basis of what has happened in the past that will be an advantage, and any memory system that makes this possible will be valuable.

One obvious adaptive structure in these terms is a general schema for what usually happens in recurrent events. Such a schema, or script, based on past experience, has the required predictive power and can be used in planning as well as acting. To the extent that the script includes optional paths, with probabilities or conditions, and variables that can fill slots, it provides the basic information that the child needs to carry through familiar activities. Thus the memory system should provide a way to build up such a script from the experience of similar episodes.

When an episode is experienced the memory system will try to fit it to one of its general scripts. This may be accomplished because the episode is given a particular name (e.g., ''going to McDonald's''), or because it occurs at the same time every day (e.g., the bedtime routine), or it may depend on actual experience of at least part of the activity itself. Any particular episode of an established script need not be remembered if it does not contain any information that is discrepant with the general script, although if it includes new variables, these may be entered as new possible slot-fillers.

If an episode does not fit the pattern of a general script, it should be retained as the possible basis for a new script. However, if a similar episode does not recur within some time limit, this memory may become inaccessible (it would be rash to claim that it disappears entirely), unless it includes some vitally important survival information (see Brown & Kulik, 1977, on flashbulb memories with respect to this point). We will not speculate on what might seem vitally important to the preschool child, although it could include matters that appear insignificant to the adult, for example, a scary dream.

This discussion suggests that episodes from a familiar script will not be retained as wholes for very long, but only in terms of the particulars they contain that fit into parts of the script structure, for example, a specific time, location, persons, or objects that occurred. The entire episode might be reconstructable from the script structure, however, and indeed, for some time might be recoverable as a vivid personal experience. How long it remains recoverable as a whole might vary depending upon how redundant it is with the general script, how frequent recurrences are, and so on.

For the human child and adult there is an additional factor that enters into the determination of whether an episode will be retained, and that of course is verbal rehearsal, to oneself or with others. Rehearsal may be the factor that determines what episodes enter into one's personal autobiographic memory stream. This type of memory is not available until the age of 3 or later (the infantile amnesia phenomenon), which fits the hypothesis of verbal rehearsal, and it varies in strength from one individual to another, apparently independently of other memory skills. It is clear from much recent research (Nelson, 1984; Nelson & Ross, 1980; Todd & Perlmutter, 1980) that even children between the ages of 1 and 3 years have episodic memories that are similar to those of older children, although they do not enter into the autobiographic memory system in later life. Moreover, since there is no evidence to date of differences in organization or structure in the memory system of the younger child and the older child, the hypothesis that lack of autobiographic memory prior to age 3 is a function of changes in cognitive structure (Schactel, 1947; White and Pillemer, 1979) lacks convincing support.

Our general functional model then envisions that an episode becomes represented in the child's mind as a specific episodic memory and whenever possible as an instance of a general script. When an episode fits a script it may be quickly fused with it, its slot-fillers entered into appropriate slots, and the episode itself may become unrecoverable except through reconstruction. Episodes that are instances of scripts may be accessed through cues of specific slot-fillers, for example, by asking about a particular story that was read yesterday (Fivush, 1984). Temporal cues are not effective in accessing such memories, probably because they are part of the general knowledge system rather than the specific memory system. However, when the episode does not fit a script, or when it is rehearsed, it may be retained as a specific memory. These memories are more easily accessed by a variety of cues and can be reported in greater detail, as the research in the previous section demonstrated. If such episodes are repeated, they too become schematized, entering into the general knowledge system, where slot-fillers can become confused with each other (Hudson, 1984; Linton, 1982; Martin et al., 1980; Slackman & Nelson, 1984; Taylor & Winkler, 1980). One further aspect of this system must be proposed in order to handle the effects observed. This is that other general knowledge structures may be derived from the experientially based schemas. In particular, categories of slot-fillers may be built up on the basis of their occurrence in the same location in a script (Nelson, 1982, 1983, 1985).

What about the effects of this system on memory for material to be learned, such as lists and stories? Where previously we considered how experienced episodes became represented as schemas, here we consider the reciprocal effect of the schema on representation of experience. When a story is presented it may be immediately recognizable as an instance of a well-known script, and the memory system may automatically therefore take advantage of that structure to remember it for future recall. Similarly, when presented with a list of items that include script-derived slot-fillers, these slot-fillers may act as cues to activate the appropriate schemas that then support memory for the list and subsequent recall.

In terms of developmental effects, we have stressed that there are few observable differences between younger and older children in their automatic use of scripts in memory. However, some developmental changes can be proposed, on the basis of our research and the present model. As we have noted at several points, preschool children appear to be schema-bound, whereas 1st-grade children have begun to be able to use their schemas more flexibly. They appear to be able to use the structure to search memory more effectively, and also to engage in reconstruction on the basis of the schema. Because of this they may be able to report plausible memories, even when such memories may be "repisodic" (Neisser, 1981), that is, contain details from several different actual episodes of a similar kind. Older children also have built up more scripts and other schemas, as well as other types of general knowledge structures, including taxonomic categories, and these enter into their memory systems as well. Moreover, they are more verbal and are more likely to engage in verbal rehearsal, not only of material to be learned as has been frequently observed, but also of everyday experiences. And finally, older children become able eventually to coordinate their memories with objective conventional temporal sequences, leading to the establishment of an autobiographical memory system marked by such cultural events as first grade, graduation, elections, and so on. Such a system enables the individual to order his or her own life experience according to a conventional pattern.

Summary

These studies of children's scripts and autobiographic memories indicate that children as young as three represent experience in memory both in the form of general event schemas and as details from specific occurrences. Together, general and episodic event knowledge provide the young child with a real-world memory system that functions at many levels: to plan and predict future activities; to attend to and remember atypical occurrences in order to modify existing knowledge structures; to build new knowledge structures such as taxonomic categories; and to coordinate one's personal life history with culturally historical events.

REFERENCES

Abelson, R. P. (1981). Psychological status of the script concept. *American Psychologist, 36,* 715–729.

Bartlett, F. C. (1932). *Remembering.* Cambridge: Cambridge University Press.

Bower, G., Black, J. B., & Turner, T. J. (1979). Scripts in memory for text. *Cognitive Psychology, 11,* 177–220.

Bjorklund, D. (1985). The role of conceptual knowledge in the development of organization in children's memory. In C. Brainerd & M. Pressley (Eds.), *Basic processes in memory development: Progress in cognitive development research.* New York: Springer-Verlag.

Brown, R., & Kulik, J. (1977). Flashbulb memories. *Cognition, 5,* 73–99.

DeLoache, J. (1980). Naturalistic studies of memory for object location in very young children. In M. Perlmutter (Ed.), *Children's memory: New directions for child development (No. 10)* (pp. 87–101). San Francisco: Jossey-Bass.

Fivush, R. (1984). Learning about school: The development of kindergarteners' school scripts, *Child Development, 55,* 1697–1709.

Fivush, R., Hudson, J., & Nelson, K. (1984). Children's long term memory for a novel event: An exploratory study. *Merrill-Palmer Quarterly, 30,* 303–316.

Graesser, A. C., Woll, S. B., Kowalski, D. J., & Smith, D. A. (1980). Memory for typical and atypical actions in scripted activities. *Journal of Experimental Psychology: Human Learning and Memory, 6,* 503–515.

Hudson, J. A. (1984). *Recollection and reconstruction in children's autobiographic memory.* Unpublished doctoral dissertation, City University of New York.

Hudson, J., & Fivush, R. (1983). Categorical and schematic organization and the development of retrieval strategies. *Journal of Experimental Child Psychology, 35,* 32–42.

Hudson, J., & Nelson, K. (1983). Effects of script structure on children's story recall. *Developmental Psychology 19,* 625–635.

Hudson, J., & Nelson, K. (1986). Repeated encounters of a similar kind: Effects of familiarity on children's autobiographic memory. *Cognitive Development, 1,* 253–271.

Istomina, Z. M. (1975). The development of voluntary memory in preschool-age children. *Soviet Psychology, 13,* 5–64.

Kyratzis, A., Lucariello, J., & Nelson K. (in preparation). *Complementary, slot-filler, and taxonomic relations as knowledge organizers for young children.*

Lange, G. (1978). Organization-related processes in children's recall. In P. A. Ornstein (Ed.), *Memory development in children.* Hillsdale, NJ: Lawrence Erlbaum Associates.

Linton, M. (1975). Memory for real-world events. In D. A. Norman & D. E. Rumelhart (Eds.), *Explorations in cognition.* San Francisco: W. H. Freeman.

Linton, M. (1982). Transformation of memory in everyday life. In U. Neisser (Ed.), *Memory observed.* San Francisco: W. H. Freeman.

Lucariello, J., & Nelson, K. (1985). Slot-filler categories as memory organizers for young children. *Developmental Psychology, 21,* 272–282.

Mandler, J. (1979). Categorical and schematic organization in memory. In C. R. Puff (Ed.), *Memory organization and structure.* New York: Academic Press.

Mandler, J. (1983). Representation. In P. Mussen (Ed.), *Manual of child psychology.* New York: Wiley.

Mandler, J., & Johnson, N. (1977). Remembrance of things parsed: Story structure and recall. *Cognitive Psychology, 9,* 111–151.

Martin, J., Harrod, W., & Siehl, C. (1980). *The development of knowledge structures.* (Research paper No. 557.) Available from the Graduate School of Business, Stanford University, Stanford, CA.

McCartney, K. A., & Nelson, K. (1981). Children's use of scripts in story recall. *Discourse Processes, 4,* 59–70.

Moely, B. E. (1977). Organizational factors in the development of memory. In R. V. Kail and J. W. Hagen (Eds.), *Perspectives on the development of memory and cognition.* Hillsdale, NJ: Lawrence Erlbaum Associates.

Myers, N., & Perlmutter, M. (1978). Memory in the years from two to five. In P. A. Ornstein (Ed.), *Memory development in children.* Hillsdale, NJ: Lawrence Erlbaum Associates.

Neisser, U. (1981). John Dean's memory: A case study. *Cognition 9,* 1–22.

Nelson, K. (1982). The syntagmatics and paradigmatics of conceptual representation. In S. Kuczaj (Ed.), *Language development: Language, thought and culture.* Hillsdale, NJ: Lawrence Erlbaum Associates.

Nelson, K. (1983). The derivation of concepts and categories from event representations. In E. Scholnick (Ed.), *New trends in conceptual representation.* Hillsdale, NJ: Lawrence Erlbaum Associates.

Nelson, K. (1984). The transition from infant to child memory. In M. Moskowitz (Ed.), *Infant memory*. New York: Prager.

Nelson, K. (1985). *Making sense: The acquisition of shared meaning*. New York: Academic Press.

Nelson, K., & Gruendel, J. (1981). Generalized event representations: Basic building blocks of cognitive development. In M. Lamb & A. Brown (Eds.), *Advances in developmental psychology* (Vol. 1). Hillsdale, NJ: Lawrence Erlbaum Associates.

Nelson, K., & Ross, G. (1980). The generalities and specifics of long-term memory in infants and young children. In M. Perlmutter (Ed.), *Children's memory: New directions for child development* (No. 10). San Francisco: Jossey Bass.

Rosner, S. R., & Hayes, D. S. (1977). *A developmental study of category item production*. Unpublished manuscript, University of Iowa.

Saussure, F. (1959). Course in general linguistics. New York: McGraw Hill. (Original work published in 1915.)

Schactel, E. G. (1947). On memory and childhood amnesia. *Psychiatry, 1,* 1–26.

Schank, R. C. (1983). *Dynamic memory: A theory of learning in computers and people*. New York: Cambridge University Press.

Schank, R. C., & Abelson (1977). *Scripts, plans, goals, and understanding*. Hillsdale, NJ: Lawrence Erlbaum Associates.

Slackman, E., & Nelson, K. (1984). Acquisition of an unfamiliar script in story form by young children. *Child Development, 55,* 329–340.

Taylor, S. C., & Winkler, J. D. (1980, August). *The development of schemas*. Presented at the meetings of the American Psychological Association, Montreal.

Todd, C. M., & Perlmutter, M. (1980). Reality recalled by preschool children. In M. Perlmutter (Ed.), *Children's memory: New directions for child development (No. 10)*. San Francisco: Jossey Bass.

Tulving, E. (1972). Episodic and semantic memory. In E. Tulving & W. Donaldson (Eds.), *Organization of memory*. New York: Academic Press.

White, S. II., & Pillemer, D. B. (1979). Childhood amnesia and the development of a socially accessible memory system. In J. F. Kihlstrom & F. J. Evans (Eds.), *Functional disorders of memory*. Hillsdale, NJ: Lawrence Erlbaum Associates.

8
Children's Lack of Access and Knowledge Reorganization: An Example from the Concept of Animism

Michelene T. H. Chi
Learning Research and Development Center,
University of Pittsburgh

Currently, a popular interpretation for young children's limited performance is the concept of lack of access. More specifically, this concept assumes that the knowledge that is needed to perform a specific task is available to the child, except that somehow, the child cannot access this knowledge or use it. This paper attempts to understand this idea in terms of knowledge organization and how knowledge might be reorganized to facilitate access. The exact nature and definition of lack of access are postulated and preliminary exploratory data to demonstrate what lack of access could mean for young children is presented in the domain of animism.

EMPIRICAL DEFINITION

"Lack of access" is an interpretation imposed upon an empirical phenomenon that is often observed in young children's cognitive performance. A few examples are offered to illustrate the phenomenon. Young children are often not capable of pairing or categorizing items on the basis of taxonomic relations. For example, if given a choice of whether to pair *scissors* with *knife* together or *scissors* and *paper* together, younger children would prefer to pair the scissors and paper because scissors cut paper, whereas older children may prefer to pair scissors and knife because they are both tools that can cut things. Thus, younger children rely on thematic relations, rather than the underlying taxonomic organization. The reason that this phenomenon is labeled *lack of access* to the relevant knowledge is because the necessary knowledge appears to be available when probed. For example, in a match-to-sample task, if children are shown a cow and asked "to find another one that is the same kind of thing," they will pick another animal (such as a pig) rather than a thematically related picture, such as milk. Markman and Hutchinson (1984) claim that the provision of a verbal label (cow) constrains the search of "another one" to another animal, thus focusing children's attention to categorical relations. This suggests that children are capable of accessing taxonomic relations when they are properly constrained.

Similarly, given a string of items to recall, younger children's recall will typically not show a clustering of items on the basis of taxonomic relationship. One byproduct of nonclustering is lower recall. Again, a current interpretation for this kind of recall pattern is not that children lack the taxonomic relations among the items, but rather, that somehow *they prefer not to use them* since their recall could be improved if their attention was drawn to the taxonomic relations (Smiley & Brown, 1979).

The thesis of my paper proposes that lack of access has to do with the way the knowledge is represented. That is, knowledge is not accessible when it is not properly represented. What constraining does (such as by providing a noun for a category member, as in the Markman & Hutchinson study) is to restrict the search for the child. Constraining the search for the child still does not explain why under normal situations, children do not access that knowledge readily. Thus, we would like to explore the idea that development is a change in the overall structure of knowledge, which permits children to access their knowledge without having their search restricted by the experimental task. Although this framework does not emphasize the existence of a limited accessing mechanism, the same set of questions would be posed as critical to our eventual understanding of cognitive development as those proposed by Gelman and Baillargeon (1983), namely: (1) what is it about the early representation of a given set of experiences that prevents them from being accessed; (2) how must this representation be changed so that it can be accessed (that is, what are the processes that can produce such changes); and finally, (3) what external experiences can foster such changes. In this paper, I focus primarily on answers to the first question, speculate on the answers to the second question, and refer to literature that addresses the third.

ENCAPSULATED MICROSTRUCTURES

It is all well-and-good to postulate that the way knowledge is represented is the culprit for lack of access. Such hypothetical statements cannot be taken seriously unless one can support it by empirical evidence. One way to understand what it means when knowledge is represented in such a way as to be inaccessible is the idea that knowledge is often not accessed because the conditions under which it needs to be retrieved does not match the conditions under which it was stored. This situation tends to produce the phenomenon that children's knowledge is contextually bound, that is, it can only be accessed in one context and not another. What this means, essentially, is that it was stored under one set of contexts, and thus it can only be retrieved under the same set of contexts.

One way to understand how this can happen is to view the knowledge that children do have as encapsulated within its own microstructure, so that its accessibility is tied to a specific set of conditions. One of the best examples of this, I think, is provided by Lawler's (1981) anecdote. Lawler noted that his daughter knew how to do mental calculation with money. She also knew how to do mental arithmetic involving pure numbers by breaking them into multiples of ten and counting up the remainders. She did not, however, connect the two techniques. For example, when asked to add 75 and 26 in terms of money, she could do so by saying "that's three quarters, four, and a penny, a dollar one" (p. 4), on the other hand, when she was adding them as numbers, she did it by adding tens and counting the remainders, such as "seventy, ninety, ninety-six, ninety-seven, ninety-eight . . ." (p. 4). Lawler (1981) refers to these separate skills as "microworlds." Although they both required the same skill in arriving at the sum by counting the leftover units, the two microworlds had distinct conditions for their activation. Only later did Lawler observe moments of *insight* when his daughter first noticed that she could combine her tens microworld with her money microworld. In a previous paper (Chi & Rees, 1983), we interpreted this data as supporting the notion of access. That is, even though the two skills might seem to an adult to be part of the same skill, to a child, they are actually separate. Access to the money microworld is limited to situations where money is explicitly mentioned, and access to numerical addition is accomplished when actual numbers are presented. One could interpret the data as showing that there are two *microstructures* (localized coherent knowledge structures) that are complete and coherent in and of themselves. Structural change can be viewed as the combining of two microstructures in some way. The critical issue is how this combination or *insight* takes place. This is the universal problem of generalization and transfer. (I prefer to use the term microstructure because my research tends to focus on the structure of declarative knowledge, whereas the term *microworld* has more of a procedural skill connotation. I will use the two terms synonymously when the knowledge domain is not clearly declarative or procedural.)

Another excellent example of lack of access that can be interpreted by an encapsulated microstructures view comes from the work on adults' misconception of the physical events in their everyday world. Much current research has shown that adults have very naive views about motion, thinking that there could be no motion without a force continuously acting on it, which violates Newton's laws. What they basically possess is the pre-Galilean impetus theory (McCloskey, 1983). The fact that students' misconceptions are resistant to change, even after having taken a course in Newtonian mechanics, suggested to McCloskey that in order to learn mechanics, students must undergo major theory change—one from Galileo's theory to Newton's theory. That is, because students continue to obey the same intuitive naive theory in making predictions about motion even after having had instruction in Newtonian theories, suggested that they have not revised their existing theory. An alternative interpretation is that students have two separate microstructures. In one, the naive theory of motion, as gained from everyday observations in real world events, obeys laws proposed by Galileo. Hence, when the student is asked to make predictions about motion that mimic everyday motion seen in the real world, his intuitive theory microstructure is accessed, and predictions are made on the basis of that microstructure. When in the classroom, however, confronted with solving textbook problems, the student activates another microstructure, one that was built from lectures and textbooks. Thus, in problem solving, this microworld with Newton's three laws is activated and used.

In order for the two microstructures to merge, I suggest that sufficient instruction must occur that forces direct confrontations between the two microworlds. That is, perhaps the conditions that would activate the one microstructure be presented in a way that request the procedures for solution from the other microstructure. This has not been the case in regular classroom instruction, which usually focuses on sterile problems, where the external world has no friction and objects have no mass.

What have we gained by saying that the reason the appropriate knowledge is not accessed is because it is encapsulated in a separate microstructure, one that is not activated by the current set of conditions? How is this interpretation any different from just saying that the relevant knowledge is not accessible, or that a major reorganization (or theory change) has not taken place? I think the advantage of using the encapsulated microstructures notion is that it presents a more concrete problem for us to solve. If we view children and beginning students' knowledge as encapsulated in microstructures, then our problem becomes one of discovering ways that can foster an integration of the two microstructures; as well as one of discovering ways of representing knowledge that can depict such reorganization. With the alternative interpretation, it's not clear how one can improve the accessing mechanism, nor foster a theory change in a general way (one in which the old theory has to be replaced by a new theory). In fact, our view of microstructures sometimes obviates the need for a definition of radical restructuring (or theory change).

The definition of radical restructuring is that (1) successive conceptual systems or theories do not have a one-to-one mapping for a set of core concepts; (2) the domain of phenomena accounted for is also different in different conceptual systems; and (3) the nature of acceptable explanations is also different (Carey, 1985). A popular example to illustrate radical restructuring in the history of science is the difference in Aristotelian and Galilean theories of mechanics. For example, Aristotle did not distinguish between average velocity and instantaneous velocity, whereas this distinction was a key insight for Galileo. Thus, the two theories do not have a one-to-one mapping in its basic set of core concepts.

Further, Aristotle considered both artificial motion (the movement of a person) as well as natural motion (such as objects falling to the earth); whereas Galileo restricted the phenomena of study to movement through space, and did not distinguish the two kinds of motion. Thus, the kind of phenomena the two theories explained were also different. Finally, different conceptual theories accept different sorts of explanations. Radical restructuring also requires the assumption that an alternative theory must be abandoned in order for the new theory to be functioning. This is a strict restriction. It is not clear that one necessarily needs to make this assumption. It is possible that large elements of one theory can be integrated with elements of another theory that may have been encapsulated (Case, 1985); or alternatively, a large number of elements of one theory can become less prominent as other elements become more salient and accessible, in the transition of one theory to another.

Consider a contemporary example that we all understand. Let us take theories in psychology in a restricted domain—memory. There are two kinds of theories that have been popular in the last decade, the information-processing approach and the levels-of-processing approach. The two theories have different core concepts: processes versus levels. The two theories explain different phenomena: Information-processing theories explain a number of phenomena, ranging from memory recall to problem solving, whereas the levels-of-processing approach concentrates on the phenomenon of incidental recognition memory. And the explanations acceptable to the two theories are clearly different: One concerns the length of time one spends to arrive at a response, the other explanation centers on the notion of whether one is focusing on the semantics or the visual feature of a word, independent of the amount of time. Since the two theories satisfy the definition of theory change, and both can be encoded by the same psychologist, to what extent then does the cognitive structure of a psychologist need to undergo radical restructuring in order for the psychologist to understand both theories? In some sense, the logical thing to conclude is that both theories can coexist in parallel (probably in separate microstructures), and each theory can be used to interpret a set of phenomena at will. Thus, this example illustrates the possibility of using an encapsulated microstructures notion (instead of the idea of radical restructuring) to interpret the phenomenon of theory change.

CHILDREN'S MISCONCEPTION OF ANIMISM

One can always argue that knowledge is not retrieved because it was not stored properly. Such handwaving is not very convincing. To make the point one must: Either show that those children who can retrieve the knowledge have it stored *differently* than those who can't, or show that those who can retrieve it properly *stored* it properly in the first place. I shall discuss some very preliminary data to illustrate both points.

A phenomenon that has been explored for several decades concerns young children's misconceptions in attributing life to inanimate objects. According to Piaget (1930, 1951), children move from a naive stage in which they attribute human qualities to inanimate objects, to the final stage in which they can accurately discriminate living from nonliving things. In the second developmental stage, children restrict this animistic view only to objects that move; in the third stage, they make this attribution only to objects that move autonomously. Finally, they reach the mature stage of discriminating biological from inanimate objects. Piaget's view has been substantiated by a number of investigators, using an interviewing and explanation-type of data.

The kind of causal explanations given by children to questions posed by Piaget are very robust and easily replicable. For example, Piaget interviewed an 8-year-old (Zimm, cited in Piaget, 1951) and asked him ''Is a cloud alive?'' and he answered ''Yes,'' ''Why?'', ''It sometimes moves.'' Thus, this child is classified at the second stage of animistic thinking.

Since Piaget's research, there has been abundant study, both replicating and extending Piaget's results (Laurendeau & Pinard, 1962), as well as clarifying and posing alternative explanations for his results. Berzonsky (1971), for example, showed that young children are more accurate in their discrimination of animistic from nonanimistic objects if the objects are familiar to them. Carey (1985) explained that children's life attribution results from their organization of biological knowledge, which centers on humans as the prototype of living things. There is also research which proposes a process model to try and predict children's answers (Richards & Siegler, 1984). Different tasks (other than explanations) have also been used to assess children's knowledge. Keil (1979), for example, found that children as young as 4-years-old could judge that a sentence is anomalous if it violated the animacy restrictions. Golinkoff and Harding (1980) showed that even 12-month-old infants will show surprise when inanimate objects that are usually stationary show spontaneous movement. Hence, the majority of the research either tries to replicate Piaget's finding, explain the sources of children's responses (such as biological knowledge or familiarity with the objects), proposes a process model to predict children's responses, or attempts to demonstrate that children much younger than the ages Piaget suggested were able to discriminate living from nonliving things.

There is no doubt that all the evidence accumulated thus far is true to a large extent. It is not difficult to conceive of children being more able to discriminate living from nonliving objects if they are familiar with the objects, or that they have increasing biological knowledge as they mature, or that the complexity of the task determines the reliability of their responses, or the type of responses required (articulation versus discrimination) determines the kind of answers children give. The goal of our research is slightly different. We want to understand *why* children produce the responses that they do, and why under alternative questioning probes, they produce alternative answers. The thesis of this paper is that the answer that one gets depends on what concepts are accessed in memory, and consequently what alternative concepts are activated. We propose two explanations. First, that the response a child gives depends on what concept node is activated in memory; and second, that the extent to which related concepts are activated and thus accessed depend on the degree to which they are associated and linked. These ideas will be expanded in what follows.

A critical set of intriguing experiments is the study by Gelman, Spelke, and Meck (1983). They first developed a taxonomy of what constitutes animism, at least for people. There are four sets of properties:

1. self-initiated actions (such as can kick, see, run, talk, hear, breath, eat)
2. has parts (such as head, feet, mouth, stomach)
3. be in a state (such as feels happy or sad, remembers, thinks)
4. can perform reciprocal action (such as returning conversation, a hug, or play).

Furthermore, Gelman et al. wanted to avoid anomalous questions such as, "Does the sun know where it is going?" as well as psychological states such as volition and thinking that young children may not understand, as well as use objects that are very familiar to the child, such as people, doll, rock, puppet, and cat. Basically, they found that children as young as 3- and 4-years-old can discriminate and answer appropriately whether certain objects can do the things listed in the taxonomy, such as run, has parts, perform reciprocal action, and so on. For example, a child of 49 months can correctly answer the questions "Can a doll run?" "No." "How do you know?" "Because she is just pretend." "Can people run?" "Yes." "How do you know?" "Because their legs grow big." "Can rocks?" "No." "How do you know" "Cause they don't have any legs or feet."

The general conclusion made by Gelman et al. (1983) was that preschoolers can clearly distinguish between animate and inanimate moving objects, such as cat and puppet. This suggests that preschool children do have organized knowledge about animate and inanimate objects that they can use to correctly classify objects. The issue of concern here is whether this result contradicts those found by Piaget. Put another way, what is the organization of a child's knowledge that will produce responses such as those gathered by Gelman et al., as well as those collected by Piaget? What kind of evidence do we need to convince ourselves that young children do have an *implicit* understanding of living things vs. nonliving things? (By *implicit* understanding, we mean that a child's responses are systematically governed by principles that discriminate living from nonliving things.) To answer such questions, we began by replicating both Piaget's type of responses and Gelman et al.'s type of responses, to see if they can be generated by the same children.

Procedure

There are four parts to this study. Each part consists of a set of questions that are asked in a given session. Each of the four children in this study came in four times, spanning a 2-week period. The ages of the children ranged from 4:8 to 5:10 years.

Session 1 constitutes three sets of questions. The first set (Question 1a) asks for definitions of what it means to be alive. The second set (1b) asks children to name objects that are alive. Then, using the objects that each child named, the child was asked to explain why the named object was alive. Session 2 is a set of questions that attempt to replicate Piaget's findings. We basically asked the same kinds of questions that Piaget asked, such as "is the sun alive?", and asked for explanation. In Session 3a, 4 objects are used to assess whether children thought they were alive. These four objects were: a blob of clay, a mechanical toy cat that moved, wagged its tail, and squalled, a doll, and a pair of shoes that can be wound up to walk. These items were carefully chosen to satisfy several constraints. The blob of clay was used because we wanted a nonliving object to be attributeless so that the child would not respond to any specific attribute that the object has, and also to see if the child would endow certain attributes to it. The mechanical cat was used because it resembled a cat but is nonliving. A doll was used because even though it resembled a living thing, it did not move. And the pair of walking shoes was used because it moved, but did not resemble any living things. We asked children not only whether each of these things are alive, but also why if they said it was, as well as what could make it alive if they said it wasn't. The idea was to get at what they consider to be salient features in determining that an object was or was not alive. Notice that the questions from Sessions 1, 2, and 3a focused on the word "alive."

Questions from Session 3b, 3c, and 4 concentrate on attributes of living things, rather than probing the concept *alive* directly. So, in some sense, they are more analogous to the type of questions Gelman et al. would ask. Questions from 3b require the children to list objects that possess certain living or nonliving attributes (e.g., Tell me all the things you know that can eat and can breath). Then in Session 3c, living things (e.g., flower, trees, and tiger) and nonliving things (e.g., table, lightbulb, and clothes hanger) were chosen to be probed more specifically about attributes that they might or might not have. Each of the living objects probed were selected from each child's own responses. Therefore, for Subject 1, because she had named in a previous session that flower and trees are alive, we probed her with those things in this session. The nonliving objects probed were chosen from a subset of the subjects' pooled responses, because some the children did not list enough nonliving exemplars. These attributes fall into the classes that Gelman et al. devised; namely, that of biological properties (Can a flower grow?), states (Can a flower feel pain?), and possession of parts (Does a flower have a brain?). The basic idea of this set of questions is to see what each child knows about individual characteristics of a living and a nonliving

176

thing, and whether this is related to their concept of aliveness. Based on Gelman et al.'s data, we would predict that children sampled in this study would correctly know many of these attributes. The point then is, how do we resolve the discrepancy between their knowing of these attributes and their false beliefs that the sun is alive. Session 4 extended the questions in Session 3c, but focused only on human attributes. All the questions are listed in Table 8.1.

Results

One of the main points that Carey (1985) makes is that developmental changes in the concept of *alive* has to do with reorganization of biological knowledge. That is, from the ages of 4–7, biological properties such as breathing, eating, sleeping, having internal organs, are only known about people, and people are children's prototypes of their *animal* category. Therefore, whether a particular animal has or does not have a given property is judged by the similarity of the animal to people, if people serve as the prototype. Indeed, in Carey's data, she found that children are more likely to attribute an animal with having a novel property (such as an omentum), the more similar the animal is to people. Conversely, the properties that are true of animals are not said to be true of people, mainly because the reference point is people, and the attribution is unidirectional. Carey's main point is that with learning and experiencing, children undergo a reorganization in which the child's initial knowledge of what are biological properties is organized around his knowledge of people, then eventually children acquire accurate biological knowledge. Carey takes this as evidence for restructuring, at least in the sense of the novice-to-expert shift. Restructuring in the sense of the novice-expert shift (henceforth called weak restructuring) has three characteristics:

1. the experts have more concepts of the domain, but do share similar concepts with novices (that is, there exists a one-to-one mapping for a subset of the concepts);

2. the experts represent different relations among the concepts that novices do not represent;

3. these new relations that are represented by the experts permit new patterns of interrelations to occur, so that the experts' structures will necessarily be more coherent than the novices.

I would like to first confirm that children's knowledge about biological properties and people properties is acquired with learning. In addition, this reorganization appears to be a cumulative process, further emphasizing that the shift or reorganization is one of the novice-expert shift kind, not one of radical restructuring. Table 8.2 shows the responses given by the 4 subjects. The responses of the two older children (S1, S2) are shown in the left panel and the right panel shows the responses of the two younger children (S3, S4). Each

TABLE 8.1
Sets of Questions Given in the Four Interview Sessions

Animism

SESSION I: Preliminary Questions

Part A--Definition

The child was asked the following five questions as a preliminary
probe of his/her distinction between animate-inaminate.

1. What does it mean to be alive?
2. How do you know if something is alive?
3. What are living things like?
4. What are nonliving things like?
5. How are living things different from nonliving things?

Part B--Name Object

The child was asked to name examples from both the living and nonliving categories:

Example:
       Tell me some things that are alive.
       Tell me some things that are not alive.

Part C--Explanation

In reference to those examples that the child named in the previous
section as belonging to either the living or nonliving category, the
child was asked:

1. Why is X alive?
2. Why is Y not alive?

SESSION II: Replication of Piaget Experiment

In this session the child was asked questions typical of the type
used in Piaget's animism research.

Example: Is the $\underline{X}$ alive? Why or why not?

Probes for $\underline{X}$:   sun . mountain . cloud.
                wind . stone . tree.
                flowers . bicycle . fire . fly.
                horse . goldfish . you . lake

SESSION III: Life Attribute Questions

Part A--Life Attributes

Following each stimulus presentation the child was asked to judge
if the stimulus was alive or not alive and what attributes determine
the distinction.

Example: Is $\underline{X}$ alive? What makes it alive or not alive?

Probes for $\underline{X}$:   blob of clay.
                moving mechanical toy cat.
                talking doll.
                walking mechanical toy shoes.
                a potted plant

Part B--Replication of Carol Smith's Experiment

The child was asked to name examples which possess properties
associated with animate or inanimate objects (but not both).

Example: Tell me all the things you know that $\underline{X}$.

Probes for $\underline{X}$:   have babies and breath.
                grow and have a heart . melt.
                have roots and can die . have bones
                and a brain . need gasoline.
                eat and die . feel pain and
                can talk . have wheels.
                see and go pee pee . get rusty

(continued)

(Table 8.1 continued)

Part C--Life Attributes

The child was asked to judge if the items named in Session I
Possess properties associated with living.

     Example: Does a clotheshanger X?
              Does a tiger X?

       Probes for X: eat . have babies . grow.
                      have a heart . have bones.
                      have a brain . have roots . die.
                      talk . see . go pee pee.
                      feel pain . cry

SESSION IV: Human Attributes

The child was asked to judge if the items in Session I possess
human attributes.

     Example: Does a clotheshanger have a X?
              Does a tiger have a X?
              Does a tree have a X?

       Probes for X: heart . intestine.
                      brain . muscles.
                      bones . blood . feet.
                      arms . legs . nose.
                      ears . mouth . eyes.
                      face

child's responses from Session 3c are divided into 4 cells. The top two cells are responses to living things, and the bottom two cells are their responses to nonliving things. The left cells are characteristics of people, and the right cells are characteristics of living things (or biological properties). There are two things to note. First that, as children mature, they acquire more knowledge about what are the biological properties of living things. This can be seen by the fact that both of the mature children ($S1$, $S2$) responded correctly that the living things possess biological properties, (that is, none of the upper-right-hand cells have a "no" response, as indicated by a 0) whereas both of the younger children ($S3$, $S4$) lack some knowledge about biological properties that animals possess (for example, $S3$ did not know that a giraffe breathes).

The second thing to note is that none of the children attribute nonliving things as having properties of people or biological properties. (That is, none of them answered "yes" to questions such as "can a table die?" as depicted in the lower 2 cells of each subject's responses. See Table 8.2.) This suggests that they may have an *implicit* understanding of what things are living and what things are not, on the basis of which set of properties are associated with each. (By *implicit* understanding, we also mean an understanding that is not accessible in standard explanation paradigm where a reason has to be articulated.) Although this evidence is not conclusive, we will discuss what alternative data should be gathered that can be more convincing.

If it is the case that children do have an implicit discrimination of living from nonliving things, why do they then make the mistakes of saying things like "The sun is alive" or, that "It's alive because it moves"? Also, why are they not able

TABLE 8.2

Responses of the Four Subjects in Session III: Part C--Life Attributes

X = Yes   O = No

Subjects s#1 and s#2

Subject / Stimulus		CHARACTERISTICS OF PEOPLE								CHARACTERISTICS OF LIVING					
		heart	see	talk	brain	pain	cry	bones	roots	die	reproduction	breath	grow	excrete	eat
s#1 LIVING	ant	X	X	X	O	X	O	X	O	X	X	X	X	X	X
	tiger	X	X	O	X	X	O	X	O	X	X	X	X	X	X
	caterpillar	X	X	O	X	X	X	X	O	X	X	X	X	X	X
NONLIVING	table	O	O	O	O	O	O	O	O	O	O	O	O	O	O
	lightbulb	O	O	O	O	O	O	O	O	O	O	O	O	O	O
	hanger	O	O	O	O	O	O	O	O	O	O	O	O	O	O
s#2 LIVING	bird	X	X	O	X	X	O	X	O	X	X	X	X	X	X
	turtle	X	O	O	X	X	O	X	O	X	X	X	X	X	X
	people	X	X	O	X	X	X	X	O	X	X	X	X	X	X
NONLIVING	table	O	O	O	O	O	O	O	O	O	O	O	O	O	O
	lightbulb	O	O	O	O	O	O	O	O	O	O	O	O	O	O
	hanger	O	O	O	O	O	O	O	O	O	O	O	O	O	O

Subjects s#3 and s#4

Stimulus		CHARACTERISTICS OF PEOPLE								CHARACTERISTICS OF LIVING					
		heart	see	talk	brain	pain	cry	bones	roots	die	reproduction	breath	grow	excrete	eat
s#3 LIVING	giraffe	O	O	O	O	X	O	O	O	X	X	O	X	O	X
	clam	O	O	O	O	O	O	O	O	X	X	O	O	O	O
	shark	O	X	O	X	O	O	X	O	X	X	O	X	O	X
NONLIVING	table	O	O	O	O	O	O	O	O	O	O	O	O	O	O
	lightbulb	O	O	O	O	O	O	O	O	O	O	O	O	O	O
s#4 LIVING	flower	X	X	O	X	X	O	X	X	X	X	X	X	X	X
	tree	X	O	O	O	O	O	O	X	X	X	X	X	O	O
	tiger	X	X	X	X	X	X	X	O	X	X	X	X	X	X
NONLIVING	table	O	O	O	O	O	O	O	O	O	O	O	O	O	O
	lightbulb	O	O	O	O	O	O	O	O	O	O	O	O	O	O
	hanger	O	O	O	O	O	O	O	O	O	O	O	O	O	O

*Blank spaces indicate that the experimenter did not probe for an attribute.

to discriminate between animate and inanimate objects, and yet be able to correctly state that "A tiger can eat or sleep," etc. The answer to these two questions may lie in the way the knowledge is represented, and what part of the knowledge structure is accessed. To illustrate this point, we present a representation of (1) our most naive subject, (2) our most sophisticated subject, and (3) an adult subject.

A semantic network representation of nodes and links is constructed using the protocol data from Sessions 1, 2, and 3a. The semantic nodes are derived from actual concepts the child used, and the links are relations that are derived from what they generate. For example, if the child said, in response to the question "What does it mean to be alive?" "It means to be alive . . . mmm . . . let's see . . . it means to be happy too", then, we would construct two nodes—an "alive" node and a "happy" node, and link them with the relation *state*. To simplify the network, we prefer to ignore the characteristics of the relations between the nodes and simply depict that a link exists. Our only constraint, one that is common among semantic networks, is to assume that there are no redundant concept nodes, unless these nodes are associated with concepts that are embedded within a different microstructure (to be elaborated later).

Figure 8.1 captures the gist of the representation of the concepts "alive" and "not alive" of our most naive child, who was 4:8 at the time. (What has been left out are additional instances and attributes that have been mentioned infre-

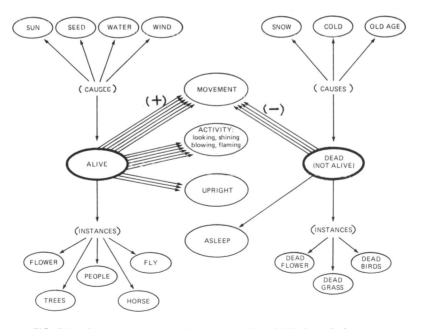

FIG. 8.1.   A representation of the most naive child's knowledge.

quently.) For this child, there is a clear error in the mapping of the semantic of the word "not alive" to the word "dead." That is, things that are not alive are things that are *dead* rather than inorganic. And also *dead things* do not have motion, and the causes of "not aliveness" are old age, cold (that is, freezing temperature), and snow. And instances of things that are not alive are dead things, like "dead birds" and "dead flowers." And, as Piaget correctly stated, this child's salient attributes for things that are alive versus things that are not center on motion and activities. (When an attribute such as "movement" is shared by both the "alive" and "dead" concepts, as shown in Fig. 8.1, positive links depict that the concept possesses that attribute, whereas negative links mean that it was explicitly mentioned by the subject that the concept does not have that attribute.)

Aside from the error in semantic mapping, this child's knowledge structure is not only meaningful (in the sense that alive things generally do have motion or can generate activity, and dead things cannot), but we further propose that this child's knowledge structure, although naive, is quite coherent in and of itself. By coherent, we mean that the two primary concepts—alive and dead—are highly integrated, as evidenced by the large number of shared attributes, especially in an inclusive and exclusive way. That is, alive things are those that have activities or have motion or are upright, whereas nonalive or dead things have the opposite attributes, which are those that have no motion or activities, and are asleep or lies down. And finally, the child has a fairly clear set of causes for what makes something alive (water, sun, seed) and what causes some things to die (old age, snow, cold temperature).

We have proposed elsewhere (Chi & Koeske, 1983; Gobbo & Chi, 1986) that a coherent structure is one that has many shared attributes between the key concepts. In the domain of dinosaurs, for example, expert children tend to use the presence and absence of a few salient features to decide whether a dinosaur is a meateater or a planteater. Hence, a dinosaur is a meateater if it has "long" and "sharp teeth," whereas it would be a planteater if these features were absent. Novice children of the same age (i.e., children who have less knowledge about dinosaurs), would have one set of attributes to decide whether a dinosaur is a meateater or not, and a separate set of attributes to decide whether or not it is a planteater. The use of one set of features to contrast two categories (meateaters and planteaters) suggested that the two categories are more coherently integrated in the expert children's knowledge representation than in the novice children's knowledge representation. This same characteristic of coherence is seen in our youngest subject's representation of dead and alive, suggesting that they see the two concepts as bipolar opposites.

An important question we want to answer from this representation is how we can understand why a given child can simultaneously answer Gelman et al.'s (1983) questions ("Can you run with a doll?" "No."), and yet incorrectly answer Piaget's question ("Is the mountain alive?" "Yes." "Why?" "It is when it makes a noise''). Our interpretation of such data is the following. From the representation of the child's protocol in Fig. 8.1, we can imagine that the child has never encountered such questions before, nor encountered such statements, so that such knowledge could not have been prestored. Therefore. in order to sensibly answer this question, the child must search the attributes in her representation that are associated with the ''alive'' concept, and postulate that the mountain is alive if it produces certain activities (such as making noise), because having the capability of producing activities is an attribute of aliveness for her. Her response protocols generally fit this characteristic—namely that she will postulate an attribute which is true of *alive* things, and state that the object in question is alive if it has that attribute. So for example, when we asked ''Is the stone alive?'', the child responded ''Yeah.'' ''Why is a stone alive?'' ''Because when it rolls I know how it is alive.'' (Presumably rolling is an activity that a stone is capable of producing. Therefore it is alive.)

What about the fact that the child can answer the Gelman et al.'s questions correctly? An ideal interpretation is to say that the reason the child can answer them correctly is because she has an implicit understanding of the concept of nonliving things, and one cannot do these things with nonliving things. That is, this interpretation would assume that the child has a hierarchical branch of nonliving things, as is shown in a hypothetical network (see Fig. 8.2, the portion of the semantic net that is depicted by the dotted lines). However, I think this would be endowing the child with greater understanding than is necessary. From such data, all one can really conclude is that the child has a ''doll'' node somewhere in memory, and associated with a doll node are attributes such as ''a doll can't run on its own,'' ''a doll can't talk unless there is a string to pull,'' and many others. So, when the child is confronted with a question such as ''Can you run with a doll?'', the child knows enough about properties of dolls to answer that question correctly. The concept of ''doll'' need not necessarily relate to their conception of living and nonliving things.

One additional thing we want to point out about Fig. 8.2 is that we believe redundant nodes do exist if they are embedded within a different microstructure. We conceptualize the ''alive'' and ''dead'' nodes as embedded within a localized coherent structure (the solid lines), and *movement* is an attribute discriminating dead from alive; yet we hypothesize that it is also an important attribute that people use to discriminate living from nonliving. Therefore, it is conceivable that movement can be represented by two separate nodes in this hypothetical network.

What kind of evidence do we need in order to be convinced that the child is sensitive to a distinction between living and nonliving things? That is, how can we assess the extent to which this child has a representation corresponding to the nonliving (dotted) branch for the tree, as shown in Fig. 8.2? One critical set of questions that we did not ask, which could provide such an assessment, would be to query the child about differences between dead things and nonliving things.

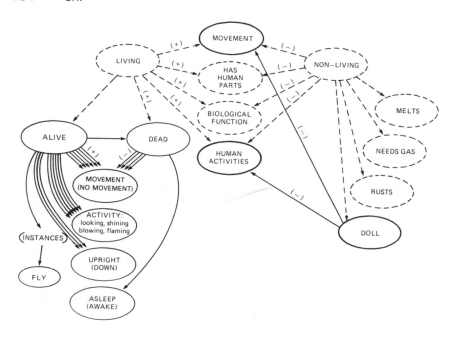

FIG. 8.2. A hypothetical representation embedding what the most naive child knows (the solid lines, taken from Fig. 1), with knowledge that the child presumably will acquire (the dotted lines).

For example, we could use an attribution paradigm of Carey's (1985), and ask the child questions such as: "If a dead cat has an omentum, would a tin can have it, versus would a bird have it?" We would predict that a child who is sensitive to the difference between living and nonliving objects would have a barrier in his or her pattern of attribution so that it would not cross the boundary between the left (LIVING) branch and the right (NONLIVING) branch of Fig. 8.2.

Although we argue that this child's microstructure of *alive* and *dead* concepts are fairly structured, coherent, and intact, what has to happen in order for this child to achieve the more mature structure in which she will correctly comprehend and discriminate living from nonliving things? Without looking at a more sophisticated subject's data, we can hypothesize that a more sophisticated structure would contain attributes that link the living with nonliving concepts in a contrasting way. Some of these shared attributes would initially be the characteristic ones, but with accumulation of greater biological knowledge, the child would come to learn the critical defining attributes.

Our oldest child subject's knowledge is represented in Fig. 8.3. Again, we did not try to capture all the utterances that she stated. But this partial representation does capture the gist of her statements. There are several major differences between her representation and that of our most naive child's (as shown in Fig.

8.1). First, this child does not map the word "not alive" onto the semantic of "dead." She correctly interprets not alive as nonliving, basically because she names the right kind of objects (such as doorknobs, clotheshanger) when we ask her for things that are not alive. Second, this child definitely uses human attributes (both human parts and human activities) as a critical feature to discriminate living from nonliving things, and movement alone is no longer a sufficient criterion. (In this representation, we indicated positive attributes with a plus sign and negative attributes with a minus sign at the links.) So for example, for this child, she claims that a cloud is not alive, and when asked why, she says "Cause it can't move. Well it can move by the wind. It can't talk. It doesn't have a face. It doesn't have a body. . . ." Therefore, she answered Piaget-type questions correctly because these objects (mountain, sun, wind, etc) do not possess human attributes or cannot perform human activities, even though they sometimes can move or can be moved. We further know that people and animals are her primary prototypes of living things because when asked "What would a flower have to be like for you to know it is alive?", she answered "Like a person. Or like a cat or a dog or an animal."

A third characteristic of her representation is that, although it is very coherent (that is, living things and nonliving things are contrasted by basically the same set of attributes), she has not acquired the defining attributes of living things (that is, the biological functions). Because *having human attributes* is still such a strong feature of living for her, she is just at the stage where she cannot resolve

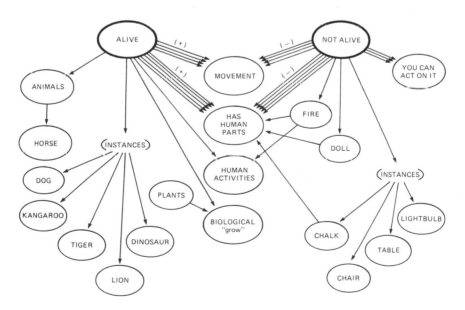

FIG. 8.3. A representation of the most mature child's knowledge.

the conflict about whether or not plants are alive. So for example, she claimed that flowers are not alive, and when probed why, she said she didn't know. But when we pushed her, as we saw earlier, her reason was that because a flower has to be like a person or an animal in order to be alive. Later on in the protocol (Session 3a), when asked if a given plant is alive, she first said no, then changed her mind, and then gave the reason that "Well, it's almost like a person . . . It can grow by itself, you have to water it. . . ." So, she is beginning to acquire some biological attributes of living things.

Figure 8.4 is a representation of an adult subject. Notice that the main attributes that this adult uses to contrast living from nonliving things are biological properties such as respiration, digestion, excretion, reproduction, growth, and movement. Thus, *having human attributes* and *human activities* which are present in the mature child's representation that was shown in (Fig. 8.3), have essentially been omitted in this adult's representation.

WHAT IS KNOWLEDGE REORGANIZATION?

Having seen three representations of the concept *alive,* what can we say about what is knowledge reorganization? What does it take to reorganize the knowledge of the sophisticated child (Fig. 8.3), to the knowledge of the adult subject (Fig. 8.4)? Our data is consistent with that presented by Carey, namely that children's primary prototype of living things focuses on people attributes (such

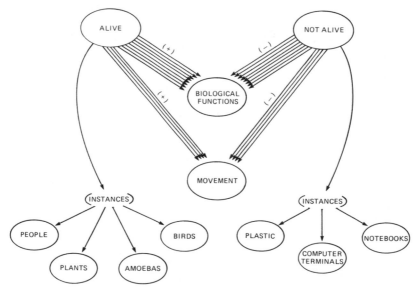

FIG. 8.4. A representation of an adult's knowledge.

as having human parts and human activities), but eventually they change or *reorganize* their knowledge so that the critical attributes contrasting living from nonliving things are biological functions. The critical issue is, how does this knowledge reorganization take place? Is the mechanism of restructuring a weak or radical one, as defined earlier?

From our data, I think we can postulate that the restructuring is a weak one. How can this take place? Well, one can imagine an incremental process by which children encounter a greater and greater number of instances of living things that do not have human parts, either through textbooks or being told. Therefore, over time and experience, the links associating living and nonliving things with "have human parts" or "have human activities" will not increase, whereas there will be an increasing number of links with the attributes of "biological function". This is not to say that the attributes of having human parts and human activities will actually be deleted from the knowledge structure, but only that these attributes will no longer be salient, in comparison to the build-up of biological functions as a salient attribute.

We know that characteristic features are not deleted from the knowledge representation because they are often cited to explain why an object is or is not alive. This may be because it is often easier to explain by using characteristic features than to cite the defining ones, especially when the defining ones are not robustly represented by the subject yet. So for example, even our adult subject first acknowledged that she knows that something is alive because "Uh, let's see, by movement," then elaborated by saying that "that's one way, except there are living things that don't move." Similarly, our sophisticated child subject, when asked why she thinks the wind is not alive, answered "Cause it doesn't have a face, and you can't see it, and but it can move." Therefore, the reorganization is a weak one in that additional concepts and links are accumulated over time, and this accumulation results in a different pattern of *emphasis* on the salient attributes. Some subset of core concepts are maintained, and the old theory (that something is alive because it moves) is abandoned, but it is not deleted. It is *abandoned* in the sense that it is not accessed, because a more salient set of attributes which can critically discriminate between living and nonliving objects has emerged and is accessed because of its dominance.

What about the reorganization from the most naive child's data (Fig. 8.1) to the more sophisticated child's data (Fig. 8.3)? What constitutes reorganization in this case? Although we do not have the critical data to defend our hypothesis, we can speculate and say that in order for the child to develop the structure in Fig. 8.3 from Fig. 8.1, the child must acquire additional structures (the dotted parts of Fig. 8.2), but the original microstructure of "alive" and "dead" remains intact. (That is, we believe that the dead–alive microstructure—the solid lines of Fig. 8.2, is available and present in the representation of the child's knowledge in Fig. 8.3. We cannot be certain that this is true because no data was gathered to query that part of the knowledge structure.)

In some sense, the issue remains: How does the child acquire the hierarchical distinction between living and nonliving things, given that she already has the lower-order distinction between dead and alive? In order to achieve this higher-order distinction (what we have sometimes called a superlink), the child needs to acquire some attributes (such as having human parts) which distinguish living from nonliving things, at least at the more advanced stage of understanding (as in the case of the child in Fig. 8.3). One way that this can happen is that we must assume that even the most naive child already has a few miscellaneous and isolated concepts of nonliving things, although they may not be integrated into a coherent microstructure. For example, even our youngest subject knows that dolls cannot run, and can name things that melt (ice, ice cream), things that rust (broken cans, broken cars). And she knows that none of these things possess any attributes of either human or other living things (as can be seen in the data in Table 8.2.) So eventually, the child will come to realize that the biological attributes listed in Table 8.2 will discriminate between one class of objects (living things) and another class of objects (nonliving things). This *realization* can be achieved by the acquisition of new links, as well as the reorganization of existing links in the sense of accentuating the prominence of some links and diminishing the strengths of others.

HOW KNOWLEDGE WAS STORED INITIALLY

This research mainly proposes that when knowledge is not accessible, it is because it was not properly stored in the first place. One way to show this, as was stated earlier, is to demonstrate that people who can retrieve the knowledge have represented it differently than those who do not. I believe the animism examples serve to illustrate this point. An alternative method, is to show that people who can retrieve and access the relevant knowledge are those who stored it properly in the first place. That is, during encoding, they have represented the knowledge in a way that is more accessible and usable later. In order to support such a claim, one has to design studies that capture knowledge representation as it is encoded during storage, and then relate it to how it is retrieved and used later. I will briefly describe a project that uses this methodology.

One project attempts to understand the sources of individual differences in the way students learn to solve physics problems. That is, for students who have comparable backgrounds, why do some students learn to solve problems better than others. Again, our answer lies in the hypothesis that good students are those who have stored procedures that are more "complete" and elaborated in some sense, so that their procedures can be accessed more readily in other problem contexts. By more complete and elaborated we mean that the rules or procedures that the student has stored while studying an example in a text has complete conditions for its use (when the conditions are not explicitly spelled out), as well as more complete implications of what else may be true, beyond the explicit

statements actually made in the text or in the worked-out examples. More specifically, we are observing how beginning students study worked-out examples
presented in the fifth chapter of a physics textbook by Halliday and Resnick
(1974). To do so, we asked students to think aloud while reading and studying
worked-out examples in Chapter 5, after having mastered the contents of Chapters 1–4. Our general prediction is that good students elaborate to a greater extent
than less successful students while studying a worked-out example, especially at
locations in the example where the reason for the use of a procedure is not clearly
explained. We surmised that studying a worked-out example in a physics problem will provide very rich protocol data because unlike algebra problems, where
sequential steps in an example problem can be used to induce a rule (Neves,
1981), physics problem examples are much more complex in the extent or degree
of reasoning involved. In algebra, for example, if two successive statements in
an example show the following steps

$$4X = 20,$$

$$X = 5$$

then the student needs to induce the rule that when X is not isolated on one side of
the equal sign, and if X has an integer multiplying it, then divide both sides of the
equation by that integer. Neves' production system can succeed in inducing this
kind of syntactic rule quite readily. Two successive statements (Statements 6 and 7
of Fig. 8.5) of a physics example are the following:

F_A, F_B, F_C are all the forces acting on the body.

Since the body is unaccelerated, $F_A + F_B + F_C = 0.$

It is not straightforward to understand why $F_A, F_B,$ and F_C are all the forces
acting on the body, nor why it is unaccelerated (that, however, can be inferred
from the statement in the problem that the body is at rest), and therefore the sum
of the forces should be zero. Perhaps the difference in difficulty of reasoning
between an algebraic problem and a physics problem is that in algebra, at least
the kind of problems Neves worked with, the student needs to induce a numerical
operation, whereas in the kind of physics problems we are dealing with, the
student has to induce the rationale underlying the construction of the mental
model of the problem.

Analyses of the transcripts (protocols) showed that, consistent with the general prediction, the most successful learners (as determined by subsequent problem-solving successes as well as general grade point average), elaborated extensively through self-explanations during the reading of each statement of the
worked-out example. The poorest students, on the other hand, almost never
added any explanations. Furthermore, the successful solvers produced the greatest number of explanations at places where justifications for a particular step
were not clearly spelled out.

The most interesting analysis is to understand the characteristics of the expla-

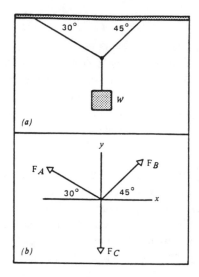

Figure 5-6 Example 5. *(a)* A block of weight *W* is suspended by strings. *(b)* A free-body diagram showing all the forces acting on the knot. The strings are assumed to be weightless.

1. Figure 5-6a shows an object of weight W hung by massless strings.

2. Consider the knot at the junction of the three strings to be "the body".

3. The body remains at rest under the action of the three forces shown Fig. 5-6.

4. Suppose we are given the magnitude of one of these forces.

5. How can we find the magnitude of the other forces?

6. F_A, F_B, and F_C are *all* the forces acting on the body.

7. Since the body is unaccelerated, $F_A + F_B + F_C = 0$

8. Choosing the x- and y-axes as shown, we can write this vector equation as three scalar equations:

9. $F_{Ax} + F_{Bx} = 0$,

10. $F_{Ay} + F_{By} + F_{Cy} = 0$

11. using Eq. 5-2. The third scalar equation for the z-axis is simply:

12. $F_{As} = F_{Bs} = F_{Cs} = 0$.

13. That is, the vectors all lie in the x-y plane so that they have no z components.

14.   From the figure we see that

15. $F_{Ax} = -F_A \cos 30^\circ = -0.866 F_A$,

16. $F_{Ay} = F_A \sin 30^\circ = 0.500 F_A$,

17. and

18. $F_{Bx} = F_B \cos 45^\circ = 0.707 F_B$,

19. $F_{By} = F_B \sin 45^\circ = 0.707 F_B$.

FIG. 8.5.   An example taken directly from a physics text (Halliday & Resnick, 1974).

nation. We find that students who are successful at subsequent problem solving are those who are building *rich* rules during the studying of the worked-out examples. They tend to do one of three things. They often add new relations that were not specified in the example. That is, the students add knowledge to their representations by inferring additional information beyond that presented. For example, in Fig. 8.5, which is an actual example taken from a text (Halliday & Resnick 1974), after reading Statement 3, the student said "So, that means that they have to cancel out, only the body would not be at rest." Another good student inferred, after reading Statements 4 and 5, "So the sum of the forces should be zero." It is easy to see how the rules stored by these successful students are more complete and enriched because of the additions of new relations of these kinds.

Another way that good students elaborate is to specify or expand the conditions under which a procedure is to be applied. For example, after reading Statement 8, one student said, "So it's convenient because you save one of the . . ., you put one of the axis on one of the force's . . . line, on the W force." This is an extremely important specification of the condition under which the reference frame (the coordinate axes) was chosen as shown in the lower panel of the free-body diagram in Fig. 8.5. The building of this kind of rule can explain why under slightly different problem conditions, the good students who have built this kind of rule can know how to choose a reference frame, whereas a poor student who did not build such a rule may associate the choice of the reference frame simply with the vertical and horizontal components of the diagram. Thus, a poor student will not know what to do in situations where the forces are slightly rotated from the ones shown in the figure. We actually have such evidence.

Notice that statement 8 simply provided the action part of a procedure (we are assuming that a procedure is a condition-action rule). Statement 8 stated only that one should choose the x- and y-axes as shown, without providing the conditions under which such a choice would be made. Therefore, what the student did in this case was to expand on the conditions under which such an action should be taken. Without providing the explicit conditions, the learner would have stored a rule that has no specific conditions attached to its action. This would create difficulties later, when the student would not know when or how one should choose a specific reference frame and what constraints to consider. In some of our previous work, we have seen evidence that unsuccessful learners have rules with no specific conditions (see also Chi, Glaser, & Rees, 1982). Expanding on the conditions of a procedure allows the good learner to build complete rules for subsequent use in a problem-solving context.

A third kind of explanation that good learners make is to recognize that a set of specific procedures serve the same goal. As a result, a procedural "chunk" is formed and the learner avoids being immersed in detail. After reading Statement 14, for example, one good student said, "Now they are going to do the same thing with it to the y," meaning that the equations of Statement 14 describe what has to be done to Force A in the y direction in the same way that it was done to Force A in the x direction in Statement 13. Hence, what the student has done is define a goal of what this set of equations accomplishes, and then proceeded to elaborate on what these equations actually mean. Her subsequent elaborations were "In the y axis, and umm, they are going to say that this times sine, so x is sine, or y is sine, at this angle. And here the angle is here is equal to, yeah okay, I'll agree with that. Umm, sine 30, okay, .5 times the force." We consider the initial elaboration after reading Statement 14 a way of understanding the global intent of the equations before proceeding to unpack the details. This allows the students to *see* that the next set of procedures serves the same goal and to generalize the purpose of a set of specific procedures.

The characteristics of the explanations that we have identified clearly suggest that in order for students to fully understand each statement of a worked-out example, they must explain the implications, the conditions, and the goals of the procedures. That is, they must infer what is true after reading each statement or set of statements, explain why a procedure is applied in the way specified, and apply a general goal to a set of detailed procedures. By engaging in such explanations, the good students are storing more complete rules that can be accessed and used in later problem-solving situations. For instance, by supplying and specifying the conditions under which one chooses a reference frame, a student will be more able to decide later how a reference frame should be chosen in a problem-solving situation. Hence, the success with which he or she uses and accesses that procedure depends on how it was stored initially. The actual linkage between the exact procedure the student has stored and whether it is subsequently used will be an analysis that we will pursue. (For other findings concerning the role of self-explanations, see Chi, Bassok, Lewis, Reimann, & Glaser, in press).

CONCLUSION

In summary, this chapter attempts to present a framework in which lack of access is seen as a mismatch between the way the relevant knowledge is actually represented, and the conditions under which it has to be retrieved. The possibilities of how knowledge can be reorganized so that it can be accessed are also proposed. Basically, the idea is that not only are new concept nodes and links acquired with experience, but a reorganization can also occur as a result of a changing shift in emphasis of what might constitute the relevant discriminating features between concepts. Such reorganization must be considered to be one of the novice-to-expert shift kind, and not a radical one.

Using the example from children's concept of living and nonliving things, we also argue that the apparent contradictions in children's ability to answer Piaget's type of questions incorrectly and Gelman et al.'s type of questions correctly has to do with how their knowledge of these concepts are represented. Mappings of two children's and an adult's knowledge, as gathered from their protocols, are presented to illustrate the point. The main idea is that responses are determined by what parts of the knowledge structure are probed, as well as what attributes are linked to the concepts. In order to decide whether children truly have an implicit understanding of living versus nonliving things, questions have to be designed to probe *not* only the local nodes, but the hierarchical structure itself. Many studies, including our own, have not accomplished this.

I have also discussed alternative ways of demonstrating that lack of access may have to do with a mismatch of the context of conditions under which the relevant knowledge is stored, and the conditions under which it has to be retrieved, by presenting another line of research that is underway. Hopefully, both tactics will converge on a better understanding of what it means to say that the relevant knowledge is there but not accessible.

ACKNOWLEDGMENT

I am grateful for comments and contributions provided by Robbie Case, Rochel Gelman, Peter Gordon, Mary Means, Terry Greene, Clauss Strauch, Anne Robin, and Mark Detweiler.

REFERENCES

Berzonsky, M. (1971). The role of familiarity in children's explanations of physical causality. *Child Development, 42,* 705–715.

Carey, S. (1986). *Childhood animism revisited: On the acquisition of natural kind terms.* Cambridge, MA: Bradford Books.

Case, R. (1985). *Intellectual development: Birth to adulthood.* New York: Academic Press.

Chi, M. T. H., Bassok, M., Lewis, M., Reimann, P., & Glaser, R. (in press). Self-explanations: How students study and use examples in learning problem solving. *Cognitive Science.*

Chi, M. T. H., Glaser, R., & Rees, E. (1982). Expertise in problem solving. In R. Sternberg (Ed.), *Advances in the psychology of human intelligence* (Vol. 1, pp. 7–75). Hillsdale, NJ: Lawrence Erlbaum Associates.

Chi, M. T. H., & Koeske, R. D. (1983). Network representation of a child's dinosaur knowledge. *Developmental Psychology, 19*(1), 29–39.

Chi, M. T. H., & Rees, E. (1983). A learning framework for development. *Contributions to Human Development, 9,* 71–107.

Gelman, R., & Baillargeon, R. (1983). A review of some Piagetian concepts. In P. H. Mussen (Ed.), *Handbook of child psychology* (pp. 231–262). New York: Wiley.

Gelman, R., Spelke, E., & Meck, E. (1983). What preschoolers know about animate and inanimate objects. In D. Rogers & J. A. Sloboda (Eds.), *The acquisition of symbolic skills.*, (pp. 297–326). New York: Plenum Press.

Gobbo, C., & Chi, M. T. H. (1986). How knowledge is structured and used by expert and novice children. *Cognitive Development, 3,* 221–237.

Golinkoff, R., & Harding, C. (1980). *Infants' expectations of the movement potential of inanimate objects.* Paper presented at the International Conference on Infant Studies, New Haven, CT.

Halliday, D., & Resnick, R. (1974). *Fundamentals of physics* (2nd ed.). New York: Wiley.

Keil, F. C. (1979). *Semantic and conceptual development: An ontological perspective.* Cambridge, MA: Harvard University Press.

Laurendeau, M., & Pinard, A. (1982). *Causal thinking in the child: A genetic and experimental approach.* New York: International University Press.

Lawler, R. W. (1981). The progressive constructions of mind. *Cognitive Science, 5,* 1–30.

Markman, E. M., & Hutchinson, J. E. (1984). Children's sensitivity to constraints on word meaning: Taxonomic versus thematic relations. *Cognitive Psychology, 16,* 1–27.

McCloskey, M. (1983). Naive theories of motion. In D. Gentner & A. L. Stevens (Eds.), *Mental models.* (pp. 299–324). Hillsdale, NJ: Lawrence Erlbaum Associates.

Neves, D. (1981). *Learning procedures from examples.* Unpublished doctoral dissertation, Carnegie-Mellon University.

Piaget, J. (1930). *The child's conception of physical causality.* London: Routledge & Kegan Paul.

Piaget, J. (1951). *The child's conception of the world.* London: Routledge & Kegan Paul.

Richards, D., & Siegler, R. (1984). The effects of task requirements on children's life judgments. *Child Development, 55,* 1687–1696.

Smiley, S. S., & Brown, A. L. (1979). Conceptual preference for thematic or taxonomic relations: A monotomic age trend from preschool to old age. *Journal of Child Psychology, 28*(2), 249–257.

Story Comprehension and Memorization by Children: The Role of Input-, Conservation-, and Output Processes

G. Denhière
Groupe TEXTIMA
Université de Paris VIII

The current state of knowledge in the area of text processing has resulted from simultaneous progress in connected sciences, including linguistics, artificial intelligence, and cognitive psychology. For example:

• the work of linguists (Brémond, 1973; Grimes, 1975; Labov & Waletzky, 1967) has inspired psychological hypotheses about the representation of textual structures in human memory (Clements, 1979; Kintsch & van Dijk, 1978; Meyer, 1975);

• concepts formulated by computer scientists such as frames, scripts, and augmented transition networks (Woods, 1980) have directly influenced conceptualizations of human processing of semantic information (Black & Bower, 1980; DeBeaugrande, 1980);

• psychological considerations have guided the construction of computer programs devoted to the understanding of natural language. For instance, results of psychological experiments (Black, Bower, & Turner, 1979) have prompted Schank (1982) to modify his original definition of "scripts" and to introduce the idea of MOP (Memory Organization Package).

Considering the field of cognitive psychology alone, we can see that its evolution and interaction with other connected sciences have enabled it to progress in such a way that its most prevalent former criticisms are rendered obsolete. For instance, some of those early criticisms concerned the artificiality of experimental situations, the use of nonsignificant verbal materials as stimuli, and the nonrepresentativeness of the psychological processes implied in these artificial situations.

The story-situation is one example of a research tool that is representative of a large class of psychological activities carried out by individuals in normal circumstances and, as such, cannot be subject to criticisms of artificiality (Ashmead & Perlmutter, 1980). More specifically,

• the materials used are complex verbal materials, structured according to syntactic and semantic rules;

• the *same* story can be presented either with verbal language, pictures (Cession, Kilen, Denhière, & Rondal, 1984; Langevin, 1980, 1982), or with film (Baggett, 1975);

• the materials which are used are not solely developed for experimental purposes; they belong to the cultural heritage which is transmitted from generation to generation;

• the story-situation corresponds to a regular modality of exchange between parents and children, and *telling a story* is often part of the ritual of *lulling to sleep* the young child;

• the story-situation is an integral part of the verbal interaction between adults and, in Europe, numerous popular radio and television programs;

• the story-situation holds an important place in school life: The pupil is often required to build and retain the global meaning of a text and afterwards to report this meaning in his own words, rather than learning by rote.

From the viewpoint of analytical research, the story-situation is one of those rare situations that can be used with very young children and with adults, regardless of age. Moreover, by means of adequate experimental manipulations, either of formal or content characteristics of texts, or of some aspects of the situation, it is possible to obtain information about the knowledge structures implied, and about the processes which use these knowledge structures.

If we temporarily set aside the social and pragmatic aspects of text comprehension and restrict ourselves to its psychological aspects we see that the research of the last 10 years has lead to a definition of comprehension as an interaction between a text and a reader/hearer (Denhière, 1984). The researcher who has placed the most emphasis on this active and constructive characteristic of understanding is probably Kintsch (Kintsch, 1974; Kintsch & Vipond, 1979; Miller & Kintsch, 1980). In other words, understanding a text does not simply consist of the mapping of textual structures in the mind of a reader, taken as a passive receptacle; rather, when a person reads a text, he or she is engaged in a series of complex activities which proceed from perceptive analysis of physical features or patterns such as letters or phonemes to semantic integration of new information with previous knowledge (Black & Bower, 1980; DeBeaugrande & Miller, 1980; Kintsch & van Dijk, 1978; Meyer, 1975; Meyer & Rice, 1982; Rumelhart, 1975, 1977; Thorndyke, 1977). An individual constructs not only a linguistic representation of successive statements of a text, but also a representation of the semantic content of the text and/or the situation evoked by the text (see Sanford & Garrod, 1981, and van Dijk & Kintsch, 1983, for two distinct positions on this last question).

Figure 9.1 portrays the main elements composing the interaction between the text and the individual. We limit ourselves here to narrative texts (DeBeaugrande, 1980; van Dijk, 1980). A narrative text consists of a representation of an event or a series of events, fictional or real, by means of language. Generally, a narrative text is often comprised of a *story* and representations of objects or characters which constitute the *description* (Bremond, 1973; Genette, 1966). The text variables can be divided into two broad categories: *Form* and *Content*. We have adopted an analytical analysis for each category (Clark & Clark, 1977). Although it has some drawbacks, this kind of exposition—from elementary units to the most complex—has the advantage of showing the different levels of analysis which are of interest. Within the content category, psychologists have examined semantic features or primitives (Gentner, 1978; Le Ny, 1976); concepts (Ehrlich & Florin, 1981), propositions (Anderson, 1980; Denhière, 1976), and macrostructures (Stein, 1982; Stein & Glenn, 1982). Finally the dichotomy Form–Content avoids the confusion between narrative superstructures and semantic macrostructures (Adam, 1984; van Dijk, 1980).

Concerning these two concepts, the fact that many narratives have common

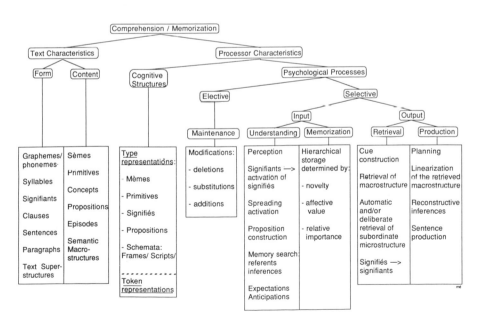

FIG. 9.1. Schematic representation of the main elements involved in text comprehension and memorization. (See text for details.)

content structures could be due to author characteristics, or reader characteristics. That is, the authors of these narratives might have common mental structures which lead them to produce similarly structured stories; or, on the other hand, hearers/readers have common mental structures which, because of social regulations such as reinforcement, lead them to favor the production of such similarly structured stories by the authors, or the survival of those stories which agreed with their mental structures (see Kintsch & Greene, 1978; Mandler, Scribner, Cole, & DeForest, 1980). At present, we are most interested in the second possibility; namely, that mental structures common to people of a specific culture govern and guide their processes of understanding and memorization of narratives. If this hypothesis is true, we must study the acquisition and the development of these structures and processes.

The "individual" branch of the tree presented in Fig. 9.1 lists most of the cognitive structures and the processes which have been recognized as influential factors in text processing.

If we discard the idiosyncratic variables, differences observed between original narratives and the stories later recalled by individuals can be ascribed to any of the three successive stages described below:

1. The input stage, including:
Perception, i.e., identification of miniunits of the surface structure of the text (letters, phonemes, syllables, words); *Comprehension,* i.e., the on-line building of the local and global meaning as one processes the narrative. These activities include:

• passage from the perceptual features of a word to the concept which is attached and the activation of this concept (Pynte & Denhière, 1982);

• construction of elementary propositions which relate concepts in an organized manner (predicates and arguments);

• memory searches to resolve problems of reference (Sanford & Garrod, 1982) and to produce bridging inferences (Clark, 1975, 1977) which are necessary to link adjacent propositions or sequences of propositions;

• the activation of formal or content schemata that guide and control the previous activities in the sense that they help to anticipate, to determine the most important propositions, and to establish semantic coherence between parts of a paragraph, an episode, and progressively, among parts of the text as a whole;

Memorization (more or less intentional according to task requirements) of the hierarchical meaningful structure which results from the previous processing and which is dependent on the degree of novelty, the affective value (Martins, 1982), and the relative importance (Clements, 1979; Denhière, 1982a; Omanson, 1982; Waters, 1983) of the information.

2. The conservation stage.

3. The output stage, including:

Retrieval of stored semantic, and occasionally phonemic and syntactic, information. Some cues (Johnson, 1982) permit access to the semantic macrostructure built during the input stage (Anderson, 1982; Anderson & Pichert, 1978; Pichert & Anderson, 1977). Search of subordinated propositions is initiated from the macrostructural retrieved information, and missing links are constructed or reconstructed (Spiro, 1977). *Production* of a new narrative if recall is requested. This production, which consists of a linearisation of the retrieved structures (Piolat & Denhière, 1984), must conform to syntactic and semantic rules of language (sentence schemata) and to the rules of construction of narratives (story schemata).

Following Le Ny (1980), we distinguish between selective and elective losses, and transformations of meaning units. The first results from active processes, i.e., collecting and processing information, mainly during the input and output phases (see Fig. 9.1). In contrast, transformations of units are attributable to passive or quasi-passive phenomena, such as forgetting and mnemonic restructuring occurring during the conservation stage. Obviously, this evolution of forgetting and restructuring is a function of the internal preexistent organization of the individual's knowledge- and belief-structures.

Although the individual's affective-motivational structures play an important role in comprehension (Bower, 1981; Denhière & Legros, 1983; Martins, 1981), we restrict our present discussion to cognitive structures. These cognitive structures have several levels of organization in the individual's semantic memory, permitting him to collect, process, conserve, and retrieve information (Mandler, 1979, 1983; Nelson, 1977, 1978, 1979). Five levels of these structures are necessary to explain semantic phenomena:

- semantic features (Clark, 1973) or mèmes (Cordier & Denhière, 1978, Le Ny, 1975, 1978);
- signifies (or, in the broad sense, concepts);
- semantic propositions, i.e., predicates and arguments (Anderson, 1980);
- frames (Minsky, 1975) or scripts (Schank & Abelson, 1977);
- text-meaning or semantic macrostructures (Kintsch, 1977).

We postulate that every structure of a given level enters in the structure of a superior one according to a determined hierarchization; we further predict that this hierarchization determines the selective and elective phenomena arising in the individual's perception, comprehension, conservation, and recall.

The above discussion about cognitive structures and processes implied in text processing applies to adults or, more precisely, to asymptotic subjects. However, the factors listed in Fig. 9.1 can be considered as so many sources of performance variation. Therefore, these factors can be examined from a differential or developmental viewpoint (Denhière & Langevin, 1981). We now undertake this task, restricting ourselves to experimental studies of some of the processes mentioned above (see Nelson, this volume, for a study of cognitive structures). We are aware of the shortcomings inherent in the proposed dichotomy between structures and processes. This tentative distinction leaves some crucial problems unanswered, such as:

- How many mnemonic stores must be postulated?
- What constraints are imposed on processes by knowledge structures?
- How is the allocation of cognitive resources to the different subsystems of the processing system controlled?
- How are automatic and deliberated processes controlled?

Our discussion focuses on two well-established experimental phenomena, which we call *Age-effect* and *Level-effect*. Several experimental paradigms have been used to determine the respective roles of input-, conservation-, and output processes in these two effects.

Only one type of text, narrative texts, has been used in these experiments. The narrative texts were analyzed at several levels of organization, especially micro- and macro-structural, but here we are mainly interested in the micro-level, the level of semantic propositions.

DEVELOPMENTAL STUDIES: AGE-EFFECT AND LEVEL-EFFECT

Two recall experiments are briefly described to illustrate the two effects. The first experiment was an immediate free-recall experiment (Denhière, 1979). The narrative, entitled "Gargantua," consisted of two independent episodes, "boat" and "house," which contained 30 and 47 underlying propositions respectively. The narrative and its predicative analysis are shown in Table 9.1.

Five groups of 25 children participated in this experiment. Mean ages of the five groups were 7, 8, 9, 10, and 11 years. The story was read aloud twice, and immediate free recall was required after each reading. Three main results should be noted:

(a) 7- and 8-year-olds' performance was significantly inferior to that of the three older groups: their performances reached only half that of older children (18 vs. 37, and 29 vs. 50 accepted propositions after first and second recalls, respectively).

TABLE 9.1
Text and Predicative Analysis of the "Gargantua" Narrative

Once upon a time, there was a giant named Gargantua. He was good and he liked to help poor people.

"boat" episode:
  One day, he was seated on a cliff. He soaked his feet in the water to wash them. The sun shone and he was hot. In his two cupped hands, he took some water to refresh himself. At the same time he grasped also a sailboat sailing nearby. When he drank, the masts tickled his throat. He told himself that he swallowed a speck of dust.

"house" episode:
  Another day, when he walked in the forest, he saw a poor old woman who was gathering dead firewood. He decided to help her. In a moment he uprooted some of the most beautiful oaks of the forest and tied them with a rope. He took the faggot and balanced it on his shoulder. The road was long and he was very happy to lay his faggot down against the wall of the old woman's house. Alas! The house fell in. The poor old woman had wood to warm herself now but she no longer had a house to shelter her.

"boat" episode:

11.TO SEAT (al)
12.ON (11, a3)
13.ONE DAY (11)
14.TO SOAK (al, a4)
15.PART OF (al, a4)
16.IN (14, a5)
17.TO WASH (al, a4)
18.FOR (14, 17)
19.TO SHINE (@1)
20.HOT (al)
21.AND (19, 20)
22.TO TAKE (al, a5)
23.SOME (a5)
24.IN (22, a6)
25.PART OF (a6, al)
26.TWO (a6)
27.CUPPED (a6)
28.TO REFRESH HIMSELF (al)
29.FOR (22, 28)
30.TO SAIL (a7)
31.SAME TIME (22, 30)
32.TO GRASP (al, a7)
33.ALSO (a5, a7)
34.TO DRINK (al, a5)
35.TO TICKLE (a8, a9)
36.PART OF (a8, a7)
37.PART OF (a9, al)
38.WHEN (34, 35)
39.TO SWALLOW (al, al0)
40.TO TELL HIMSELF (al, 39)

al : giant   a6 : hands
a3 : cliff   a7 : sailboat
a4 : feet   a8 : masts
a5 : water   a9 : throat
@1 : Sun   al0: speck of
                  dust

"house" episode:

11.TO WALK (al)
12.IN (11, all)
13.TO SEE (al, al2)
14.POOR (al2)
15.TO GATHER (al2, al3)
16.DEAD (al3)
17.WHEN (11, 13)
18.A DAY (11)
19.ANOTHER (18)
20.TO DECIDE (al, 20)
21.TO HELP (al, all)
22.TO UPROOT (al, al4)
23.BEAUTIFUL (al4)
24.THE MOST (23)
25.SOME (al4)
26.PART OF (25, 23)
27.PART OF (al4, all)
28.IN A MOMENT (22)
29.TO TIE (al, al4)
30.WITH (29, al5)
31.AND (22, 29)
32.TO TAKE (al, al6)
33.TO BALANCE (al, al6)
34.ON (33, al7)
35.PART OF (al7, al)
36.AND (32, 33)
37.LONG (al8)
38.HAPPY (al)
39.VERY (38)
40.TO LAY DOWN (al, al6)

41.AGAINST (40, al9)
42.PART OF (al9, a20)
43.TO POSSESS (al2, a20)
44.OLD (al20
45.CAUSE (38, 40)
46.AND (37, 38)
47.ALAS
48.TO FALL IN (a20)
49.TO HAVE (al2, a20)
50.TO WARMHERSELF (al2)
51.FOR (49, 50)
52.NOW (49)
53.TO HAVE (al2, a20)
54.NO LONGER (53)
55.TO SHELTER (al2)
56.FOR (43, 45)
57.BUT (49, 53)

all : forest   al6 : faggot
al2 : woman   al7 : shoulder
al3 : firewood al8 : road
al4 : oaks   al9 : wall
al5 : rope   a20 : house

TABLE 9.2
Mean Numbers of Recalled and Accepted Propositions for the Five Age Groups.
Among Accepted Propositions, Those Identicial and Similar to the Text-
Base Were Coded Separately

	FIRST RECALL					SECOND RECALL				
Groups	7	8	9	10	11	7	8	9	10	11
Recalled	24.9	27.3	45.5	44.1	51.0	36.4	43.0	58.5	54.7	62.5
Accepted	17.0	18.9	35.3	35.0	41.6	26.2	31.8	50.1	46.0	53.3
Identical	9.8	11.2	23.1	22.6	28.9	16.2	20.8	37.3	35.1	42.6
Similar	7.2	7.7	12.2	12.4	12.7	10.0	11.0	12.8	10.9	11.7
% $\frac{\text{Accepted}}{\text{Recalled}}$	68.4	70.3	77.4	79.8	81.9	71.7	74.9	84.7	84.5	87.2
% $\frac{\text{Identical}}{\text{Accepted}}$	54.7	55.4	64.2	64.4	69.1	59.3	62.4	71.4	76.6	77.6

The text-base (see Table 9.1) included 87 propositions. The two lower lines of the table refer to the mean percentages of accepted propositions to recalled ones and to the mean percentages of identical propositions to accepted ones (Denhiere, 1980, p.231).

This is an example of the *age-effect*. The increase in performance results from an increase in the number of recalled identical propositions, as is shown in Table 9.2.

(b) If we regard only those propositions that have been recalled by more than half the subjects of each group, we can observe that these propositions belong to the macrostructure of the episodes, even if the performances of the youngest groups are far from achieving recall of the complete semantic macrostructure (see Figs. 9.2 and 9.3).

(c) The similarity in recall performances among the five age groups is confirmed by the correlations computed between the accepted recalled propositions for the five groups. All the computed correlations differ significantly from zero ($p<.01$) and, for the "boat" episode, the values of these correlations decrease as the difference between the age groups increase (see Table 9.3).

TABLE 9.3
Correlations Between the Frequency of Recall of the Five Age-Groups
for the "Boat" and "House" Episodes of the "Gargantua" Narrative

	"Boat"					"House"				
Age	7	8	9	10	11	Age	7	8	9	10	11
7	--	.90	.76	.66	.55	7	--	.93	.85	.91	.91
8	.81	--	.70	.63	.49	8	.90	--	.86	.92	.90
9	.69	.71	--	.81	.70	9	.84	.73	--	.89	.90
10	.78	.77	.79	--	.77	10	.91	.82	.90	--	.95
11	.55	.71	.85	.65	--	11	.91	.84	.88	.94	--

First recall on the upper part of the diagonal, and second recall on the lower part of the diagonal.

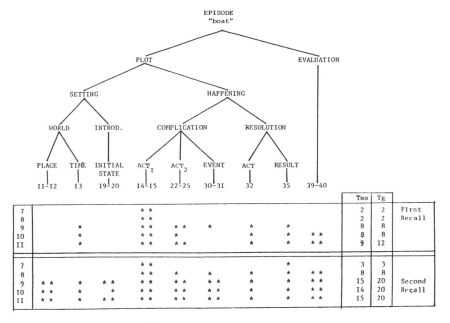

FIG. 9.2. Propositions recalled by more than half of the children of each age group. (Tms: propositions which belong to the macrostructure; Tg: total number of recalled propositions. The numbers below the story constituents refer to the number in the predicative analysis.)

LEVEL-EFFECT

The second recall experiment was devoted to the "level-effect" (Kintsch, 1974). Four narratives were constructed whose statements can be classified according to three levels of decreasing importance:

• kernel-statements (K) expressed the semantic macrostructure of the narratives, and contained 55 underlying propositions;
• important expansion-statements (E.1) were subordinated to kernel statements, and contained 65 underlying propositions;
• nonimportant expansion-statements (E.2) were subordinated to E.1 statements and contained the same number of propositions (n=65).

As shown in Table 9.4 each narrative was composed of a series of triplets, K–E.1–E.2, which were always presented in the same order. The four narratives were equivalent in linguistic signs, words, sentences, underlying propositions,

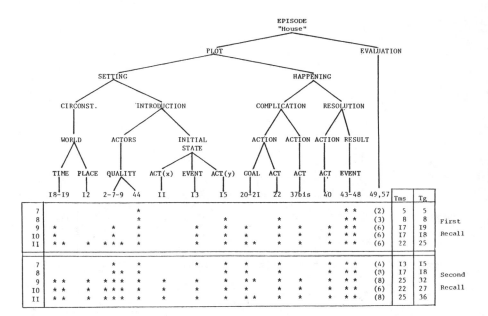

FIG. 9.3. Propositions recalled by more than half of the children of each age group. (Tms: propositions which belong to the macrostructure; Tg: total number of recalled propositions. The numbers below the story constituents refer to the number in the predicative analysis.)

and number of different arguments, but differed in number of episodes "Bear-Cub," " "Bull" and "Giant" and "Spider" and the nature of the links between the two two-episodes stories.

The results of two groups of children 8.6 and 9.6 years old show a clear level-effect. The mean percentages of recalled propositions decreased steadily from kernel-statements to expansion-statements, from 33.4% to 4.8% for the youngest group of children, as shown in Table 9.5.

The hierarchy of adult performances (n=40) in an incidental learning situation were similar to those of the children, with the following mean percentages of recalled propositions: 54.0%, 27.6% and 17.7% for kernel (K), important expansions (E.1), and nonimportant expansions (E.2), respectively (Denhière, 1987). Thus, given the same number of underlying propositions, both children and adults are sensitive to variations in the episodic structure of narratives, and in the relative importance of information in narratives. We do not consider the influence of the episodic structure here; instead we concentrate on explanations of the age-effect and the level-effect.

How can these effects be explained? As stated earlier, we consider input-, conservation-, and output processes to be responsible (Britton, Meyer, Simpson, Holdredge, & Curry, 1979).

TABLE 9.4
Excerpt of the "Gargantua" Narrative ("House" Episode)

"house" episode:

K   : The giant walked in the forest.
E.1: It was a magnificent forest.
E.2: Trees of all sizes mingled their foliages.

K   : The giant/He was a poor old woman who gathered dead wood.
E.1: The giant/He decided to help her.
E.2: Dressed in old clothes, the woman/she was bent double.

K   : The giant/He uprooted some oaks in a moment.
E.1: The giant/He tied them up with a thick rope.
E.2: The oaks/They were some of the most beautiful oaks of the forest.

K   : The giant/He went with the woman up to her very door
E.1: The road was long and the oaks were heavy.
E.2: The old woman could not keep up with him.

K = kernel statement; E.1 = important expansion-statement; E.2 = nonimportant
expansion-statement.

INPUT PROCESSES

We first report a study that examined how subjects of different ages explicitly attribute relative importance to the statements of a narrative, and compared this behavioral expression with free recall of these same narratives. Eight-year-old children, 11-year-old children, and adults were asked to judge the relative importance of idea units in the narratives (Denhière & Le Ny, 1980). Four 1-episode narratives were used. Each narrative was divided into 22 sentences, and subjects identified which of the eight they considered *most important* in each narrative, i.e., "the ones that would most completely relate the whole story." After this task was completed, the subjects identified the eight *least important* sentences.

TABLE 9.5
Mean Percentages of Recalled Propositions as a Function
of Their Relative Importance

Levels of Importance	Bear-Cub (1)	Spider (3)	Bull (2)	Giant (2)	Mean
K (n=55)	30.1	33.8	31.3	38.3	33.4
(A) E.1. (n=65)	4.8	17.1	8.4	12.3	10.6
E.2. (n=65)	3.1	4.1	3.8	8.3	4.8
K (n=55)	50.3	54.5	50.5	60.5	54.0
(B) E.1. (n=65)	18.7	28.1	28.5	34.6	27.6
E.2. (n=65)	11.2	23.7	11.1	24.7	17.7

K = kernel statements; E.1 = important expansion-statements; E.2 = non-important expansion-statements for the four narratives (A: children; B: adults).

Three main results will be highlighted:

1. The mean number of sentences chosen by at least 50% of the subjects increased with age: 4.75, 6.75, and 8.00 for 8-year-olds, 11-year-olds, and adults, respectively.

2. The mean correlation values between each pair of groups differ significantly from zero as can be seen in Table 9.6. Further, the adults' judgments are in closer agreement with the 11-year-old children's judgments than with the 8-year-old children's judgments. Second, the correlations between the two children's groups are lower than those obtained between adults and 11-year-olds.

3. The correlations between importance ratings and free recall of the same four narratives by three other children groups (7, 8.6, and 11-year-olds) showed that although recall of the three groups was unrelated to 8-year-olds' importance ratings, all correlations were significant between recall of the three groups and importance ratings of 11-year-olds and adults (see Table 9.7).

CONCLUSION

We do not suppose that the hierarchy expressed by the younger children in their judgments is actually used in some stage of their memorization of narratives (Brown & Smiley, 1977; Waters, 1978, 1981, 1983; Young & Schumacher, 1983; Yussen, Matthews, Buss, & Kane, 1980). A plausible explanation is that the postulated schemata or cognitive macrostructures in younger children already play a prominent role in retrieval of semantic information and production of a new narrative as a report of the original.

CONSERVATION PROCESSES

Another origin of the age-effect and the level-effect may be found in conservation processes. Two recall experiments were conducted to test the hypothesis that forgetting varies with age and relative importance of semantic information.

TABLE 9.6
Mean Correlation Values (Spearman's p) Between Judgment
Rankings (Most and Least Important Sentences) for Each
Pair of Groups Through the Four Narratives

	Adults-11	Adults-8	8-11
The most important	.86*	.49*	.66**
The least important	.81**	.47*	.46*

(Denhiere & Le Ny, 1980, p. 156)

TABLE 9.7
Mean Correlation Values (Spearman's p) Between Importance
Ratings of 8- and 11-Year-Old Children and Adults, and Those
Obtained from Free Recall Reports of the Same "Gargantua"
Narrative ("House" Episode) by Three Other Children Groups
(7-, 8.6-, and 11-Year-Olds)

RECALL \ JUDGMENTS	8	11	Adults
IMMEDIATE			
7	.30	.53*	.57*
8.6	.29	.50*	.61**
11	.12	.68**	.65**
DELAYED			
8.6	.27	.73**	.75**
11	.18	.75**	.67**

(Denhiere & Le Ny, 1980, p.157)

In the first experiment we used the four narratives described previously to compare immediate and delayed recall of 8.6 and 11-year-olds (Denhière, 1982a).

The results were disappointing: The mean of forgetting after a delay of 10 minutes was equal to one proposition; this effect did not vary with age or with relative importance level of the information.

In a second experiment (Denhière & Larget, 1983), we used two episodes of one narrative, "Gargantua." The two episodes were equivalent in linguistic signs, words, sentences, underlying propositions, and number of arguments. Moreover, the structures of the two episodes were tentatively equivalent according to the Kintsch and van Dijk (1975) system and Mandler and Johnson's (1977) story grammar.

Three groups of 20 children, 7.6, 8.6, and 11-years-old, participated in this experiment, with a 7-day delay between the two recalls.

The results (see Table 9.8) were again disappointing: The mean of forgetting was two propositions, and did not vary with age or with relative importance level. This last result differs from the findings of Stein and Glenn (1979). We concluded from these results that the age-effect and the level-effect cannot be attributed to different rates of forgetting depending on age or relative importance of information.

OUTPUT PROCESSES

Output processes might explain the level-effect in one of two ways. A first hypothesis, called here "differential forgetting" states that the deeper the level of information in the hierarchical text representation of the subject, the greater the probability of decay.

TABLE 9.8
Mean Numbers of Recalled and Accepted Propositions for the Three Age Groups
for Immediate and Delayed Recall Conditions

| | RECALL | | | | | |
| | IMMEDIATE | | | DELAYED | | |
	7.6	8.6	11	7.6	8.6	11
Recalled	9.8	14.5	24.1	8.0	12.6	21.1
Accepted	7.4	10.6	18.4	5.4	8.4	16.4
Identical	4.5	5.8	10.9	3.0	3.9	8.7
Similar	2.9	4.8	7.5	2.4	4.5	7.7
Recalled	16.8	22.3	29.9	15.6	19.6	29.1
Accepted	13.0	16.0	25.6	10.8	13.1	23.5
Identical	8.0	9.8	17.6	6.1	7.2	14.9
Similar	5.0	6.2	8.0	4.7	5.9	8.6

According to an alternate hypothesis, called "differential loss of access," the deeper the information is within the hierarchical structure, the greater the number of steps that are necessary to reach this information, and the greater the probability that it will not be accessed.

We used a cued recall situation to contrast these two hypotheses. Materials were the four narratives previously described as a series of triplets of kernel (K), important expansions (E.1), and nonimportant expansions (E.2). The recall cues consisted of the important and nonimportant expansions; subjects were asked to recall the kernel statements and the complementary expansions (E.2 when E.1 was used as cue, and E.1 when E.2 was used).

If information is not recalled because it is *forgotten* (i.e., if the trace of this information has disappeared), nonimportant expansions, which were less frequently recalled than important expansions in all previous experiments, would be more frequently forgotten than important expansions and, consequently, nonimportant expansions would be a less effective recall cue than important expansions. Indeed, if E.2 information, which corresponds to E.2 statements, is forgotten, it cannot allow an access to the superordinated E.1 expansions and, therefore, to go further, to the kernel information. If a piece of information is not recalled because of a *failure to gain access* to the stored information, then the prediction is the reverse: Nonimportant expansions (E.2) would be more effective cues than important expansions (E.1). Indeed, when we present E.2 expansions to the subjects, we increase the probability of retrieving the superordinated information (E.1) and, in this way, of going further up towards the kernel information (K). However, when we use E.1 expansions, the probability of retrieving the subordinated information E.2 is not increased. Finally, if our hypotheses is true that subjects try to first retrieve the kernel information in a free recall paradigm, then the two kinds of cues (E.1 and E.2) would not affect the recall of kernel information.

TABLE 9.9
Mean Numbers of Recalled Propositions as a Function of the
Nature of the Cue (E.1 or E.2) and Experimental Condition

Conditions	Cues	Kernel	E.1.	E.2.	Total
Imagery value	E.1.	10.8	---	2.1	12.9
	E.2.	11.5	4.3	---	15.8
Predictability	E.1.	12.8	---	3.1	15.9
	E.2.	12.4	6.1	---	18.5

The experiment involved two steps. In the first step, the subjects—40 psychology students—judged the importance level of narrative statements on a 4-point scale. Each subject read four narratives; for two of them the students judged the "imagery value" of the statement, and for the two others, they predicted the recall probability of each statement by a group of 11- to 12-year-old children.

A week later, the same subjects were presented with four lists (one list per narrative) of only E.1 or E.2 expansion statements, and blank open spaces between them. Their task was to supply the missing statements, K and E.2, or K and E.1. Naturally, the subjects had not been informed of this recall task during the first phase of the experiment.

The main results are depicted in Table 9.9.

1. Nonimportant expansions, which were recalled the least frequently in a free recall situation, were significantly more effective as cues than important expansions. This result was observed across both conditions: 15.8 vs 12.9 recalled propositions for the *imagery value* condition and 18.5 vs 15.9 propositions for the *recall probability* condition.

2. The recall of the kernel statements was not affected by the nature of expansions used as recall cues since the recall means are approximately equal across the two conditions.

Thus, the level-effect (K > E.1 > E.2) previously obtained in the free-recall experiments likely results from increasing difficulty of access to subordinated information rather than from an increasing rate of forgetting in relation to depth within the hierarchy.

Conclusion

We are now faced with an apparent paradox: the least frequently recalled statements are the best recall cues. If this result is valid and if the level-effect is really due to an increasing difficulty of access as a function of the depth of information within the hierarchy, specific predictions could be made when we compare recall and recognition performances.

RECOGNITION

Regarding the previous results, the comparison between recall and recognition raised two interesting points. It is generally accepted that recognition does not imply as exhaustive a memory search as does recall (Lecocq & Tiberghien, 1981; Tiberghien & Lecocq, 1973). However, it seems that recognition is less influenced by the relative importance of information than is recall.

Two main hypotheses can be proposed regarding the origin of the level-effect:

1. If *input processes* are responsible for the level-effect, and if we postulate that subjects differentially process information according to its relative importance, the rate of correct recognition will reflect the level-effect. If the conservation of information preserves the resulting hierarchy of the initial processing, we should find the same effect in delayed recognition, probably amplified corresponding to increases of the delay.

2. If *output processes* are responsible for the level-effect, as the results of the cued-recall experiment suggest, different predictions must be made. If we accept that the subject initiates a top-down search process controlled by some schemata, then, at recall, the subject would begin by searching information corresponding to the first constituents (the beginning, for instance) and then proceed down within the hierarchy (e.g., Who was the main character? What was his or her state? What did he or she want to do? etc . . .). When the relevant information is retrieved, the subject returns to the node that would permit him or her to gain access to the information of the next constituent.

Thus, if the level-effect observed in recall resulted mainly from a top-down search process and if, in addition, the recognition did not imply this process to the same degree, we would not observe a level-effect in recognition.

The same line of reasoning can also be applied to the age-effect.

1. If *input processes* are responsible for the age-effect observed in free recall, we would have an age-effect—and a level-effect—in recognition: the difference between the recognition performances of 7- and 8-year-olds and older children would be similar to their recall differences (see Table 9.2), and the probability of correct responses would decrease with depth in the hierarchy.

2. If *output processes* are responsible for the age-effect observed in free recall, we would not observe a level-effect (see above), and the differences among age groups would be considerably weaker in recognition than in recall.

Three groups of 60 children (7, 8, and 10-year-old) participated in an immediate and delayed (8 days) recognition experiment. Three 2-episode narratives, equivalent in the number of linguistic signs, words, sentences, underlying propositions, and number of different arguments, were used. Each narrative was divided into 20 statements. The experimenter read the story, and during recognition the child answered "yes" or "no" to 50 statements according to whether or not they were presented in the original narrative. Ten statements were semantically similar to the original ones; 10 were semantically distant; and 10 were semantically unrelated; a "no" answer was required for these last 30 statements (see Denhière & Lecoutre, 1983, for a detailed description of the procedure).

The differences among the mean frequencies of correct responses (recognition of "old" statements and rejection of "new" distractor statements) of the three age groups, although significant ($p < .01$), were relatively small: .661, .691, and .723 for 7-, 8-, and 10-year-old children respectively.

As immediate recognition was significantly better than delayed recognition (.721 vs. .663), we did not observe any level-effect in immediate and delayed recognition. Thus, the kernel statements which express the semantic macrostructure of the narratives were not recognized any better than the expansions. In fact a reverse tendancy is obtained: .681 for kernel- and .701 for expansion-statements. None of the interactions between age, relative importance of the statements, and delay was statistically significant.

Conclusion

As predicted by the output hypothesis, we did not obtain a level-effect in immediate recognition, a result which is in agreement with several studies conducted with adults (Caccamise & Kintsch, 1978; McKoon, 1977; Miller, Perry, & Cunningham, 1977; Walker & Meyer, 1980; Yekovich & Thorndyke, 1981). However, we did not observe a level-effect in delayed recognition, as obtained by Caccamise and Kintsch (1978) and McKoon (1977).

As also predicted by the output hypothesis, the differences among the three age groups were predominantly weaker in recognition than in recall: The mean difference among correct recognition responses for the three age groups taken 2 × 2 was about one statement, while recall of the same narratives by 7- and 8-year-old children was only half the recall of the older children.

GENERAL CONCLUSIONS

These results have important implications for theories of children's cognitive development. Free-recall performances vary as a function of children's ages: The mean number of recalled propositions doubles between 7- to 8-year-old children and 9- to 11-year-olds. However, these quantitative differences should not mask the qualitative similarities exemplified by the frequency distributions of the recalled propositions and the significant correlations among these frequencies across the five age-groups. Moreover, a level-effect is observed in all groups of children: even the youngest children recall the most important information in narrative texts with greatest frequency, as do older children and adults. Therefore, we can conclude that cognitive structures underlying the hierarchization of semantic information observed in the recall of narratives are built—for the most part—before the mean age of 7 years (Mandler, 1978; Poulsen, Kintsch, Kintsch, & Premack, 1979; Stein & Glenn, 1979).

If this explanation is correct, most of the performance differences among age groups could be attributed to the nature of the processes used by the children: Either these processes are qualitatively different, or they are the same but are used in different ways, or else the allocation of resources to the different sub-processes varies according to age (Britton, Graesser, Glynn, Hamilton, & Penland, 1983). The variability of the pattern of differences among the age groups which is observed in the four kinds of tasks previously described (importance ratings, free recall, cued recall, and recognition experiments) is in agreement with this tentative interpretation. The results of the judgment task corroborate those reported by other researchers (Brown & Smiley, 1977; Hidi, Baird, & Hildyard, 1982; Waters, 1978, 1983) and indicate that it is necessary to make a clear-cut methodological distinction between metalinguistic and metacognitive processes on the one hand, and cognitive activities on the other (Brown, 1975, 1978; Hasselhorn & Körkel, 1984; Schneider, 1984; Weinert & Kluwe, 1984). However, simply labeling a phenomenon does not explain it.

In our study the most paradoxical result was that younger children did not recall most frequently those units that they judged as most important, but rather, the units that adults and older children had judged as most important. Taken together, these two sets of correlations show that younger children have at least two different series of hierarchies or rules, one already similar to the adults' hierarchy, and the other not yet as fully developed. We have no reason to believe that the hierarchy expressed by the younger children in their importance ratings is actually used in their comprehension or memorization of the narrative. It is impossible to suppose that these subjects process the semantic information during perception and understanding, according to the importance norms they express in their judgments: Obviously they could not report information which they could not have stored, even though they could indeed omit, in their recall, information which they actually had conserved in memory.

A plausible explanation would be that the postulated cognitive macrostructures play a major role when younger children retrieve semantic information and produce a new narrative as a report of the story. Following this line of reasoning, we could postulate that these children, despite what is expressed in their judgments, have stored in memory almost all of the information of the story that is necessary for recalling it. At the time of recall, they select the stored meaningful units according to the hierarchy or rules, which are otherwise described as macrostructures.

This explanation, more cognitive than metacognitive, can be experimentally investigated. It leads us to suppose that: (1) the youngest children are able to construct a hierarchy of the semantic information that is similar to that of the older subjects, and that (2) the major differences among different age groups lie in the retrieval of information stored in memory.

These suppositions are confirmed by results such as the significant correlations among the recall of the five age-groups and the level-effect, mentioned earlier. The results of the cued recall experiment further clarifies supposition (2): The decreasing probability of recall according to depth in the hierarchy seems to be due to an increasing difficulty of access and not to an increasing rate of forgetting, a result which is also in agreement with delayed recall experiments. Finally, the interpretation is strongly supported by the results of the recognition experiment: The reduced role of the search process in recognition (compared to recall) is accompanied by an important decrement in the differences among age-groups and the disappearance of the level-effect.

Given this explanation, it is difficult to reconcile oneself to the general assumption that memory structures are not only used to provide expectations during understanding, but are also used as retrieval structures (Reiser & Black, 1982). Even if this is true, the main difficulty of young children would be to produce effective cues which enable them to use the memory structures built during reading (see Johnson, 1982, for a review). The nonrecall of whole episodes by young children (Denhière, 1982a) is clearly an argument in favor of this hypothesis (see also Baudet, 1984a, 1984b).

However, if differential retrieval is an adequate explanation of our present results, it does not mean that selective encoding (Meyer & Rice, 1982), or differential encoding (Kintsch & van Dijk, 1978) do not play a role in producing the age-effect and the level-effect. More likely, the relative contribution of each of these processes varies with the properties of the population, the text materials, and the nature of the task. It is one of the tasks of future research to shed some light on this area.

ACKNOWLEDGMENT

This chapter was written while the author was benefiting from the program of exchanges between the Centre National de la Recherche Scientifique (France) and the Centre National de la Recherche du Canada (Canada) and was a visiting professor at the Département de Psychopédagogie, de la Faculté des Sciences de l'Education de l'Université Laval à Québec (Canada). We are grateful for helpful discussions held with Jocelyne Glasson, Claude Langevin and Régine Pierre and for the technical and financial support of Laval University. Support for the research described in this paper came from the Centre National de la Recherche scientifique (E.R.A. Nr. 235).

We would like to thank Patrick Roach and Beth Kurtz for help in the translation and editing of this paper.

REFERENCES

Adam, J. M. (1984). *Le récit.* Paris: Que sais-je?

Anderson, J. R. (1980). Concepts, propositions and schemata: What are the cognitive units? *(Technical Report.)* Carnegie-Mellon University.

Anderson, R. C. (1982). Allocation of attention during reading. In A. Flammer & W. Kintsch (Eds.), *Discourse processing.* Amsterdam: North Holland.

Anderson, R. C., & Pichert, J. W. (1978). Recall of previously unrecallable information following a shift in perspective. *Journal of Verbal Learning and Verbal Behavior, 17,* 1–12.

Ashmead, D. H., & Perlmutter, M. (1980). Infant memory in everyday life. In M. Perlmutter (Ed.), *New directions for child development: Children's memory.* (Vol. 10). San Francisco: Jossey-Bass.

Baggett, P. (1975). Memory for explicit and implicit information in picture stories. *Journal of Verbal Learning and Verbal Behavior, 14,* 538–548.

Baudet, S. (1984). Comprehension et mémorisation de récits chez l'enfant d'âge préscolaire: Effet de l'origine sociale. *Psychologica Belgica,* **24**(1), 1–26.

Baudet, S. (1986). La mémorisation de récits chez l'enfant d'âge préscolaire: L'accès à l'information stockée en mémoire en function de l'origine sociale. *L'Année Psychologigus, 86,* 124–136.

Black, J. B., & Bower, G. H. (1980). Story understanding as problem-solving. *Poetics, 9,* 223–250.

Black, J. B., Bower, G. H., & Turner, T. J. (1979). Scripts in memory for text. *Cognitive Psychology, 11,* 177–220.

Bower, G. H. (1981). Mood and memory. *American Psychologist, 36,* 129–148.

Bremond, C. (1973). *Logique du récit.* Paris: Seuil.

Britton, B. K., Graesser, A. C., Glynn, S. M., Hamilton, T., & Penland, M. (1983). Use of cognitive capacity in reading: Effects of some content features of text. *Discourse Processes, 6,* 39–57.

Britton, B., Meyer, B. J. F., Simpson, R., Holdredge, T., & Curry, C. (1979). Effects of the organization of text on memory: Test of two implications of a selective attention hypothesis. *Journal of Experimental Psychology: Human Learning and Memory, 5,* 496–506.

Brown, A. L. (1975). Recognition, reconstruction, and recall of narrative sequences by preoperational children. *Child Development, 46,* 156–166.

Brown, A. L. (1978). Knowing when, where, and how to remember: A problem of metacognition. In R. Glaser (Ed.). *Advances in instructional psychology* (Vol. 1). Hillsdale, NJ: Lawrence Erlbaum Associates.

Brown, A. L., & Smiley, S. S. (1977). Rating the importance of structural units of prose passages: A problem of metacognitive development. *Child Development, 48,* 1–8.

Caccamise, D., & Kintsch, W. (1978). Recognition of important and unimportant statements from stories. *American Journal of Psychology, 91,* 651–657.

Cession, A., Kilen, A., Denhière, G., & Rondal, J. A. (1988). Maman, une histoire! Influence du milieu social et de l'âge des enfants sur la mémorisation de récits standard et de récits produits par la mère. *Enfance,* sous presse.

Clark, E. (1973). What's in a word? On the child's acquisition of semantics in his first language. In

T. E. Moore (Ed.), *Cognitive development and the acquisition of language*. New York: Academic Press.

Clark, H. H. (1975). Bridging. In R. C. Schank & B. Nash-Webber (Eds.), *Theoretical issues in natural language processing*. Proceedings of a Conference at M.I.T.

Clark, H. H. (1977). Inferences in comprehension. In D. La Berge & J. Samuels (Eds.), *Basic processes in reading: Perception and comprehension*. Hillsdale, NJ: Lawrence Erlbaum Associates.

Clark, H. H., & Clark, E. (1977). *Psychology and language: An introduction to psycholinguistics*. New York: Harcourt Brace Jovanovich.

Clements, P. (1979). The effects of staging on recall from prose. In R. O. Freedle (Ed.), *New directions in discourse processing*, (Vol. 2). Norwood, NJ: Ablex.

Cordier, F., & Denhière, G. (1978). L'influence de la composition sémique et propositionnelle de textes sur le temps de lecture. *Psychologie et Education, Numéro spécial*, 185–194.

DeBeaugrande, R. (1980). *Text, discourse, and process*. Norwood, NJ: Ablex.

DeBeaugrande, R., & Miller, G. W. (1980). Processing models for children's story comprehension. *Poetics, 9*, 181–201.

Denhière, G. (1976). Influence de la composition sémique de phrases sur le temps d'étude: Etude comparative. *Journal de Psychologie, 2*, 217–235.

Denhière, G. (1979). Comprehension et rappel d'un récit par des enfants de 6 à 12 ans. *Bulletin de Psychologie, 341*, 803–818.

Denhière, G. (1980). Narrative recall and recognition by children. In F. Klix & J. Hoffmann (Eds.), *Cognition and memory*. Amsterdam: North Holland.

Denhière, G. (1982). Do we really mean schemata? In J. F. Le Ny & W. Kintsch (Eds.), *Language and Comprehension*. Amsterdam: North Holland.

Denhière, G. (1985). Statut psychologique du paragraphe et structure de récit. In S. Laufer (Ed.), *La notion de paragraphe*. Paris Editions du C.N.R.S.

Denhière, G. (1984). *Il était une fois, . . . Comprendre et retenir un récit*. Lille: Presses Universitaires de Lille.

Denhière, G. (1987). Il y a bien longtemps, . . . Aspects de la genèse de la compréhension et de la mémorisation de récits. In J. Pieraut- Le Bonniec (Ed.), *Connaître et le dire*, Liège, Mardaga.

Denhière, G., & Langevin, J. (1981). La compréhension et la mémorisation de récits: Aspects génétiques et comparatifs. In J. A. Rondal, J. L. Lambert, & H. H. Chipman (Eds.), *Psycholinguistique et handicap mental*. Liège: Mardaga.

Denhière, G., & Larget, E. (1983). Rappel immédiat et différé de récit: Influence de la nature des épisodes, de leur ordre de présentation et de l'âge des enfants. *Document E.R.A. 235*. Université de Paris VIII.

Denhière, G., & Lecoutre, B. (1983). Memorisation de récits: Reconnaissance immédiate et différée d'énoncés par des enfants de 7, 8 et 10 ans. *L'Année Psychologique, 83*, 345–376.

Denhière, G., & Legros, D. (1983). Comprendre un texte: Construire quoi? Avec quoi? Comment? *Revue Française de Pédagogie, 65*, 19–29.

Denhière, G., & Le Ny, J. F. (1980). Relative importance of meaningful units in comprehension and recall of narratives by children and adults. *Poetics, 9*, 147–161.

Ehrlich, S., & Florin, A. (1981). *Niveaux de compréhension et production d'un récit*. Bordeaux: C.N.R.S.

Genette, G. (1966). Frontières du récit. *Communications, 8*, 152–163.

Gentner, D. (1978). On relational meaning: The acquisition of verb meaning. *Child Development, 49*, 988–998.

Grimes, J. (1975). *The thread of discourse*. The Hague: Mouton.

Hasselhorn, M. & Körkel, J. (1984). *The role of metacognition and domain-specific knowledge in the processing of texts: Analysis of a training study with 6-grade children*. Working Paper. Max-Planck-Institute for Psychological Research, Munich.

Hidi, S., Baird, W., & Hildyard, A. (1982). That's important but is it interesting? Two factors in text processing. In A. Flammer & W. Kintsch (Eds.), *Discourse processing*. Amsterdam: North Holland.

Johnson, R. E. (1982). Retrieval cues and the remembering of prose: A review. In A. Flammer & W. Kintsch (Eds.), *Discourse processing*. Amsterdam: North Holland.

Kintsch, W. (1974). *The representation of meaning in memory*. Hillsdale, NJ: Lawrence Erlbaum Associates.

Kintsch, W. (1977). On comprehending stories. In M. A. Just & P. A. Carpenter (Eds.), *Cognitive processes in comprehension*. Hillsdale, NJ: Lawrence Erlbaum Associates.

Kintsch, W., & van Dijk, T. A. (1975). Comment on se rappelle et on résume des histoires. *Langages, 40*, 98–116.

Kintsch, W., & van Dijk, T. A. (1978). Toward a model of text comprehension and production. *Psychological Review, 85*, 363–394.

Kintsch, W., & Vipond, D. (1979). Reading comprehension and readibility in educational practice and psychological theory. In L. G. Nillson (Ed.), *Perspectives on memory research*. Hillsdale, NJ: Lawrence Erlbaum Associates.

Labov, W. J., & Waletzky, J. (1967). Narrative analysis: Oral versions of personal experience. In J. Helm (Ed.), *Essays on the verbal and visual arts*. Seattle: Washington University Press.

Lecocq, P., & Tiberghien, G. (1981). *Mémoire et décision*. Lille: Presses Universitaires de Lille.

Langevin, J. (1980). La mémorisation des versions verbale et figurative de récits par des déficients mentaux et de jeunes enfants. *Thèse de Doctorat de 3 cycle*. Université de Paris VIII.

Langevin, J. (1982). La mémorisation de textes et les personnes handicapées sur le plan cognitif. *Repères, 2*, 5–61.

Le Ny, J. F. (1975). Sémantique et psychologie. *Language, 40*, 3–29.

Le Ny, J. F. (1976). Sèmes ou mèmes? *Bulletin de Psychologie, 46–54*.

Le Ny, J. F. (1978). De la structure de la signification d'une phrase. *Bulletin de Psychologie, 341*, 833–843.

Le Ny, J. F. (1980). Selective activities and elective forgetting in the process of understanding and in the recall of semantic contents. In F. Klix & J. Hoffmann (Eds.), *Cognition and memory*. Amsterdam: North Holland.

Mandler, J. M. (1978). A code in the node: The use of a story schema in retrieval. *Discourse Processes, 1*, 14–35.

Mandler, J. M. (1979). Categorical and schematic organization in memory. In C. R. Puff (Ed.), *Memory organization and structure*. New York: Academic Press.

Mandler, J. M. (1983). Representation. In P. Mussen (Ed.), *Manual of child psychology* (Vol.3). New York: Wiley.

Mandler, J. M. & Johnson, N. S. (1977). Remembrance of things parsed: Story structure and recall. *Cognitive Psychology, 9*, 111–151.

Mandler, J. M., Scribner, S., Cole, B., & DeForest, M. (1980). Cross-cultural invariance in story recall. *Child Development, 51*, 19–26.

Martins, D. (1981). Affectivité, personnalité et mémoire verbale. *L'Année Psychologique, 2*, 485–510.

Martins, D. (1982). Influence of affect on comprehension of a text. *Text, 2*, 141–154.

McKoon, G. (1977). Organization of information in text memory. *Journal of Verbal Learning and Verbal Behavior, 16*, 247–260.

Meyer, B. J. F. (1975). *The organization of prose and its effect on recall*. Amsterdam: North Holland.

Meyer, B. J. F., & Rice, G. E. (1982). The interaction of reader strategies and the organization of text. *Text, 2*, 155–192.

Miller, J. R., & Kintsch, W. (1980). Readability and recall of short prose passages: A theoretical analysis. *Journal of Experimental Psychology: Human Learning and Memory, 6*, 335–354.

Miller, R., Perry, F., & Cunningham, D. (1977). Differential forgetting of superordinate and subordinate information acquired from prose material. *Journal of Educational Psychology, 69,* 730–735.

Minsky, M. (1975). A framework for representing knowledge. In P. H. Winston (Ed.), *The psychology of computer vision.* New York: McGraw-Hill.

Nelson, K. E. (1977). Cognitive development and the acquisition of concepts. In R. C. Anderson, R. J. Spiro, & W. E. Montague (Eds.), *Schooling and the acquisition of knowledge.* Hillsdale, NJ: Lawrence Erlbaum Associates.

Nelson, K. E. (1978). Semantic development and the development of semantic memory. In K. E. Nelson (Ed.), *Children's language* (Vol. 1). New York: Gardner Press.

Nelson, K. E. (1979). Explorations in the development of a functional semantic system. In W. A. Collins (Ed.), *Minnesota Symposia on Child Psychology.* (Vol. 12). Hillsdale, NJ: Lawrence Erlbaum Associates.

Omanson, R. C. (1982). An analysis of narratives: Identifying central, supportive, and distracting content. *Discourse Processes, 5,* 195–224.

Pichert, J. W., & Anderson, R. C. (1977). Taking different perspectives on a story. *Journal of Educational Psychology, 69,* 309–315.

Piolat, A., & Denhière, G. (1984). Restitution orale et écrite d'un récit lu, entendu et présenté en images. *Bulletin de Psychologie,* à paraître.

Poulsen, D., Kintsch, E., Kintsch, E., & Premack, D. (1979). Children's comprehension and memory for stories. *Journal of Experimental Child Psychology, 28,* 379–403.

Pynte, J., & Denhière, G. (1982). Influence de la thématisation et du statut syntaxique des propositions sur le traitement de récits. *L'Année Psychologique, 2,* 101–129.

Reiser, B. J., & Black, J. B. (1982). Processing and structural models of comprehension. *Text, 2,* 225–252.

Rumelhart, D. E. (1975). Notes on a schema for stories. In D. G. Bobrow & A. Collins (Eds.), *Representation and understanding: Studies in cognitive science.* New York: Academic Press.

Rummelhart, D. E. (1977). Understanding and summarizing brief stories. In D. LaBerge & S. J. Samuels (Eds.), *Basic processes in reading: Perception and comprehension.* Hillsdale, NJ: Lawrence Erlbaum Associates.

Sanford, A. J., & Garrod, S. C. (1981). *Understanding written language.* Chichester: Wiley.

Sanford, A. J., & Garrod, S. C. (1982). Towards a processing account of reference. In A. Flammer & W. Kintsch (Eds.), *Discourse processing.* Amsterdam: North-Holland.

Schank, R. S. (1982). *Dynamic memory: A theory of reminding and learning in computers and people.* Cambridge, England: Cambridge University Press.

Schank, R. C., & Abelson, R. (1977). *Scripts, plans, goals. and understanding.* Hillsdale, NJ: Lawrence Erlbaum Associates.

Schneider, W. (1984). Developmental trends in the meta-memory-memory behavior relationship: An integrative review. In D. L. Forrest-Pressley, G. E. McKinnon, & T. G. Waller (Eds.), *Cognition, metacognition, and performance.* New York: Academic Press.

Spiro, R. J. (1977). Inferential reconstruction in memory for connected discourse. In R. C. Anderson, R. J. Spiro, & W. E. Montague (Eds.), *Schooling and the acquisition of knowledge.* Hillsdale, NJ: Lawrence Erlbaum Associates.

Stein, N. L. (1982). The definition of a story. *Journal of Pragmatics, 6,* 487–507.

Stein, N. L., & Glenn, C. G. (1979). An analysis of story comprehension in elementary school children. In R. O. Freedle (Ed.), *New directions in discourse processing* (Vol. 2). Norwood, NJ: Ablex.

Stein, N. L., & Glenn, C. G. (1982). Children's concept of time: The development of a story schema. In W. J. Friedman (Ed.), *The developmental psychology of time.* New York: Academic Press.

Thorndyke, P. W. (1977). Cognitive structures in comprehension and memory of narrative discourse. *Cognitive Psychology, 9,* 77–110.

Tiberghien, G., & Lecocq, P. (1973). Rappel et reconnaissance: I. Hypothèses dualistes. *L'Année Psychologique, 1*, 225–260.

van Dijk, T. A. (1980). *Macrostructures*. Hillsdale, NJ: Lawrence Erlbaum Associates.

van Dijk, T. A., & Kintsch, W. (1983). *Strategies of discourse comprehension*. New York: Academic Press.

Walker, C., & Meyer, B. J. F. (1980). Integrating different types of information in text. *Journal of Verbal Learning and Verbal Behavior, 19*, 263–275.

Waters, H. S. (1978). Superordinate-subordinate structure in semantic memory: The role of comprehension and retrieval processes. *Journal of Verbal Learning and Verbal Behavior, 17*, 587–597.

Waters, H. S. (1981). Organizational strategies in memory for prose: A developmental analysis. *Journal of Experimental Psychology, 32*, 223–246.

Waters, H. S. (1983). Superordinate-subordinate structure in prose passages and the importance of propositions. *Journal of Experimental Psychology: Learning, Memory, and Cognition, 9*, 294–299.

Weinert, F. E., & Kluwe, R. H. (Eds.) (1984). *Metakognition, Motivation und Lernen*. Stuttgart: Kohlhammer.

Woods, W. A. (1980). Cascaded ATN grammars. *American Journal of Computational Linguistics, 6*, 1–12.

Yekovich, F. R., & Thorndyke, P. W. (1981). An evaluation of alternative functional models of narrative schemata. *Journal of Verbal Learning and Verbal Behavior, 20*, 454–469.

Young, D. R., & Schumacher, G. M. (1983). Context effects in young children's sensitivity to the importance level of prose information. *Child Development, 54*, 1446–1456.

Yussen, S. R., Mathews, S. R., II., Buss, R. R., & Kane, P. T. (1980). Developmental change in judging important and critical elements of stories. *Developmental Psychology, 16*, 213–219.

IV

SOCIAL AND MOTIVATIONAL CONTEXTS OF MEMORY DEVELOPMENT

10 Motivated Remembering

Scott G. Paris
University of Michigan

Imagine how 8 year-olds might try to remember 20 pictures spread out on a table. They might scan the items systematically, group similar pictures together, and proceed to label and rehearse them as study techniques. Recall would probably be very good and children would be credited with effective use of appropriate strategies. But what is the interpretation of performance if children only stare at the pictures and exhibit no overt grouping, labeling, or rehearsal? A cognitive interpretation might attribute poor recall to (a) lack of organized knowledge about the stimuli (Chi, 1978), (b) inadequate knowledge and control of cognitive strategies (Pressley, Forrest-Pressley, Elliot-Faust, & Miller, 1985), or (c) poor metacognition (Brown, 1978). Cognitive deficiencies, though, are not the only possible explanations for apparently nonstrategic behavior and poor recall. Children may have beliefs and attitudes that interfere with effective remembering. For example, they might believe that grouping and rehearsal are silly or time-consuming. Some children might believe that they are unable to place pictures into groups properly or that some other tactic, perhaps staring, is better. More generally, children may believe that the consequences for failure are minimal or severe and thus act in a manner that will remove them quickly from the situation to more appealing options elsewhere.

The critical issue in the example is why children do not use skills independently as mnemonic aids that they are able to use when directed by others, the familiar "production deficiencies" observed in countless studies of memory development (Flavell, 1970). In this chapter, a cognitive strategy view of memory difficulties is contrasted with social motivational perspectives derived from expectancy-value and decision-making models. These perspectives are considered to be heuristic alternatives for studying individual and developmental differences in remembering because they encompass motivational variables such as beliefs, values, expectancies, and coping behavior. The three approaches are compared within situations that elicit deliberate remembering because such tasks depend on controlled memory processes and voluntary decision making. Deliberate attempts to remember are only a subset of memory functions but they are commonly observed in everyday situations, they reflect explicit experimental procedures, and they are important for academic learning. Remembering lists of items to buy on shopping errands, recalling procedural steps in games or work, and studying material for later recall are typical examples of intentional remembering.

Four characteristics of intentional remembering are especially pertinent to this chapter because they are often neglected in theories of memory and cognitive development that emphasize only the acquisition of a repertoire of mnemonic skills. First, remembering is often directed to achieve specific purposes that are embedded in other activities that serve larger functions for the individual. Rarely is recall the only objective. Second, there are extrinsic and intrinsic consequences for remembering. Some may entail small rewards or penalties, such as additional shopping errands, while others may be stressful or critical (e.g., remembering frequency and dosage of medication). Anticipation of memory outcomes and consequences can lead to different strategic behavior depending on the values and expectations that are associated with the task. Third, everyday memory demands usually afford alternatives. One can choose to use one strategy rather than another, to try with more or less effort, or to avoid the situation entirely. Fourth, common tasks include environmental supports for performance such as physical cues, external models or standards, and periodic feedback, instruction, and encouragement from other people. It is suggested in this chapter that these four factors are not confounds in the assessment of memory but rather they are significant determinants of how people ordinarily remember. They mediate expressions of memory ability.

THE INSTRUMENTAL FUNCTION OF STRATEGIES

The heart of strategic remembering is the deliberate selection of appropriate actions to achieve specific ends. Intent is signaled by selection of an action among alternatives and a belief that it will promote a particular outcome. But the action must be appropriate or there is only intent without benefit. Likewise, the person must be capable of performing the action if the connection is to be more than wishful thinking. It has been suggested that one of the early concepts that young children may form about remembering is that some actions are instrumental as mnemonic aids (Paris, Newman, & Jacobs, 1985). For example, 3- 4-year-olds spontaneously look at and touch a cup that conceals an object in order to remember it (Wellman, Ritter, & Flavell, 1975). Some actions, perhaps staring, touching, attending, and labeling, are welded to tasks and readily elicited. Children may gain an appreciation of their value sooner than more abstract strategies such as grouping, imagery, or elaboration.

Brief instruction usually enhances children's remembering significantly (Flavell, 1970). Similar results have been obtained with adolescents (Pressley, Levin, & Bryant, 1983) and elderly adults. But brief instruction does not provide an enduring amelioration of spontaneous production deficiencies which suggests that the problem is not due to just lack of knowledge. Perhaps subjects gain only partial understanding of how instructed strategies operate, or they hold conflicting beliefs about their value, or the new options appear less effective than well-practiced alternatives. These types of misconceptions have been investigated in recent studies of the instrumental function of mnemonic strategies.

Initial studies of children's conceptions of the instrumental effectiveness of memory strategies manipulated feedback. Kennedy and Miller (1976), for example, told two groups of 7-year-olds to label and rehearse the names of pictures. Only one group was given feedback that the strategies had helped them remember better. This retroactive attribution apparently altered children's evaluations of the usefulness of strategies because they subsequently produced rehearsal spontaneously more often than children given no feedback. Borkowski, Levers, and Gruenenfelder (1976) demonstrated that simple observation of successful strategy use can also promote children's subsequent use of the tactics. Despite these apparent changes in the correlated understanding and use of mnemonic strategies, though, evidence for the influence of metamemory on performance remained sparse (Cavanaugh & Perlmutter, 1982).

Paris, Newman, and McVey (1982) designed a study to test explicitly the influence of children's conceptions of the instrumental value of strategies on their self-controlled use of those strategies. Seven and 8-year-old children were given two memory trials with 24 different pictures on each of 5 consecutive days. Days 1 and 2 provided baseline data, Day 3 included strategy training, and Days 4 and 5 provided measures of strategy maintenance. The microgenetic study was designed to measure changes in children's understanding and use of cognitive strategies so children's evaluations of strategies were assessed following recall on Days 2, 3, and 5. The critical issue was to determine if training altered children's judgments about strategies as well as their performance. Training included two conditions; elaborated and nonelaborated instructions. The nonelaborated condition directed children to group, label, and rehearse the items as well as to test their own memories and to use blocked recall. Children were told how to perform each action but the instructions were traditional, spare descriptions rather than explanations about strategies, conditions that Brown, Bransford, Ferrara, and Campione (1983) contrast as blind versus informed training studies. The elaborated conditions provided identical descriptions and prescriptions to use the strategies but the instructions also included brief explanations *why* the tactics would be beneficial. In our view, this additional information provided a meaningful rationale for children to use the actions and thus transformed instructed mnemonic actions into personal strategies.

Did the two training conditions result in different outcomes? Yes. The two groups of children did not differ in recall, clustering, study behavior, or metacognitive judgments about strategies before training. However, on Days 3, 4, and 5 children in the elaborated instructional group (a) recalled significantly more pictures (approximately a 20% advantage), (b) clustered recall significantly more, and (c) used overt labeling, rehearsal, and physical grouping more often. Metacognitive judgments were measured in two ways; by answers to open-ended questions (How did you try to remember the pictures today? What plan worked best? What's the very best thing to do to help you remember?) and by ratings of the effectiveness of ten strategies on a 5-point scale. Sorting pictures by groups was the strategy that changed the most during training and most distinguished subjects in the two groups. Other strategies, such as rhyming or rehearsal, remained relatively stable over training. This means that children perceived some actions such as rehearsal as familiar and effective throughout the study and the principal effect of training was to persuade children that sorting is actually a useful memory strategy. Indeed, on Day 5, 7% of children with below average recall exhibited low awareness of the value of sorting while 87% of children with above average recall demonstrated awareness of the useful instrumental function of sorting. Structural modeling with hierarchical path analysis confirmed the strong relations among training, metacognitive judgments, study behavior, and memory performance. Thus, the study demonstrated that children's conceptions of the instrumental effectiveness of strategies mediates children's production and maintenance of the mnemonic tactics.

A variety of research supports the importance of subjective understanding about cognitive strategies. Elaborated instructions that describe how, when, and why to apply memory strategies promote spontaneous use and transfer of the strategies better than nonelaborated instructions or practice (Fabricius & Hagen, 1984; Ringel & Springer, 1980). In these studies, subjects in elaborated training conditions reported more positive evaluations and intentional use of the instructed strategies. Research on reading comprehension strategies confirms the results of memory studies. When children are thoroughly informed about how to use strategies such as paraphrasing, rereading, or summarizing, they learn to use the strategies more effectively and spontaneously (Palincsar & Brown, 1984; Paris, Cross, & Lipson, 1984). Paris and Jacobs (1984) demonstrated that children's metacognitive understanding about the instrumental value of reading strategies can be fostered through direct instruction and that such awareness is related significantly to strategic reading.

Pressley, Ross, Levin, and Ghatala (1984) demonstrated that children's perceptions of strategy efficacy influence their choice of strategies. In that study, 10- 12-year-olds were taught two methods for learning new vocabulary words; the keyword method and generating a sentence with the word used appropriately in context. (The keyword method is demonstrably more effective in this task.) There were four conditions in which memory performance and children's understanding of strategy effectiveness was compared; a control condition in which two methods were described, a practice condition in which children practiced both strategies on one list, a practice plus prompt condition in which children were asked (after recall) to reflect on which strategy was most helpful, and a practice plus feedback condition in which children were told exactly how many words they had learned with each strategy. The practice plus feedback condition led to the highest level of recall and the most positive evaluations and use of the keyword method. It hardly seems surprising that the greatest amount of information clarified the ambiguous task and novel strategies the most but the study does confirm that subjective perceptions of strategy efficacy are important determinants of strategy use, choice, maintenance, and transfer.

Analyses of subjective conceptions of the instrumental function of mnemonic tactics help to explain performance variations among training conditions and levels of understanding about strategies but the approach may also illuminate reasons for developmental changes in remembering skills. Children and elderly adults may maintain their use of familiar strategies, even though they may not be effective, because the well-practiced tactics are known to be manageable and reasonably useful. Thus, the choice to eschew some strategies even after feedback or demonstration might reveal personal decisions that are based on calculations of perceived ease, economy, and effectiveness of alternative tactics and not just stubbornness or ignorance. Cox and Paris (1978) asked children (9–10-year-olds), college students (20–22 year-olds), and elderly adults (65–75 year-olds), to study and recall a list of 30 nouns that included five instances of six conceptual categories. Three different groups of subjects at each age level participated in three distinct conditions; the *Remember* condition included no strategy instruction, the *Categorize* condition included a prescription to sort pictures by group, and the *Generate* condition included a prompt to think of a good strategy. Following recall, subjects reported strategies that they used and then rank-ordered 20 different memory tactics with regard to their beneficial effects for each individual on a list learning task.

The data revealed expected differences in recall and clustering by age level but the subjective data revealed distinct reasons for the differences. Children reported using categorization as a strategy only when directed, otherwise they reported nearly exclusive reliance on rehearsal. Both groups of adults, though, reported a richer variety and larger number of strategies, including conceptual grouping, in all three conditions. As might be expected, children rated rehearsal positively while categorization was perceived as useful only by those children told to use it. Adults had the opposite ratings: categorization was more valued than rehearsal by all groups. When asked which strategies they would use on another list learning task, children responded with a large number of ineffective strategies, thus displaying poor understanding of instrumental efficacy. Both groups of adults, though, responded with a small number of related and effective strategies that would be employed on future tasks. Thus, children's poor understanding of instrumental and effective strategies (as evident in all three conditions) may underlie their inefficient strategy use and lower levels of recall. Elderly adults, by contrast, exhibited poor recall, clustering, and use of strategies only in the uninstructed *Remember* condition. When they were provided with general prompts to devise a strategy or with explicit directions to categorize words, they performed strategically and significantly better. Thus, their problem was not lack of knowledge like the children, but failure to enlist knowledge about strategy efficacy spontaneously for intentional remembering.

A subsequent study by Cox and Paris (1979) substantiated the findings. Subjects at the same three age levels studied and recalled the same 30 nouns and were then shown ten concrete methods of marking the list of words as study aids. These concrete representations of memory strategies (e.g., repetitive copying represented rehearsal, listing by groups depicted categorization, adding words to form semantic or rhyming associates, pictures represented imagery, etc.) were evaluated for their personal and relative effectiveness. There were expected main effects of age for both recall and clustering measures. Again, children reported using rehearsal almost exclusively while adults reported categorization as their predominant, but not sole, strategy. When shown actual strategies that could be used, children rated categorization and self-testing best but failed to distinguish clearly among other strategies. Ratings by adults were more discriminating and revealed significantly more positive evaluations of categorization and personal grouping than children.

Subjects were also asked how the various strategies might be combined. Children reported that they would use one tactic and then relearn the list of words with another while adults nearly always reported coordinated strategies such as alphabetization within groups followed by rehearsal. Such differences in reported metamemory may not be due to age alone, though. Zivian and Darjes (1983) replicated the Cox and Paris (1978) study with university women (young adults in school), 35–49 year-old women (middle-aged women in school and middle-aged women out of school), and 60–86 year-olds (elderly women out of school). Despite the small sample size, single sex, and incomplete experimental design, there was evidence that the in-school groups and out-of-school groups were most alike. Thus, schooling rather than age may contribute to metacognitive judgments about the perceived instrumental function of memory strategies.

AN EXPECTANCY-VALUE MODEL OF INTENTIONAL REMEMBERING

Research on subjective conceptions of memory strategies clearly reveals that people select means that they value positively in order to aid memory. Judgments about strategy effectiveness lead to expectations that recall will be fostered, which motivates decisions to use particular tactics as mnemonic strategies. Terms such as "strategy efficacy," "personal rationale," and "perceived utility" have been used to describe knowledge about strategies that appears to underlie their motivated production, selection, and continued use. These beliefs can be interpreted as metacognitive evaluations of the instrumental effectiveness of strategies or they can be examined as combinations of personal expectations about successful performance and incentives to use the tactics. The latter framework is examined in this section as both a more comprehensive and more specified model of choice behavior for intentional remembering.

Expectancy value models of choice behavior postulate that a person will choose to act in fashion A rather than B if the (probability of success with A) x(the incentive value of A) is greater than the similar product of alternative B. Obviously this is an oversimplified representation; see Atkinson (1982) and Feather (1982a) for complex extensions of such models that include internal dispositions, perceived control, and inhibiting or facilitative effects of ongoing tendencies. Expectations about likelihood and value of behavioral options include subjective conceptions about the effectiveness and effort required of cognitive strategies as well as the costs/benefits associated with each option in different situations. The expectations and values involved in intentional remembering can be unpacked by considering the links in the sequence of Person-Action-Outcome-Consequences.

Subjective Expected Utility

Research on strategic remembering examines perceived effectiveness of various strategies or more specifically, personal beliefs about the Action-Outcome relation. Effectiveness, though, is not the only dimension of strategies that can influence perceived utility. It seems plausible that a person might evaluate the relative effectiveness of two strategies correctly but choose the less effective one if it is considerably easier. Adults, for example, commonly eschew proven study techniques because they appear to require too much work. Thus, economy of effort, or perceived *workload,* may be another critical dimension of the utility of memory strategies.

Informal observations of children struggling to learn categorization as a memory strategy suggest that many children may discount the tactic as irrelevant or demanding (or both). Decisions to use or forego particular strategies are therefore influenced both by informational and motivational properties of strategies. The concept of workload expands the frame of reference for judging utility in two ways. First, there is the effort required for the person to produce the action (e.g., imagine the effort required to generate keywords for foreign vocabulary items), and, second, there is the effort required in order for the action to have a positive influence on the outcome (e.g., consider the number of rehearsals required in order to memorize a difficult list of stimuli). Effort to produce a strategy and the work required to achieve a desired criterion level of consequence can be represented schematically as workload expectations between Person-Action and Action-Outcome-Consequences relations. Both can be included in subjective perceptions of effort required by different strategies.

Judgments about workload can be combined with conceptions about strategy effectiveness in an inverse relation to yield judgments about strategy *efficiency*. For example, rehearsal may be adequate and most efficient for remembering a list of four items while learning a list of 14 items would require more effective strategies or more work at rehearsal. Kreutzer, Leonard, and Flavell (1975) provide an anecdote of a child who reported an elaborate mnemonic association for remembering a telephone number but when asked if that is how he usually remembered, he replied no, he would write the number on a piece of paper. The ability to select efficient strategies means that people can calculate tradeoffs between effectiveness and workload. The actual choice of a strategy therefore includes both beliefs about strategy effectiveness and one's willingness to work on a particular task.

Judgments about strategy efficiency, though, are not absolute. The use of efficient strategies is tempered by personal and situational limitations. For example, categorization may be an efficient strategy for remembering a group of related pictures but 10-year-olds may choose it more often (and use it more successfully) than 7-year-olds by virtue of practice, familiarity, and knowledge organization. In a similar vein, situational constraints, limited time, or anxiety might prevent the use of efficient strategies. Overt cumulative rehearsal may be an efficient strategy for memorizing a list of words but it is not appropriate for remembering the names of people at a party. Failure to use effective strategies might be explained by individual and situational differences in workload, or in perceptions of self-efficacy, which are discussed later.

The point of this discussion is that judgments about strategy utility are not the same across people and tasks. Nor are they absolute evaluations of the instrumental effectiveness of mnemonic tactics. They are personal choices made in situations that answer such questions as, "Is this a good thing to do? Will it help me achieve adequate recall? How much effort is required? Can I do it? Is it the best available option?" The answers to these queries are embedded in judgments about the subjective expected utility (SEU) of various options. The mathematical expression of SEU for a strategy such as rehearsal (R) is:

$$SEU_{(R)} = \frac{P_{(R)} \times E_{(R)}}{W_{(R)}}$$

where $P_{(R)}$ represents the probability of successfully using rehearsal, $E_{(R)}$ indicates the perceived effectiveness of rehearsal, and $W_{(R)}$ is a measure of its perceived workload.

There are several advantages to an SEU characterization of memory strategies. First, the relevant parameters are expanded to include workload and probability of the behavior in order to provide a more thorough conceptualization of utility than evaluations of only perceived effectiveness of instrumental value. The mathematical expression of the relations among variables also permit (indeed invite) empirical hypothesis testing that is not possible in contemporary approaches to strategy utility. Second, the SEU characterization clearly emphasizes personal conceptions about memory strategies that are judged relative to one's abilities to perform a task in a particular situation. Third, an SEU orientation provides a bridge from expectancy value models of social motivation to cognitive competence models of memory development. The constructs imported from motivational research illuminate a variety of plausible processes that may influence intentional remembering as well as memory development. For example, production deficiencies for strategies may not be due to ignorance or cognitive inability. Subjects could decline to use strategies that they possess or are directed to use because the required effort appears too great or their personal expectations for success are low. More simply, the tactic is not worth doing well in the situation.

Incentives for Intentional Remembering

The previous discussion unpacked variables that affect personal expectations for successful recall but ignored incentives for the choices. SEU is a "cold" cognitive evaluation in some ways; behavioral choices will be affected by perceived values of the consequences of the actions in addition to their usefulness. The goal of intentional remembering is successful recall but this outcome is followed by other consequences because memory goals are embedded in ongoing behavior. Thus, successful recall might enable you to find your car keys and drive to work or it might bolster self-confidence. The outcomes of intentional remembering lead to other consequences and provide incentives for performance—not just as energizers for effort but as incentives to invest effort in particular strategies.

Goal attainment can influence intentional remembering in two basic ways. First, there is an extrinsic value generated by the Outcome-Consequences relation. The consequences provide incentives for effort and efficient strategy selection. It seems reasonable to expect people to engage in more work or to tolerate inefficient strategies if the prize for recall is valued highly. The second manner of influence involves the intrinsic value of successful remembering. Some tasks are interesting, challenging, or satisfying; people approach them because they are inherently enjoyable. But other tasks may provoke stress, negative reactions, and avoidance. It is easy to imagine situations in which subjects are highly anxious about the quality of their memory performance because they believe it reflects on their personal ability or intellect. High anxiety may interfere with strategic processing just as indifference may lead to a lack of effort or strategy use (Feather, 1982b). Schematically, the intrinsic value can be represented as Person-Outcome-Consequences because the value and probability of achieving the consequences depends on the personal frame of reference. Depending upon one's past performance and expectations, 50% recall can be subjectively defined as success or failure.

Goal values and consequences of memory outcomes signal the importance of personal gains and losses derived from remembering activities. There are personal attributions made about one's performance that can lay blame or credit memory to other people, task difficulty, effort, or ability. These variables figure prominently in attribution theories of motivation and schooling (Nicholls, 1983; Weiner, 1979). Three types of self-oriented relations can influence intentional remembering. First, the Person-Action link permits expectations about *self-efficacy,* i.e., Do I have the ability and can I muster the effort to succeed? Second, the Person-Action-Outcome sequence reflects one's intentionality and, thus, *perceived control* over one's own behavior. Third, the Person-Action-Outcome-Consequences sequence, the entire chain of intentional remembering, is a demonstration of competence that contributes to social displays of ability as well as personal evaluations of *self-esteem.* These feelings of efficacy, control, and esteem operate prospectively as motives for behavior and retrospectively as attributions. Considerable research has demonstrated that people use these expectations to guide their behavior in achievment-related situations (e.g., Covington, 1983; Dweck & Elliot, 1983; Weiner, 1979). It seems plausible that intentional remembering should be likewise influenced by expectancies and values regarding self-efficacy, control, and esteem.

The expectancies and values associated with instrumental efficiency, goal attainment, and self-worth are summarized in Fig. 10.1. It is postulated that intentional remembering is a function of the interactions among values for strategy SEU, goal attainment, and self-worth. Although the relations among the expanded set of motivational variables may already appear complicated, it is necessary to add context as a factor that can influence all variables. The tasks, people, and objects in the situation can influence each construct. First, instrumental efficiency can be facilitated by provision of structured tasks, feedback, informed instruction, external cues, and so forth. The probability of successful behavior can also be manipulated by social guidance or support. Second, goal values can be altered by extrinsic consequences, the nature of the task, social dynamics, and ego involvement (Maehr, 1983). Third, situations can change the importance attributed to one's own performance depending on the expectancies and values attached to success or failure. Thus, situational variability is to be expected because self-perceptions of intentional remembering depend on particular tasks, strategies, outcomes, and consequences.

INTENTIONAL REMEMBERING AS DECISION-MAKING

Decision making also provides a theoretical framework for analyzing developmental and individual differences in memory performance. The kinds of reflective analyses and judgments involved in optimal decision making are shown in

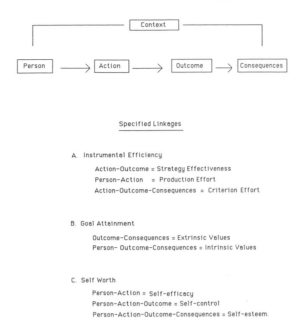

FIG. 10.1. Schematic diagram of variables linked in an SEU model.

Table 10.1 and they reveal procedural steps for comparing alternatives and choosing the best option for a particular situation. Bransford and Stein (1984) provide a similar model of IDEAL problem solving where I = identify the problem, D = define and represent the problem, E = explore possible strategies, A = act on the strategies, and L = look back and evaluate the effects of your activities. These procedures are clearly relevant to intentional remembering in which decisions are made about effective strategies, expectations, and values. Three models of decision making, conflict theory, judgmental heuristics, and habits, are considered in this section as heuristic frameworks for studying intentional remembering.

Conflict Theory

Conflict theory attempts to describe the processes used by people to derive decisions as opposed to expectancy-value models that emphasize the actual choices. Mann and Janis (1982) propose a conflict theory that has direct implications for understanding intentional remembering.

> Psychological stress arising from decisional conflict stems from two principal sources. First, the decision-maker is concerned about the material and social losses he might suffer from whichever course of action he chooses—including the costs of failing to live up to prior commitments. Second, he recognizes that his reputation

TABLE 10.1
Optimal Decision-Making Procedures

1. Decompose the problem to identify goals and subgoals.
2. List all feasible courses of action to achieve the goals.
3. For each action, enumerate all possible consequences.
4. For each consequence, assess the relative value and probability of its occurrence.
5. Compute the expected worth of an option by multiplying the value of its probability of occurrence.
6. Sum the expected worths of all possible consequences for each action.
7. Compare options and choose the action with the greatest expected worth.

and self-esteem as a competent decision-maker are at stake. The distinction between the two sources of stress is potentially important. The first source of stress relates to expected gains and losses *intrinsic* to the choice alternatives themselves. The second source of stress relates to the *generalized* expectation that the decision as a whole—how one goes about making it as well as its outcome—could prove to be satisfying or damaging. We see then, that the concept of expectancy is implicit in conflict theory. (1982, p.343)

Mann and Janis (1982) propose that the following five coping patterns reveal how people with different expectancies and levels of stress derive decisions.

1. *Unconflicted adherence* is a decision to continue previous behavior, perhaps because information about potential gains or losses has been neglected or discounted. For example, a child who continues to rehearse words one at a time even after being shown other strategies may simply not be convinced to change a prior habit.

2. *Unconflicted change* is a decision to accept uncritically a salient or recommended course of action. A child who obediently categorizes pictures when directed, for example, may be demonstrating compliance more than a personal choice of an effective mnemonic strategy.

3. *Defensive avoidance* involves escape by procrastination, shifting responsibility to someone else, or rationalizing the choice of the least objectionable alternative. Mann and Janis (1982) point out that the first two options are low-effort coping responses and are more prevalent than rationalizations that require time and effort. It is interesting to note that two frequent tactics for rationalizing one's choice in defensive situations are to (a) distort the value or utility of an option, or (b) distort the probability of an outcome. Examples of the first type include exaggeration of the reward value, minimization of loss value, or denial of aversive consequences. Examples of the second type include exaggeration of the remoteness in time of the consequences of the action and minimization of social surveillance so that one *gets away with* a poor choice. This category of

decision making is remarkably consistent with defensive coping patterns, excuses, and attributions discussed by Covington (1983).

4. *Hypervigilance* is characteristic of *panic* situations in which a person impulsively seizes upon a solution that promises immediate relief. Extreme affect disrupts reasoning, as may happen for example, in frantic but illogical search for any method to recall information during an examination.

5. *Vigilance* is a pattern of careful, exhaustive, unbiased appraisal of possible courses of action. According to Mann and Janis (1982), a vigilant decision maker:

1. thoroughly canvasses a wide range of alternative courses of action;

2. takes account of the full range of objectives to be fulfilled and the values implicated by the choice;

3. carefully weighs whatever he or she knows about the costs or drawbacks and the uncertain risks of negative consequences, as well as the positive consequences, that could flow from each alternative;

4. intensively searches for new information relevant for further evaluation of the alternative;

5. conscientiously takes account of any new information or expert judgment to which he or she is exposed, even when the information or judgment does not support the course of action he or she initially prefers;

6. re-examines the positive and negative consequences of all known alternatives, including those originally regarded as unacceptable, before making a final choice; and

7. makes detailed provisions for implementing or executing the chosen course of action, with special attention to contingency plans that might be required if various known risks were to materialize. (p. 348)

These processes are idealistic but they include far more than expectancy-value models that are usually confined to an analysis of only the first three activities. Vigilant decision making also includes the same kinds of logical, executive control embodied in metacognition (Brown et al., 1983).

Conflict theory, as represented by the work of Mann and Janis (1982), complements expectancy-value theories with a focus on inadequate information processing and distorted coping patterns that arise from stressful decisions. The coping patterns outline conditions under which nonoptimal SEUs are constructed and describe different behavioral patterns that preserve self-values by distorting optimal decision-making steps. Stress drives the model and self-protective values are the overriding criteria, not accuracy of calculating optimal decisions. Clearly, the models of logical SEU analysis and conflict resolution complement each other by illuminating conditions under which expectancies and values are preserved or distorted in predictable ways.

Judgmental Heuristics

A second model of decision making is less idealized and emphasizes how biases influence judgment and choice. Kahneman and Tversky (1979) present evidence for two general violations of SEU theory. The first bias is called the "certainty effect" and is revealed in judgments where highly certain consequences, whether positive or negative, are given more weight than uncertain consequences. This suggests more than the simple claim that people cannot estimate probability well or multiply it by outcome value. The claim is that people are unduly influenced by what they perceive to be certain consequences. This has implications for risk taking because we know that moderate uncertainty provides more challenge than likely failure or success (Atkinson, 1982). For example, if a person believes that recall of 30 words is nearly impossible, he or she might not try at all because the certainty of failure looms large. This may lead to behavior like learned helplessness. Conversely, if successful recall is nearly certain, effort may be diminished because the task is not challenging and the value of the consequences drops precipitously. (And failure at easy tasks is humiliating.) Thus, certainty, or probability of particular outcomes, may not operate linearly as a scale of probabilities. People may distort their judgments to avoid nearly certain consequences.

Kahneman and Tversky's (1979) second biased heuristic is the "reference effect." This principle suggests that people make judgments relative to current status, expectations, or adaptation levels rather than absolute judgments of value or probability. In the previous discussion, this bias was incorporated in situational and developmental factors that may cause criteria for judgments to fluctuate. Mann and Janis (1982) also ascribe such variable reference points to situational factors. All of these views regard SEU as relative to the contexts in which the judgments are made rather than absolute evaluations. Other biases in judgment noted by Tversky and Kahneman (1974) may also be incorporated into developmental and situational factors. For example, "representativeness" and "availability" influence decision making because people attach inordinate importance to familiarity, salience, recency, and ease of recognition. Children and elderly adults who lack knowledge and confidence for intentional remembering may be especially influenced by situationally salient information. Options that are convenient or handy may be chosen not out of ignorance but because of poor decision-making procedures.

Satisficers

A third model of decision making minimizes the role of reflective analysis and comparison of alternative actions by emphasizing default strategies. In a sharp criticism of the comprehensive rationality embodied in some expectancy-value and decision-making models, Fischoff, Goitein, and Shapira (1982) said,

what else could people do besides trying to list and assess the expected consequences of all courses of action open to them? For one, they could try not to think at
all, but rely on non-analytic decision rules like 'this is (most like) what I've always
done' or 'this is what my (most expert) friends tell me to do' or 'this is what
everyone else is doing'. Or they could refuse to make one final decision, preferring
to muddle through by trial and error, making small incremental decisions that
afford an opportunity to change courses if things aren't going well. (p.326)

This characterization emphasizes short-sightedness and fuzzy-mindedness but
may portray realistic situations better than idealized versions of decision making.
Habits or trial and error decisions are consistent with Simon's (1967) notion of
"satisficing" in which a decision is made as soon as a partially acceptable
alternative has been identified. Here, decisions are not derived from multiplicative calculations nor exhaustive searching of alternatives. "Good enough
for now" seems to be the main criterion. Each of these options also externalizes
decision making and relieves the decision maker of cognitive burdens because
the decisions follow one's own immediate experiences (habits) or the prior
experience of others (traditions) or the current behavior of peers (norms) or the
recommendations of experts (instruction). Trial and error decisions that conform
to some external or familiar standard are certainly easier to make than IDEAL or
vigilant decisions. This view of decision making may characterize how naive
subjects act in experimental tests of memory ability that may be threatening or
ambiguous. Subjects typically receive little feedback or incentive as they remember nor are they penalized for muddling through. Poor use of memory
strategies could reflect biases in decisions as well as lack of mnemonic knowledge.

TOWARD A THEORY OF MOTIVATED REMEMBERING

Traditional accounts of memory development have neglected how remembering
is affected by motivational variables such as beliefs, expectancies, and incentive
values. We seemed to have forgotten Miller, Galanter, and Pribram's (1960)
admonition that ". . . knowing is for the sake of doing and doing is rooted in
valuing . . . " (p.71) and that any theory that does not recognize the connection
among knowledge, evaluation, and action ". . . allows a reflex being to behave
at random or leaves it lost in thought or overwhelmed by blind passion" (p.71).
The premise of this chapter is that there may be large differences between
cognitive competence and memory performance that are mediated by beliefs and
values. Motivational factors in turn may amplify or disguise memory differences
with age and skill. For example, cognitive expertise about chess may be accompanied by affect, expectations, and values that lead experts to invest their efforts

and talents in distinctly different ways from novices or people who dislike chess. Failure to measure motivational constructs does not mean that they are not operative. In a similar manner, the production deficiencies for mnemonic strategies often observed among young children, retarded people, or elderly adults may be confounded with a host of motivational factors that have simply been ignored by researchers. A theory of motivated remembering is required to account for the relative impact of affect, beliefs, expectancies, and decision making on people's memory performance.

The three views of intentional remembering presented here provide some outlines of variables that may be important for such a theory. Research has only begun on subjective beliefs about remembering but studies have shown clearly that (a) people often use mnemonic strategies that they believe are instrumentally useful and effective, (b) misconceptions about strategy utility are common among children, elderly adults, and students learning new tactics, and (c) misconceptions can diminish memory performance. Research on strategic remembering has yet to examine perceptions of effort and expectancies of successful use but the construal of these factors may also impact on subjective conceptions of strategy utility. Although an SEU orientation to mnemonic strategy production may help to explain why subjects choose to use or not use strategies, it may not be entirely adequate. Critics point to the following problems with SEU characterizations:

(a) probabilities and values of a potentially large number of options cannot be calculated or compared (Fischoff et al., 1982);

(b) the search for new information, compromise solutions, and refusals to act are neglected (Mann & Janis, 1982);

(c) biases distort SEU computations (Kahneman & Tversky, 1979); and

(d) individual motives and risk-taking influence choice behavior (Atkinson, 1982; Coombs, 1975).

Extrapolations of SEU models to intentional remembering must address these issues.

Expectancy-value models contribute a large potential pool of additional variables to consider. Incentives related to goals, consequences, and self-worth were mentioned briefly. More elaborate discussions can be found in Harter (1981), Feather (1982a), Heckhausen (1977), Nicholls (1983), Kuhl, (1982), Rokeach (1979), and Weiner (1979). Although expectancy-value models have been promulgated in social psychology to explain choice behavior, they have direct implications for developmental and educational analyses of cognition. Paris and Cross (1983), for example, have proposed an interactive model of learning that combines cognitive abilities and motivational factors. Finally, decision-making models provide different perspectives on the ways that stress, bias, and habits might influence problem solving.

It is not suggested that these various models can be glued together into an elegant theory. Each embodies serious problems that deserve at least brief notice. First, all three views are cognitive theories about skills, strategies, beliefs, values, and expectations. People in these models may be lost in thought, like Tolman's rats, trying to consider how to attack the task. More attention needs to be given to the translation of intentions into actions and how such actions are influenced by affect and enduring motives of individuals. Second, research in all three areas has been criticized for possible distortions in self-reports or remote inferences about motivations for observed behavior. Third, there has been a paucity of research on any of these motivational variables within developmental studies of learning and memory, and, perhaps because of this, theories in all three domains are based on models of adult performance and need to be elaborated for developmental variables.

Finally, all three views face serious problems defining core constructs, e.g., strategy, belief, and heuristic. For example, researchers have incredible difficulty agreeing on definitions of a *cognitive strategy* and distinguishing it from tactic, process, skill, metacognitive strategy, metacomponent, and the like. Inconsistency has led some researchers to define strategies explicitly as deliberate and selective coordination of mnemonic means and goals (e.g., Paris, 1978; Wellman, 1977). But some have reduced *strategy* to a vacuous, inclusive term like Pressley et al. (1985) who exclude deliberate and voluntary thinking as attributes of strategies and conclude, "Indeed, it is generally becoming recognized that strategy functioning at its very best has a mindless, reflexive character to it" (p.3).

On a more positive note, all three views provide optimal models of logical, thorough, reflective problem solving as well as descriptions of how performance can be degraded. For example, strategic remembering can be inefficient (or absent) due to inadequate procedural, declarative, or conditional knowledge about strategies (Paris, Lipson, & Wixson, 1983) or inadequate metacognitive understanding of strategies (Paris & Lindauer, 1982). Or effort can be diminished if the task goals are devalued, perceived as unattainable, or regarded as threats to self-competence. Alternatively, vigilant decisions can be shortcircuited by stress, biases, or trial and error muddling. The collective value of the views is that they implicate a larger variety of cognitive and affective variables that may enhance or undermine remembering. This is valuable for developmental assessments as well as for the design of instructional programs to teach strategies for learning and remembering. These implications are considered next.

Developmental Constraints and Interpretations

A theory of motivated remembering has several implications for developmental research and theories. Habitual use of personalized strategies, reactions to instruction, and inclinations to transfer skills can all be influenced by expectancies, beliefs, and decision-making rules. Thus, developmental differences in remembering may be due partly to differing conceptions of Person-Action-Outcome-Consequences relations that shape intentions and actions. Current accounts of memory development ignore or confound such motivational characteristics and new methods are needed to disentangle the relative contributions of these variables. It follows from this orientation that developmental constraints may reflect several different kinds of limitations on remembering including: (a) misconceptions of instrumental functions of strategies; (b) devaluation of effective techniques due to rationalization, forgetting, disuse, or perceived effort; (c) lack of effort due to self-perceived inability; (d) avoidance due to perceived threats to self-esteem; or (e) trial and error tactics in ambiguous situations. Half-hearted effort, defensive avoidance, or lack of persistence can lead subjects to adopt convenient or familiar tactics that meet some internal criterion of combined acceptable effort, effectiveness, and risk. These choices do not reflect decontextualized levels of mnemonic knowledge or motivation but rather a personal and functional approach to particular situations. If these characteristics of motivated remembering were included in assessments of metamemory, there might be stronger relations between subjective reports and memory performance.

Developmental constraints include more than misconceptions and nonoptimal effort, though. Idealized versions of metacognition, SEU, and decision making all include careful, logical comparisons of a large number of options. Very young and very old people may be unable to consider the range of options simultaneously or to calculate the multiplicative values of likelihood, value, and workload. The exhaustive listing of alternatives, predicting consequences of each, and weighing the pros and cons is a tremendous cognitive load for anyone. Children and elderly adults may be expected to perform these operations less effectively than young adults. Finally, we should recognize that reliance on external aids is related to age. Adults help children to remember and elderly adults may learn to use external memonic cues to compensate for poorer internal memory strategies. Familiar habits and illogical heuristics for remembering may also exert differential influences across the life span as compensatory strategies for remembering.

Instructional Episodes

Motivated remembering also has clear implications for instruction related to mnemonic skills because self-controlled strategies, both maintenance and transfer, depend on personal willingness to employ the tactics in a range of situations. Understanding how to use a strategy is no guarantee that the tactic will be generalized or followed vigorously. Theoretical attempts to explain strategy transfer in terms of *cold* cognitive knowledge neglect motivational beliefs, values, and expectancies as well as social guidance. Current research has rediscovered the social context of instruction after years of barren experimental techniques, "blind training" (cf. Brown et al., 1983), that masqueraded as cognitive instruction. The popularity of Vygotsky's views and the "zone of proximal development" reflect renewed interest in social guidance and the motivation transferred from teacher to pupil during instruction (Rogoff & Wertsch, 1984). The concepts, beliefs, values, and motivation that are actually transferred in "zones" remain to be articulated but the framework highlights the importance of socially transmitted knowledge and motivation. Instructional episodes are usually brief, intensive, and recurrent opportunities for teachers or adults to impart information about strategies directly to pupils. During these episodes, successful teachers convince students that strategies are important to use so that students understand that extra effort leads to enhanced performance. Utility and workload are taught along with values related to goals, consequences, and self. Adults reinforce feelings of self-efficacy, control, and esteem in instructional episodes as cognitive coaches. Pride and mastery arise from socially guided interactions and they help to motivate future efforts at strategic remembering.

CONCLUSION

In this chapter I have tried to assemble cognitive and developmental aspects of motivated remembering. The starting point was research on memory strategies and the illustration that subjective perceptions of strategy effectiveness vary with age and contribute to developmental changes in spontaneous production of appropriate strategies. Subsequently, the concept of perceived strategy utility was enlarged to include dimensions of workload and probability that are similar to notions of SEU in expectancy value models of social motivation. Expectancy value models of choice behavior may be heuristic also because they include subjective perceptions of the intrinsic and extrinsic consequences of memory success or failure. These may change with age, ability, and situation to influence strategy choices, vigor, or persistence. Consequences of memory also influence how people view their own abilities so that successful strategic remembering may promote feelings of efficacy, control, and esteem. The importance of these variables in other behavioral domains, and theories of social motivation, argue for empirical research on how they affect memory development.

The formation of expectancies and values relevant for remembering reveals that lack of knowledge, misconceptions, or partial knowledge may all contribute to age-related changes in memory skills. But these cognitive concepts and competencies should not leave people buried in thought, trying to determine how to remember. Decision-making procedures serve as frames of reference for evaluating how people compare alternatives for action. An idealized set of procedures was contrasted with emotional coping patterns, illogical heuristics, and habits. Under conditions of stress or incomplete information processing, people may act intentionally yet inefficiently in their attempts to remember. Identification of these conditions may help illuminate situational factors that influence memory and complement views of cognitive naivite.

The outline of motivated remembering presented in this chapter is intended to expand upon cognitive competence models and to provide performance mediators that function in everyday situations of intentional remembering. The approach is a field theory because it considers how people behave as a function of their ecological contexts. It is a developmental theory because it is necessary to chart behavior longitudinally in order to understand its use. The theory is social, motivational, and functional because intentional remembering is influenced by other people and it serves larger purposes in the individual's stream of behavior. The focus of the theory is explaining individual and situational differences by considering the constellation of variables that influence choices, expectancies, and decision making. Neither stability nor transfer are assumed across individuals or situations as opposed to the normative, universal assumptions of current theories. It is hoped that this combination of theoretical and pragmatic perspectives will provide viable alternatives to Piagetian and information-processing accounts of memory development. The frameworks suggest many new variables to study and invite new methods and ideas from social, motivational, and instructional psychology to help explain memory development.

ACKNOWLEDGMENT

This chapter was written while the author was a visiting scholar at Flinders University and the University of Newcastle in Australia. I appreciate the support of these universities and especially the stimulating conversations with Norm Feather, Leon Mann, Mary Luszcz, John Biggs, John Kirby, and Phil Moore.

REFERENCES

Atkinson, J. W. (1982). Old and new conceptions of how expected consequences influence actions. In N. Feather (Ed.), *Expectations and actions: Expectancy value models in psychology*. Hillsdale, NJ: Lawrence Erlbaum Associates.

Borkowski, J. G., Levers, S. R., & Gruenenfelder, T. A. (1976). Transfer of mediational strategies in children: The role of activity and awareness during strategy acquisition. *Child Development, 47*, 779–786.

Bransford, J., & Stein, B. (1984). *The IDEAL problem-solver*. San Francisco: Freeman.

Brown, A. L. (1978). Knowing when, where, and how to remember: A problem of metacognition. In R. Glaser (Ed.), *Advances in instructional psychology* (Vol. 1). Hillsdale, NJ: Lawrence Erlbaum Associates.

Brown, A. L., Bransford, J. D., Ferrara, R. A., & Campione, J. C. (1983). Learning, remembering, and understanding. In P. H. Mussen (Ed.), *Handbook of child psychology* (Vol. III). New York: Wiley.

Cavanaugh, J. C., & Perlmutter, M. (1982). Metamemory: A critical examination. *Child Development, 53*, 11–28.

Chi, M. T. H. (1978). Knowledge structure and memory development. In R. Siegler (Ed.), *Children's thinking: What develops?* Hillsdale, NJ: Lawrence Erlbaum Associates.

Coombs, C. (1975). Portfolio theory and the measurement of risk. In M. F. Kaplan & S. Schwartz (Eds.), *Human judgment and decision processes.* New York: Academic Press.

Covington, M. V. (1983). Motivated cognitions. In S. Paris, G. Olson, & H. Stevenson (Eds.), *Learning and motivation in the classroom.* Hillsdale. NJ: Lawrence Erlbaum Associates.

Cox, G., & Paris, S. G. (1978, November). *Memory skills of young and elderly: What is a production deficiency?* Paper presented at the Gerontological Society Meeting, Dallas.

Cox, G., & Paris, S. G. (1979, April). *The nature of mnemonic production deficiencies: A lifespan analysis.* Paper presented at the Society for Research in Child Development, San Francisco.

Dweck, C. S., & Elliot, E. S. (1983). Achievement motivation. In P. H. Mussen (Ed.), *Handbook of child psychology* (Vol.IV). New York: Wiley.

Fabricius, W. V., & Hagen, J. W. (1984). Use of causal attributions about recall performance to assess metamemory and predict strategic memory behavior in young children. *Developmental Psychology, 20,* 975–987.

Feather, N. T. (1982a). *Expectations and actions: Expectancy-value models in psychology.* Hillsdale, NJ: Lawrence Erlbaum Associates.

Feather, N. T. (1982b). Actions in relation to expected consequences: An overview of a research program. In N. Feather (Ed.), *Expectations and actions: Expectancy-value models in psychology.* Hillsdale, NJ: Lawrence Erlbaum Associates.

Fischoff, B., Goitein, B., & Shapira, Z. (1982). The experienced utility of expected utility approaches. In N. Feather (Ed.), *Expectations and actions: Expectancy-value models in psychology.* Hillsdale, NJ: Lawrence Erlbaum Associates.

Flavell, J. H. (1970). Developmental studies of mediated memory. In H. W. Reese & L. P. Lipsitt (Eds.), *Advances in child development and behavior* (Vol.5). New York: Academic Press.

Harter, S. (1981). A model of mastery motivation in children: Individual differences and developmental change. In W. A. Collins (Ed.), *Minnesota symposium on child psychology* (Vol.14). Hillsdale, NJ: Lawrence Erlbaum Associates.

Heckhausen, H. (1977). Achievement motivation and its constructs: A cognitive model. *Motivation and Emotion, 1,* 283–329.

Kahneman, D., & Tversky, A. (1979). Prospect theory. *Econometrica, 47,* 263–291.

Kennedy, B. A., & Miller, D. J. (1976). Persistent use of verbal rehearsal as a function of information about its value. *Child Development, 47,* 566–569.

Kreutzer, M. A., Leonard, C., & Flavell, J. H. (1975). An interview study of children's knowledge about memory. *Monographs of the Society for Research in Child Development, 40* (1, Serial No. 159).

Kuhl, J. (1982). The expectancy-value approach within the theory of social motivation: Elaborations, extensions, critique. In N. Feather (Ed.), *Expectations and actions: Expectancy-value models in psychology.* Hillsdale, NJ: Lawrence Erlbaum Associates.

Maehr, M. (1983). On doing well in science: Why Johnny no longer excels; Why Sarah never did. In S. Paris, G. Olson, & H. Stevenson (Eds.), *Learning and motivation in the classroom.* Hillsdale, NJ: Lawrence Erlbaum Associates.

Mann, L., & Janis, I. (1982). Conflict theory of decision making and the expectancy-value approach. In N. Feather (Ed.), *Expectations and actions: Expectancy-value models in psychology.* Hillsdale, NJ: Lawrence Erlbaum Associates.

Miller, G., Galanter, E., & Pribram, K. (1960). *Plans and the structure of behavior.* New York: Holt.

Nicholls, J. G. (1983). Conceptions of ability and achievement motivation: A theory and its implications for education. In S. Paris, G. Olson, & H. W. Stevenson (Eds.), *Learning and motivation in the classroom.* Hillsdale, NJ: Lawrence Erlbaum Associates.

Palincsar, A. S., & Brown, A. L. (1984). Reciprocal teaching of comprehension-fostering and comprehension-monitoring activities. *Cognition and Instruction, 1,* 117–175.

Paris, S. G. (1978). Coordination of means and goals in the development of mnemonic skills. In P. Ornstein (Ed.), *Memory development in children.* Hillsdale, NJ: Lawrence Erlbaum Associates.

Paris, S. G., & Cross, D. R. (1983). Ordinary learning: Pragmatic connections among children's beliefs, motives, and actions. In J. Bisanz, G. Bisanz, & R. Kail (Eds.), *Learning in children.* New York: Springer-Verlag.

Paris, S. G., Cross, D. R., & Lipson, M. Y. (1984). Informed strategies for learning: A program to improve children's reading awareness and comprehension. *Journal of Educational Psychology, 76,* 1239–1252.

Paris, S. G., & Jacobs, J. E. (1984). The benefits of informed instruction for children's reading awareness and comprehension skills. *Child Development, 55,* 2083–2093.

Paris, S. G., & Lindauer, B. K. (1982). The development of cognitive skills during childhood. In B. Wolman (Ed.), *Handbook of developmental psychology.* Englewood Cliffs, NJ: Prentice-Hall.

Paris, S. G., Lipson, M. Y., & Wixson, K. K. (1983). Becoming a strategic reader. *Contemporary Educational Psychology, 8,* 293–316.

Paris, S. G., Newman, D. R., & Jacobs, J. E. (1985). Social contexts and functions of children's remembering. In C. J. Brainerd & M. Pressley (Ed.), *The cognitive side of memory development.* New York: Springer-Verlag.

Paris, S. G., Newman, R. S., & McVey, K. A. (1982). Learning the functional significance of mnemonic actions: A microgenetic study of strategy acquisition. *Journal of Experimental Child Psychology, 34,* 490–509.

Pressley, M., Forrest-Pressley, D. L., Elliot-Faust, D., & Miller, G. (1985). Children's use of cognitive strategies, how to teach strategies, and what to do if they can't be taught. In M. Pressley & C. J. Brainerd (Eds.), *Cognitive learning and memory in children.* New York: Springer-Verlag.

Pressley, M., Levin, T. R., & Bryant, S. L. (1983). Memory strategy instruction during adolescence: When is explicit instruction needed? In M. Pressley & T. R. Levin (Eds.), *Cognitive strategy research: Psychological foundations.* New York: Springer-Verlag.

Pressley, M., Ross, K. A., Levin, J. R., & Ghatala, E. S. (1984). The role of strategy utility knowledge in children's strategy decision making. *Journal of Experimental Child Psychology, 38,* 491–504.

Ringel, B. A., & Springer, C. J. (1980). On knowing how well one is remembering: The persistence of strategy use during transfer. *Journal of Experimental Child Psychology, 29,* 322–333.

Rogoff, B., & Wertsch, J. V. (Eds.). (1984). *Children's learning in the "Zone of Proximal Development".* San Francisco: Jossey-Bass.

Rokeach, M. (1979). Some unresolved issues in theories of beliefs, attitudes, and values. In H. J. Howe & M. M. Page (Eds.), *Nebraska symposium on motivation* (Vol.27). Lincoln: University of Nebraska Press.

Simon, H. A. (1967). Motivation and emotional controls of cognition. *Psychological Review, 74,* 29–39.

Tversky, A., & Kahneman, D. (1974). Judgment under uncertainty: Heuristics and biases. *Science, 185,* 1124–1131.

Weiner, B. (1979). A theory of motivation for some classroom experiences. *Journal of Educational Psychology, 71,* 3–25.

Wellman, H. M. (1977). The early development of intentional memory behavior. *Human Development, 22,* 86–101.

Wellman, H. M., Ritter, K., & Flavell, J. H. (1975). Deliberate memory behavior in the delayed reactions of very young children. *Developmental Psychology, 11,* 780–787.

Zivian, M. T., & Darjes, R. W. (1983). Free recall by in-school and out-of-school adults: Performance and metory. *Developmental Psychology, 19,* 513–520.

11 Memory in Context: The Case of Prospective Remembering

S. J. Ceci
U. Bronfenbrenner
J. G. Baker
Cornell University

In the last few years there has been a resurgence of interest by cognitive psychologists in the influence of *context* on development (see Dixon & Hertzog, this volume; Scribner, 1984). Evidence for this renewed interest can be found in the growing body of research concerned with *functional* or *everyday* forms of cognition. An implicit assumption underlying this research is the belief that the context in which cognition takes place is not simply an adjunct to the cognition, but a constituent of it. Adjunctive views of cognition have given way to a view that recognizes the importance of the physical and psychological setting in which cognition unfolds. The social and physical context has been shown to influence a subject's perception of a problem as well as to shape his or her solution to it (Lave, Murtaugh, & de la Roche, 1984). This interest in *context* has been especially visible among memory researchers (Chi, 1978; Wagner, 1978), and at Cornell University our colleagues and ourselves have been part of this chorus (Ceci & Bronfenbrenner, 1985; Neisser, 1982).

In this chapter we shall describe a series of experiments that have been conducted over the last few years. We briefly present our methods and results, and suggest what we believe they tell us about the ecology of human memory. These studies differ from traditional studies in one important way. They *embed* memory processes in a larger social context, thus focusing on the adaptive nature of memory rather than on a particular set of disembedded information-processing subroutines.

Before we describe our experiments, it may be useful to alert our readers to three different levels of discourse that will be entertained. On the most narrow level, we present evidence for the existence of a strategy that we call *strategic time-monitoring* and demonstrate that children as young as 10-years-of-age appreciate its utility and cognitive efficiency. On a somewhat broader plane, we show how various contextual factors influence the likelihood that children will deploy this strategy, and argue that even young children respond differentially to changes in context. Finally, on the broadest level of discourse, we present what we believe our findings suggest about the need to incorporate more ecological complexity into models of memory development than we have heretofore been inclined to do. We argue that the context in which remembering takes place should be regarded not as something adjunctive to memory but as a constituent of it.

At the outset, however, we want to acknowledge the incompleteness and inadequacies of this early effort to develop an ecological description of memory development. Even though this might seem to be a simple undertaking at first glance, the issue of the ecology of human memory is a complex one, and this attempt is but a crude beginning.

RETROSPECTIVE VERSUS PROSPECTIVE MEMORY

After nearly 2 decades of vigorous inquiry by memory researchers, a great deal is known about developmental changes in processes that support *retrospective* memory. By *retrospective* memory we are referring to the encoding, storage, and retrieval of previously presented information, whether this information is something as disconnected from the cognitive system as nonsense syllables, or something as inextricable as connected discourse—and all of the levels in-between (e.g., isolated pictures and words, photographs of faces, etc).

In contrast to our vast reservoir of knowledge concerning *retrospective* memory, very little is knows about the development of processes that support *prospective* memory, i.e., remembering to do something in the future. This lack of knowledge about *prospective* memory is somewhat surprising given its ubiquitousness in our daily lives. Individuals of all ages would appear to be confronted with demands for prospective memory on a regular basis, e.g., remembering to file income tax returns by April 15th, to take one's medicine every 3 hours, or even to turn off the bath water in 15 minutes to prevent a flood!

In chapter 5, Mike Pressley reported the results of a literature survey he and his colleagues conducted on *retrospective* memory. During the last decade there have been over 4000 articles and chapters that have dealt with some feature of *retrospective* memory. According to Pressley, over 1000 of these articles were concerned specifically with *developmental* aspects of *retrospective* memory. Our own survey on *prospective* memory has revealed that, up to the beginning of 1984, there existed very little research on this topic. In fact, the number of published studies could be counted on the fingers of one's two hands. And those articles that dealt specifically with *developmental* aspects of *prospective* memory could be counted on the fingers of a single hand! All of these studies (N = 3) were concerned with one aspect of *prospective* memory, the use of external retrieval cues to facilitate remembering to undertake some action in the future (Kreutzer, Leonard, & Flavell, 1975; Meacham, 1982; Meacham & Colombo, 1981). In this chapter we attempt to redress this imbalance, albeit in a rather modest way.

External retrieval cues are an undeniably useful means of fostering *prospective* memory, one that seems to have been appreciated by individuals from time immemorial (consider the familiar folk strategy of tying a ribbon around one's finger). Flavell and his colleagues were the first to examine age differences in the appreciation of external retrieval cues, showing that even the youngest children they interviewed exhibited a knowledge of the benefits. For example, 6-year-olds reported that they remembered to bring their ice skates to school on the following day, either by placing notes to themselves in conspicuous places or by putting their skates by the front door so that they might serve as reminders as they departed for school (Kreutzer et al., 1975).

In many *prospective* memory situations, however, external retrieval cues are either inefficient or unfeasable. Indeed, an entire class of activities exist for which the use of external aids are impractical. These activities have in common a need to undertake some act during a narrowly specified range of time. In order to react promptly, at the desired time, one needs to be constantly aware of the passage of time. A good example of such an activity is getting a suntan. During one's first encounter of the season with direct sun (or with a sunlamp) it is important not to become over-exposed. If one's tolerance is, for example, 10 minutes, then forgetting to turn off the sunlamp by even a few minutes can have unpleasant consequences.

On the basis of our interpretation of some empirical data on adults' efforts to remember to take specific future actions (Harris & Wilkins, 1982), as well as introspections into our own attempts of this kind, we reasoned that adults try to *calibrate* their psychological clocks by frequently comparing their subjective estimates of the passage of time with the actual passage of clock time. We suspected that adults become proficient at monitoring the passage of time through early and frequent clock checks. These clock checks, we reasoned, help one to gain confidence in his or her subjective estimates of elapsed time and permit one increasingly more freedom from the constraints of clock watching. The frequent comparison of one's temporal estimates with the amount of time that has actually transpired during the early part of a waiting period, enables one to delay subsequent clock checks for progressively longer intervals.

It is possible that the *calibration* of one's psychological clock might initially entail extra effort at the beginning of a prospective memory task. In the long run, however, calibration is likely to result in a reduced need for clock checking, once it is accomplished. In this sense calibration would appear to be a *low-effort* cognitively efficient solution because it not only allows one to undertake multiple tasks simultaneously (i.e., once it is accomplished a subject is freed from the repetitive demands of clock watching), but it also is associated with less overall clock-checking. In our work we have been interested in modeling the calibration process and examining systematic variations in it as a function of context. But an adequately complex account of the calibration process must go beyond the knowledge of that process in an adult's head and model the acquisition of this process. In the two studies that follow we briefly attempt to chart the development of calibration in children and adolescents. We began by posing the three following hypotheses:

Hypothesis 1

A high frequency of clock checking during the early part of a waiting period, followed by a long period of inactive clock watching, and finally some last-minute clock-checking, is a cognitively efficient means of remembering to commit some future action. Namely, a U-shaped distribution of clock checking is expected. This is because the frequent early clock checking enables individuals to calibrate their psychological clocks so that they can eventually disregard the clock for long periods without sacrificing promptness.

Hypothesis 2

The willingness to engage in calibration (i.e., the U-shaped distribution of clock-checking) will be influenced by the context in which the remembering occurs. Based on Bronfenbrenner's (1977) comparative evaluation of experiments by nature and by design, we expect that the laboratory setting will induce anxiety, especially in the youngest children, that is incompatible with the adoption of a low-effort solution to the problem of remembering to commit some future act. The more familiar and less threatening context of children's own homes on the other hand, will lead to increased use of the calibration strategy.

Hypothesis 3

The use of the cognitively efficient, low-effort calibration strategy will interact with certain biologically based variables (age and sex) and certain social variables (sex-role expectations of the task). These predictions were derived from the knowledge that the processes of socialization encourage different expectations and preferences between boys and girls, as well as between older and younger children. Specifically, on a traditionally female sex-typed task (baking) girls would be less likely to engage in a low-effort solution whereas on a traditionally male sex-typed task (changing a motorcycle battery) boys would be less likely to do so. Given its predominantly learned nature, this sex-typing is expected to be greatest among the younger aged children.

BAKING CAKES AND CHARGING BATTERIES

In order to test our hypothesis about the presence of the *calibration* strategy and specific contextual influences on its use, we asked 96 10- and 14-year-old boys and girls to perform one of two identically structured tasks, either bake cupcakes for 30 minutes or charge a motorcycle battery for 30 minutes. Half of the children were asked to perform this task in their own homes and the rest were asked to perform it in a psychophysics laboratory at Cornell University. While the children waited for the cupcakes to bake, or the battery to charge, they were permitted the free and unlimited use of a video game, *PacMan*. Children who conducted the task in their home were allowed to play the video game in whatever room of their home they normally played games or watched television. Children who performed the tasks in the laboratory played the video game in an adjoining office. While they waited for the tasks to be completed, all children were secretly observed to determine how often they checked a wall clock. For those children who conducted the tasks in their homes, the observer was an older sibling who was trained by one of the researchers to observe their younger sibling unobtrusively. Although these older siblings pretended to be reading in another part of the same room, in actuality, they recorded each instance when the child turned away from the video game in order to check on the clock. In the laboratory, this task was performed by unfamiliar peers of the children's older siblings.

We utilized a number of methods in order to test our first hypothesis—that a U-shaped distribution would characterize the frequency of clock checking by children who were involved in either the task of baking cupcakes or charging a motorcycle battery. First, the 30 minute experimental period was broken into six consecutive time periods of 5 minutes each. A cursory visual inspection of a distribution of the frequency of clock checking for these time periods (Fig. 11.1), lends qualitative support to our hypothesis. As expected, clock checking was most frequent during early involvement in the task as well as just prior to either the removal of the batch of cupcakes from the oven or the removal of battery cables from the charger. During intermediate time periods, the frequency of clock checking was minimal. It appears that by this time children had already calibrated their psychological clocks, resulting in reduced clock checking and increased attention directed towards the video game.

In order to evaluate this first hypothesis quantitatively, an orthogonal polynomial regression analysis was performed and, indeed, revealed a parabolic curve as the best descriptor of clock-checking over time.

Although the previous analysis lends support to the existence of *strategic time monitoring* as cognitive phenomenon, probably the most striking finding was the confirmation of our second hypothesis which revealed dramatic variations in the amount of clock checking as a function of the experimental context. Figures 11.1 and 11.2 clearly reveal disparate curves that vary according to whether the child

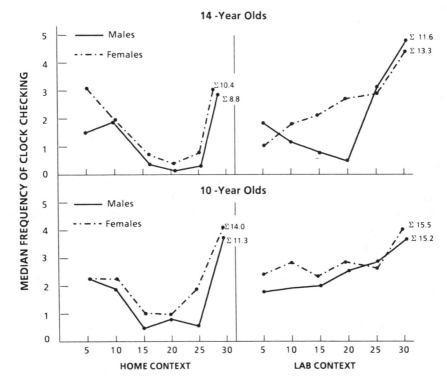

FIG. 11.1. Children's clock-checking frequencies on the cupcake baking task. Late responders excluded. (Σ = Mean total number of clock checks.)

performed the task in the home—a familiar setting complete with customary appliances and furnishings as well as in the presence of an older sibling, or whether the task was conducted in the laboratory—a strange environment filled with psychophysics instrumentation and the presence of an unfamiliar adult. Whereas the graph for the home context is parabolic, thereby confirming our notion that children utilize the strategy of time monitoring in the home, the graph documenting the frequency of clock checking for subjects in the laboratory appears almost linear. Statistical analyses confirm the existence of a significant main effect for context ($p<.001$).

This second hypothesis was tested by comparing the overall number of clock checks. For each age and sex comparison, the total number of clock checks was greater in the laboratory setting than in the home. On the one hand, these results suggest that children in the home setting not only utilized a calibration strategy (as evidenced by the larger quadratic components), but they used this strategy in an efficient manner, as indicated by less total time spent monitoring the clock.

On the other hand, it appears that children who conducted the tasks in the laboratory were less efficient overall. As opposed to the child who engaged in strategic time monitoring in the home context, children in the laboratory context exhibited what we termed *anxious time monitoring*. That is to say, children in an unfamiliar laboratory setting did not strategically monitor time to their benefit, but instead they appeared more apprehensive, which resulted in an incremental (rather than U-shaped) rate of clock checking throughout the course of the 30 minute experimental period.

Taken together, the results associated with the first two hypotheses suggest that young children are able to use complex cognitive strategies in order to remember to perform a future task (remove cupcakes from the oven or disconnect battery charger cables). Whether children *do* indeed use these strategies, however, is often a function of the experimental context in which memory occurs. We found that all children, but especially young children, were more likely to employ strategic time monitoring in the more comfortable and familiar environment of the home than in the strange and unfamiliar setting of the university psychophysics laboratory. Specifically, young children in the home conserved

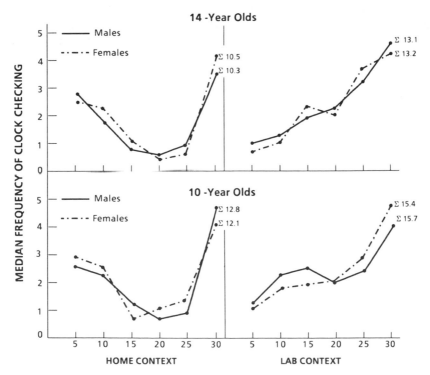

FIG. 11.2. Children's clock-checking frequencies on the battery-charging task. Late responders are excluded. (Σ = Mean total number of clock checks.)

time overall, while young children in the psychophysics laboratory displayed both increased vigilance and decreased efficiency, with the latter reflected in a steadily increasing frequency of clock checking throughout the duration of the experimental period. Although this latter method of time monitoring suggests both more anxiety and more concern surrounding task performance, both methods appear equally predictive of a child's ability to remember to take the cupcakes out of the oven or to remove the battery cables from the charger. In sharp contrast, 21 children who missed the 30 minute deadline by more than 1 minute exhibited an altogether different pattern of clock monitoring (see Fig. 11.3). *All* children who failed to perform the task on time decreased their clock checks throughout the course of the experiment. Not a single one of these late responders engaged in strategic time-monitoring. We found that within the group of late responders, children who checked the clock the most infrequently were also the children who were the latest to remove the cupcakes or battery cables.

All of these findings can be qualified by the results of our third hypothesis, which anticipated these effects to vary as a function of the age and sex of the child. Overall adolescents utilized a more efficient time-monitoring strategy than did younger children. Not only did older children spend less total time engaged in clock monitoring, but they also made more use of the calibration strategy. These age differences, however, only prevailed in the laboratory setting. In the home setting, children of both ages were just as likely to engage in strategic time-monitoring.

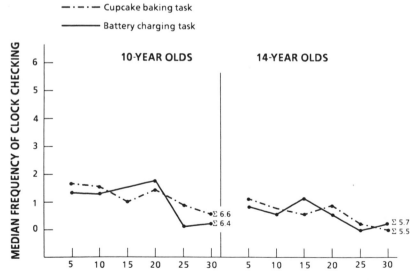

FIG. 11.3. Clock-checking frequencies of "late responders" in the HOME context. No cases of late responding occurred in the LAB context. (Σ = Mean total number of clock checks.)

Beyond age differences, we hypothesized that the traditionally female task of baking would engender a pattern of anxious time-monitoring in girls, while correspondingly boys would manifest this "anxious pattern" while engaged in the motorcycle battery task. Our analyses did not fully support this hypothesized two-way interaction between the sex of the child and the sex role expectations of the task the child was asked to perform. Instead, we found a more complex interaction between age, sex, context, and type of task. To reiterate our central theme, with hardly an exception, significant interactions were restricted to the *laboratory environment!* Specifically, older boys within the laboratory context, who baked cupcakes, utilized the most efficient calibration strategy of any of the groups tested in the laboratory. We found that of the four different groups of subjects that were examined in the laboratory, adolescent males manifested the least anxious and most efficient pattern of strategic time-monitoring. The particular task of baking cupcakes, along with the context of the laboratory, holds few sex-typed expectations of success for boys. Although there was a trend towards significance, girls did not evidence a pattern of time monitoring congruent with sex role expectations in either context.

An examination of the overall frequency of clock checks, by sex, revealed that, regardless of age, boys who engaged in the battery charging task glanced at the clock most often. Correspondingly, girls (particularly in the home context), who were involved in the cupcake baking task checked the clock the most frequently.

Overall, we suggest that the various strategies that aid prospective memory have different costs and benefits. On the one hand, strategic time-monitoring offers a period of time for secondary activities (e.g., playing PacMan). However, because the total time spent monitoring the clock is reduced, the child runs the risk of failing to remember to perform the task at all. On the other hand, anxious time-monitoring insured completion of the primary task, but the child now runs the risk of neglecting secondary tasks. Finally, the failure to use any apparent strategy seems to result in increased attention directed towards secondary tasks, with the primary task left undone (see Fig. 11.3).

Although interesting in and of themselves, these findings leave a number of issues and alternative hypotheses open for speculation. For example, is it not reasonable to suggest that children in the home context viewed their participation and the outcome of this participation as less important than did children in the laboratory setting? Likewise, although children in the laboratory setting may typically be able to engage in strategic time monitoring in the course of everyday events, when placed in an unfamiliar and more demanding setting do they revert to a strategy which insures success but with reduced efficiency? Finally, exactly which aspect of the laboratory context was responsible for the observed reduction in strategic time-monitoring? Was it the presence of strange observance and/or strange equipment or some as yet unidentified feature of the laboratory? In order to address these speculations empirically, we conducted one final experiment.

Twenty-four children were asked to bake cupcakes in a kitchen on campus—a residential apartment located within Cornell University's home economics department. It was our expectation that this new setting would be viewed by children as less familiar than their own kitchen, yet more familiar than the university psychophysics laboratory. Moreover, this kitchen-on-campus context allowed us to separate the effects of strange observers and strange equipment, as it was a normally finished kitchen (and adjacent living room), although the person assigned to observe the child was unfamiliar.

The results of this subexperiment revealed a pattern of clock checking by younger children that was indistinguishable from their age mates' anxious time-monitoring in the previous study. By contrast, older children, utilized a U-shaped calibration strategy similar to their peers' previous pattern of strategic time monitoring in the home environment. In other words, it appears that for younger children the unfamiliarity of the university setting outweighs the familiarity of an ordinary kitchen. This *strange situation,* in turn, resulted in a pattern of anxious time monitoring and a cumulative number of clock checks no different from the pattern of results that were obtained in the psychophysics laboratory. Conversely, adolescents responded to a kitchen in a university setting in the same way their peers reacted to a kitchen in their own home. Thus, for these older children, it appears that the causative factor in the failure of their peers to engage in strategic time-monitoring in the laboratory was the presence of strange equipment and not strange observers. We hesitate to press the point, however, because the outcome may very well have been different if we had used different stimuli, observers, and/or equipment.

Beyond Memory Development: Cognitive Development in Context.   Moving beyond the kitchen-on-campus experiment, to a more general level, the question arises as to whether and how children's prospective memory strategies might vary if this same experiment were to be conducted in other settings besides those included in the present investigation, for example, in a classroom, or a neighborhood youth center? Would the former induce more cautious and strained responses resembling those engendered in the laboratory? And, would the latter invite more complex and efficient cognitive strategies akin to those that arose in the more familiar and relaxed atmosphere of the home? As Dixon and Hertzog (this volume) argue, there is a need for memory researchers to address the issue of *intra*individual variation and challenge the implicit *trait-like* assumptions about memory that have characterized much of the past literature.

Such questions can be raised at a still broader level of context, perhaps of even greater significance for behavior and development (Bronfenbrenner & Crouter, 1982). For example, what would have been the result of this series of experiments had they been conducted with children from different social classes or cultural backgrounds, from a single parent versus two-parent homes, from families in which the mother worked for pay versus those in which she remained at home? To the extent that these contextual shifts imply shifts in children's roles and experiences, we would expect them to adapt their cognitive behavior in keeping with our functionalist perspective.

These questions can also be extended beyond the domain of prospective memory to a broad range of cognitive processes. Indeed, it would be surprising if the robust ecological variation that we observed in children's use of time-monitoring strategies was but a single instance of a more general phenomenon, that of contextual constraints on cognition. Many aspects of cognitive functioning originate in response to specific environmental challenges and appear to be evoked most readily by the reinstatement of these challenges (Ceci, Baker, & Nightingale, in press; Ceci & Liker, 1986). According to this view, we might expect that laboratory assessments of one's cognitive developmental level would match one's cognitive capability only to the extent that the laboratory task is embedded in an appropriate social context that reinstates important environmental challenges. We turn next to some preliminary evidence bearing on this issue.

Recently, we began a project that aimed to assess the influence of context on problem solving. We are not yet finished with the aspects of this study, therefore our findings must be viewed tentatively. Children aged 10 to 12 were asked to predict the distance traversed on a computer screen by a geometric shape (circle, square, triangle). The shapes were one of two colors (black, white) and two sizes (small, large). A mathematical function that weighted each level of these variables (shape, color, size) and their interactions was developed to determine the distance traversed by each shape on the screen. For example, one function that we developed specified that all white shapes traveled upward and all black shapes downward; all circles traveled leftward, all squares went rightward, and all triangles remained in the center of the screen. Finally, all large shapes traveled to a far location while all small shapes traveled to a nearby location. (It will be noted that this function is a "main effects" algorithm because it can determine the screen destination of a particular shape without considering interactions among the variables.) Children were given 750 feedback trials in which a shape appeared at the center of the screen and they were asked to indicate its likely termination point. We measured (in screen pixels) the distance between their estimated termination point and the actual termination point. Of interest to us was the ability of the children to employ interactive and multivariate forms of reasoning to estimate the distance traversed by the shapes. There is some suggestion in the cognitive literature that college students have a great deal of difficulty using three variables in an interactive model (Klayman, 1985; Nisbett & Ross, 1980). Rather, it appears that they rely on what might be regarded as *main effects* models, for example, estimating the distance on the basis of the unique variance associated with each color size, and shape, but not considering their interactive variance.

As might be expected, our 10- to 12-year-olds fared no better than college students, rarely demonstrating an appreciation of the interactive nature of the three variables when a curvilinear function was used to determine the shapes' distances. We did not give a great deal of thought to this finding until one day while visiting a game arcade at a local shopping mall one of us noticed youngsters playing a video game in which successful performers appeared to require an understanding of the manner in which the levels of one variable influences the value of another variable. In short, children in this game arcade were exhibiting the type of cognitive complexity that we had failed to observe in our laboratory. The impression was so strong that we felt impelled to rerun the distance estimation task with one important amendment: The mathematical function that we had used to determine a shape's distance was now used to control the distance traversed by a flying object (balloon, butterfly, bee). These objects were either white or black, and either large or small. As in the earlier task, successful prediction required one to consider all three variables, in some cases interactively, and in others only additively. Children were instructed to type a number on the keyboard that represented their best prediction of where the object would terminate on the screen. (The screen was subdivided into sectors, each with a corresponding number.)

If you guessed that the children were able to conquer this task once it was embedded in a context of known entities such as flying objects you would be wrong. They were not better then their peers had been in the original experiment with geometric shapes. So, we decided to add some additional realism to the task. Instead of typing numbers on the keyboard to represent children's estimates of the objects' termination point, we asked them to *shoot down* the objects with a cannon that was under the control of a joystick. They were awarded different amounts of points for *hits* of varying objects, sizes, and colors. In this final form the task resembled a video game, and children took to it with great enthusiasm. Their success in estimating the flying objects' distances was assessed by the degree to which their cannon shots intersected them. As before, this often required an appreciation of the effects of the three variables *interactively*. Even our youngest children fared significantly better than chance at estimating the objects' termination points (and better than their peers in their earlier experiments—see Fig. 11.4).

In explaining these results, we have taken a cue from the Soviet activity theorists and suggested that complex cognition can proceed in the absence of intention, provided the subject is emerged in the physical activity of the task (Wertsch, 1981). By adding the physical component of shooting a cannon at the flying objects—and the accompanying visceral sensation—children shifted from a conscious mode of cognizing to an automatic one. It is not that the video game contest improved children's ability to think more complexly by providing familiar cues; rather the added context allowed the children to cognize naturally and effortlessly. In the future we plan to follow the implications of this assertion.

ADDITIVE DISTANCE ESTIMATION TASK

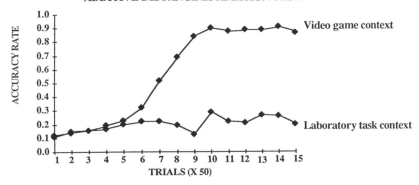

FIG. 11.4. Children's mean proportion of accurate estimates of a moving object in game versus laboratory contexts. (Simple main effects algorithm).

CONCLUDING THOUGHTS

Taken together, the results from our prospective memory study and the distance estimation study converge on a view of cognition that is notable for its contextual constraints. Information-processing models of memory and cognition, though elegant in their formal properties, are by themselves insufficient devices for understanding the capabilities of children, as well as for charting the transitional mechanisms of development. It is only through adding real-world complexity to our models that we can hope to capture the sheer unrest of mental functioning. As the cognitive anthropologist Jean Lave has argued, the context in which cognition occurs shapes not only our perception of a problem but also our choice of its solutions (Lave et al., 1984). As we begin to understand more about the nature of cognitive development, it is likely that the importance of context and function will become even more apparent.

ACKNOWLEDGMENT

Portions of the research reported in this chapter were supported by grants from the Graduate School of Cornell University and the College of Human Ecology.

REFERENCES

Bronfenbrenner, U. (1977). *The ecology of human development*. Cambridge, MA: Harvard University Press.

Bronfenbrenner, U., & Crouter, A. C. (1982). Work and family through time and space. In S. B.

Kamerman & C. D. Hayes (Eds.), *Families that work: Children in a changing world.* Washington, D.C.: National Academy Press.

Ceci, S. J., & Bronfenbrenner, U. (1985). Don't forget to take the cupcakes out of the oven: Prospective memory, strategic time-monitoring, and context. *Child Development, 56,* 150–165.

Ceci, S. J., & Liker, J. (1986). A day at the races: IQ, expertise, and cognitive complexity. *Journal of Experimental Psychology: General, 115,* 255–266.

Ceci, S. J., Baker, J. G., & Nightingale, N. N. (in press). The ecologies of intelligence: challenges to traditional views. In D. Detterman (Ed.), *Issues in Human Intelligence Vol. 2.* Norwood, NJ: Ablex.

Chi, M. T. H. (1978). Knowledge structures and memory development. In R. Siegler (Ed.), *Children's thinking: What develops?* Hillsdale, NJ: Lawrence Erlbaum Associates.

Harris, J., & Wilkins, A. (1982). Remembering to do things: A theoretical framework and an illustrative experiment. *Human Learning, 1,* 1–14.

Klayman, J. (1983). Learning from feedback in probablistic environments. University of Chicago, Center for Decision Research Monograph.

Kreutzer, M., Leonard, C., & Flavell, J. (1975). An interview study of children's knowledge about memory. *Monographs of the Society for Research in Child Development, 40,* Serial No. 159.

Lave, J., Murtaugh, M., & De la Roche, O. (1984). The dialectic of arithmetic in grocery shopping. In B. Rogoff & J. Lave (Eds.), *Everyday cognition, its development in social context.* Cambridge, Ma: Harvard University Press.

Meacham, J. (1982). A note on remembering to execute planned actions. *Journal of Applied Developmental Psychology, 4,* 121–133.

Meacham, J., & Colombo, J. (1980). External retrieval cues facilitate prospective remembering in children. *Journal of Educational Psychology, 73,* 299–301.

Neisser, U. (1982). *Memory Observed.* San Francisco: Freeman.

Nisbett, R., & Ross, L. (1980). *Human Inference: Strategies and shortcomings of social judgment.* Englewood Cliffs, NJ: Prentice Hall.

Paris, S. G., Newman, R., & Jacobs, J. (1985). Social context and functions of children's remembering. In M. Pressley & C. Brainerd (Eds.), *Cognitive learning and memory in children.* New York: Springer Verlag.

Scribner, S. (1984). Studying working intelligence. In B. Rogoff & J. Lave (Eds.), *Everyday cognition: Its development in social context.* Cambridge, MA: Harvard University Press.

Wagner, D. (1978). Memories of Marocco: The influence of age, schooling and achievement on memory. *Cognitive Psychology, 10,* 1–28.

Wertsch, J. (1981). *The concept of activity in Soviet Psychology.* Armonk, NY: Sherpa.

12

Reconsidering the Context of Remembering: The Need for a Social Description of Memory Processes and their Development

Frederick Verdonik
University of Michigan

Our present day understanding of memory functions and their development is shaped predominantly by psychological and biological research. These approaches focus attention on memory functions that operate through individual processes. Moreover, it is implicitly assumed that descriptions based on individual memory processes can adequately account for reconstructions of the past under all conditions. However, while the individual may be an appropriate unit of description for memory functions carried out in isolation, memory processes that operate during social interactions are not reducible to individual processes. Rather, reconstructions of the past that occur during social interactions are best characterized as social memory processes

In the present chapter, social memory processes are described as communicative processes between participants in social interactions. The overall objective of the chapter is to foster a reconsideration of the social nature of these memory processes.[1] Toward this end, I first outline a conceptual framework for considering the operation of social memory during interactions. In the following

---

[1]The concept of memory as a social process has been researched from several theoretical traditions. Halbwachs (1980) represents a sociological approach; Perlmutter (1952) and Yukes (1954) reflect a psychological tradition that adhered to a notion of 'group mind'; Kvale (1977), Meacham (1977), and Istomina (1975) reflect a transactional and activity framework; and Ratner (1980, 1984) and Rogoff and Gardner (1984) have employed Vygotsky's notion of "zone of proximal development." These researchers differ with respect to their definitions of social memory, and dimensions of memory that they hypothesize to be social, and their adherence to a social description of memory functions. Additional research has been conducted on the topic. However, mention of these studies is not possible because of space considerations.

section, some case studies that illustrate particular social memory processes are presented. In the final section, I make some suggestions about future research on social memory processes.

AN INTRODUCTION TO SOCIAL MEMORY AS COMMUNICATIVE PROCESSES BETWEEN GROUP MEMBERS

A principal function of memory processes during social interactions is to reconstruct the past so that participants can carry out an ongoing activity. This social function is realized through an interdependency and mutual regulation of people in a communicative context. Group members structure, support, and direct each other's reconstructions of the past. Memory-products emerge from and contribute to communicative processes in the service of an activity. From this perspective, remembering is a communicative system *among* people in an activity.

As communicative processes, group reconstructions are joint efforts to establish, maintain, and/or change *shared* meanings of the past (cf. Bartlett, 1964; Halbwachs, 1980; Olson, 1979; Spence, 1982). However, the goal(s) of a particular activity also plays an important part in creating and structuring social demands to remember during interactions (cf. Istomina, 1975; Zinchenko, 1981). The relationship *among* participants during joint reconstructions is defined and redefined, in part, by the perceived goals of an activity (cf. Wertsch, 1984). Communicative processes that constitute joint reconstructions can not be considered functionally independent of an activity. Consequently, an understanding of memory as a social process of communication ultimately requires a description of how memory functions as a joint effort after shared meaning in relation to an activity.

Consider the following dialogue as an illustration of how participants of a discussion jointly act to structure, guide, and support each other's reconstructions. Imagine a mother and child engaged in a discussion about a future trip to their country house. The mother announces to her 6-year-old child that they will be going to the country again, but the child does not understand where they are going. In an attempt to bridge their understanding, the mother helps the child to reconstruct some past events from a previous visit to the country. The mother says, "Do you remember last summer when we went swimming in the lake? . . . And you saw the ducks?" The child says that he doesn't remember. The mother continues to guide his reconstruction of past events. She says, "Remember we picked wild blueberries and we made blueberry pie? The child says, "We saw a deer?" After establishing a framework of shared meaning with the child, the mother and child jointly elaborate upon and enrich the dimensions of meaning that they share for this event. The mother says, "And we tried to feed the deer." The child says, "Yeah, and it ran away."

As exemplified above, an important feature of social memory processes is the functional relationship formed between participants during these reconstructive episodes and the changes in this relationship over time. As group members, they are mutually dependent upon one another to generate and interpret information about the past. Moreover, they organize this information into a coherent framework which is related to the ongoing discussion. For example, the participation of the child who forgot about his experiences at a summer home is guided and supported by his mother's questions. Through these questions the mother invites her child to interpret and confirm information recalled. Also, timely pauses by the mother provide opportunities for the child's participation in the reconstructive process. In turn, the mother's participation in the reconstructive episode is directly contingent upon her child's communications. The mother's efforts to reconstruct information with her child and establish a shared framework of meaning about the past are constrained by the quality of her child's participation. For instance, the child's verbal and nonverbal feedback to his mother's questions regulates how his mother further elaborates and organizes information. In sum, memory-products that are reconstructed during social exchanges frequently reflect cooperative efforts. Memory-products emerge from the interlocking behaviors of both participants over the course of a reconstructive episode.

Social processes that constitute group remembering are similar in *function* to processes that constitute individual remembering. For example, information is often inferred, elaborated upon, contextualized, and checked during individual and joint reconstructions (Perlmutter, 1952; Yukes, 1954). Despite the functional similarities, the operation and orchestration of these functions during social exchanges are realized through different processes, when compared to their occurrence under individual conditions. Social exchanges constrain and afford the reconstruction of the past in ways that are different from individual remembering. While individual processes contribute to social constraints and affordances, they do not fully determine how memory functions are realized during social interactions. Rather, the communicative functions of remembering create unique constraints on, and affordances for remembering during social interactions.

There are several characteristics of communication that create a different set of potentials to actualize memory functions. First, group reconstructions entail two or more people who have different interpretations of information already remembered or to be remembered. While group members share some interpretations, the fact that group members do not fully share the same meaning of information creates a need for group members to negotiate a shared meaning of information. The construction of a shared framework of meaning to interpret information constitutes an important constraint on how information can be reconstructed between group members. In contrast, when individuals reconstruct information outside of group interactions, it is not necessary to construct a shared framework of meaning with themselves. An individual as a self-system does not have to share meaning with her or himself, or take the perspective of her or himself since she or he is the self. Thus, the specific constraints on remembering as an individual effort after meaning are different from those constraints on group reconstruction as joint efforts after shared meaning.

Second, affordances to reconstruct information among group members differ from those that operate solely within individuals (Perlmutter, 1952). During social reconstructions, group members can help each other to generate information about the past (Ratner, 1980, 1984). If a group member cannot remember information, then other group members can support, direct, and structure this group member's reconstruction of information. In this way the competencies of each group member are potentially amplified through cooperative interactions with other group members. As illustrated in the example of the mother and child, a person who has forgotten information participates in social processes that create a joint potential to actualize a memory product. Moreover, joint reconstructions increase the probability that group members will share a similar interpretation of memory products. Thus, the cooperation of group members creates a set of affordances to reconstruct information which is qualitatively different from individual potentials to reconstruct information.

EMPIRICAL DESCRIPTIONS OF SOCIAL MEMORY PROCESSES

Empirical descriptions of social memory processes are given in the form of case studies. The objective of presenting these case studies is to describe social exchanges that are considered joint reconstructions of the past. These descriptions reflect upon the previous discussion of social memory processes as communicative efforts after shared meaning about the past in relation to an ongoing activity.

Method for Studying Social Memory Processes

A model-building activity was employed as a context to describe social memory processes between mothers and their children. Specifically, mothers and their children were paired together and instructed to build with blocks places that truly exist in their community. They were told not to build imaginary places or to incorporate information about other communities. The instructions also emphasize that both participants could build places and contribute to the completion of the model.

Children who participated in the study were ages 4 and 7 years, and the ages of the mothers ranged from 30 to 33 years. All participants were from middle-class backgrounds, and they were selected from the same eastern metropolitan area.

Each dyad was provided with wooden blocks of different shapes, colors, and sizes to construct their model. A 6' × 6' plastic sheet was positioned on the floor and served as a surface to make the model. The model-building session for each dyad group was conducted in the home of the participants. Each session lasted approximately 45 minutes. All sessions were videotaped. The verbatim transcripts of the interactions between dyad members during the model-building session constitute the data to be reported.

The model-building activity was specifically designed to examine social memory processes. However, the mothers and children who participated in the study were not informed that the primary aim was to study social memory processes until the end of the project. The research was introduced to participants as a study of what parents and their children know about their local environment. Presented in this way, the contents of their discussions were emphasized rather than the reconstructive processes per se.

The instructions and goals of the model-building activity create demands to remember information about a local environment. In addition, they create constraints on the information that is appropriate to the activity. While participants define and redefine the task and its goals over the course of the activity, dyad members must manage these task demands to some degree if they are to complete the model-building activity as defined by the researcher. At minimum, participants *must* remember places in order to represent them in their model. Depending upon the dyad, memory demands may also include information about the properties of the places to be modeled. For example, a swing set and sand box may represent their local playground, because the playground in their community consists of these objects. Also, the relation of places to each other may be represented in some form. For example, a drug store may be constructed next to a florist shop, because this spatial arrangement reflects the locations of these places in their community. In addition to the demands to remember information about their community as it truly exists, the construction of the model per se creates its own set of memory demands. As participants represent more places in their community, there are more places for participants to identify and locate in their model.

A model-building task was chosen as an activity to describe joint reconstructions of information between mothers and their children for several reasons. First, the task involves a knowledge domain which is familiar to children and their parents through their daily activities. In fact, they routinely share experiences in their local environment. The familiarity of mothers and their children with places in their community increases the potential for both participants to remember places and contribute to the activity. Second, the parents who participated in the study regarded knowledge about the local environment as important for their children's safety and involvement in everyday activities. Comments by the parents suggest that the task information is considered to be culturally significant. Third, the children and parents who participated in the study were familiar with the use of building blocks to represent places and things. They often expressed excitement about building a model of their community. In sum, all three factors suggest that participation in the activity by children and their parents was a meaningful experience.

Case Studies of Social Memory Processes

In the following case studies, descriptions of social memory processes will focus on joint reconstructive episodes between mothers and their children. A joint reconstructive episode is defined as a sequence of exchanges in which children and their parents direct, support, and guide each other's understanding of the past, as a means to inform the ongoing activity of constructing a model. These descriptions highlight the communicative functions of joint reconstructive episodes in the model-building activity. The implications of these episodes for social memory development are discussed.

Examples of Joint Reconstructive Episodes as Mutual Regulations

In the model-building activity, joint reconstructive episodes often functioned to establish the meaning of places and their locations for both participants. The following transcript illustrates how a mother structures and supports her child's participation during a joint reconstruction. In this interaction, a mother and her 4-year-old son have just finished constructing a place called 'Leslie's House.' They are trying to remember another place in their community so that they can construct it in their model.

> *Mother:* What do you want to make?
> *Child:* Gonna make a friend's house.
> *Mother:* We have to make only . . . Remember the rule? . . . Only make *REAL* buildings.(Mother stresses the word 'real' by the tone of her voice and her hand movements)
> *Child:* (Child nods his head to indicate that he understands).
> *Mother:* So, near where we live we have our house (Mother motions with her hands to a previous construction and then she pauses). . . . We have Leslie's house (Mother motions with her hands to a previous construction and then she pauses). . . And where do we go shopping?
> *Child:* I don't . . .
> *Mother:* Usually . . . We always have an argument because you ask me to buy gum there?
> *Child:* (Looks at the model)
> *Mother:* Where?
> *Child:* J.G. (Quick and confident voice)
> *Mother:* Where would J.G. be here? (She motions to the places already constructed and then she pauses) . . . In this town?

In the example above, the joint process of remembering is an important and necessary step for the mother and child to complete the activity of making a model of their community. Toward this end, the mother helps her child to construct an *attitude* about the places to be remembered in relation to the goal. First, she restates the goals of the activity and obtains her child's agreement that information should service this goal. She then structures her child's participation in reconstructing information by using places already constructed in their model community. Furthermore, she invites his participation through asking questions about salient events that she knows her child has experienced. Together these exchanges constrain the child's thinking about their town. The mother and child gradually construct a shared framework which directs and organizes their interpretation about information to be remembered.

There are certain stylistic qualities about the exchanges in this reconstructive episode that seem to possess some generality within a current sample of 32 dyads. For instance, the mother starts the joint reconstructive episode with a general question which functions to orient her child to reconstruct information. This general question is then followed by specific questions that build upon one another. In addition, she personalizes her inquiries and the meaning of places in subsequent questions by referencing shared experiences. The mother and child gradually *resonate* to each other as a shared context of meaning unfolds through these inquiries. These supportive processes by the mother complement and supplement the child's contributions and efforts to reconstruct information.

It is noteworthy that in the previous example the child plays a somewhat passive role in the reconstructive episode. He does not actively contribute information during the reconstructive process, or structure the mother's reconstruction. However, the child does regulate his mother's participation through his actions. For instance, he acknowledges the mother's efforts and provides feedback to the questions asked. During the reconstructive episode, the child's nonverbal expressions indicated to his mother the relative success of her inquiries. The child's attention to his mother's pointing and his facial expressions during her pauses seemed to influence the structure of her messages (e.g., degree of specificity).

A second example of a joint reconstructive episode illustrates how a mother displays a strategy for remembering. In this interaction, the child has just finished building the neighborhood playground. The mother helps her 4-year-old child to use their previous experiences in the local environment to remember other places.

Mother: So, that's the playground?
Child: Yeah.
Mother: So this is our street, and you are going toward the playground. (Pause)
   What do you see along the way?
Child: Ah, the fire station.

In the example above, the mother relates the playground to other places experienced by her child. The mother supports and directs her son's remembrance of the fire house by taking an *imaginary walk* through the environment with her child. Similar to the first example, the mother helps her child to generate a shared framework to remember places in their neighborhood. The framework established by both participants creates a continuity between places already constructed and places to be constructed.

A third example of a reconstructive episode is an instance of a 7-year-old child who plays a more active role in directing her mother's participation. In this interaction, the mother and child are constructing a model of the child's school. The mother starts to build a kindergarten classroom. The child stops her mother from building the classroom, because the child is unsure about how many doors should be built and where they should go.

Mother: Here is the kind . . . Here's the wall for the kindergarten classrooms.
Child: Wait.
Mother: What?
Child: How many doors are there? How many kindergartens?
Mother: Oh, forget all about the doors.
Child: Wait. How many kindergartens?
Mother: Well, there's Mrs. McPadden's. (Pause) And Mrs. Lipton's. And Mrs. Morgan's . . . Miss Morgan. And Miss Lindoff's, right?
Child: So how many is that?
Mother: Mmm.
Child: There're two doors. (Pause) No. There are three doors. (Pause) I think. (Pause) Can't remember. Is . . . Is the first door before the first kindergarten?
Mother: No. You know what I think it might be? Don't the classrooms share outside doors?
Child: Yes. Two classrooms and one door? That's what I'm thinking. Is there a classroom here or is there just the door?
Mother: Okay. There would be a classroom here? and then a door?
Child: Classroom here and then a door.
Mother: And then a door (Stated simultaneously with her child).

The example above clearly illustrates the emergence of a memory-product from the interlocking behaviors of the participants. The child's active role in the reconstructive process generates new demands for the mother to remember information. Also, the child's questions serve a variety of functions in the reconstructive episode. For instance, the child's questions initiate the goal of the reconstructive episode, redefine the goal of the reconstruction, invite the mother's participation, and regulate the mother's contributions. Thus, the active role of the child in organizing and supporting the mother's participation seems to create new potentials for the dyad to realize the memory-product.

To summarize: The three case studies illustrate the ways in which participants structure and support each other's reconstructions of the past during social interactions. This joint functioning of participants to reconstruct information is more than a stimulus-response sequence. For instance, mothers do more than simply elicit a memory in the child. The social interdependence of participants during reconstructive episodes is more accurately described as a process of mutual regulation. It is through these mutual regulations that participants jointly establish, maintain, and/or change shared meanings about places in their model community. The social exchanges constitute an interdependent relationship through which a memory-product gradually emerges. Furthermore, in the present case studies, it is observed that the relationship between participants can change over the course of a single reconstructive episode. As participants restructure and negotiate their involvement in a reconstructive process, the constraints on and affordances for reconstructing information change. Based on these observations, it is hypothesized that the quality of participation in joint reconstructive episodes by both participants has important consequences for the development of their memory functions during social interactions.

Use of a Joint Reconstructive Episode to Resolve a Memory Conflict

Interestingly, joint reconstructive episodes were often employed by participants to resolve the disputes about the accuracy of information and the goals of the task. An example of how a joint reconstruction is used to resolve a conflict about the locations of places is illustrated in the following transcript. In the interaction sequence below, the conflict has already been initiated by the mother. In brief, the mother wants to move a building that was labeled 'Dillon's House' to a new location so that it accurately reflects its location in real life. She claims that its current location is incorrect. She also suggests that they move their house to a different corner so that it accurately represents its true location. The child objects to these changes in their model. The interaction sequence below begins with the mother helping her 4-year-old child to remember the location of their house relative to other places in their neighborhood.

> *Mother:* Which is the 'Y'? Why don't you show me which way we go if we're going to the 'Y,' then you'll know how to tell me.
> *Child:* See, if we're goin' to the 'Y' we should park right here because (Inaudible). Then we walk that way, and then we go that way, and we're right here. Straight to the Empire State building.
> (Mother returns after a brief interruption)
> *Child:* Jeremy's house is away from Joan's house. Joan's house is way uptown. So Jeremy's house is way over here across from my house. So we want to go downtown. We have to go . . . we have to walk over the road that says walk, and go over this road to those small cars, and then we could go over to Jeremy's house. This time we have to park over here.

Mother: First we get buildings to be other buildings besides the 'Y,' like daddy's office.

Child: No. Daddy's office is somewhere over that corner next to our house. That's where daddy's office go, here.

Mother: What do we see when we go down on the bus toward Dillon's house?

Child: The 'Y'.

Mother: And what do we see on the other side of the street?

Child: Daddy's office.

Mother: No. Before we get to daddy's office? (Pause) Big white building?

Child: The Empire State building

Mother: No. Before we get there. The big white building? (Pause) The shopping center?

Child: Jeremy's house.

This excerpt from a conflict sequence suggests that joint reconstructions can function to reestablish a shared framework of meaning between the mother and her child. Similar to previous reconstructive episodes in the session, the mother tries to engage her child in an imaginary walk through the environment. In this strategy, routine experiences are employed once again by participants. These shared experiences function to support the efforts of participants to infer information about places and further elaborate on the meaning of places. As a result of their participation in this strategy, the mother and child gradually reestablish shared meanings about these places.

In this episode, the mother initiates once again the *walking method* to structure her child's participation in the reconstructive process. At this point in the interaction, the mother and child have successfully employed this strategy to mediate their participation. It has emerged as a *practice* between participants. However, the structure of this strategy in a conflict situation appears to be different from its structure during reconstructions that are not related to conflicts. As illustrated in the example above, the use of joint reconstructions to resolve a conflict included more monitoring of the child's interpretation of place meanings by the mother; the mother's voice was more exaggerated in its intonation than in nonconflict reconstructions; and the mother's breakdown of the *walking* process into smaller components, and linking of the components seems more detailed and explicit in the conflict episode, than in the nonconflict reconstructions.

The use of reconstructions to resolve conflicts was observed in a number of dyads. Within this model-building activity, participation in joint reconstructions to resolve conflicts seemed to be a turning point in the interactions between the dyad members. In particular, these joint reconstructive episodes may have affected the expectations between participants about the function and structure of joint reconstructions. Although the following is speculation at this point, I wish to suggest that these joint reconstructions represent *critical memory episodes* for micro-development of social memory processes within this activity. For instance, in the previous example, the child employed the *walking method* to orient his mother and negotiate the meaning of places. Although the mother had initiated this strategy on several occasions prior to the conflict, this was the first instance in which the child tried to employ this strategy to structure his mother's reconstruction and interpretation of places. As evidenced in this example, over multiple participations in memory conflicts during this activity, children may become sensitive to the need to structure actively the participation of their mothers during the resolution of memory conflicts. Children may learn task-specific strategies to initiate, continue, and terminate reconstructive processes that function to resolve conflicts. However, a more detailed description of these episodes is needed to verify their role in microgenetic developments of social memory processes and their stability within and across dyads and activities.

Challenges for Adult Participation in Joint Reconstructive Episodes and the Potential Development of Social Memory Processes

Most studies of adult-child interactions overlook the potential development of adults. These studies ignore the experiences of adults during social interactions. Adults are considered to be models of cognitive development, as opposed to the objects of cognitive development. This perspective has important implications for the present work on social memory processes. For instance, a mother's support and guidance of her child during joint reconstructive episodes in the present activity would be typically regarded by reseachers as evidence of a mother's individual competency to carry out the activity by herself. The mother's individual memory abilities are merely displayed under social conditions. With respect to adult participation in joint reconstructions, the traditional models of adult-child interactions would assume that memory processes operating on an individual level are isomorphic to memory processes that operate between group members. This presumed relation between individual and social context of remembering would preclude any recognition of memory development for adults through supporting and guiding the participation of their children in joint reconstructions.

In the present research, a mothers and child's actions are considered to be a dependent system of interactions. During cooperative efforts, mothers also encounter challenges to their present memory competencies to organize and reconstruct information. For instance, communicative processes used by a mother to organize information about the environment with her child are not identical to her reconstruction of environmental knowledge outside of a social interaction. During joint reconstructive episodes with her child, a mother is processing information on a more explicit level, processing the child's comprehension of places remembered and to be remembered, communicating her intentions to act and the meanings of places to the child, and changing her intentions to act and meanings of places in relation to the intentions and meanings communicated by her child.

These efforts by a mother to support and guide her child's participation in joint reconstructions may require memory skills that develop through interactions with her child.

The following dialogue illustrates a task-specific challenge for a mother to reconstruct information with her 4-year-old son. As the challenge unfolds, participants organize and reorganize information in relation to each other and the goals of the activity. In this interaction sequence, a memory challenge begins with her child changing the meaning of places already constructed in their model.

Mother: Okay. Okay. Okay. What . . . Whose house should I put down?
Child: Ah, I don't have Dillon's house over here.
Mother: Well, Dillon's house would be way uptown . . . and Jeremy's house is pretty close to the playground.
Child: Yes, but Dillon's house is not way uptown. It's close to our house.
Mother: I thought this was our house.
Child: No!
Mother: Okay, we changed it.
Child: That's the Empire State building.
Mother: Swooo! That one's big. Okay, if that's the Empire State building, then it would be very tall and go all the way down here.
Child: And Jeremy's house is right here. But . . . But . . . (Mother interrupts)
Mother: Which one is Jeremy's house? (Tone of confusion)
Child: That one, and Dillon's house is way towards that river so it's uptown from our house.

During this reconstructive episode the mother and her child try to reestablish shared meanings for places already constructed in their model. The mother expresses a genuine confusion about the present meaning of places. She tries to understand her child's *new* meanings for places in relation to their previously established and shared framework of meanings. In contrast, the child does not seem disturbed by the changes. Rather, he objects to his mother's maintenance of the previous meanings of places. When questioned about the places constructed, he confidently asserts a different set of meanings for places. It is noteworthy that the mother does not rebuke her child's redefinition of places. Instead, she attempts to think within a new framework of meanings.

The child's role in the memory episode creates certain challenges for the mother's role in the modeling activity. She is still directing her child's participation in the memory episode, but the child also plays a more dominant role in directing and structuring the mother's meaning of places. The management of these task-specific roles in the reconstructive episode generates a variety of demands that may be unfamiliar to the mother, as well as the child. Indeed, during and after the session the mother explicitly mentioned her difficulty and confusion in remembering the identities and locations of places in their model.

In trying to meet the challenges of their new roles, the mother in relation to her son may also develop task-specific strategies to reconstruct stable meanings about places represented in their model. For instance, the mother helped her child to organize information so that he could help her to participate in the activity. This was accomplished through the mother asking questions about the present meaning of places based on their prior meanings, and then elaborating upon the new meanings of places. Again, emergence of these social strategies during memory challenges may represent task-specific microgenetic developments of social memory processes.

In sum, researchers of memory suggest that social demands facilitate memory development during early childhood (e.g., Ratner, 1980, 1984). If social memory demands are an integral part of memory development, then it follows that adults may also be learning, refining, and/or developing memory skills in relation to the participation of children. These changes in adult memory skills over the course of interactions reflect developments of group reconstructive processes. Future research on social memory processes between adults and children should recognize the potential developments of adults, as well as children. For instance, the types of social challenges that enhance memory development for adults during social activities need to be described. Moreover, memory challenges encountered by mothers in the present research resulted from their children's participation in the activity. This suggests that we need to examine the interdependency of memory between the adults and children during social interactions. In particular, it will be important to describe how adults (e.g., parents and teachers) and children develop memory strategies in relation to the practical demands that they encounter as consequences of their interlocking behaviors in activities.

DIRECTION OF FUTURE RESEARCH

The aim of this chapter has been to stimulate thinking about memory as a social process of reconstruction between participants in an activity. The work presented is not intended to be a formal theory of social memory processes. It is a perspective which suggests a need to describe memory functions as social processes of communication. The value of this social perspective lies in its long-term potential to enhance our current understanding of memory functioning during social activities, differences in memory functioning among members of the same and different cultures, and the changes in memory functioning over the course of the life span. A handful of researchers have already begun to move in this direction (Ratner, 1984; Rogoff & Gardner, 1984; White, 1984). However, further research is required to construct theories that can fulfill the potential contributions of a social memory perspective. Toward this end, the descriptive and speculative tone of this chapter attempts to generate a reconsideration of, and interest in, social memory processes and their development.

With respect to future research, a detailed description of social memory processes is a necessary first step. These descriptions must identify the range of social processes that regulate participation in joint reconstructions. In addition, it is essential for researchers to describe *how* these social exchanges function to support, organize, and/or direct memory functions. A primary focus should be on the emergence and unfolding of memory processes between participants over a single interaction and across multiple interactions. Adequate social descriptions of memory functions during interactions must proceed research on social memory processes as potential explanations of individual memory functions and their development.

To conclude: It is necessary for researchers of memory to reconsider some basic assumptions about the adequacy of individual processes to describe memory functions during social interactions. However, individual and social descriptions should not be considered polar perspectives. These levels of description must be recognized as complementary dimensions of memory functions from the very start. Indeed, future research can potentially enhance our understanding of memory functions through clarifying the relation of memory functions operating between participants during social interactions to their operation outside of social interactions.

ACKNOWLEDGMENTS

I would like to thank S. Paris, R. Dixon, I. Sigel, and L. Sherrod for their thoughtful comments on the chapter; and K. Nelson and M. Perlmutter for their encouragement of and discussions about the research. Finally, a special thanks to the children and parents for their assistance and understanding.

REFERENCES

Bartlett, F. (1964). *Remembering: A study in experimental and social psychology.* (rev. ed.) London: White Friars Press.

Halbwachs, M. (1980). *Collective memory.* (F. Ditter & V. Ditter Trans.). New York: Harper & row (Original work published 1952).

Istomina, Z. (1975). The development of voluntary-memory in school age children. *Soviet Psychology, 13*,(4), 5–64.

Kvale, S. (1977). Dialectics and research on remembering. In N. Datan & H. Reese (Eds.), *Life-span developmental psychology: Dialectical perspectives on experimental research* New York: Academic Press.

Meacham, J. (1977). A transactional model of remembering. In N. Datan & H. Reese (Eds.), *Life-span developmental psychology: Dialectical perspectives on experimental research* New York: Academic Press.

Olson, R. (1979). *The constitutive processes of memory in organizational communication.* Unpublished doctoral dissertation, Ohio State University.

Perlmutter, H. (1952). *A study of group and individual memory-products.* Unpublished doctoral dissertation, University Of Kansas.

Ratner, H. (1980). The role of social context in memory development. In M. Perlmutter (Ed.), *Children's memory: New directions For child development,* No. 10. San Francisco: Jossey-Boss.

Ratner, H. (1984). Memory demands and the development of young children's memory. *Child Development, 55,* 2173–2191.

Rogoff, B., Gardner, W. (1984). Adult guidance of cognitive development. In B. Rogoff & J. Lave (Eds.), *Everyday cognition: Its development in a social context* Cambridge, MA: Harvard University Press.

Spence, D. (1982). *Narrative truth and historical truth: Meaning and interpretation in psychoanalysis.* New York: W. W. Norton.

Verdonik, F. (1981). *Memory development through social processes.* Unpublished manuscript, City University Of New York, Graduate and University Center.

Wertsch, J. (1984). The zone of proximal development: some conceptual issues. In B. Rogoff & J. Wertsch (Eds.), *Children's learning in the "zone of proximal development": New directions for child development,* No. 23. San Francisco: Jossey-Boss.

White, S. (1984, May). *Distinguished Lecture: Development and learning.* Paper presented as invited address at the meeting of the Fourteenth Annual Piaget Society, Philadelphia.

Yukes, H. (1954). *Some effects of group properties upon recall.* Unpublished doctoral dissertation, New York University.

Zinchenko, P. (1981). Involuntary memory and the goal directed nature of activity. In J. Wertsch (Ed.), *The concept of activity in Soviet psychology* New York: M. E. Sharpe.

V

THEORETICAL APPROACHES
OF UNIVERSAL CHANGES
AND INDIVIDUAL
DIFFERENCES IN MEMORY
DEVELOPMENT ACROSS THE
LIFE SPAN

On Cognitive Operators in Information Processing and Their Effects on Short-term Memory Performance in Different Age Groups

Walter Hussy
Alexander von Eye
Universität Trier
West Germany

INTRODUCTION

The experiment on age differences in memory presented in this chapter was conducted in the traditions of life-span developmental psychology and the information processing approach to cognitive psychology. The memory phenomena of interest in this paper concern both short- as well as long-term memory. In general, we investigate how short-term memory is related to other processes of cognitive functioning, long-term memory, and age. The main assumption that underlies the experiment is that performance on selected short-term memory tasks does not vary as a function of age within the age-range under study; however, it is assumed that other domains of cognitive functioning do show age-related variation. In addition, it is assumed that, because of the effects that cognitive functioning exerts on memory, an age-related variation in memory performance can be observed (cf. Craik, 1977). This variation, however, does not reflect changes in short-term memory performance per se; rather, it indicates changes in other cognitive functions, e.g., performance in problem solving.

Before describing a model which integrates both short- and long-term memory, a brief introduction to the two kinds of tasks with which the subjects (Ss) were presented is given. The first task was to recall a list of items which consisted either of meaningful or meaningless material. This task can be solved using short-term memory; in the following we refer to it as memory task. Problem solving was required to solve the second task. In this task Ss were asked to make sequential predictions of symbols. To be successful Ss had also to use long-term memory. This task is referred to as concept forming because the Ss had to realize the rules (concepts) of the sequences to make successful predictions.

So far as the general goal of the paper is concerned we now can be a bit more concrete: We assume that Ss of different age groups differ in performance on both the memory and the concept-forming tasks. The main hypothesis, however, is that interindividual differences in concept forming performance (or in the effectiveness of cognitive operators) account for differences in memory task performance within and between different age groups. In the following discussion the theoretical background of this hypothesis is presented.

A STRUCTURAL AND PROCESSUAL MODEL
OF COMPLEX INFORMATION PROCESSING

The structural and processual model of *complex information processing* (CIP; Hussy, 1979, 1983, 1984; in German: SPIV-model, where SPIV is the acronym of "*S*truktur- und *P*rozeßmodell komplexer *I*nformations*v*erarbeitung") was designed to cover both structural and processual features of complex information processing. Here, the term 'complex' includes not only perception and memory performance but also problem solving. In Fig. 13.1 the CIP model is depicted.

Information Processing Structures

As indicated in Fig. 13.1, on the basis of retention time three components of the memory structure are postulated: Very-short-term (perceptual), short-term, and long-term memory. We will not elaborate on the components of perceptual memory (IA = input analysis, IT = input trace) which is conceived in accordance with Craik and Lockhart's (1972) dimension of sensory/semantic elaboration. More pertinent to the present context are the remaining two main components, that is short-term (STM) and long-term memory (LTM).

Figure 13.1 shows that retention times covering periods up to about 20 sec-

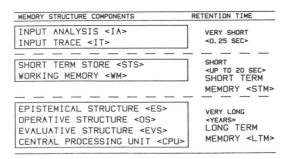

FIG. 13.1.   The eight substructures of the CIP-model.

onds are needed for short-term memory, which is subdivided into a *short-term store* (STS; Atkinson & Shiffrin, 1968) and a *working memory* (WM; Baddeley & Hitch, 1974). Whereas in STS information is gathered in a time-related—i.e., sequential—way, in WM information can be processed in a flexible, time-unrelated way.

Information that can be retrieved after this time interval of 20 seconds is assumed to be stored in long-term memory. Long-term memory is differentiated into three substructures, namely, the epistemical, operative, and evaluative structure. The *epistemical structure* (ES; Dörner, 1979) contains the entire lexical knowledge of an individual. According to several conceptions of semantic memory (e.g., Collins & Quillian, 1969), information in this structure is organized with respect to part-whole and concreteness-abstractness relations. Episodical features (Tulving, 1983) of the epistemical structure are taken into account by temporal and spatial relations.

The *operative structure* (OS) contains knowledge that is characterized by its function, i.e., information in WM is viewed with respect to its capacity to generate new relations. Information in the OS can be grouped into functional units, that are called *cognitive operators*. To put it in other terms, cognitive operators are defined as mental methods or algorithms of problem solving. Cognitive operators can be either elementary such as activating, inhibiting, linking, or disunifying, or complex, such as classifying, generalizing, or concept forming. The cognitive operations involved in concept forming are of particular interest in this chapter and are discussed in more detail later.

It is important to note that in the OS there is no strong relation defined between operators and problems. Thus, the appropriateness or effectiveness of operators applied to a given task (to a set of information stored in WM) must be evaluated. Criteria for this cognitive function, the so-called *evaluators,* are stored in the *evaluative structure* (EVS). This structure provides a functional basis for evaluating how effective operators can be (when they must be selected), or how effective they are (when they are applied).

Finally, there is a *central processing unit* (CPU) which can be thought of as organizing, monitoring, and controlling all ongoing processes (Weinert & Kluwe, 1984). Hence, it is excluded that structural components interact directly with each other. The CPU involves the processual features of problem solving which we discuss in the following section.

Processes in Problem Solving

As far as the processual part of the model is concerned four different phases are postulated that are assumed to be present in all problem-solving activities. In Fig. 13.2 the organizing, monitoring, and controlling activities of the CPU during these four phases of complex information processing are depicted. In the first phase of the process the CPU controls *the definition of the problem and the*

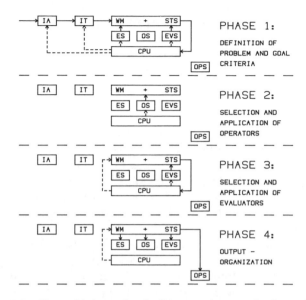

FIG. 13.2.   Flow of information (solid arrows) - organized, monitored and controlled by the CPU (dotted arrows) - during the four phases of complex information processing.

criteria to be met by gathering information from outside the organism (e.g., through instruction) and inside (ES) and checking it using an evaluator of the EVS. If the information processing is not terminated by these activities the subject is engaged in a problem and proceeds to the second phase during which an appropriate *operator from the OS has to be selected and applied.* The effectiveness of the applied operator is tested in the third phase by *selecting and applying an evaluator from the EVS.* If application of the selected evaluator suggests a match of problem definition and criteria the problem is solved and the output system (OPS) can be triggered by the CPU. We shall discuss further processual features of the CIP model in the section on the concept forming task below (for more details on the CIP model, see Hussy, 1983, 1984).

EXPERIMENTS

The Memory Task

As was mentioned earlier, it is assumed that memory performance measured in recall rates varies with age. To test this assumption, Ss from six age groups were presented, each with two lists of learning material. The first list contained the so-called *meaningful material,* which consisted of 20 pre- and suffixes with either two, three, or four letters. The presentation was done both acoustically and visually (tape and slides simultaneously presented, 2 seconds per item). Immediately after the presentation of the items written free recall was required. This procedure was repeated twice, each time with a different sequence of pre- and suffixes. The second list consisted of 20 meaningless CVC-syllables. This list was presented in exactly the same way as the first one. Half of the Ss were first presented with the meaningful material, the other half with the second list, which will be referred to in the following as the *meaningless material*. In the data analyses recall rates of the third trial are used.

The Concept Forming Task

In order to measure age differences in complex information processing performance (problem solving) a task was constructed that can be solved only if the concept forming operator mentioned earlier is effectively applied. In this part of the experiment, Ss were presented with a 2-dimensional matrix on a screen of a micro computer. As depicted in Figure 13.3, each cell of the matrix contains a symbol, e.g., *hearts* or *clubs,* as in a card game. The subject is asked to guess and predict what symbol will appear next. The predicted symbol has to be keyed in the computer. Irrespective of what Ss do, a program determines the sequences of blinking symbols and responds after each prediction with the ''correct'' symbol blinking. The subject has to predict the next symbol, receives feedback, and so on. The goal is to correctly predict as many symbols as possible.

The program that determines the sequence of blinking symbols has two features (rules) that are important for the following psychological considerations:

a. Not necessarily all symbols of the matrix are part of the sequence of blinking symbols, and

b. the sequence of the symbols is determined by rules that define the conditional probabilities of the symbols; it follows from this rule that symbol x is followed by symbol y not by chance but by a given conditional probability. The sequence of symbols is not fully determined by this kind of conditional probability (*first order*), rather, *higher order conditional probabilities* (e.g., third

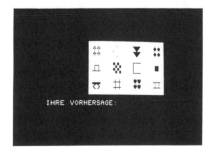

FIG. 13.3. The symbol matrix of concept forming (Task 2) as presented on the screen of a personal computer.

order, fifth order) must be taken into account to come to perfect predictions. For the Ss, this second rule implies that more than the last symbol (e.g., last three, last five symbols) must be taken into account to be able to perfectly predict the next symbol, i.e., with a probability of $p = 1.0$. In the following passage the conditional probabilities are called "concepts."

Ss were presented with two tasks that differed in two aspects:

1. Whereas in task 1, four out of a set of eight symbols were involved in the sequence, in task 2, five out of a set of twelve symbols were involved;

2. As far as the order of conditional probabilities needed for correct prediction is concerned, the first task is fully determined by fifth-order concepts, whereas the second task requires realizing concepts of up to the eleventh order.

These tasks are described in Table 13.1. The symbols of the sequences are encoded row-wise by numbers (from 1 to 12). Compared to Fig. 13.3, which represents task 2, the matrix for the first task consists of two rows. The next section gives a detailed explanation of the measures of the amount of information (Shannon, 1948) that characterize the two tasks at the beginning of the problem solving process and after successful application of the different cognitive operators.

For reasons of comparability the use of concepts of only the first, third, and fifth order is analyzed. The dependent variable in the experiment is concept-forming performance, measured by the number of first-, third-, and fifth-order concepts realized when dealing with the tasks.

Task Description in Terms of the CIP Model

To illustrate the CIP model and the hypotheses to be formulated later we give a description of the two tasks used thereby referring mainly to the concept of cognitive operators in general and of concept forming in particular.

Memory task.   In terms of the CIP model, the two degrees of meaningfulness realized in the memory tasks differ with respect to both the structural components and the processes involved. So far as the meaningless material is concerned, the main structural components involved are WM and STS. Because the storage capacity of these components is assumed to comprise not more than the magic number of seven $\pm$ 2 items, twenty items cannot be processed by these memory structure components alone. To handle this overload of information some operators of the OS must be applied. For example, Ss may engage in rehearsal, i.e., repeating mentally as many of the earlier items as they can in the interval between the presentation of two new items (primary rehearsal; Atkinson &

TABLE 13.1

Descriptive Information to Both the Concept Forming Tasks, Concerning Their Problem
Structure and the Effects of Processing by the Adequate Cognitive Operators

| Sequence | Number of Symbols | | Example | Amount of Information (Bit) | | | | |
	Total	Involved		Beginning	Rote Learning	C1[b]	C3	C5
1	8	4	2,3,7,3,7,[a] 5,3,7,3,7, 2,3,7,3,7,...	3.00	2.00	0.60	0.19	0.00
2	12	5	1,4,12,9,11,4,1, 1,4,12,9,11,4,1, 4,12,9,1,11,4,1, 4,12,9,1,11,4,1, 12,9,1,4,11,4,1,...	3.58	2.32	1.20	0.59	0.21

[a]The symbols are encoded by numbers (from 1 to 12) from the left to the right side of the symbol matrix, row by row.

[b]C1 means first order concept forming operator (correspondingly C3 and C5).

Shiffrin, 1968). Application of this operator leads to exhausting the storage capacity of STM.

The main difference between the processing of meaningless and meaningful material can be seen in this last operation. Processing meaningful material implies that connections (associations, relations) to the knowledge that is stored in the ES can be established by means of an operator of the OS, which can be called "retrieve associated information from ES and compare the features." This operator corresponds to both "secondary rehearsal" (Atkinson & Shiffrin, 1968) and the concept of "semantic elaboration" (Craik & Lockhart, 1972). By means of this operation the amount of information contained in the list of items can be reduced to a considerable degree; this results in better retrieval performance than that observed when irreduceable (meaningless) information is used.

Concept Forming Task.   Again, information overload is the problem in the concept forming task. The number of symbols entering the WM soon exceeds its capacity so that the Ss are forced to find ways to reduce the amount of information carried by each symbol. Two operators can be useful tools for reaching this goal: (1) rote learning. and (2) concept forming. By applying rote learning Ss are able to distinguish between the entire set of symbols in the matrix and the proper subset of symbols that occur in the sequence. In the following passages, elements of this subset are called involved symbols. When dealing with the simpler concept forming task (task 1, T1) the amount of information unexplained in the prediction of the next symbol is reduced by this operator. If applied successfully information is reduced by one third, or—in concrete terms—from 3 bit (at the beginning) to 2 bit. In task 2 (T2) information can be reduced from 3.58 bit to 2.32 bit (see Table 13.1). However, in both tasks there is still too much information left to avoid information overload.

Further reduction of information is possible when applying a concept-forming operator by which relations between symbols involved in the WM are established. The conditional probabilities (of different order) mentioned earlier are examples of this kind of relation. To form a first-order concept (abbreviated as C1 in Table 13.1) in this experiment means to relate symbol x_i to symbol $x_{i\$}PL_1$ in terms of conditional probabilities. The sequential nature of those concepts to be established becomes even more clear in the case of third- (C3) or fifth-order concepts (C5). These concepts are defined by a defined sequence of symbols, followed by the next one with a defined conditional probability. Concept forming in this sense implies changing the level of analysis from considering only one element to paying attention to a combination of elements.

To control the problem-solving process the CPU first initiates the definition of the problem (predict correctly as many symbols as possible), then the search and application of one or more operators start to rearrange information in the WM such that the definition can be met (for example to select the involved symbols by means of rote learning). Finally, the CPU organizes the evaluation of the operation (e.g., did the number of correct predictions increase? are there still incorrect predictions?). As long as there is a discrepancy between the goal and the present state of problem solving, these processes will continue, thereby eventually leading to the selection of concept-forming operators which—if higher-order operators are applied—at least yield positive evaluations. As seen in Table 13.1, first-order concept forming further reduces the information of a prediction in task 1 to 0.60 bit, whereas with the successful application of the fifth-order concept-forming operator the task is solved because there is no more information left to be processed, or, in other words, because there is no longer a discrepancy between goal and current problem solving state. It is also indicated in Table 13.1 that in task 2 the information remaining after the application of the corresponding operators is always greater than in task 1, thus illustrating the higher problem difficulty of task 2. In addition, Table 13.1 shows that task 2 cannot be solved by applying fifth-order concept formation because there is 0.21 bit left, which results in incorrect predictions and a goal-state discrepancy.

SUBJECTS AND EXPERIMENTAL PROCEDURE

Altogether n = 189 Ss participated in the experiment. They represent seven age groups with an average age of 8, 10, 12, 15, 20, 40, and 60 years. Further information on group size and sex-distribution is given in Table 13.2. Up to the age-group of 20 Ss were randomly selected from local schools. Additionally, to complete the age groups of 20, 40, and 60 advertisements were put in the local newspaper.

Half of the Ss in each age group started the experiments with the memory tasks, and the other half began with the concept-forming task. The memory tasks were administered in group sessions whereas the concept-forming tasks required single subject sessions. As previously mentioned a micro computer was used to

TABLE 13.2
Description of the Ss in Terms of Age, Sex, and Number

Age Group	Mean Age	Sex		Total Number
		Male	Female	
8	8;2	11	14	25
10	10;1	14	12	26
12	12;2	20	7	27
15	15;3	19	17	36
20	20;4	17	10	27
40	40;7	12	9	21
60	60;1	11	16	27
		104	85	189

control the experiments. The computer presented the symbols stepwise on the screen, provided feedback on the predictions and registered the predictions and the time needed for them. The average time for both sessions was about 2 hours.

HYPOTHESES

In general, we expect age-differences in both memory performance and concept forming. In a first hypothesis (H1) we assume that recall rates increase with age because the content of the ES increases with age. This hypothesis applies to both meaningful and meaningless material. In addition, we hypothesize (H2) that, across age groups, recall rates of meaningful material are higher than recall rates of meaningless material (cf. Miller & Selfridge, 1950), because the number of possible (associative) connections between data basis (ES) and meaningful material is per definition greater than the number of associations possible with meaningless material.

Age-related variation in concept forming is also postulated (H3). In particular, Ss younger and older than 20-years-of-age are assumed to be less capable than 20-year-old Ss in forming any concept of the orders under study (H4). This hypothesis is based on the assumption that both richness and effectiveness of the OS increase up to an age of about 30 and decline thereafter. An even more differentiated hypothesis concerns the order of concept forming. It is assumed that higher-order concepts are formed less frequently than lower-order concepts (H5) and that this order applies especially to the groups both younger and older than 20-years-of-age (H6).

The link between memory and the concept-forming task is provided by the following hypothesis: Together with age, concept forming is a powerful predictor of performance of WM and STS (H7). This last hypothesis should be explained a bit more in terms of the CIP model because it represents the central assumption. As far as the development of cognitive structures and processes is concerned, H7 implies that no increase in storage capacity, neither of the components of the STM nor of the LTM, is postulated in the present age range. Rather, the postulated improvements in both tasks up to the age-group of 20 is due to an enrichment of the components of the LTM and a more effective functioning of the CPU, resulting in more flexible and effective processing of information. Here, flexibility and effectiveness are measured in terms of information reduction by means of application and evaluation of cognitive operators under the control of the CPU. The frequently observed age-related decline in cognitive performance—especially on fluid intelligence items (e.g., Horn & Cattell, 1967; Sattler, 1982; Schaie & Baltes, 1977)—is attributed to less flexible and effective application and evaluation of cognitive operators. This issue is discussed with respect to the experimental findings in the last section.

RESULTS

Hypotheses H1 to H6 are tested by means of analyses of variance, H7 by fitting a structural equation model.

H1 and H2 are tested by a two-factorial analysis of variance. The first factor is "age" with seven levels (the 7 age groups), the second factor is "memory performance" with two levels (meaningful and meaningless material; repeated measurement). With reference to Kirk (1969) the notation is a SPF 7.2-design. The average performance of the different age groups in the two memory tasks is shown in Fig. 13.4. It illustrates the postulated age and material effects. H1 is confirmed by the main effect of "age" ($F(6, 182) = 9.803$; $p < 2 \cdot 10^{-9}$), H2 by "material" ($F(1, 182) = 11.148$; $p = 0.001$). Formulated in words, the age effect can be described as a monotonous increase in recall rates from the youngest age group to the 20-year-old group. The 40-year-old subjects show slightly poorer performance, i.e., recall rates that are not much higher than the recall rates in the group of the 12-year-old subjects. Furthermore, the 60-year-old subjects recall in the average about one item more than the 10-year-old subjects. As far as the material effect is concerned, the more meaningful material is

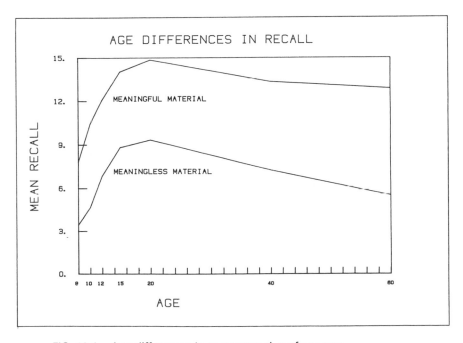

FIG. 13.4. Age differences in memory task performance.

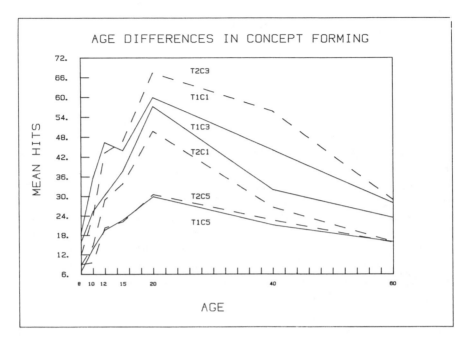

FIG. 13.5.   Age differences in concept forming task performance.

recalled better than the meaningless material by all age groups. There is no age by material interaction, i.e., the material effect can be assumed to be constant across age groups.

H3 to H6 are confirmed by a second two-factorial analysis of variance with age as the first factor (six levels) and concept-forming performance as the second factor (three levels with repeated measurement), in the notation of Kirk, a SPF 6.3-design. H3 is confirmed by the main effect of "age" ($F(6, 182) = 12.301; p = 1 \cdot 10^{-11}$), H4 by comparison of "treatment means," H5 by the main effect of "concept-forming performance" ($F(2, 182) = 8.776; p = 0.0002$), and H6 by significant simple main effects. The age-related relative frequencies of concept forming of first-, third-, and fifth-order in both tasks are depicted in Fig. 13.5.

Hypothesis H7 will be tested by means of a structural equation model. The model was specified according to the entire set of hypotheses to meet the following criteria:

1. Cognitive performance as measured by the concept-forming tasks can be treated as a unique class of behavior, termed concept forming;

2. Concept forming in Task 1 can be distinguished from concept forming in Task 2;

3. Recall performance as measured by the memory tasks can be treated as a unique class of behavior;

4. Recall of meaningless material can be distinguished from recall of meaningful material;

5. Recall performance is determined uniquely by concept forming;

6. Age is related to concept forming only.

To meet criterion 1 a first factor, named F1 in Fig. 13.6, was introduced that represents what was termed concept forming. This factor was designed to have as indicators the six concept-forming measures, i.e., the values of the extent to which first-, third-, and fifth-order concepts were formed when dealing with both the first and the second task. In general, it was assumed that the formation of concepts of any order is causally determined by F1.

Criterion 2 requires that within the unique behavior of class of concept forming there is a distinction between indicators belonging to Task 1 and indicators belonging to Task 2. In order to meet this criterion the errors associated with each indicator of Task 1 were allowed to correlate with any other error of indicators of Task 1. In the same way, errors of Task 2 indicators were allowed to correlate only with each other.

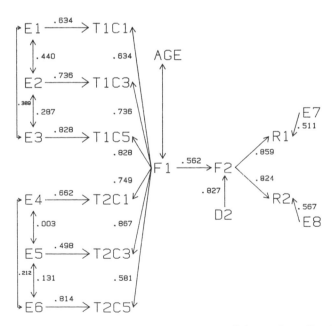

FIG. 13.6.   The model, the estimated path coefficients, the estimated correlations.

In criterion 3, recall performance is required to be a unique behavior class in the same way as concept forming. Therefore, a second factor, F2, the recall performance factor, was introduced. This factor has two indicators, namely R1, the recall rates of meaningful material, and R2, the recall rates of meaningless material. To meet criterion 4, the errors of these indicators were not allowed to correlate with each other. As compared to F1, every single indicator of F2 plays the same role as every group of indicators of either one of the concept forming tasks.

The core of the model is given with criteria 5 and 6. It is assumed that both recall rates R1 and R2 are causally determined by F2, and that, in general, recall performance is determined by concept forming. This assumption leads to the assignment of a status to F1 that differs from the status of F2. In this model, F1 is the only independent variable (except for the error terms). F2, on the other hand, is a dependent variable, like all measured concept forming and recall variables.

In criterion 6, age is introduced into the model. It is assumed that memory performance does not vary with age. Therefore, there is no direct causal or correlational relationship between age and the recall variables in the model (criterion 5). Age is only related to F1, the cognitive performance factor. In the model, age is treated neither as a dependent variable that is determined by a given factor nor as an independent variable. Age is considered to be correlated with concept forming. In this role, it is independent without, however, exerting any causal effect. This particular status of the age variable was assumed because of the lack of clarity in the psychological meaning of age. However, it is implicitly assumed that the age variable can be taken as a predictor of changes in concept forming across time.

In formal terms, application of the 6 criteria led to the following structural equations:

a. *causal relations*

$$T1C1 = a_1 F_1 + b_1 E_1,$$
$$T1C3 = a_2 F_1 + b_2 E_2,$$
$$T1C5 = a_3 F_1 + b_3 E_3,$$
$$T2C1 = a_4 F_1 + b_4 E_4,$$
$$T2C3 = a_5 F_1 + b_5 E_5,$$
$$T2C5 = a_6 F_1 + b_6 E_6,$$
$$F2 = a_7 F_1 + b_7 D_2,$$
$$R1 = a_8 F_2 + b_8 E_7,$$
$$R2 = a_9 F_2 + b_9 E_8,$$

b. *correlations*

$$E_1 E_2, \; E_1 E_3, \; E_2 E_3, \; E_4 E_5, \; E_4 E_6, \; E_5 E_6, \; AGE \; F_1.$$

In these equations, the TiCj denote the jth-order concept in the ith task $(j = \{1, 3, 5\}, \; i = \{1, 2\})$, the Ri denote the ith recall task $(i = \{1, 2\})$, the a_i are path coefficients and the b_i error weights. The variance of all errors were set a priori to 1.0; this does not include the error associated with the second factor, the disturbance D_2. For numerical reasons the correlation E_5E_6 was set to r = 0.8. The model fit was done with Bentler's structural equations program EQS (Bentler, 1983, 1984; cf. Bentler & Bonett, 1980). The model, the estimated path coefficients, and the estimated correlations are depicted in Fig. 13.6.

The overall χ^2 indicates that the fit is statistically acceptably good (χ^2_{14} = 21.717; $p(\chi^2)$ = 0.0846). The tested model does not deviate significantly from the best possible, i.e., the fully saturated model. The normed fit index of Bentler and Bonett (1980), Δ = 0.979, looks high if compared with its range of 0 $\leq \Delta$ $\leq$ 1, where Δ denotes the index. However, it cannot be interpreted as squared multiple correlations. Therefore, the degree to which this index is associated with meaningfully good fits is yet to be determined. Nevertheless, in the present data set, Δ = 0.979 seems to indicate a good fit, because it lies above Δ = 0.9. This latter value and smaller ones of the overall fit index can usually be improved substantially (Bentler & Bonett, 1980).

The path coefficients that depict causal relationships between factors and measured variables were tested with respect to their magnitude by checking against their standard errors. The smallest resulting test statistic is z = 7.458. Even if α is adjusted according to Bonferroni to $\alpha^* = \alpha/$ (number of tests) every single coefficient is significant. In Table 13.3 the measurement equations and the respective standard errors and test statistics are summarized.

DISCUSSION

As expected, there are age differences in both memory performance and concept-forming performance (H1 and H3). Most interesting are the differences between the age groups of 20 and 40 years. Whereas in memory performance no significant decline from 20- to 40-years-of-age could be observed, there is a significant

TABLE 13.3
Measurement Equations with Standard Errors and Test Statistics

Equation	SE	z
T1C1 = 22.556*F1 + 1.0 E1	1.890	11.932
T1C3 = 19.309*F1 + 1.0 E2	1.963	9.836
T1C5 = 10.959*F1 + 1.0 E3	1.420	7.716
T2C1 = 19.130*F2 + 1.0 E4	1.665	11.487
T2C3 = 28.545*F1 = 1.0 E5	2.042	13.977
T2C5 = 10.794*F1 + 1.0 E6	1.447	7.458
R1 = 1.000 F2 + 1.0 E7	–	–
R2 = 0/893*F2 + 1.0 E8	0.106	8.403

*Estimated values are denoted by asterisks.

decline of the concept-forming performance (H4). In both, memory and concept formation performance the 60-year-olds score significantly poorer than the 20-year-olds. The resulting question, whether these age-performance relations are independent from each other, is answered by the structural equation model. The model suggests that age is only related to concept-forming performance but not to memory performance. As mentioned earlier this relation does not imply a causal relationship. Rather, it means that all cognitive structures and processes involved in concept forming—as described for example by the CIP model—differ in effectiveness with age. The model also suggests that the same relation does not obtain for memory performance as measured in this experiment, that is performed of STM. Age is not directly related to this class of cognitive operations; rather, the model supports the notion of a causal relationship between concept forming and memory.

In terms of the cognitive model used to describe the underlying cognitive functions this last result can be regarded as development of cognitive operators—such as concept forming—with age. This interpretation implies that the ability to reduce information in WM by means of application of operators from OS to such a degree that the remaining information can be handled by the STM storage capacity increases up to an age of about 20 years and slowly starts to decline thereafter. It also implies, as shown by the confirmation of H5 and H6, that this effect can be demonstrated particularly in the case of high problem difficulty. At the level of measured variables, the storage capacity of the STM components does not change with age. However, the observable differences are due to developmental changes in the OS (H7). In this sense, there is only an indirect relationship between memory performance and age.

This interpretation of the results will be taken as a starting point of the attempt to incorporate concepts of development into the CIP model. A further step in this direction is the additional assumption (H8) that the ES also develops with age as far as its enrichment, integration, and differentiation is concerned. The assumption of maximal performance in the range from 25- to 35-years-of-age is not made in this case. With this additional assumption the different courses of the age differences of memory and concept-forming performance can be explained. Where there should be a decrease in memory performance beginning at about the age of 30 years (cf. H7), H8 suggests that further development of the ES compensates for this effect, resulting in an unchanged memory performance.

A particular problem concerns the question whether the EVS and the CPU show developmental changes that could also account for the age differences in problem-solving performance. Primary evidence comes from metacognitive research on memory development which shows the developmental character of control and executive processes (Kluwe & Schiebler, 1984). However, these results must be complemented by research on developmental aspects of evaluation and control structures and processes in problem solving.

ACKNOWLEDGMENT

The research reported in this paper was granted by Stiftung Volkswagenwerk, FRG, AZ.: II/25450. The authors are indebted to Roger A. Dixon for his very helpful comments on an earlier version of this paper.

REFERENCES

Atkinson, R. L., & Shiffrin, R. M. (1968). Human memory: A proposed system and its control processes. In K. W. Spence & J. T. Spence (Eds.), *The Psychology of motivation and learning* (Vol. 2, pp. 89–195). New York: Academic Press.

Baddeley, A. D., & Hitch, G. (1974). Working memory. In G. H. Bower (Ed.), *The psychology of motivation and learning* (Vol. 8, pp. 47–90). New York: Academic Press.

Bentler, P. M. (1983). Some contributions to efficient statistics in structural models: Specification and estimation of moment structures. *Psychometrika, 48,* 493–517.

Bentler, P. M. (1984). *Theory and implementation of EQS, a structural equations program.* Unpublished program manual.

Bentler, P. M., & Bonett, D. G. (1980). Significance task and goodness of fit in the analysis of covariance structures. *Psychological Bulletin, 88,* 588–606.

Craik, F. I. M. (1977). Age differences in human memory. In J. E. Birren & K. W. Schaie (Eds.), *Handbook of the Psychology of aging.* New York: Van Nostrand Reinhold.

Craik, F. I. M., & Lockhart, R. S. (1972). Levels of processing: A framework for memory research. *Journal of Verbal Learning and Verbal Behavior, 11,* 268–294.

Collins, A. M., & Quillian, M. R. (1969). Retrieval time from semantic memory. *Journal of Verbal Learning and Verbal Behavior, 8,* 240–247.

Dörner, D. (1979). Problemlösen als Informationsverarbeitung. Stuttgart: Kohlhammer.

Horn, J. C., & Cattell, R. B. (1967). Age differences in fluid and crystallized intelligence. *Acta Psychologica, 26,* 107–129.

Hussy, W. (1979). Informationsverarbeitende Strukturen und Prozesse: Versuch einer allgemein- und entwicklungspsychologischen Modellbildung. *Trierer Psychologische Berichte, 6.*

Hussy, W. (1983). Komplexe menschliche Informationsverarbeitung: Das SPIV-Modell. *Sprache & Kognition, 2, 47 62.*

Hussy, W. (1984). *Denkpsychologie, Band 1.* Stuttgart: Kohlhammer.

Kirk, R. E. (1969). *Experimental design: Procedures for the behavioral sciences.* Belmont, CA: Brooks/Cole.

Kluwe, R. H., & Schiebler, K. (1984). Entwicklung exekutiver Prozesse und kognitive Leistungen. In F. E. Weinert & R. H. Kluwe (Eds.), *Metakognition, Motivation und Lernen.* Stuttgart: Kohlhammer.

Miller, G. A., & Selfridge, J. A. (1950). Verbal context and the recall of meaningful material. *American Journal of Psychology, 63,* 176–185.

Sattler, J. M. (1982). Age effects on Wechsler's Adult Intelligence Scale-Revised Tests. *Journal of Consulting and Clinical Psychology, 50,* 785–786.

Schaie, K. W., & Baltes, P. B. (1977). Some faith helps to see the forest: A final comment of the Baltes-Schaie position on adult intelligence. *American Psychologist, 32,* 1118–1120.

Shannon, C. E. (1948). A mathematic theory of communication. *The Bell System Technical Journal, 27,* 379–423 and 623–656.

Tulving, E. (1983). *Elements of episodic memory.* Oxford: Clarendon Press.

Weinert, F. E., & Kluwe, R. H. (Eds.). (1984). *Metakognition, Motivation und Lernen.* Stuttgart: Kohlhammer.

14

A Functional Approach to Memory and Metamemory Development in Adulthood

Roger A. Dixon
University of Victoria

Christopher Hertzog
Georgia Institute of Technology

INTRODUCTION

Our overall goal in this chapter is to clarify the relevance of contextualism to theory and research on adult memory and metamemory. Nevertheless, we shall not attempt an exhaustive review of this metatheory, or the contextual perspective on theories of development (see, rather, Dixon, 1986; Lerner, Hultsch, & Dixon, 1983; Pepper, 1970; Rosnow & Georgoudi, 1986; Sarbin, 1977). Instead, we focus more attention on a related (if not derivative) approach to the study of psychological problems, viz., functionalism. It has long been clear that contextualism and functionalism are not identical (e.g., Angell, 1907), although their common philosophical roots—i.e., that they derive from similar "logical motivation" (Angell's term)—and similar theoretical and methodological strengths and weaknesses are evident. In the first section of this chapter, we summarize the major features of the functionalism present in the early part of this century (of, e.g., Angell, Baldwin, Dewey, and James), thereby setting the stage for our discussion of its application to the study of memory phenomena.

In the subsequent two sections we attempt to make the application of functionalism to cognitive development more explicit by focusing on some aspects of a functional approach to memory and metamemory. Afterward, we attempt to interpret metamemory development in adulthood in functional terms, i.e., emphasizing the development, adaptiveness, and ecological dependency of knowledge of and beliefs about memory and of the use of memory strategies and aids. In the final section, we focus some attention on how the investigation of these phenomena might profit from the application of selected tenets of a functional approach to the study of cognitive developmental psychology.

THE FUNCTIONAL APPROACH TO PSYCHOLOGY

At first glance, it appears that since William James, the history of contextual psychology is spotted at best. Insofar as contextualism was a tangible sponsor of an approach to psychology, that approach portrayed psychological development as an active, continuing, adaptive life-long process, related to other internal or mental processes, and interacting with external activities and sociohistorical processes. Thus, a contextual psychology is related to (and occasionally identified with) psychologies derived from pragmatism, dialecticism, and functionalism. Contextual psychology, placing such emphasis on change and novelty, as well as chance and unpredictability, is threatened with indeterminateness and lack of precision. Such threats leave the status of analysis—not to mention knowledge—seemingly problematic. If there are many ways of analzying a given event, and none of them may be taken to ultimate completion, then analysis, like knowledge, is never final. This pragmatic, fallibilistic view of knowledge derives in part from evolutionary theory and may be associated with a natural selection epistemology (see Campbell, 1970, 1974; Plotkin, 1982; Popper, 1965; Rescher, 1980; Toulmin, 1961). Because of its serious consideration of multilevel change, contextualism would seem logically to imply a temporal approach to psychological investigation. Nevertheless, its application to developmental psychology has been only recently addressed (Blank, 1986; Dixon, 1986; Lerner et al., 1983; Lerner & Lerner, 1986).

Since J. R. Angell (1907, p. 61) devoted his presidential address before the convention of the American Psychological Association of 1906 to a characterization of functional psychology, several comprehensive historical and theoretical accounts of this approach to psychology have appeared (see, e.g., Beilin, 1984; Boring, 1957; Heidbreder, 1933; McKinney, 1978; Petrinovich, 1979; Raphelson, 1973; Sahakian, 1975). In an earlier paper, the relationship between contextualism and functional psychology was explored (Dixon, 1986). Our purpose in this section is to abstract from these accounts the main features of the functional approach, especially as they may inform our understanding of cognitive development in adulthood.

Functionalism, as a movement in psychology, was founded in the late 19th century at the University of Chicago (Raphelson, 1973). There, under the tutelage of such philosophers and psychologists as John Dewey, James R. Angell, George H. Mead, A. W. Moore, and Harvey Carr it flourished throughout the early decades of the twentieth century. It was, however, as Boring (1957) notes, a prototypically American psychology and thus may be found in the writings of numerous American psychologists (e.g., James Mark Baldwin, James McKeen Cattell, G. Stanley Hall, George T. Ladd, Edward L. Thorndike) at several locations (e.g., Columbia University) in several subdisciplines (e.g., developmental psychology, educational psychology, and mental testing). The subject matter of functional psychology was mental activity, a generic term incorporating such mental processes as perception, memory, and will (Carr, 1925; Heid-breder, 1933). Although it was methodologically pluralistic, it did place more emphasis on objective observation than on introspection (in contrast to the structuralists).

Overall, according to Boring (1957), functional psychology is concerned with: "success in living, with the adaptation of the organism to its environment, and with the organism's adaptation of its environment to itself" (p. 551). To this end, functional psychologists adapted the concept of function, which was inherited in part from Darwin's theory of evolution (Dallenbach, 1915; Ghiselin, 1969; Morris, 1970; Wiener, 1949). The biological version of this concept suggested that anatomical structures, shaped as they were by natural selection, functioned so as to further the survival of the organism. Psychologists (e.g., James, 1890, 1907) reasoned that consciousness (or selective systems of knowledge), although having no mechanical function, is useful in securing the survival needs of the organism because of its presumed causal efficaciousness. It was thought that the mind is an organ selected for its utility in benefiting the adaptation of the complex human organism to a complex environment. Key issues pertaining to this concept—for example, (a) the relationship of functional to structural, behavioral, and Gestalt approaches, (b) the relative activity (vs. passivity) implied in a functional account, and (c) the relationship between teleological and nonteleological explanations of functional behavior—have been addressed elsewhere (see, Beilin, 1984; Campbell, 1970; Carr, 1925, 1930; Dallenbach, 1915; Dewey, 1944; Dixon, 1986; Ghiselin, 1969; James, 1880; McKinney, 1978; Mead, 1934; Plotkin, 1982; Titchener, 1898, 1899).

Several ramifications of this approach to the study of mental phenomena have been identified. First, as alluded to earlier, many functionalists focused on the dynamic, temporal nature of mental and behavioral activity (Carr, 1925). Consistent with (and in part inspired by) the Darwinian approach to human social and psychological phenomena, this temporization was associated with more vigorously pursued developmental research questions and methods (Angell, 1907, 1908; Baldwin, 1895; Dewey, 1910; Dixon & Lerner, 1985, 1988; Toulmin & Goodfield, 1965; White, 1968). Second, the temporization of psychological phenomena occurred, as well, on another level of analysis. That is, some attention was devoted to the transitory, state-like nature of mental contents. As with biological phenomena, the contents were believed to be evanescent, but because the functions endured, still subject to empirical study (Angell, 1907). Although there are several methodological and theoretical problems attendant to such a view, we shall see later that this conceptualization engenders intraindividual research on the functional relationships among affective processes, mood states, goals, and external circumstances, on the one hand, and cognitive changes, on the other (Angell, 1907, 1908; Nesselroade, 1987).

Third, the functionalists were early advocates of investigating psychological operations as they occur under actual living conditions. In part, due to a resistance to elementism (Dewey, 1896), the functionalists argued for more research on mental precesses in terms of how they operate, their utilities, and what they accomplish in the biological and ecological conditions in which they function (Angell, 1907, 1908; Heidbreder, 1933). The methodological ramifications of this approach to psychological problems—including a concern with the ecology of behavior, adaptive significance of behavior, ecological validity, and representativeness of situations sampled as part of the measurement of behavior—is evident in numerous recent publications (e.g., Bronfenbrenner, 1977; Bruce, 1985; Brunswik, 1952; Petrinovich, 1979).

In sum, the early functional approach to psychology focused attention on: (a) the instrumentality and selectivity of mental operations, (b) the developmental or temporal nature of behavior, (c) the transitory or state-like nature of some mental contents, and (d) the usefulness of investigating psychological activity in ecologically or biologically relevant conditions. Together, these otherwise unexceptional (by contemporary standards) observations constitute the principal guidelines for comprehensive and programmatic life-span psychological research. In the following section we describe some ways in which these guidelines have been integrated into research on life-span memory development.

FUNCTIONALISM AND THE STUDY OF MEMORY

Because a wide range of 19th-century research on memory has been reviewed elsewhere (Murray, 1976), we focus in this section on some principal features of the functional approach, especially as they foreshadow selected contemporary developments. James (1890), for example, defined memory in terms of knowledge, but suggested that the remembering of an object or fact involves the emotion of belief insofar as the object is imagined to be in one's own past. He argued that the setting of the to-be-recalled event or experience is an important part of remembering, for it is the setting that makes one recognize the thought as a recollection. Without the setting, or with a vague indefinite setting, the thought is indistinguishable from "a mere creation of fancy" (James, 1890, p. 658). Memory, as a mental function, is portrayed as a process, a "chain of events whereby the mental life of the past is retained and utilized in the present" (Baldwin, 1893, p. 133). The notion of process is central: A given image (or a given memory) is not a thing stored in one's subconsciousness, but rather a state dependent upon a process (Baldwin, 1893, p. 137). Note that the instrumental, temporal, and state-like features of memory are paramount.

In addition, the functional, adaptive service of remembering is considered. The continuous functioning of cognition, as a selecting instrument of survival (James, 1890, 1907), eventuates in the individual learning enough to partake of social reservoirs of knowledge (Baldwin, 1909). The successful application of trial-and-error learning sequences—whether actual or vicarious, as in mnemonically supported thinking (Campbell, 1970)—thus results in knowledge gain that enhances the survival potential of the individual (Baldwin, 1909), but not in infallible knowledge (Campbell, 1974). Indeed, in modern terms, it is because of the dynamic representation of the encounters between an active organism and a changing (and ill-structured ecology), that the knowledge with which the organism faces problem-solving situations is fallible (Campbell, 1974; Dixon & Baltes, 1986; Lewontin, 1978; Plotkin & Odling-Smee, 1982; Popper, 1965, 1972.) Complementing ongoing empirical research in this period, the functionalists were not remiss in noting the practical and functional value of forgetting (Angell, 1908; James, 1890). Indeed, James (1890) argued that "in the practical use of our intellect, forgetting is as important a function as recollecting" (p. 679). Consciousness is not only selective in its attentiveness to the objective field but in its recollection of that to which it attends.

In addition, the early functionalists were actively concerned with such contemporary issues as: (a) irregularities in the process of remembering (and forgetting); (b) the physical and mental conditions of encoding and retrieval; (c) exceptionality in memory skills; (d) the occasionally problematic nature of nomothetic and trait-like portrayals of memory ability, especially when such depictions are based on methods that are insensitive to intraindividual differences across both time and contexts; as well as (e) mnemonics and other aids to knowledge activation and use.

Several of these issues have been raised more recently by memory researchers identified with a contextual or functional approach, a cross-cultural approach, a comparative developmental approach, and a sociohistorical or dialectical approach (e.g., Bartlett, 1932; Cole, Gay, Glick, & Sharp, 1971; Hoffman, in press; Hultsch & Pentz, 1980; Jenkins, 1974, 1979; Neisser, 1978; Nilsson, 1979, 1984; Paris & Cross, 1983; Smirnov & Zinchenko, 1969; Wagner, 1978a, 1978b; Wagner & Paris, 1981), and even by sociologists writing about cognitive theory (e.g., Coulter, 1983, 1987). It would be excessive to assert that these approaches cohere, for numerous fundamental differences could be overlooked or underestimated in such an amalgamation. Nevertheless, it may be instructive to note that, insofar as these approaches overlap, the major themes of confluence are generally functional ones. For example, recent observers conclude that comparative developmental research must consider the influence of motivation, affect, and context in the development of functionally significant memory skills (Wagner & Paris, 1981).

That the functional perspective on remembering has attained a certain common-sense status is evinced, perhaps, by the notable range of approaches converging upon many of its most prominent themes. For the most part, however, these approaches are intellectually descended from earlier functionalists and constructivists (e.g., Bartlett, 1932; James, 1890). In the interim memory research was dominated by general memory theories in the form of, first, the behavioral verbal learning model and, second, the cybernetic, information processing perspective (see, e.g., Jenkins, 1974; Kolers & Roediger, 1984; Lachman, Lachman,& Butterfield, 1979; Miller, Galanter, & Pribram, 1960; Nilsson, 1979; Postman, 1972, 1975), each of which has contributed enormously to the understanding of human memory. The re-emergence of efforts to link the science of memory with the pragmatics of memory can be seen in the recent stirrings of the approaches mentioned above.

Of course, if these putatively "new" views of memory are to have a significant impact, they must delineate persuasively the ways in which they interpenetrate and build upon extant approaches and the ways in which they depart from them. The intellectual gain must be registered in both theoretical and empirical arenas. At present, the advances made—taken one by one—by practitioners of these new views of memory are usually consistent with at least one problem area of extant models. Thus, it appears that the gain is registered primarily at the level of interactions (new combinations of factors considered) and interpretations (new reasons for considering these factors together). For example, the following recommendations of proponents of the new functional approach do not require complete severance of connections with the verbal learning or information processing perspectives: (a) to adopt a more tentative posture regarding the pursuit of general theory, (b) to consider critically models that reify components of memory, or (c) to take into consideration issues of ecological relevance (Bruce, 1985; Hoffman, in press; Jenkins, 1979; Neisser, 1976, 1978; Nilsson, 1979, 1984). These recommendations suggest that it may be empirically useful to consider memory as "one aspect of adequate cognitive functioning in a given situation" (Nilsson, 1979, p. 8). This portrayal turns attention specifically and directly to the study of interactions among different cognitive and affective functions, as well as the relationships between one's past and one's present memory skills, on the one hand, and adaptive functioning in specific ecological and social settings on the other.

The potential utility and scope of the functional view, as well as its indebtedness to extant models, can be illustrated by two related contemporary approaches to memory, viz., *schema theory* and the *situation model*. Although neither one is (or is intended to be) a functional theory of memory per se, both have certain relevant functional tenets. In the first case, schemata, as units of knowledge, are thought to be useful in the interpretation of sensory data, the determination of goals, and the organization of appropriate action (Bartlett, 1932; Bobrow & Norman, 1975; Rumelhart, 1975, 1980; Schank & Abelson, 1977; for a comprehensive review see Alba & Hasher, 1983). That is, schema theory is concerned with both the representation of knowledge (usually about a particular domain) and the use to which that representation is put. In principle, schemata may be conceived of as functional (or adaptive) not only in that they reduce the amount of information stored, but also in that redundancies (and even some details) may be ignored while more attention is focused on the processing (selection, abstraction, interpretation, and integration) of incoming information. Like problem-solving heuristics, schemata are adaptive in that they may lead to a solution ("true" understanding) with minimal ratiocination, i.e., with cognitive economy. However, also like heuristics, they may lead the problem solver successively away from the (veridical) solution (Anderson, 1981; Bartlett, 1932; Bransford, Barclay, & Franks, 1972; Bransford & Johnson, 1973; Rumelhart, 1975, 1980).

The second illustration of a functional approach is the perspective of van Dijk and Kintsch (1983) on text comprehension and recall. In addition to their well-known framework for the representation of text, these authors have recently proposed a cognitive model of the process of discourse comprehension, a model that attempts to take account of the activation and use of flexible, dynamic knowledge systems. Briefly, this situation model suggests that the reader or hearer constructs an interpretation of a (for example) text that is not necessarily identical to the true text representation, that is, the reader constructs a representation of the situation denoted by the text. To understand a text one must construct a representation of what the text is about. Several elements and ramifications are important in the present context. First, van Dijk and Kintsch suggest that it is through the construction of individualized situation models—e.g., reading the same text but, because of episodic, subjective experiential clusters, taking it to mean something different—that some individual differences (due to differential goals, interests, familiarity, and domains of knowledge) in recall rates may be generated.

Second, this suggests that the comprehender's active "control system"— i.e., goals, purposes, wishes, interests, moods, emotions, as well as various knowledge structures—interact with the text and influence the interpretation of the text's meaning. It should be noted that this active control structure may operate unconsciously, influencing short-term memory without necessarily being a part of it. Van Dijk and Kintsch (1983) note the similarity of this view to the functional (and in particular James') perspective on consciousness. That the aspects of the control system—like knowledge structures—influence discourse processing unconsciously (and yet can, in principle, be brought into consciousness) is roughly analogous to recent schematic approaches to self-knowledge and social cognition (e.g., Cantor & Kihlstrom, 1983; Chanowitz & Langer, 1980; Kihlstrom, 1983; Langer, 1978, 1981; Markus, 1983). A third relevant point is that it is the availability of a situation model that makes the efficient comprehender analogous to the expert in other domains of memory (e.g., Chase & Ericsson, 1981; Ericsson, 1985; Ericsson & Chase, 1982; Hatano & Osawa, 1983; Kliegl & Baltes, 1987; Yates, 1966). In both cases, within the domain of competence or familiarity, and after considerable effort in acquisition, efficient use of mnemonic devices—highly over-learned strategies, chunking mechanisms, retrieval systems—are brought to bear. Similarly, in both cases, for material outside the domain of competence, or for which an appropriate knowledge base is lacking, memory performance is not enhanced.

Briefly, the empirical and developmental relevance of such functional models of memory has been demonstrated in several studies. For example, adult developmental work manipulating uniqueness and datedness of stimuli (Poon & Fozard, 1978), memory for entertainment and sociohistorical events (Botwinick & Storandt, 1980), and memory for cohort-related biographical texts (Hultsch & Dixon, 1983) indicates that when the expertise of older adults is invoked— when, in the present terminology, a situation model of the task materials can be generated—they perform at higher levels than on control (unfamiliar) materials, and often as well as younger adults. The implication, of course, although fascinating, can be tendered only provisionally: As may also be the case with adult intelligence (Dixon & Baltes, 1986; Dixon, Kramer, & Baltes, 1985), *some* of the apparent age-related memory performance decline in adulthood may be related to the familiarity, ecological relevance, adaptive significance of the testing conditions and materials, i.e., the ease with which an appropriate schema or situation model can be invoked by the older learner.

In sum, the functional approach to memory has long proposed a consistent collection of principles. Among these principles are the following:

1. Both one's personal history and one's present memory skills can be conceptualized on a dimension of adaptiveness in human cognition;

2. Memory is a process, a series of operations and changes;

3. Multiple factors affect memory performance in a given situation, including motivation, beliefs and perceptions, prior knowledge and skills, mood states, as well as characteristics of the external context; and

4. Some account of ecological relevance should be taken.

That, in large measure, these principles continue to be espoused by proponents of this view—and that the differences between the research implied by these principles and that which is possible within the realm of extant models is not large— testifies to their conceptual vibrancy and augers well for their empirical prospects.

FUNCTIONALISM AND THE STUDY
OF METAMEMORY

Since the early 1970s cognitive psychologists have focused increasing attention on putatively higher mental processes. In an effort to describe the evolving complexities of human mental functioning, multifaceted, occasionally hierarchical, models of thinking have been proffered. The question of whether such multifaceted or hierarchical models are simply useful representations of mental processes or are also adequate portraits of how such processes actually occur will not be addressed here. Nevertheless, the present focus is derived from those experimental and psychometrically oriented psychologists who have retained the descriptive emphasis of these models of human cognition. Thus, in employing terms such as "metacognition" and "higher mental processes" the emphasis is on the manipulation or measurement of these processes and not on their explanatory adequacy. In this regard such terms as metamemory (Cavanaugh & Perlmutter, 1982; Flavell, 1971; Flavell & Wellman, 1977; Pressley, Borkowski, & O'Sullivan, 1984, 1985; Wellman, 1983), metacognition (Borkowski, 1985; Brown, 1978; Brown, Bransford, Ferrara, & Campione, 1983; Forrest-Pressley, MacKinnon, & Waller, 1985; Kitchener, 1983), metacomponents (Borkowski, 1980; Sternberg, 1980), metaattention (Loper & Hallahan, 1982), metalanguage (Gleitman, Gleitman, & Shipley, 1972) and metalinguistic awareness (Smith & Tager-Flusberg, 1982), executive cognitive function (Butterfield & Belmont, 1975), adaptive production system (Simon, 1979), general reasoning (Osherson, 1975), control system or plans (Bruce, 1980; Das, 1980; Freedle, 1972), modern homunculus (Butterfield, 1978, 1980), and voluntary memory (Smirnov & Zinchenko, 1969; Yendovitskaya, 1971) have emerged to describe apparently related facets of human cognition. Especially in the case of the "metas" the terms refer only obliquely to a hypothetical higher order process. That is, these terms refer less to another *level* of processing than to another measurable variety of knowledge, beliefs, or perceptions. In the case of metamemory this other variety is knowledge, beliefs, and perceptions about memory (Brown, 1975). Metamemory, in brief, is knowledge and beliefs about the functioning, development, limitations, and capacities of (a) one's own memory, and (b) the human memory system.

It is unnecessary to review thoroughly the imposing body of literature on life-span metamemory development (see Cavanaugh, in press; Cavanaugh & Perlmutter, 1982; Dixon, in press; Schneider, 1985). It may be useful, however, to summarize briefly our perspective vis-à-vis this literature. At present, metamemory is described most fruitfully as a potentially useful representation of a particular class of mental processing, a subset of the larger category of metacognition. The fact that numerous independent attempts have been made to examine a class of seemingly similar mental phenomena is taken as nominal (but convergent) evidence for their relative autonomy and thus potential descriptive usefulness. The questions of whether (a) they sufficiently diverge from one another to be independently measurable and useful, or (b) whether as a class they sufficiently diverge from other well-defined and measurable classes of behavior, are empirical, but not yet answered, questions. Nevertheless, some recent reviews (Cavanaugh, in press; Cavanaugh & Perlmutter, 1982; Dixon, in press; Schneider, 1985) suggest that, although the concept of metamemory has been frequently ill-defined and inadequately assessed, there are recoverable dimensions and robust, if somewhat modest, predictive relationships. In the remainder of this section we discuss briefly some recent conceptions of metamemory (and similar phenomena) with special attention to uncovering their potential functional tenets.

Functionalism and Metamemory

The writings of early functional psychologists are also illuminating with respect to metamemory. As we have seen, these early writers conceived of memory in the context of environmental demands, as one of several cognitive functions. No small amount of attention was devoted to aspects of remembering, reminiscence, recollection, reproduction, retention (etc.) that bear striking resemblance to aspects of what is now known as metamemory (and associated phenomena). There are several examples of intellectual precursors to conceptions related to metamemory such as memory aids, memory monitoring, voluntary memory, tip-of-the-tongue phenomena, mnemonic and memory skill training, and knowledge of imagery strategies. Besides the obvious historical interest, it is interesting to note that all of these phenomena were couched in the same functional framework as was memory. Indeed, those functionalists addressing issues of memory rarely failed to simultaneously consider related issues of metamemory and mnemotechny. To be sure, the important point is not that the functionalists confused the two domains, but that, even then, questions of memory implied questions of metamemory and that both were seen from the viewpoint of cognitive adaptiveness.

A few illustrations will suffice. William James (1890) discussed both the feeling-of-knowing and such "vulgar" but useful external memory aids as knowing about tying a knot in a handerkerchief. James also argued (and offered experimental evidence to support the notion) that exercise and instruction in memory skills within a particular domain do not result in skills generalizable to other domains or overall memory capacity; i.e., "concept systems" (or retrieval structures) are generally domain-specific. Similarly, as an integrated part of his deliberations regarding memory, Angell (1908) discussed knowledge and use of such mnemonic aids as repetition, imagery (vividness), recency, and number of associations. Even a more rational method—i.e., "knitting" up a fact with other well-known and related facts—is also discussed. Because memory and metamemory (here, broadly defined) are adaptive—i.e., they function to enhance one's control over past, present, and future experience—the "sooner and oftener we can apply to some practical undertaking a fact we wish to remember, the better the chance of its remaining in our minds" (Angell, 1908, p. 242). Baldwin (1893), in his discussion of "the mental conditions of memory," also suggested that, because mental experiences are never isolated, the more integrated (or "bound together by relations") they are, the more likely they are to be permanent. James, Angell, and Baldwin all devoted considerable attention to the idea of exceptional memory, and to metamemory procedures through which one may attain such performance levels. Again, by contemporary standards the concept of metamemory was considerably more fuzzy at the turn of the century, and we are not suggesting that we abandon the advances of the ensuing 90 years. Rather, we find it instructive to consider that metamemory and memory were discussed not in hierarchical terms, but in terms of their empirical relationship to one another and in terms of their functional utility in cognitive adaptation.

In sum, when metamemory is, like memory, considered in terms of "metamemory functions," the relationship between the "internal" and the "external," the mind and the environment, as well as various internal processes, become paramount concerns. In the abstract, the differential memorability of certain events may be related to evolutionary factors (Bruce, 1985; Nilsson, 1979). But, as we have seen, early functionalists recognized that differential retention and differential reproducibility was, in part, a function of individual goals, as reflected in differential levels of applied attention and coordination of means and goals (for recent work see Miroshkhina, 1973–74; Paris, 1978; Paris & Cross, 1983; Vygotsky, 1962, 1978). At this level, then, metamemory functions are efficient and adaptive within specified domains and insofar as they contribute to the active manipulation of the conditions of memorability and application of memory aids. In addition to motivation, memorability is a function of knowledge and beliefs about memory, as well as of interests, moods, emotions, and personality (for recent work see Bower, 1981; Bower, Gilligan, & Monteiro, 1981; Bower, Monteiro, & Gilligan, 1978; Snyder & White, 1982; Zeigarnik, 1972–73). Finally, it should be re-emphasized that the early functionalists wrote about putative metamemory functions in the context of memory functions. That is, metamemory was distinguished, but empirically not separated, from memory. Although it was implicitly dimensionalized, it was not reified, nor was it placed as a higher order or executive process. Rather, it was functional and developmental; it functioned in the selection, accumulation, and evaluation of experience and, in so doing, in the construction of individuality. In the following two subsections we discuss in more detail a tentative functional interpretation of some of these metamemory (broadly defined) phenomena. We apply such an interpretation to, first, the relationship between memory knowledge and mnemonics and, second, memory knowledge and memory beliefs.

Mnemonics and Memory Knowledge

Mnemotechny—"the skill of assisting the memory, especially by the employment of artificial aids" (Rawles, 1978, p. 164)—has been the subject of considerable interest throughout recorded history (Brown & Deffenbacher, 1975; Ericsson, 1985; Rawles, 1978; Yates, 1966). Many varieties of mnemonics, or memory aids, have been catalogued, and reports of their use in such contexts as narration, theatre, and education have been plentiful. Accounts of prodigious mnemonic feats (by both otherwise normal people and idiots savants), as well as an interest in personal mental efficiency, have, for more than a century, inspired books devoted to memory training and improvement (a few of the formidable number are: Bellezza, 1982a; Cermak, 1976; Datas, 1904; Dineen, 1977; Evans, 1889; Furst, 1944; Grey, 1844; Higbee, 1977; Lorayne & Lucas, 1976). Further, as we have already seen, scientific research in mnemonics has a long (albeit somewhat disconnected) history (Brown & Deffenbacher, 1975; Yates, 1966).

Nevertheless, mnemonic research was not integrated into all memory research traditions. Ebbinghaus (1885) for example, attempted to preclude explicitly the use of mnemonics in memorizing activities, and the S—R tradition, although recognizing their presence, argued that they were of negligible importance in the prediction of recall rates (Bellezza, 1981; see Underwood & Schulz, 1960). More recently, the surge of interest in mnemonics in arenas such as practical memory and learning psychology has been accompanied by an apparent wider acceptance in traditional cognitive psychology (Bellezza, 1981, 1982b; Ericsson, 1985). Thus, mnemonics are no longer seen as tantamount to tricks, crutches, or to "artificial memory." However, it is still uncertain the extent to which mnemonics can be viewed as practical means of using well-known principles of learning in the service of achieving efficiency in the tasks of daily living and in establishing and maintaining control over memory functioning (Bellezza & Reddy, 1978; Bower, 1970; Higbee, 1977, 1978; Pressley, 1982; Pressley, Levin, & Delaney, 1982). Higbee (1978) argued that even some famous cases of bizarre and exceptional memories (such as those recorded by Gordon, Valentine, & Wilding, 1984; Hunter, 1977; Luria, 1969; Wilding & Valentine, 1985) are, to a considerable extent, examples of natural memory processes. That is, the possession of exceptional basic memory abilities is not a prerequisite for the acquisition of techniques that lead to exceptional performances.

Mnemonic devices function to organize or encode information such that the probability of recalling it is enhanced. Although in functional terms their outcomes may be similar, it is important to distinguish between internal memory procedures and external memory aids. Well-known internal mnemonic devices include the story mnemonic (Bower & Clark, 1969), the method of loci, the peg-word mnemonic, and the first-letter mnemonic (see Bellezza, 1981; Morris, 1977, for reviews). Well-known external memory aids include shopping lists, appointment calendars, alarm clocks and timers, memos, and, of course, James' "vulgar" tying knots (Harris, 1978). Although, in general, both forms may be adaptive, their appearance and use may be specific to a given culture or set of life experiences (Cole et al., 1971; Wagner, 1978a).

Whereas internal mnemonic devices are normally used to facilitate effective learning, external memory aids are normally employed as reminders of future events and actions. There is some evidence to suggest that, although external memory aids are less frequently studied, they are more frequently used by adults

(Harris, 1978, 1980). Some external aids are useful simply as external storage mechanisms and others are useful as cues for the future (Harris, 1978). In both cases, they are practical insofar as they successfully manipulate the environment (Harris, 1980).

Internal mnemonic devices, in contrast, are portrayed by some observers as contrived and less practical (Harris, 1978; Higbee, 1978; but see West, in press; Yesavage, in press). Nevertheless, in recent years the effective application of mnemonic devices to general vocabulary learning (Pressley, Levin, & Miller, 1982; Sweeney & Bellezza, 1982) and to second language learning (Atkinson, 1975; Atkinson & Raugh, 1975; see also Hall, Wilson, & Patterson, 1981; Pressley, Levin, & Delaney, 1982) has been demonstrated. As we have seen, several mnemonic devices have been associated with enormous gains in forward memory span (Chase & Ericsson, 1981; see also Kliegl & Baltes, 1987, who used the method of loci) and words (Battig & Bellezza, 1979, using the peg-word mnemonic), as well as with the functionally important process of updating memory (Bellezza, 1982b). In addition, work with practical mnemonics and older adults is proceeding (e.g., Anschutz, Camp, Markley, & Kramer, 1985; West, in press; Yesavage, in press; Yesavage & Rose, 1984). As Higbee (1977, 1978) noted, the important point of this research is not so much that one wants to memorize prodigious numbers of words or digits (Battig & Bellezza, 1979), for such exceptional performances have been known to psychologists for a century. Rather, it is of interest that most normal individuals can in principle achieve mastery of a given mnemonic and that this skill may be useful in practical situations. That is, such evidence of reserve capacity suggests that mnemonic devices may contribute to the successful social and professional adaptation of most normal adults (e.g., in remembering important names, facts, and places), especially if it is shown that they are transferable (West, in press; Yesavage, in press).

In the earlier discussions of schema theory and the situation model, the notion of retrieval dynamics and structures was introduced (see Baddeley, 1976, 1982). In general, successful comprehension was dependent upon the (often spontaneous) generation of a rich retrieval structure. In considering mnemonic procedures an analogous notion has been interposed, that of cognitive cuing structures (Bellezza, 1981). Although these cuing structures act as mediators, it is not necessary that they be conceptually related to the to-be-remembered material. Rather, their purpose is to facilitate a process of self-cuing. The apparent parallel between cognitive cuing structures and retrieval structures suggests a higher-order analogy between mnemonic devices and memory schemata. As Battig and Bellezza (1979) have noted, however, an important difference is one of automaticity. We have already emphasized that memory schemata are activated relatively automatically. The use of a mnemonic device, on the other hand, reflects an intent to remember; it is a deliberate strategy, often requiring a great deal of effort to master. Thus, at least at the outset mnemonic devices represent the effortful side of efficient memory functioning, although less effortful (and, within a given domain, more effective) than rote learning. Nevertheless, after they are acquired their actual use may be relatively automatic.

In closing this subsection, one under-investigated and quite adaptive class of mnemonics should be mentioned. The focus of the present discussion has been on internal memory procedures. Although occasionally leading to spectacular memory feats, such mnemonics may not be as broadly applicable, easily transferable, and functionally valuable as external memory aids. In addition, the use of external aids—including lists, calendars, memos, and clocks—is easy to learn (or train) and their use involves comparatively little cognitive effort. Further research on the knowledge and use of external aids throughout adulthood, and perhaps especially in late adulthood, would be valuable.

Memory Knowledge, Beliefs, and Performance

Mnemonics and external aids, of course, cannot be used unless they are somehow (tacitly or otherwise) known. Beginning with research on the tip-of-the-tongue phenomenon (Brown & McNeil, 1966) and the feeling-of-knowing phenomenon (Hart, 1965), knowledge and beliefs about memory contents, abilities, and strategies have received considerable attention. Under the feeling-of-knowing condition the subject perceives that the target information is indeed stored and that further retrieval efforts may result in recapturing the elusive memory (Hart, 1965). The situation in which the target is on the tip-of-the-tongue is often accompanied with increased motivation to remember, and relatively good success rates (Hart, 1965; Ryan, Petty, & Wenzlaff, 1982). Under these specific conditions the metamemory-memory relationship is respectably high. As has been pointed out elsewhere (Cavanaugh & Perlmutter, 1982; Herrmann, 1982) there are many other conditions in which the obtained correlations between metamemory phenomena and memory performance are moderate (e.g., .3 to .5) at best. Is it a prerequisite for the conceptual viability of metamemory that it be related empirically to memory performance?

Throughout the many investigations of metamemory-memory relationships in childhood runs the thread of several assumptions about the nature of the two domains (Dixon, in press). As Brown (1975) and others (e.g., Cavanaugh & Perlmutter, 1982; Flavell, 1981; Flavell & Wellman, 1977; Wellman, 1978) have articulated it, one important assumption is that metamemory and memory performance are indeed closely related. The more specific assumption, however, is evident: viz., metamemory beliefs and knowledge, like self-knowledge and the feeling-of-knowing, is a causal antecedent of strategic memory behavior and of subsequent memory performance. Flavell (1981) portrayed this relationship in dynamic, interactional terms. Knowledge and beliefs about cognition develop as a function of experiences with a succession of cognitive goals, conjectural cognitive actions, strategies, and solutions (Flavell, 1981; see also Markus, 1983, regarding self-knowledge). A major demonstration of support for this model, and for the attendant developmental hypothesis that metacognitive knowledge and evaluations would increase through at least early adulthood, was conducted by Pressley, Levin, and Ghatala (1984). Neither Flavell's model (1981) nor the Pressley et al. (1984) study were cast in a functional framework and yet both speak to several issues upon which a functional interpretation might focus. Salient among these is the question of how to account for the frequently modest observed relationships between metamemory and memory.

One important issue pertains to the multiple, yet seemingly problematic, methods of measuring metamemory. Certainly one naturalistic way of investigating memory knowledge and beliefs is through the use of field studies and diaries. However, it is the alternative, the use of memory questionnaires and inventories, that has proliferated in recent years (see Herrmann, 1982, for a review). In part, the motivation for such proliferation has been to simplify ecological investigation of everyday or practical memory performance. As Herrmann's (1982) review suggests, however, memory questionnaires are (thus far) not suitable as comprehensive substitute indicators of ecological memory performance. The tentative evidence pertaining to the validity of such questionnaires—the memory knowledge/beliefs and performance relationships—is both inconclusive and, where conclusive, weak.

Several conceptual and methodological reasons for the merely moderate level of empirical validity evidence have been proffered (Herrmann, 1982, 1984), at least three of which are related to the functional tenets we have described above. First, memory and metamemory phenomena may not be unitary processes. Rather, they should be conceived of in terms of both general and specific aptitudes (Herrmann, 1982; Herrmann & Neisser, 1978; Sehulster, 1981b) and, in the case of metamemory, empirically (as well as phenomenologically) distributed into multiple first-order dimensions. Although these dimensions may themselves be organizable into such higher order factors as memory knowledge and memory beliefs (Dixon & Hultsch, 1983b; Hertzog, Dixon, Schulenberg, & Hultsch, 1987; Hultsch, Hertzog, Dixon, & Davidson, in press), failure to consider carefully which dimensions of metamemory might be related to which dimensions of memory, and then failure to measure the appropriate dimensions could lead to small validity coefficients (Dixon, in press; Herrmann, 1982; Herrmann & Neisser, 1978). Second, the reliability with which each metamemory and memory variable can be measured limits the correlation between them. In the literature, a metamemory variable with low or unknown reliability may not be correlated highly with even a reliably measured memory variable. In such a situation the inference that the constructs are unrelated must be tempered by methodological shortcomings.

Third, there may be, across occasions, considerable intraindividual variability in memory knowledge and beliefs; i.e., as the functionalists might have suggested, metamemory may be more state-like than trait-like. That self-reports are intraindividually inconsistent does not necessarily imply that the "error" variance is unwieldly or uninteresting. For, if coherent patterns may be recovered from this intraindividual variability—if such variability may be linked, for example, to variability in other labile aspects of the individual (e.g., mood states such as anxiety and fatigue, self-efficacy, control, motivation, health, or other cognitive experiences)—then the observed variability is potentially interpretable and psychologically meaningful (Nesselroade, 1987). This is a logical confluence of the functional approach and Flavell's (1981) model of metacognition. Two elaborations on this confluence should be mentioned. From a phenomenological perspective research on self-theories of memory (e.g., Sehulster, 1981a, 1982) indicates that memory beliefs may be integrated into a larger system of self-beliefs; the structure of these self-theories are neither static (Sehulster, 1981b) nor isolated from other cognitive or affective dimensions (Sehulster, 1981a). Other investigators have reached similar conclusions (Lachman, 1983; Lachman & Jelalian, 1984; West, Boatwright, & Schleser, 1984). From an ecological perspective, the relationship between memory experiences and memory performances may imply that there is ecological specificity in metamemory-memory relationships. Thus, metamemory knowledge and beliefs may be uniquely associated with particular situations and be differentially related to memory performance as conditions vary. These conditions can include aspects of the "internal" context (e.g., other cognitive or affective processes) or "external" context (e.g., other memory experiences or demands).

Conclusion

Overall, the functional approach does not provide an answer to the problem of low observed validity coefficients between metamemory measures and memory performance measures. But it does provide a rationale for turning attention to several apparently significant lacunae in the metamemory literature. Indeed, more than a passive rationale for answering unasked questions, these lacunae, in many ways, represent the heart of the functional approach. As indicated above, the implicit assumption in the metamemory/memory work is that there is a causal sequence such that metamemory knowledge leads to strategy use, which in turn results in good memory performance. With respect to individual differences, the prediction becomes as follows: individuals with higher metamemory knowledge are more likely to employ optimal mnemonic strategies and therefore remember better, thereby producing a correlation between degree of metamemory knowledge and level of memory task performance (Pressley, Levin, & Ghatala, 1984). A functional perspective suggests multiple ways in which metamemory/memory correlations, as typically measured, may be diluted. We can understand each of the three points raised above as pointing to multiple additional causes of individual differences in strategy use other than memory knowledge. These influences, such as situation-specific memory experiences or subjective beliefs about one's own memorial efficacy, either operate independently of veridical memory knowledge or mediate its relationship to strategy use. These methodological interpretations and some of the associated alternative influences on memory performance deserve further empirical attention. One would expect, for example, that the multiple dimensions of metamemory—including perceptions, beliefs and veridical knowledge—might be differentially related to memory performances, i.e., there might be task-specific or context-specific prediction patterns. Thus, the variation (or absence of cross-validation) in the results of univariate studies of metamemory and memory task performance is not surprising.

Our orientation to metamemory underscores the importance of incorporating studies of metamemory/memory relationships into a larger theoretical framework which emphasizes the functional relations of self-perceptions, appraisal of environmental situations and situational demands, behavioral intentions, and behavioral goals in predicting memory performances, both in the laboratory and everyday life (e.g., Brown, 1979, 1982; Cantor & Kihlstrom, 1983; Hultsch, Dixon, & Hertzog, 1985; Markus, 1983). That is, if we wish to predict accurately individuals' successful and unsuccessful use of memory, we must achieve a functional integration of concepts and methods deriving from social and personality psychology on the one hand (e.g., self- and person-perception, attributional style) and cognitive psychology on the other (e.g., metamemory, memory strategy utilization). It also indicates to us the critical need to consider alternative research questions and methods that will help us identify cross-situational consistency and inconsistency in metamemory/memory performance relations (e.g., Mischel & Peake, 1982, 1983). As discussed below, in our own research we seek to use self-report instruments to identify multiple dimensions of metamemory in adults. However, we are cognizant of the applicability to such research of Mischel's (1979, 1984) admonition regarding personality research; viz, it is not the most useful deployment of scientific resources to identify through elegant psychometric techniques dimensions of personality that are often poor predictors of behaviors in specific situations.

Thus far in this chapter we have attempted to communicate our understanding of a functional approach to psychology, in general, and to the study of memory and metamemory, in particular. In the following section we focus more specifically on the investigation of metamemory development throughout adulthood. In particular, we clarify the applicability of the functional approach to research on this topic. We use a research program with which we have been involved, together with David F. Hultsch, as the principal illustration.

TOWARD FUNCTIONAL RESEARCH
ON METAMEMORY IN ADULTHOOD

Previous Research: Metamemory/Memory Relationships

Although the corpus of research on metamemory in adulthood is not as large as that in childhood, several recent reviews have summarized and integrated selected subsets of the data base. For example, Cavanaugh (in press) reviewed the metamemory and aging literature where metamemory was operationally defined with any of multiple experimental (often on-line laboratory) tasks. Complementing this review, the metamemory and aging literature, where metamemory is indicated by verbal report (especially questionnaire) date, has been discussed by Dixon (in press) and, with a focus on clinical applications, by Gilewski and Zelinski (1986). Because these reviews are comprehensive and, at this writing, up to date, we offer here only a brief sketch of this literature, highlighting those issues that bear upon the functional approach or inform our own program of research. For further details regarding the contexts or procedures of given studies. the interested reader is directed to the original sources or to the recent reviews cited above.

There is a small but growing literature on metamemory/memory connections in adulthood. In a study of young (18–31), young–old (60–69) and old–old (70–79) adults, Bruce, Coyne, and Botwinick (1982), found that when metamemory was operationalized as the ability to assess memory task demands older subjects performed significantly poorer than younger subjects. In addition when metamemory was operationalized as prediction of recall prior to exposure to the memory task age differences in the same direction (with young adults more accurate than older adults, who erred on the side of overestimation) were found. When the "feeling-of-knowing" phenomenon was investigated with younger and older adults no age differences in accuracy were found (Lachman & Lachman, 1979). Similarly, when metamemory was operationalized as recall prediction accuracy after the learning tasks, no age differences were found (Bruce et al., 1982). A similar conclusion was reached by Lachman, Lachman, and Thronesbery (1979) and by Perlmutter (1978). In her comparison of young (20–25) and old (60–65) adults, Perlmutter found no age differences in metamemory (as indicated by memory prediction and memory confidence rating). One major age difference that did occur was in the spontaneous use of effective acquisition strategies. Thus, although older and younger adults performed similarly in metamemory knowledge, memory monitoring, memory prediction, memory confidence rating, and in the attempt to use effective strategies, older subjects did not spontaneously use as effective acquisition strategies as younger subjects. However, the introduction of acquisition instructions attenuated this observed age

310

difference. As is the case with young children, for these older subjects appropriate strategy instructions appeared to result in more effective memory performance.

This apparent trend, however, is not readily extended to all laboratory memory tasks. In a study comparing college age (mean = 20 years) and older adults (mean = 69 years), Murphy, Sanders, Gabriesheski, and Schmitt (1981) found that within the old age group strategy training (emphasizing chunking and rehearsal) resulted in recall performance superior to that of a control (intentional learning) group, but inferior to that of a group given no strategy training but simply required to engage in extra study time. In a separate analysis, Murphy et al. (1981) found age differences (favoring the young subjects) in recall readiness accuracy, but no age differences in memory span prediction accuracy. In previous research (e.g., Hulicka & Grossman, 1967; Hultsch, 1975; Reese, 1976) memory performance deficits associated with aging have been hypothesized to covary with deficiencies in the use of recall strategies or mediators. The research of Murphy et al. (1981), although not solving this issue, suggests that deficiencies in other realms of metamemory may control a portion of the performance difference variance. Such additional controlling factors may include knowledge of task demands, memory capacity, memory monitoring, and memory motivation (Bruce et al., 1982; Carroll & Gray, 1981; Flavell & Wellman, 1977; Kreutzer, Leonard, & Flavell, 1975; Murphy et al., 1981).

There is some evidence to suggest that strategies in the form of physical reminders are useful in maintenance of naturalistic memory performance in older adults (Carroll & Gray, 1981). There is mixed evidence regarding the type, purpose, and frequency of memory aids used by older adults (Cavanaugh, Grady, & Perlmutter, 1983; Dixon & Hultsch, 1983b). Effortful mental imagery mnemonics are rarely spontaneously used by older adults (Camp, Markley, & Kramer, 1983), who are, like some younger adults, generally unaware of their potentially functional effects (Rabinowitz, Ackerman, Craik, & Hinchley, 1982; Weinstein, Duffy, Underwood, MacDonald, & Gott, 1981). Nevertheless, in the Camp et al. (1983) study, evidence of some spontaneous generation of sophisticated mnemonics was found. Furthermore, in a study comparing children and a mixed group of young adults (18–39 years), the latter group demonstrated that knowledge about the relative efficacy of two strategies could be gained from practice with to-be-remembered material despite (in one condition) misleading experimental training (Pressley, Levin, & Ghatala, 1984). In another study, Weinstein et al. (1981) found that those strategies that were used were often specific to the type of material, e.g., invoking a familiar schema to interpret and comprehend a reading task.

Rabinowitz et al. (1982) concluded that because no age differences were found for their metamemory indicators (relatedness and imagery), metamemory was an insignificant contributor to age decrements in memory performance.

Given the apparent multidimensional nature of metamemory and the potential for differential relationships by tasks (Poon & Fozard, 1980), such a conclusion appears a bit premature. Although the results are mixed, at least two avenues of research support this counter-assertion. First, research in mnemonic training, especially employing the peg system or the method of loci, has revealed some (however sporadic) support for the proposition that knowledge and use of mnemonics are predictive of recall rates (Camp et al., 1983; Kliegl & Baltes, 1987; Robertson-Tchabo, Hausman, & Arenberg, 1976). That there are interindividual differences within cohorts in knowledge and use and substantial variation in situation- and technique-specificity is clear.

This specificity is revealed even more clearly when results from the second avenue of research supporting the metamemory-memory connection in adulthood are considered. When multidimensional self-assessment indicators, largely psychometric batteries, are considered, some evidence of a connection is apparent. For example, Zelinski, Gilewski, & Thompson (1980) found evidence for more metamemory accuracy in older adults than in younger adults. These authors used what came to be known as the Memory Functioning Questionnaire (see also Gilewski & Zelinski, 1986; Gilewski, Zelinski, Schaie, & Thompson, 1983). Similarly, Dixon and Hultsch (1983a) found some evidence for relationships among several dimensions of metamemory and memory for text performance. In the latter study, whereas affective dimensions of metamemory were more closely related to memory for text performance in older adults than younger adults, knowledge dimensions of metamemory were more closely related to memory performance in younger adults than older adults. In a more recent study of the relationship between multiple aspects of metamemory and a wide range of cognitive abilities, Dixon, Hertzog, and Hultsch (1986), found predictable, significant, but highly domain-specific correlations. Such selective relationships in adulthood have been found by other users of self-report instruments (e.g., Bennett-Levy & Powell, 1980; Broadbent, Cooper, Fitzgerald, & Parkes, 1982; Sunderland, Harris, & Baddeley, 1984).

In our own work, we have used the Metamemory in Adulthood (MIA) instrument (Dixon & Hultsch, 1983b, 1984). In the following subsection we describe the motivation for, and the characteristics of, this instrument in more detail.

The Metamemory in Adulthood (MIA) Instrument

In general, the mixed results from studies of adult age differences in metamemory and in metamemory/memory relationships parallels the results obtained with children. Somewhat restricted evidence regarding memory knowledge/memory task performance relationships has been found (but see Pressley, Forrest-Pressley, Elliott-Faust, & Miller, 1985; Schneider, 1985; Schneider, Körkel, & Weinert, 1987). Three possible sources of explanations of these inconsistencies interest us now. First, metamemory appears to be a multidimensional construct and perhaps only certain dimensions of knowledge and beliefs about memory are relevant for specific memory performance tasks. Second, investigations of metamemory to date have generally not attended to a distinction between what might be termed "objective" knowledge about memory systems (principles about mnemonic strategies, benefits of distributed versus massed practice, etc., which apply to *all* individuals) and the dimension of "subjective" beliefs about one's own memory capacity, expectations of performance level, and motivation to perform (Hertzog, Dixon, Schulenberg, & Hultsch, 1987). These subjective dimensions may be more critical determinants of memory performance in older persons than are the levels of veridical knowledge about memory function and mnemonics (Hultsch et al., 1985). Third, adult individual differences in memory may be to a great degree situation-specific. That is, they may be contingent upon specific prior experiences, or evoked only upon a recognition of the similarity of a current memory-demanding situation to situations in which memory strategies have been effectively used. In other words, memory knowledge and beliefs may be schematic or situational, as implied by the text model of van Dijk and Kintsch (1983) discussed previously. If so, then adequate explication of metamemory/memory relationships requires not only evaluation of situational memory demands but also, and perhaps more importantly, subjective representations of these demands as a precursor to memory-related behaviors (strategic or otherwise).

As indicated in the previous section, some research on metamemory development in adulthood that is partly consistent with the functional approach described herein has begun to appear. As an illustration, one ongoing program of research in which several features of this functional approach are included will be discussed (Dixon & Hultsch, 1983a, 1983b, 1984; Hultsch et al., in press; Zelinski et al., 1980). Generally, this program may be categorized by: (a) its methods (a combination of questionnaire and experimental), (b) its approach to the construct of metamemory (multidimensional), (c) its concern for ecologically relevant constituent metamemory behaviors and for a range of memory tasks varying along a continuum of ecological validity, and (d) the explicit attention given to the interrelationships of knowledge, practical, and affective dimensions of metamemory.

In designing a multidimensional instrument to represent selected facets of the content domain of metamemory, we consulted functional and epistemological, general psychometric, and the extant empirical literatures. In brief, the construct of metamemory was to be tapped indirectly through a self-report instrument. The construct was perceived to serve a useful summarizing function—i.e., it was theoretically rich—and a potentially fertile empirical function (Beck, 1950; Cook & Campbell, 1979; Loevinger, 1957; Messick, 1981). Because the construct was hypothesized to be multidimensional, a battery of diverse subscales tapping diverse subconstructs was designed. Methodologically, this approach entailed that a multiple factor pattern would emerge and that the pattern of intertask (or interfactor) correlations would differ from that of more unidimensional instruments (Messick, 1981; Nunnally, 1978). Specifically, interfactor correlations would be smaller in the multidimensional (heterogeneous) case than in the unidimensional case. It is important to note that a prominent source of validation of the instrument would come from observed relationships between the construct and actual psychological performance, but also from observed relationships among specific subscales of the instrument and other scales or other instruments theoretically either similar (convergent validity) or dissimilar (discriminant validity).

On the basis of the above considerations our first efforts in developing the Metamemory in Adulthood (MIA) instrument were directed at enriching the construct of metamemory. We examined multiple semantic memory, episodic memory, metamemory, metacognition, and self-perception questionnaires and interviews (only those available to about 1980 were consulted). With the context of cognitive aging research in mind, we abstracted eight theoretically meaningful dimensions. These dimensions—operationalized with items designed to reflect everyday, ecologically relevant activities, behavior, or conditions—are summarized in Table 14.1.

Several avenues of empirical work have been pursued. In the initial phase, after content validity was established for a pool of 206 items, the instrument was administered sequentially to three separate samples of community-dwelling adults ranging in age from 18–84 years (see Dixon & Hultsch, 1983b, for further sample information). Computation of internal consistency estimates (by age and sample) and factorial validity (by sample) resulted in a 120-item instrument, with acceptable psychometric properties for seven of the eight subscales. The seven subscales with acceptable reliability (internal consistency) and factorial validity (iterative principal axis with promax rotation) were: Strategy, Task, Capacity, Change, Anxiety, Achievement, and Locus. However, the Capacity and Change subscales were highly correlated. The Activity subscale behaved consistently across samples, but with more modest psychometric properties.

Substantive developmental analyses of this initial data set followed the establishment of psychometric reliability and validity. Multivariate analyses of variance revealed robust significant age differences on the Task, Capacity, Change, and Locus subscales, with young adults evincing higher levels of knowledge or perceptions regarding the first three of these dimensions, and more internality on the fourth, than older adults (Dixon & Hultsch, 1983b). In an early effort to investigate empirical validity the MIA was correlated with recall performance on ecologically relevant materials (texts). These analyses and, especially, stepwise multiple regression analyses revealed that, whereas the text recall performance of both younger and older adults was related to "knowledge" dimensions of metamemory (Strategy, Change, and Task), the performance of older adults was also predicted by "affective" dimensions (Strategy, Task, Achievement, and Anxiety) (Dixon & Hultsch, 1983a). In addition, there was suggestive evidence from

TABLE 14.1
The Eight Dimensions of the Metamemory in Adulthood (MIA) Instrument

Dimension	Description	Sample Item
1. Strategy	Knowledge of one's remembering abilities such that performance in given instances is potentially improved; reported use of mnemonics, strategies, and memory aids.	Do you write appointments on a calendar to help you remember them?
2. Task	Knowledge of basic memory processes, especially as evidenced by how most people perform.	For most people, facts that are interesting are easier to remember than facts that are not.
3. Capacity	Perception of memory capacities as evidenced by predictive report of performance on given tasks.	I am good at remembering names.
4. Change	Perception of memory abilities as generally stable or subject to long-term decline.	The older I get the harder it is to remember things clearly.
5. Activity	Regularity with which respondent seeks and engages in activities that might support cognitive performance.	How often do you read newspapers?
6. Anxiety	Rating of influence of anxiety and stress on performance.	I do not get flustered when I am put on the spot to remember things.
7. Achievement	Perceived importance of having a good memory and performing well on memory tasks.	It is important that I am very accurate when remembering names of people.
8. Locus	Perceived personal control over remembering abilities.	It's up to me to keep my remembering abilities from deteriorating.

Based on Dixon & Hultsch (1983b, 1984).

these studies that the relationships among the metamemory subscales changes during the adult life-span. The correlations among the Capacity and Change subscales were higher in older adults, indicating in all probability that more older adults who perceive themselves as having poor memories perceive this low capacity to be a function of age-related change. The Change scale also appeared to correlate more highly with the affective metamemory dimensions in the elderly. We investigated these issues further in later research.

In two subsequent studies the factor structure of the MIA issue and a second form of the empirical validity issue were addressed. In the first study, Hertzog et al. (1987) examined data on seven MIA subscales (omitting Activity) from six separate samples (age range = 18–84 years, total N = 750). These samples were combined to yield two half samples for cross-validation purposes. A multiple groups confirmatory factor analysis—using the first half sample to develop a model and the second half sample to validate it—revealed that, although the models did not fully cross-validate, there are at least two higher-order factors in the MIA. As suggested earlier, these factors correspond to knowledge about memory functioning and beliefs about self-efficacy in using memory. Thus, the evidence pertaining to the functionally relevant hypotheses of the (a) multi-dimensions nature of metamemory, and (b) differentiation of memory knowledge and memory beliefs in adulthood, is now more complete.

The second form of the empirical validity issue was addressed by Dixon et al. (1986). As summarized above, the initial evidence suggested that there were differential prediction patterns for memory for text performance for young and old adults. The second research question pertained to whether the MIA was related to performance also on laboratory cognitive and memory tasks. To investigate this problem, performance on a wide range of ability measures—including two indicators each of Verbal Comprehension (Vocabulary 1, Advanced Vocabulary), Induction (Letter Sets, Letter Series), Span (Forward, Backward), Associative Memory (Object Number Test, Memory for Words), Associational Fluency (Controlled Associations, Figures of Speech), and Ideational Fluency (Topics Test, Theme Test) (Ekstrom, French, Harman, & Derman, 1976)—was correlated with performance on the MIA. The sample included three adult age groups, young ($\bar{X} = 32.0$; n = 50), middle-age ($\bar{X} = 49.5$; n = 50) and old ($\bar{X} = 68.9$; n = 50). A series of hypotheses guided the inspection of the correlation matrix. Overall, predictable patterns of relationships were found, especially with the knowledge dimensions of the MIA. In contrast to the memory for text results (Dixon & Hultsch, 1983a), no evidence was found that the affect subscales predicted performance on laboratory cognitive tasks. Thus, again, the earlier argument concerning the specificity of prediction patterns among the multiple dimensions of metamemory and the multiple dimensions of memory performance is supported. This implies, as well, that metamemory/memory correlations are unlikely to be significant when global or unselected measures are employed.

Our most recent research efforts have been directed to expanding our understanding of (a) the construct validity of the MIA, and (b) patterns of adult age-related differences in knowledge and beliefs about memory. In two recent papers we have described more completely the issue of construct validity and our approach to investigating the convergent and discriminant validity of metamemory questionnaires (Hertzog, Hultsch, & Dixon, 1987; Hultsch et al., in press). Data were collected from two samples drawn from rather different populations. One sample, consisting of 378 individuals (100 university students, 278 adults aged 55–78 years), was drawn from Victoria, British Columbia, a medium-size west coast Canadian city. The second sample, consisting of 447 adults (age range 20–78 years), was drawn from a semi-rural area in the eastern United States (Annville, Pennsylvania). As described above, there is some theoretical utility in describing metamemory as multidimensional, with factorially differentiated memory beliefs and memory knowledge components. In an earlier cross-validated factor analysis, Hertzog et al. (1987) found evidence that the MIA scales Capacity, Change, Anxiety, and Locus loaded on a dimension interpreted as Memory Self-Efficacy. The important tasks in the present construct validation study were to assess the extent to which (a) multiple-scale questionnaires actually measure the same underlying construct (convergent validity), and (b) the target construct can be shown to be distinct from other theoretically related constructs (discriminant validity). Thus, we were interested in the extent to which, for example, memory self-efficacy is measured in another metamemory questionnaire (the MFQ; see Gilewski & Zelinski, 1986) and the extent to which memory self-efficacy can be differentiated from such well-known constructs as locus of control and global self-efficacy. The results of Hertzog, Hultsch, & Dixon (1987) indicated that, indeed, in both samples, selected scales of the MIA and the MFQ converge to measure the memory self-efficacy construct. In addition, the memory self-efficacy factor in both questionnaires seems to be defined equivalently in different age groups. Finally, the discriminant validity results suggested that memory self-efficacy, as measured by the MIA and MFQ, may be differentiated from basic personality dimensions such as neuroticism and extraversion and, to some extent, global self-efficacy. Thus, as is the case with the relationship between internal control to perceptions of control in the specific domain of intelligence (Lachman, 1983, 1986), memory self-efficacy is related to but distinct from general self-efficacy.

A cross-validation study of age differences was reported recently by Hultsch et al. (1987). Data on responses to the MIA and MFQ from the Victoria, B.C., and Annville, PA, samples (described above) were analyzed. Overall, the results indicated a pattern of age differences similar to that observed in earlier samples (e.g., Dixon & Hultsch, 1983b). Age differences were found on the MIA scales measuring memory self-efficacy (Capacity, Change, Locus) for both samples, and on the MFQ scales for the Victoria sample only (which compared students to older adults). In this study, we also investigated sex differences in MIA responses for the first time. Some evidence was found that women reported more strategy use and greater anxiety associated with memory-demanding situations than men (Hultsch et al., 1987).

Conclusion: To this point, then, our research has been addressed to several aspects of memory and metamemory phenomena in adulthood. These aspects are logically derivable from our understanding of a functional approach to the study of life-span cognitive development. Some examples of these compatible aspects are as follows: (a) metamemory has been represented explicitly as multidimensional; (b) metamemory is composed of related but distinct dimensions of knowledge and subjective beliefs about memory; (c) adult age and sex differences were examined and found to be reliably domain specific, (d) metamemory/memory prediction patterns were examined and found to be at a low to moderate level but also domain specific, and (e) construct validity work has been undertaken such that the relationship of the MIA to other metamemory scales and global scales of related constructs was examined. In the following section we describe some current research directions and goals. This agenda is designed to enrich our understanding of metamemory and memory development in adulthood through the pursuit of selected research questions as derived from the functional perspective on life-span cognitive development.

CONCLUSION: A RESEARCH AGENDA

Our current research agenda is based on: (a) suggestions of early functional psychologists, and (b) our appraisal of the current research situation, including our own work as sketched in the previous section. In this conclusion we argue that one important avenue for future research is the investigation of intraindividual change. In particular, our evaluation of the current research situation suggests the need to identify short term change and variability in subjective dimensions of metamemory as influenced by processes of situational appraisal and self-evaluation involving memory and related processes. From our perspective, a functional view of both metamemory and memory performance implies an extension of research on metamemory to the analysis of intraindividual variation. To date, both cognitive performance measures and metamemory measures have been assumed to provide a valid indication of abilities. Thus, the assumption is that these abilities are stable over the adult life span, except for age-related (generally decremental) change. Inextricably interwoven with this assumption is the position that the observed cognitive performance is more trait-like than state-like, that there is relatively little intraindividual variation, relatively little intraindividual fluctuation, due to corresponding changes in labile characteristics of individuals such as interest patterns, motivations, mood states, familiarity, and perceptions of self-efficacy in cognitive situations.

One of the key elements in our proposal is the recognition that ontogenetic change in underlying mental processes is but one contributing factor to age-correlated changes in complex cognitive behaviors. Our present efforts are directed at examining critically two common (often implicit) assumptions in cognitive aging research: (a) that memory performance measures supply a valid indication of memory processing "traits"—for example, working memory capacity or quality of informational elaboration during encoding—which are stable over time except for (in adulthood) age-related decremental change, and (b) that these memory measures are relatively unaffected by the above labile "performance characteristics."

Our perspective derives from the general functional approach to cognitive research, and from a life-span conceptualization of cognitive performance that includes the following points: (a) individual cognitive performance differences among older adults are at least partly determined by the familiarity of environmentally determined cognitive demand characteristics; (b) there are fluctuations in the cognitive performance of older individuals, associated with lability in physiological and psychological states and these are conceptually distinct from age change per se; (c) perceptions of self-efficacy in cognitive situations (including feelings of mastery or control) have a substantial impact on the cognitive performance of older adults (and vice-versa); (d) there are individual differences among older adults in both the accuracy of cognitive self-perceptions and in the degree to which these perceptions are influenced by salient experiences demanding cognitive competence.

This perspective does not deny (or attempt to explain away) age-related changes in memory "mechanisms." Such changes undoubtedly do exist. However, it does presume that: (a) there are substantial interindividual differences in the rate and degree of such change, and (b) observed changes in memory functioning in adulthood are directly influenced by factors which are conceptually distinct from ontogenetic change.

Evidence of substantial temporal fluctuation on measures of memory performance (from different memory domains) would challenge the assumption that single session memory assessment procedures inevitably identify stable individual differences in memory processes. Moreover, evidence that these fluctuations were predicted by contemporaneous fluctuations in affective states or perceptions of cognitive competence might suggest that a major component of variance in elderly individuals' cognitive performance may be only indirectly related to memory skills per se. Instead, it may be more directly a function of attitudes and expectations regarding performance in (possibly unfamiliar, especially for older adults) cognitive situations. Such evidence might also provide an alternative explanation for empirically observed interindividual differences in memory functioning; that is, such differences could be, in part, artifacts of assessing individuals at different points on labile subjective state dimensions affecting memory performance.

Given this general perspective, it becomes critical to follow two related avenues of research inquiry: (a) extended attempts to validate measures of metamemory and chart their differential relations to memory performance, and (b) a new line of research designed to assess intraindividual fluctuations in metamemory and memory performance, introducing thereby one means of identifying situational effects on these variables. Four specific research issues may be derived from these two related avenues of inquiry:

1. Examination of the convergent factorial validity of multiple measures of metamemory;

2. Determination of the divergence of dimensions of metamemory from more general constructs of self-perception, personality, and affect;

3. Investigation in large samples of the measurement equivalence of meta-

memory measures across multiple age groups. In particular, we are interested in determining whether the shifting correlations among metamemory scales indicate differential relationships among constructs or different measurement properties of the scales; and

4. Delineation of intraindividual fluctuation in perceptions of memory-related self-efficacy and affect. In particular, we want to know if fluctuations in these dimensions covary with perceived memory failures in the elderly, and if so, whether these shifting perceptions influence memory performance.

As summarized in the previous section, results pertaining to the first three issues are beginning to appear. Our own multiple-occasion work on the fourth issue is presently underway. In order to address these (inherently multivariate) research questions advanced statistical techniques (covariance structures analysis, etc.; Jöreskog & Sörbom, 1979) are being used. It is well known that such techniques are appropriate for large sample analysis of causal models; it can also be shown that such techniques are appropriate for multivariate intraindividual research designs (Nesselroade, 1987). Carefully designed intraindividual models could be used, for example, to disentangle the memory-related anxiety/memory performance relationship identified by Dixon and Hultsch (1983a). Are some older persons anxious about accurately perceived loss of memory function, or are their anxieties, based on expectations of (and fears about) senile memory decline, producing poorer memory performance? From a functional perspective, such a question is not an "either-or" proposition. Both phenomena are probably occurring for different individuals, and for the same individual at different points in time. We hope that the type of research approach we are pursuing can begin to assess the intertwined relationships among multiple dimensions of metamemory and memory performance in specific situations across the adult life span.

ACKNOWLEDGMENT

The authors appreciate the helpful comments of Stephen J. Ceci, Reinhold Kliegl, Michael Pressley, and Jacqui Smith on an earlier version of this chapter. In addition, numerous discussions with David F. Hultsch have contributed to the formulation of many of the present ideas.

REFERENCES

Alba, J. W., & Hasher, L. (1983). Is memory schematic? *Psychological Bulletin, 93,* 203–231.
Anderson, J. R. (1981). Effects of prior knowledge on memory for new information. *Memory & Cognition, 9,* 237–246.

Angell, J. R. (1907). The province of functional psychology. *Psychological Review, 14,* 61–91.

Angell, J. R. (1908). *Psychology: An introduction to the structure and function of human consciousness* (4th ed.). New York: Henry Holt.

Anschutz, L., Camp, C. J., Markley, R. P., & Kramer, J. J. (1985). Maintenance and generalization of mnemonics for grocery shopping by older adults. *Experimental Aging Research, 11,* 157–160.

Atkinson, R. C. (1975). Mnemotechnic in second-language learning. *American Psychologist, 30,* 821–828.

Atkinson, R. C., & Raugh, M. R. (1975). An application of the menmonic keyword technique to the acquisition of a Russian vocabulary. *Journal of Experimental Psychology: Human Learning and Memory, 1,* 126–133.

Baddeley, A. D. (1976). *The psychology of memory.* New York: Harper & Row.

Baddeley, A. D. (1982). *Your memory: A user's guide.* New York: Macmillan.

Baldwin, J. M. (1893). *Elements of psychology.* New York: Henry Holt.

Baldwin, J. M. (1895). *Mental development in the child and the race.* New York: Macmillan.

Baldwin, J. M. (1909). *Darwin and the humanities.* Baltimore: Review Publishing.

Bartlett, F. C. (1932). *Remembering: A study in experimental and social psychology.* Cambridge: Cambridge University Press.

Battig, W. F., & Bellezza, F. S. (1979). Organization and levels of processing. In C. R. Puff (Ed.), *Memory organization and structure.* New York: Academic Press.

Beck, L. W. (1950). Constructions and inferred entities. *Philosophy of Science, 17,* 74–86.

Beilin, H. (1984). Functionalist and structuralist research programs in developmental psychology: Incommensurability or synthesis? In H. W. Reese (Ed.), *Advances in child development and behavior* (Vol. 18). Orlando, FL: Academic Press.

Bellezza, F. S. (1981). Mnemonic devices: Classification, characteristics, and criteria. *Review of Educational Research, 51,* 247–275.

Bellezza, F. S. (1982a). *Improve your memory skills.* Englewood Cliffs, NJ: Prentice-Hall.

Bellezza, F. S. (1982b). Updating memory using mnemonic devices. *Cognitive Psychology, 14,* 301–327.

Bellezza, F. S., & Reddy, B. G. (1978). Mnemonic devices and natural memory. *Bulletin of the Psychonomic Society, 11,* 277–280.

Bennett-Levy, J., & Powell, G. E. (1980). The Subjective Memory Questionnaire (SMQ). An investigation into the self-reporting of 'real-life' memory skills. *British Journal of Social and Clinical Psychology, 19,* 177–188.

Blank, T. O. (1986). Contextual and relational perspectives on adult psychology. In R. L. Rosnow & M. Georgoudi (Eds.), *Contextualism and understanding in behavioral science.* New York: Praeger.

Bobrow, D. G., & Norman, D. A. (1975). Some principles of memory schemata. In D. G. Bobrow & A. M. Collins (Eds.), *Representation and understanding: Studies in cognitive science.* New York: Academic Press.

Boring, E. G. (1957). *A history of experimental psychology* (2nd ed.). Englewood Cliffs, NJ: Prentice-Hall.

Borkowski, J. G. (1980). On the nature and measure of metacomponents. *The Behavioral and Brain Sciences, 3,* 585–586.

Borkowski, J. G. (1985). Signs of intelligence: Strategy generalization and metacognition. In S. Yussen (Ed.), *The growth of reflection in children.* Orlando FL: Academic Press.

Botwinick, J., & Storandt, M. (1980). Recall and recognition of old information in relation to age and sex. *Journal of Gerontology, 35,* 70–76.

Bower, G. H. (1970). Analysis of an mnemonic device. *American Scientist, 58,* 496–510.

Bower, G. H. (1981). Mood and memory. *American Psychologist, 36,* 129–148.

Bower, G. H., & Clark, M. C. (1969). Narrative stories as mediators for serial learning. *Psychonomic Science, 14,* 181–182.

Bower, G. H., Gilligan, S. G., & Monteiro, K. P. (1981). Selectivity of learning caused by affective states. *Journal of Experimental Psychology: General, 110,* 451–473.

Bower, G. H., Monteiro, K. P., & Gilligan, S. G. (1978). Emotional mood as a context for learning and recall. *Journal of Verbal Learning and Verbal Behavior, 17,* 573–585.

Bransford, J. D., Barclay, J. R., & Franks, J. J. (1972). Sentence memory: A constructive versus interpretive approach. *Cognitive Psychology, 3,* 193–209.

Bransford, J. D., & Johnson, M. K. (1973). Consideration of some problems of comprehension. In W. G. Chase (Ed.), *Visual information processing.* New York: Academic Press.

Broadbent, D. E., Cooper, P. F., Fitzgerald, P., & Parkes, K. R. (1982). The Cognitive Failures Questionnaire (CFQ) and its correlates. *British Journal of Clinical Psychology, 21,* 1–16.

Bronfenbrenner, U. (1977). Toward an experimental ecology of human development. *American Psychologist, 32,* 513–531.

Brown, A. L. (1975). The development of memory: Knowing, knowing about knowing, and knowing how to know. In H. W. Reese (Ed.), *Advances in child development and behavior* (Vol. 10). New York: Academic Press.

Brown, A. L. (1978). Knowing when, where, and how to remember: A problem of metacognition. In R. Glaser (Ed.), *Advances in instructional psychology.* Hillsdale, NJ: Lawrence Erlbaum Associates.

Brown, A. L. (1979). Theories of memory and the problems of development: Activity, growth, and knowledge. In L. S. Cermak & F. I. M. Craik (Eds.), *Levels of processing in human memory.* Hillsdale, NJ: Lawrence Erlbaum Associates.

Brown, A. L. (1982). Learning and development: The problem of compatibility, access and induction. *Human Development, 25,* 89–115.

Brown, A. L., Bransford, J. D., Ferrara, R. A., & Campione, J. C. (1983). Learning, remembering, and understanding. In J. H. Flavell & E. M. Markman (Eds.), *Handbook of Child Psychology, Vol. 3: Cognitive Development.* New York: Wiley.

Brown, E., & Deffenbacher, K. (1975). Forgotten mnemonists. *Journal of the History of the Behavioral Sciences, 11,* 342–349.

Brown, R., & McNeil, D. (1966). The 'tip of the tongue' phenomenon. *Journal of Verbal Learning and Verbal Behavior, 5,* 325–337.

Bruce, B. C. (1980). Plans and social actions. In R. J. Spiro, B. C. Bruce, & W. F. Brewer (Eds.), *Theoretical issues in reading comprehension.* Hillsdale, NJ: Lawrence Erlbaum Associates.

Bruce, D. (1985). The how and why of ecological memory. *Journal of Experimental Psychology: General, 114,* 78–90.

Bruce, P. R., Coyne, A. C., & Botwinick, J. (1982). Adult age differences in metamemory. *Journal of Gerontology, 37,* 354–357.

Brunswik, E. (1952). *The conceptual framework of psychology.* Chicago: The University of Chicago Press.

Butterfield, E. C. (1978). On studying cognitive development. In J. P. Sackett (Ed.), *Observing behavior: Theory and application in mental retardation.* Baltimore: University Park Press.

Butterfield, E. C. (1980). On Sternberg's translation of g into metacomponents and on questions of parsimony. *The Behavioral and Brain Sciences, 3,* 586–587.

Butterfield, E. C., & Belmont, J. M. (1975). Assessing and improving the executive cognition functions of mentally retarded people. In I. Bialer & M. Sternlicht (Eds.), *Psychological issues in mentally retarded people.* Chicago: Aldine.

Camp, C. J., Markley, R. P., & Kramer, J. J. (1983). Spontaneous use of mnemonics by elderly individuals. *Educational Gerontology, 9,* 57–71.

Campbell, D. T. (1970). Natural selection as an epistemological model. In R. Naroll & R. Cohen

(Eds.), *A handbook of method in cultural anthropology* (pp. 51–85). Garden City, NY: The Natural History Press.

Campbell, D. T. (1974). Evolutionary epistemology. In P. A. Schilpp (Ed.), *The philosophy of Karl Popper.* La Salle: Open Court.

Cantor, N., & Kihlstrom, J. (1983). Social intelligence: The cognitive basis of personality. Unpublished manuscript, Department of Psychology, University of Michigan.

Carr, H. A. (1925). *Psychology.* New York: Longmans, Green.

Carr, H. A. (1930). Functionalism. In C. Murchison (Ed.), *Psychologies of 1930.* Worcester, MA: Clark University Press.

Carroll, K., & Gray, K. (1981). Memory development: An approach to the mentally impaired elderly in the long-term care setting. *International Journal of Aging and Human Development, 13,* 15–35.

Cavanaugh, J. C. (in press). The place of awareness in memory development across adulthood. In L. W. Poon, D. C. Rubin, & B. A. Wilson (Eds.), *Everyday cognition in adulthood and old age.* New York: Cambridge University Press.

Cavanaugh, J. C., Grady, J. G., & Perlmutter, M. (1983). Forgetting and use of memory aids in 20 to 70 year olds everyday life. *International Journal of Aging and Human Development, 17,* 113–122.

Cavanaugh, J. C., & Perlmutter, M. (1982). Metamemory: A critical examination. *Child Development, 53,* 11–28.

Cermak, L. S. (1976). *Improving your memory.* New York: McGraw-Hill.

Chanowitz, B., & Langer, E. (1980). Knowing more (or less) than you can show: Understanding control through the mindlessness-mindfulness distinction. In J. Garber & M. Seligman (Eds.), *Human helplessness: Theory and applications.* New York: Academic Press.

Chase, W. G., & Ericsson, K. A. (1981). Skilled memory. In J. R. Anderson (Ed.), *Cognitive skills and their acquisition.* Hillsdale, NJ: Lawrence Erlbaum Associates.

Cole, M., Gay, J., Glick, J. A., & Sharp, D. W. (1971). *The cultural context of learning and thinking.* New York: Basic Books.

Cook, T. D., & Campbell, D. T. (1979). *Quasi-experimentation: Design and analysis issues for field settings.* Chicago: Rand McNally.

Coulter, J. (1983). *Rethinking cognitive theory.* London: Macmillan.

Coulter, J. (1987). Recognition in Wittgenstein and contemporary thought. In M. Chapman & R. A. Dixon (Eds.), *Meaning and the growth of understanding: Wittgenstein's significance for developmental psychology.* Berlin: Springer-Verlag.

Dallenbach, K. M. (1915). The history and derivation of the word 'function' as a systematic term in psychology. *American Journal of Psychology, 26,* 473–484.

Das, J. P. (1980). Planning: Theoretical considerations and empirical evidence. *Psychological Research, 41,* 141–151.

Datas, J. (1904). *A simple system of memory training.* London: Gale & Polden.

Dewey, J. (1896). The reflex arc concept in psychology. *Psychological Review, 3,* 357–370.

Dewey, J. (1910). *The influence of Darwin on philosophy.* New York: Henry Holt.

Dewey, J. (1944) *Democracy and Education.* New York: The Free Press.

Dineen, J. (1977. *Remembering made easy.* Wellingborough: Thorsons.

Dixon, R. A. (1986). Contextualism and life-span developmental psychology. In R. L. Rosnow & M. Georgoudi (Eds.), *Contextualism and understanding in behavioral science.* New York: Praeger.

Dixon, R. A. (in press). Questionnaire research on metamemory and aging: Issues of structure and function. In L. W. Poon, D. C. Rubin & B. A. Wilson (Eds.), *Everyday cognition in adulthood and old age.* New York: Cambridge University Press.

Dixon, R. A., & Baltes, P. B. (1986). Toward life-span research on the functions and pragmatics of intelligence. In R. J. Sternberg & R. K. Wagner (Eds.), *Practical intelligence: Nature and origins of competence in the everyday world*. New York: Cambridge University Press.

Dixon, R. A., Hertzog, C., & Hultsch, D. F. (1986). The multiple relationships among Metamemory in Adulthood (MIA) scales and cognitive abilities in adulthood. *Human Learning, 5*, 165–177.

Dixon, R. A., & Hultsch, D. F. (1983a). Metamemory and memory for text relationships in adulthood: A cross-validation study. *Journal of Gerontology, 38*, 689–694.

Dixon, R. A., & Hultsch, D. F. (1983b). Structure and development of metamemory in adulthood. *Journal of Gerontology, 38*, 682–688.

Dixon, R. A., & Hultsch, D. F. (1984). The Metamemory in Adulthood (MIA) instrument. *Psychological Documents, 14*, 3.

Dixon, R. A., Kramer, D. A., & Baltes, P. B. (1985). Intelligence: Its life-span development. In B. B. Wolman (Ed.), *Handbook of intelligence: Theories, measurements, and applications*. New York: Wiley.

Dixon, R. A., & Lerner, R. M. (1985). Darwinism and the emergence of developmental psychology. In G. Eckhardt, W. G. Bringmann, & L. Sprung (Eds.), *Contributions to a history of developmental psychology*. The Hague: Mouton.

Dixon, R. A., & Lerner, R. M. (1988). A history of systems in developmental psychology. In M. H. Bornstein & M. E. Lamb (Eds.), *Developmental psychology: An advanced textbook*. (2nd edition). Hillsdale, NJ: Lawrence Erlbaum Associates.

Ebbinghaus, H. (1885). *Über das Gedächtnis*. Leipzig: Duncker.

Ekstrom, R. B., French, J. W., Harman, H. H., & Derman, D. (1976). *Manual for kit of factor-inferences cognitive tests*. Princeton, NJ: Educational Testing Services.

Ericsson, K. A. (1985). Memory skill. *Canadian Journal of Psychology, 39*, 188–231.

Ericsson, K. A., & Chase, W. G. (1982). Exceptional memory. *American Scientist, 70*, 607–615.

Evans, W. L. (1889). *Memory training: A complete and practical system for developing and confirming the memory* (2nd ed.). New York: A. S. Barnes.

Flavell, J. H. (1971). First discussant's comments: What is memory development the development of? *Human Development, 14*, 272–278.

Flavell, J. H. (1981). Cognitive monitoring. In W. P. Dickson (Ed.), *Children's oral communication skills*. New York: Academic Press.

Flavell, J. H., & Wellman, H. M. (1977). Metamemory. In R. V. Kail, Jr., & J. W. Hagen (Eds.), *Perspectives on the development of memory and cognition*. Hillsdale, NJ: Lawrence Erlbaum Associates.

Forrest-Pressley, D. L., MacKinnon, G. E. & Waller, T. G. (Eds.) (1985). *Metacognition, cognition, and human performance*. New York: Academic Press.

Freedle, R. O. (1972). Language users as fallible information-processors: Implications for measuring and modeling comprehension. In J. B. Carroll & R. O. Freedle (Eds.), *Language comprehension and the acquisition of knowledge*. Washington, D.C.: V. H. Winston.

Furst, B. (1944). *How to remember*. New York: Greenberg.

Ghiselin, M. (1969). *The triumph of the Darwinian method*. Berkeley: University of California Press.

Gilewski, M. J., & Zelinski, E. M. (1986). Questionnaire assessment of memory complaints. In L. W. Poon (Ed.), *Handbook for clinical memory assessment of older adults*. Washington, D.C.: American Psychological Association.

Gilewski, M. J., Zelinski, E. M., Schaie, K. W., & Thompson, L. W. (1983, August). *Abbreviating the Metamemory Questionnaire: Factor structure and norms for adults*. Paper presented at the annual meeting of the American Psychological Association, Anaheim, CA.

Gleitman, L. R., Gleitman, H., & Shipley, E. F. (1972). The emergence of the child as grammarian. *Cognition, 1*, 137–164.

Gordon, P., Valentine, E., & Wilding, J. (1984). One man's memory: A study of a mnemonist. *British Journal of Psychology, 75.* 1–14.

Grey, R. (1844). *Memoria technica, or method of artificial memory.* Oxford: Whittaker.

Hall, J. P., Wilson, K. P., & Patterson, R. J. (1981). Mnemotechnics: Some limitations of the mnemonic keyword method for the study of foreign language vocabulary. *Journal of Educational Psychology, 73,* 345–357.

Harris, J. E. (1978). External memory aids. In M. M. Gruneberg, P. E. Morris, & R. N. Sykes (Eds.), *Practical aspects of memory.* London: Academic Press.

Harris, J. E. (1980). Memory aids people use: Two interview studies. *Memory & Cognition, 8,* 31–38.

Hart, J. T. (1965). Memory and the feeling-of-knowing experience. *Journal of Educational Psychology, 56,* 208–216.

Hatano, G., & Osawa, K. (1983). Digit memory of grand experts in abacus-derived mental calculation. *Cognition, 15,* 95–110.

Heidbreder, E. (1933). *Seven psychologies.* Englewood Cliffs, NJ: Prentice-Hall.

Herrmann, D. J. (1982). Know thy memory: The use of questionnaires to assess and study memory. *Psychological Bulletin, 92,* 434–452.

Herrmann, D. J. (1984). Questionnaires about memory. In J. E. Harris & P. E. Morris (Eds.), *Everyday memory, actions and absent-mindedness.* London: Academic Press.

Herrmann, D. J., & Neisser, U. (1978). An inventory of everyday memory experiences. In M. M. Gruneberg, P. E. Morris, & R. N. Sykes (Eds.), *Practical aspects of memory.* London: Academic Press.

Hertzog, C., Dixon, R. A., Schulenberg, J., & Hultsch, D. F. (1987). On the differentiation of memory beliefs from memory knowledge: The factor structure of the Metamemory in Adulthood Scale. *Experimental Aging Research, 13,* 101–107.

Hertzog, C., Hultsch, D. F., & Dixon, R. A. (1987, August). *What do metamemory questionnaires measure? A construct validation study.* Paper presented at the Annual Meeting of the American Psychological Association, New York.

Higbee, K. L. (1977). *Your memory: How it works and how to improve it.* Englewood Cliffs, NJ: Prentice-Hall.

Higbee, K. L. (1978). Some pseudo-limitations of mnemonics. In M. M. Gruneberg, P. E. Morris, & R. N. Sykes (Eds.), *Practical aspects of memory.* London: Academic Press.

Hoffman, R. R. (in press). Context and contextualism in the psychology of learning. *Cahiers de Psychologie Cognitive.*

Hulicka, I. M., & Grossman, U. L. (1967). Age group comparisons for the use of mediators in paired-associate learning. *Journal of Gerontology, 22,* 46–51.

Hultsch, D. F. (1975). Adult age differences in retrieval: Trace-dependent and cue-dependent forgetting. *Developmental Psychology, 11,* 197–201.

Hultsch, D. F., & Dixon, R. A. (1983). The role of pre-experimental knowledge in text processing in adulthood. *Experimental Aging Research, 9,* 17–22.

Hultsch, D. F., Dixon, R. A., & Hertzog, C. (1985). Memory perceptions and memory performance in adulthood and aging. *Canadian Journal on Aging, 4,* 179–187.

Hultsch, D. F., Hertzog, C., & Dixon, R. A. (1987). Age differences in metamemory: Resolving the inconsistencies. *Canadian Journal of Psychology, 41,* 193–208.

Hultsch, D. F., Hertzog, C., Dixon, R. A., & Davidson, H. (in press). Memory self-knowledge and self-efficacy in the aged. In M. L. Howe & C. J. Brainerd (Eds.), *Cognitive development in adulthood: Progress in cognitive development research.* New York: Springer-Verlag.

Hultsch, D. F., & Pentz, C. A. (1980). Encoding, storage, and retrieval in adult memory: The role of model assumptions. In L. W. Poon, J. L. Fozard, L. S. Cermak, D. Arenberg, & L. W. Thompson (Eds.), *New directions in memory and aging: Proceedings of the George A. Talland Memorial Conference.* Hillsdale, NJ: Lawrence Erlbaum Associates.

Hunter, I. M. L. (1977). An exceptional memory. *British Journal of Psychology, 68,* 155–164.

James, W. (1880). Great men, great thoughts, and the environment. *The Atlantic Monthly, 46,* 441–459.

James, W. (1890). *The principles of psychology* (Vol. 1). New York: Dover.

James, W. (1907). The function of cognition. In *Pragmatism and four essays from the Meaning of Truth.* New York: New American Library.

Jenkins, J. J. (1974). Remember that old theory of memory? Well, forget it! *American Psychologist, 29,* 785–795.

Jenkins, J. J. (1979). Four points to remember: A tetrahedral model of memory experiments. In L. S. Cermak & F. I. M. Craik (Eds.), *Levels of processing in human memory.* Hillsdale, NJ: Lawrence Erlbaum Associates.

Jöreskog, K., & Sörbom, D. (1979). *Advances in factor analysis and structural equation models.* Cambridge, MA: Abt.

Kihlstrom, J. F. (1983). Conscious, subconscious, unconscious. In K. S. Bowers & D. Meichenbaum (Eds.), *Unconscious processes: Several perspectives.* New York: Wiley.

Kitchener, K. S. (1983). Cognition, metacognition, and epistemic cognition: A three-level model of cognitive processing. *Human Development, 26,* 222–232.

Kliegl, R., & Baltes, P. B. (1987). Theory-guided analysis of development and aging mechanisms through testing-the-limits and research on expertise. In C. Schooler & K. W. Schaie (Eds.), *Cognitive functioning and social structure over the life course.* Norwood, NJ: Ablex.

Kolers, P. A., & Roediger, H. L., III. (1984). Procedures of mind. *Journal of Verbal Learning and Verbal Behavior, 23,* 425–449.

Kreutzer, M. A., Leonard, C., & Flavell, J. H. (1975). An interview study of children's knowledge about memory. *Monographs of the Society for Research in Child Development, 40* (1, Serial No. 159).

Lachman, J. L., & Lachman, R. (1979). Comprehension and cognition: A state of the art inquiry. In L. S. Cermak & F. I. M. Craik (Eds.), *Levels of processing in human memory.* Hillsdale, NJ: Lawrence Erlbaum Associates.

Lachman, J. L., Lachman, R., & Thronesbery, C. (1979). Metamemory through the adult life span. *Developmental Psychology, 15,* 543–551.

Lachman, M. E. (1983). Perceptions of intellectual aging: Antecedent or consequence of intellectual functioning? *Developmental Psychology, 19,* 482–498.

Lachman, M. E. (1986). Locus of control in aging research: A case for multidimensional and domain specific assessment. *Psychology and Aging, 1,* 34–40.

Lachman, M. E., & Jelalian, E. (1984). Self-efficacy and attributions for intellectual performance in young and elderly adults. *Journal of Gerontology, 39,* 577–582.

Lachman, R., Lachman, J. L., & Butterfield, E. C. (1979). *Cognitive psychology and information processing: An introduction.* Hillsdale, NJ: Lawrence Erlbaum Associates.

Langer, E. J. (1978). Rethinking the role of thought in social interaction. In J. H. Harvey, W. Ickes, & R. F. Kidd (Eds.), *New directions in attribution research* (Vol. 2, pp. 35–58). Hillsdale, NJ: Lawrence Erlbaum Associates.

Langer, E. J. (1981). Old age: An artifact? In J. McGaugh & S. Kiesler (Eds.), *Aging: Biology and Behavior.* New York: Academic Press.

Lerner, R. M., Hultsch, D. F., & Dixon, R. A. (1983). Contextualism and the character of developmental psychology in the 1970s. *Annals of the New York Academy of Sciences, 241,* 101–128.

Lerner, R. M., & Lerner, J. V. (1986). Contextualism and the study of child effects in personality and social development. In R. L. Rosnow & M. Georgoudi (Eds.), *Contextualism and understanding in behavioral research.* New York: Praeger.

Lewontin, R. C. (1978). Adaptation. *Scientific American, 239,* 157–169.

Loevinger, J. (1957). Objective tests as instruments of psychological theory. *Psychological Reports, 3,* 635–694. (Monograph Supplement 9)

Loper, A. B., & Hallahan, D. P. (1982). Meta-attention: The development of awareness of the attentional process. *The Journal of General Psychology, 106,* 27–33.

Lorayne, H., & Lucas, J. (1976). *The memory book.* London: W. H. Allen.

Luria, A. R. (1969). *The mind of a mnemonist* (L. Solotaroff, Trans.). New York: Avon Books.

Markus, H. (1983). Self-knowledge: An expanded view. *Journal of Personality, 51,* 543–565.

McKinney, F. (1978). Functionalism at Chicago—Memories of a graduate student: 1929–1931. *Journal of the History of the Behavioral Sciences, 14,* 142–148.

Mead, G. H. (1934). *Mind, self, and society.* Chicago: University of Chicago Press.

Messick, S. (1981). Constructs and their vicissitudes in educational and psychological measurement. *Psychological Bulletin, 89,* 575–588.

Miller, G. A., Galanter, E., & Pribram, K. H. (1960). *Plans and the structure of behavior.* New York: Holt, Rinehart & Winston.

Miroshkhina, E. A. (1973–74). Strategies of verbal problem solving. *Soviet Psychology, 12,* 53–71.

Mischel, W. (1979). On the interface of cognition and personality. *American Psychologist, 34,* 740–754.

Mischel, W. (1984). Convergences and challenges in the search for consistency. *American Psychologist, 39,* 351–364.

Mischel, W., & Peake, P. K. (1982). Beyond deja vu in the search for cross-situational consistency. *Psychological Review, 89,* 730–755.

Mischel, W., & Peake, P. K. (1983). Some facets of consistency: Replies to Epstein, Funder and Bem. *Psychological Review, 90,* 394–402.

Morris, C. (1970). *The pragmatic movement in American philosophy.* New York: Braziller.

Morris, P. E. (1977). Practical strategies for human learning and remembering. In M. J. A. Howe (Ed.), *Human learning.* London: Wiley.

Murphy, M. D., Sanders. R. E., Gabriesheski, A. S., & Schmitt, F. A. (1981). Metamemory in the aged. *Journal of Gerontology, 36,* 185–193.

Murray, D. J. (1976). Research on human memory in the nineteenth century. *Canadian Journal of Psychology, 30,* 201–220.

Neisser, U. (1976). *Cognition and reality.* San Francisco: Freeman.

Neisser, U. (1978). Memory: What are the important questions? In M. M. Gruneberg, P. Morris, & R. H. Sykes (Eds.), *Practical aspects of memory.* New York: Academic Press.

Nesselroade, J. R. (1987) Some implications of the trait-state distinction for the study of development over the life span: The case of personality. In P. B. Baltes, D. L. Featherman, & R. M. Lerner (Eds.), *Life-span development and behavior* (Vol. 8). Hillsdale, NJ: Lawrence Erlbaum Associates.

Nilsson, L.-G. (1979). Functions of memory. In L.-G. Nilsson (Ed.), *Perspectives on memory research: Essays in honor of Uppsala University's 500th Anniversary.* Hillsdale, NJ: Lawrence Erlbaum Associates.

Nilsson, L.-G. (1984). New functionalism in memory research. In K. W. J. Lagerspertz & P. Niemi (Eds.), *Psychology in the 1990s.* Amsterdam: North-Holland.

Nunnally, J. C. (1978). *Psychometric theory* (2nd ed.). New York: McGraw-Hill.

Osherson, D. N. (1975). *Logical abilities in children: Vol. 3. Reasoning in adolescence: Deductive inference.* Hillsdale, NJ: Lawrence Erlbaum Associates.

Paris, S. G. (1978). Coordination of means and goals in the development of mnemonic skills. In P. A. Ornstein (Eds.), *Memory development in children.* Hillsdale, NJ: Lawrence Erlbaum Associates.

Paris, S. G., & Cross, D. R. (1983). Ordinary learning: Pragmatic connections among children's beliefs, motives, and actions. In J. Bisanz, G. L. Bisanz, & R. Kail (Eds.), *Learning in children: Progress in cognitive development research.* New York: Springer-Verlag.

Pepper, S. C. (1970). *World hypotheses* (2nd ed.). Berkeley: University of California Press.

Perlmutter, M. (1978). What is memory aging the aging of? *Developmental Psychology, 14,* 330–345.

Petrinovich, L. (1979). Probabilistic functionalism: A conception of research method. *American Psychologist, 34,* 373–390.

Plotkin, H. C. (1982). Evolutionary epistemology and evolutionary theory. In H. C. Plotkin (Ed.), *Learning, development, and culture.* New York: Wiley.

Plotkin, H. C., & Odling-Smee, F. J. (1982). Learning in the context of a hierarchy of knowledge gaining processes. In H. C. Plotkin (Ed.), *Learning, development, and culture.* New York: Wiley.

Poon, L. W., & Fozard, J. L. (1978). Speed of retrieval from long-term memory in relation to age, familiarity, and datedness of information. *Journal of Gerontology, 33,* 711–717.

Poon, L. W., & Fozard, J. L. (1980). Epilogue: New directions in memory and aging research. In L. W. Poon, J. L. Fozard, L. S. Cermak, D. Arenberg, & L. W. Thompson (Eds.), *New directions in memory and aging: Proceedings of the George A. Talland Memorial Conference.* Hillsdale, NJ: Lawrence Erlbaum Associates.

Popper, K. R. (1965). *Conjectures and refutations: The growth of scientific knowledge.* New York: Harper & Row.

Popper, K. R. (1972). *Objective knowledge: An evolutionary approach.* Oxford: Clarendon Press.

Postman, L. (1972). A pragmatic view of organization theory. In E. Tulving & W. Donaldson (Eds.), *Organization of memory.* New York: Academic Press.

Postman, L. (1975). Verbal learning and memory. *Annual Review of Psychology, 26,* 291–335.

Pressley, M. (1982). Elaboration and memory development. *Child Development, 53,* 296–309.

Pressley, M., Borkowski, J. G., & O'Sullivan, J. T. (1984). Memory strategy instruction is made of this: Metamemory and durable strategy use. *Educational Psychologist, 19,* 94–107.

Pressley, M., Borkowski, J. G., & O'Sullivan, J. T. (1985). Children's metamemory and the teaching of memory strategies. In D. L. Forrest-Pressley, G. E. MacKinnon, & T. G. Waller (Eds.), *Metacognition, cognition, and human performance.* New York: Academic Press.

Pressley, M., Forrest-Pressley, D. L., Elliott-Faust, D., & Miller, G. (1985). Children's use of cognitive strategies, how to teach strategies, and what to do if they can't be taught. In M. Pressley & C. Brainerd (Eds.), *Cognitive learning and memory in children.* New York: Springer Verlag.

Pressley, M., Levin, J. R., & Delaney, H. D. (1982). The mnemonic keyword method. *Review of Educational Research, 52,* 61–91.

Pressley, M., Levin, J. R., & Ghatala, E. S. (1984). Memory strategy monitoring in adults and children. *Journal of Verbal Learning and Verbal Behavior, 23,* 270–288.

Pressley, M., Levin, J. R., & Miller, G. E. (1982). The keyword method compared to alternative vocabulary-learning strategies. *Contemporary Educational Psychology, 7,* 50–60.

Rabinowitz, J. C., Ackerman, B. P., Craik, F. I. M., & Hinchley, J. L. (1982). Aging and metamemory: The roles of relatedness and imagery. *Journal of Gerontology, 37,* 688–695.

Raphelson, A. C. (1973). The pre-Chicago association of the early functionalists. *Journal of the History of the Behavioral Sciences, 9,* 115–122.

Rawles, R. E. (1978). The past and present of mnemotechny. In M. M. Gruneberg, P. E. Morris, & R. N. Sykes (Eds.), *Practical aspects of memory.* London: Academic Press.

Reese, H. W. (1976). The development of memory: Life-span perspectives. In H. W. Reese (Ed.), *Advances in child development and behavior* (Vol. 11). New York: Academic Press.

Rescher, N. (1980). *Scepticism: A critical reappraisal.* Oxford: Blackwell.

Robertson-Tchabo, E. A., Hausman, C. P., & Arenberg, D. (1976). A classical mnemonic for older learners: A trip that works! *Educational Gerontology, 1,* 215–226.

Rosnow, R., & Georgoudi, M. (Eds.) (1986). *Contextualism and understanding in behavioral science.* New York: Praeger.

Rumelhart, D. E. (1975). Notes on a schema for stories. In D. G. Bobrow & A. M. Collins (Eds.), *Representation and understanding: Studies in cognitive science.* New York: Academic Press.

Rumelhart, D. E. (1980). Schemata: The building blocks of cognition. In R. J. Spiro, B. C. Bruce, & W. F. Brewer (Eds.), *Theoretical issues in reading comprehension*. Hillsdale, NJ: Lawrence Erlbaum Associates.

Ryan, M. P., Petty, C. R., & Wenzlaff, R. M. (1982). Motivated remembering efforts during tip-of-the-tongue states. *Acta Psychologica, 51*, 137–147.

Sahakian, W. S. (1975). *History and systems of psychology*. New York: Schenkman.

Sarbin, T. R. (1977). Contextualism: A world view for modern psychology. In J. K. Cole & A. W. Landfield (Eds.), *Nebraska Symposium on Motivation 1976* (Vol. 24). Lincoln: University of Nebraska Press.

Schank, R. C., & Abelson, R. P. (1977). *Scripts, plans, goals, and understanding*. Hillsdale, NJ: Lawrence Erlbaum Associates.

Schneider, W. (1985). Developmental trends in the metamemory-memory behavior relationship: An integrative review. In D. L. Forrest-Pressley, G. E. MacKinnon, & T. G. Waller (Eds.), *Cognition, metacognition, and human performance* (Vol. 1). Orlando, FL: Academic Press.

Schneider, W., Körkel, J., & Weinert, F. E. (1987). The effects of intelligence, self-concept, and attributional style on metamemory and memory behavior. *International Journal of Behavioral Development, 10*, 281–299.

Sehulster, J. R. (1981a). Phenomenological correlates of a self theory of memory. *American Journal of Psychology, 94*, 527–537.

Sehulster, J. R. (1981b). Structure and pragmatics of a self-theory of memory. *Memory & Cognition, 9*, 263–276.

Sehulster, J. R. (1982). Phenomenological correlates of a self theory of memory II: Dimensions of memory experience. *American Journal of Psychology, 95*, 441–454.

Simon, H. A. (1979). Information processing models of cognition. *Annual Review of Psychology, 30*, 363–396.

Smirnov, A. A., & Zinchenko, P. I. (1969). Problems in the psychology of memory. In M. Cole & I. Maltzman (Eds.), *A handbook of contemporary Soviet psychology*. New York: Basic Books.

Smith, C. L., & Tager-Flusberg, H. (1982). Metalinguistic awareness and language development. *Journal of Experimental Child Psychology, 34*, 449–468.

Snyder, M., & White, P. (1982). Moods and memories: Elation, depression, and the remembering of the events of one's life. *Journal of Personality, 50*, 149–167.

Sternberg, R. J. (1980). Sketch of a componential subtheory of human intelligence. *The Behavioral and Brain Sciences, 3*, 573–614.

Sunderland, A., Harris, J. E., & Baddeley, A. D. (1984). Assessing everyday memory after severe head injury. In J. E. Harris & P. E. Morris (Eds.), *Everyday memory, actions and absent-mindedness*. London: Academic Press.

Sweeney, C. A., & Bellezza, F. S. (1982). Use of the keyword mnemonic in learning English vocabulary. *Human Learning, 1*, 155–163.

Titchener, E. B. (1898). Postulates of a structural psychology. *Philosophical Review, 7*, 449–465.

Titchener, E. B. (1899). Structural and functional psychology. *Philosophical Review, 8*, 290–299.

Toulmin, S. (1961). *Foresight and understanding: An inquiry into the aims of science*. New York: Harper Torchbook.

Toulmin, S., & Goodfield, J. (1965). *The discovery of time*. Chicago: The University of Chicago Press.

Underwood, B. J., & Schulz, R. W. (1960). *Meaningfulness and verbal learning*. Philadelphia: Lippincott.

van Dijk, T. A., & Kintsch, W. (1983). *Strategies of discourse comprehension*. New York: Academic Press.

Vygotsky, L. S. (1962). *Thought and language*. Cambridge: M.I.T. Press. (E. Harfmann & G. Vakar, Trans. and Ed.) (Original work published 1934)

Vygotsky, L. S. (1978). *Mind in society.* Cambridge, MA: Harvard University Press. (M. Cole, V. John-Steiner, S. Scribner, & E. Souberman, Eds.)

Wagner, D. A. (1978a). Culture and mnemonics. In M. M. Gruneberg, P. E. Morris, & R. N. Sykes (Eds.), *Practical aspects of memory.* London: Academic Press.

Wagner, D. A. (1978b). Memories of Morocco: The influence of age, schooling, and environment on memory. *Cognitive Psychology, 10,* 1–28.

Wagner, D. A., & Paris, S. G. (1981). Problems and prospects in comparative studies of memory. *Human Development, 24,* 412–424.

Weinstein, C. E., Duffy, M., Underwood, V. L., MacDonald, J., & Gott, S. P. (1981). Memory strategies reported by older adults for experimental and everyday learning tasks. *Educational Gerontology, 7,* 205–213.

Wellman, H. M. (1978). Knowledge of the interaction of memory variables: A developmental study of metamemory. *Developmental Psychology, 14,* 24–29.

Wellman, H. M. (1983). Metamemory revisited. In M. T. H. Chi (Ed.), Trends in memory development (Contribution to *Human Development,* Vol. 9, pp. 31–51). New York: S. Karger.

West, R. L. (in press). Practical memory mnemonics for the aged. In L. W. Poon, D. C. Rubin, & B. A. Wilson (Eds.), *Everyday cognition in adulthood and old age.* New York: Cambridge University Press.

West, R. L., Boatwright, L. K., & Schleser, R. (1984). The link between memory performance, self-assessment, and affective status. *Experimental Aging Research, 10,* 197–200.

White, S. H. (1968). The learning-maturation controversy: Hall to Hull. *Merrill-Palmer Quarterly, 14,* 187–196.

Wiener, P. P. (1949). *Evolution and the founders of pragmatism.* Cambridge: Harvard University Press.

Wilding, J., & Valentine, E. (1985). One man's memory for prose, faces and names. *British Journal of Psychology, 76,* 215–219.

Yates, F. A. (1966). *The art of memory.* London: Routledge & Kegan Paul.

Yendovitskaya, T. V. (1971). Development of memory. In A. V. Zaporozhets & D. B. Elkonin (Eds.), *The psychology of preschool children.* Cambridge, MA: M.I.T. Press.

Yesavage, J. A. (in press). Mnemonics as modified for use by the elderly. In L. W. Poon, D. C. Rubin, & B. A. Wilson (Eds.), *Everyday cognition in adulthood and old age.* New York: Cambridge University Press.

Yesavage, J. A., & Rose, T. L. (1984). Semantic elaboration and the method of loci: A new trip for older learners. *Experimental Aging Research, 10,* 155–159.

Zeigarnik, B. V. (1972–73). Excerpts from B. V. Zeigarnik's monograph "Personality and the pathology of activity." *Soviet Psychology, 11,* 3–89.

Zelinski, E. M., Gilewski, M. J., & Thompson, L. W. (1980). Do laboratory tests relate to self-assessment of memory ability in the young and old? In L. W. Poon, J. L. Fozard, L. S. Cermak, D. Arenberg, & L. W. Thompson (Eds.), *New directions in memory and aging: Proceedings of the George A. Talland Memorial Conference.* Hillsdale, NJ: Lawrence Erlbaum Associates.

15

Human Memory as a Faculty Versus Human Memory as a Set of Specific Abilities: Evidence from a Life-Span Approach

Monika Knopf
J. Körkel
W. Schneider
F. E. Weinert
Max Planck Institute for Psychological Research, Munich

INTRODUCTION

Since the very beginning of memory research in psychology, a most controversial issue has been the question if memory represents a general, unitary human faculty or rather a variety of specific and probably independent abilities. Everyday-life experiences lead us to believe that one can distinguish between people with a generally good memory who are able to remember various incidents and facts even after a long period of time, and those who easily forget whatever they have been told to keep in mind. On the other hand, pioneers of experimental research in memory like Ebbinghaus (1885) or Meumann (1907) already considered the possibility of extreme intraindividual differences in tasks covering different memory contents (e.g., assessing memory for prose versus memory for numbers). Meumann's position was not very clear, however; in his earlier studies (cf. Meumann 1907), he proposed a distinction between a "general memory" and several "task-specific memories," whereas he doubted the existence of a "general memory" in a later publication (Meumann, 1918), emphasizing the fact that—according to his empirical investigations—only special memories could be found.

A number of studies conducted in the 20s and 30s within the psychometric approach (e.g., Anastasi, 1932; Bolton, 1931; Lee, 1925) confirmed Meumann's (1918) later position in that only low correlations were found among memory tests varying either with regard to test materials (e.g., pictures versus words) or with regard to the type of assessment procedure (e.g., recognition versus recall).

In one of the most comprehensive investigations into the problem, Katzenberger (1964) tested 109 college students using 20 different memory tests which

331

were systematically varied according to type of assessment (recall vs. recognition), test material (numbers, syllables, words, sentences, and pictures), and the time interval between task presentation and actual memory test (short- vs. long-term memory). The pattern of intercorrelations among his memory tasks corresponded to that found in the earlier studies, and a factor analysis computed on the intercorrelation matrix led to an eight-factor solution. Consequently, there was reason to conclude that the memory refers to a variety of different abilities or dimensions.

Within the psychometric approach, the most prominent hypothesis specifying developmental aspects of memory postulated the differentiation of special abilities during later childhood and early adulthood out of a fairly unified and general cognitive ability. For late adulthood the occurrence of de-differentiation was assumed (differentiation/de-differentation-hypothesis; Balinsky, 1941; Burt, 1954; Garrett, 1946). This hypothesis received empirical support in several studies (e.g., Friedman, 1974). Thus, in this research tradition the existence of relatively independent memory abilities was demonstrated at least for the age group of younger adults. On the other hand, a number of investigators have failed to find evidence for the validity of this hypothesis (summarized in Reinert, 1970).

The study of interindividual differences has been a traditional topic and issue of differential psychology. Within this discipline, it was claimed that most cognitive performances are likely immutable. Therefore performance tests were designed and test items were selected on which individuals maintained their relative position over time. Within the field of developmental psychology, however, individual differences have been neglected in favor of an emphasis on universal processes of development. This seems to be due to the predominance of the experimental model and the evolutionary approach in developmental psychology (McCall, 1977), treating individual differences as trivial, unstable variations that can have only little impact upon later development. Cronbach (1957) and others (e.g., Estes, 1974; Gagné, 1967) have commented on this lack of interest in more detail.

With the advent of information-processing models in the late 60s the conceptualization of memory changed essentially. In brief, the modal information-processing model specified three components of memory: structural features or hardware, the system architecture, and the programs or software (see e.g., Atkinson & Shiffrin, 1968; summarized in Campione, Brown, & Bryant, 1985; Hunt & Lansman, 1975). Whereas it was assumed that the structural features as well as the system architecture are relatively invariant components of the memory system, large individual differences were expected in the programable parts of the memory system both across subjects and within subjects. Psychologists interested in the question of intraindividual and interindividual differences began to search for tasks that require considerable strategic effort for effective execution. The idea was that the magnitude of performance differences between subjects as well as within subjects would be largest in strategy-intensive tasks (Brown, 1975).

A great deal of research in developmental psychology in the 70s and early 80s demonstrated that age-related changes in memory performance are in fact linked to the growing child's more frequent, spontaneous, and more flexible use of mnemonic strategies (cf. Brown, Bransford, Ferrara, & Campione, 1983; Hagen, Jongeward, & Kail, 1975). Finally, the concept of metamemory has been introduced by Flavell (1971; see also Flavell & Wellman, 1977) to explain even more of the performance differences in strategic memory tasks between and within subjects that could not be explained by memory strategies. On the other hand, it often was shown that developmental differences are hard to detect in such memory tasks where strategic activities are not efficient (cf. Perlmutter & Lange, 1978). In addition, developmental psychologists comparing memory behavior in retarded and nonretarded people (e.g., Campione & Brown, 1977, 1978) identified that strategy-intensive memory tasks do not only cause age-related differences in memory performance but also the most dramatic interindividual differences.

Further, the shift in theoretical conceptualization of memory stimulated new efforts in experimental psychology to analyze the magnitude and sources of interindividual performance differences. While psychometrics were mainly interested in differences at performance level, cognitive psychologists concentrated their interest on the identification of underlying psychological mechanisms and processes. Especially short-term memory processes became a fashionable and productive area of study (cf. Chase, Lyon, & Ericsson, 1981; Cohen, 1982; Humphreys, Lynch, Revelle, & Hall, 1983; Hunt, Frost, & Lunneborg, 1973; Kirby, 1980).

However, a review of the literature makes clear that only a few studies addressed the topic of the development of intraindividual patterns of memory performance. One line of research addressing this issue is strongly linked to the theoretical concepts and the techniques favored in the experimental approach to interindividual differences. Accordingly, the question has been to identify such memory processes that are causing interindividual variances as well as developmental differences in memory span tasks. Somewhat surprisingly, Dempster (1981) stresses that there is no conclusive evidence that any of the strategic memory processes (e.g., chunking, rehearsal, grouping) or the overall capacity of the system plays a role in interindividual memory span variance. By contrast, the investigations reviewed by Dempster suggest that the important factors underlying span differences are nonstrategic ones. Especially, the speed with which stimuli can be identified proved as a major source of both individual as well as developmental differences in memory span. Should these conclusions prove valid after further investigations it would be necessary to broaden the scope of memory tasks traditionally used in developmental psychology. Although Dempster (1981) does not explicitly address the question if memory should be treated as faculty or as a variety of specific abilities/skills, the rather low intraindividual correlations between different memory processes involved in memory span tasks are clear evidences for the second conceptualization.

In another line of research investigating the development of memory differences, the hypothesis was tested that interindividual differences in memory may reflect a general strategic factor. According to that assumption, some individuals may use memory strategies consistently and perform well, whereas others may use strategies poorly and thus remember inaccurately. For example, in a study by Kail (1979) 3rd- and 6th-graders were tested on three memory tasks. From each task, a strategy-free and a strategy-based measure was derived. The results of a factor analysis seemed to confirm the hypothesis, at least for the 6th-graders: here, all three strategy-based measures loaded heavily on one factor, which appeared to be the validation of the role of a general strategic factor. For the 3rd-graders, no such factor could be found. Although this finding suggests the existence of developmental changes in the interrelations among tasks, this cannot be inferred by a visual inspection of the intercorrelations among measures. Another problem with the interpretation of a general strategic factor is that this should correspond with highly significant correlations among the strategy-based measures. But as Kail (1979) pointed out, correlations, when significant, were rather small. Obviously, other factors must also have contributed to individual differences in 6th-graders' memory ability.

Stevenson, Hale, Klein, and Miller (1968) compared 3rd- through 7th-graders' performance on a series of learning and problem-solving tasks. As a main result, they found that correlations among the tasks were higher than those usually obtained, but that they were not, in the absolute sense, of high magnitude. The lowest intercorrelations were found for tasks that differed from one another both in structure and content. No notable developmental changes in the interrelations among tasks across the 5-year span of ages included in the study were detected. The authors concluded that their results offered little support for the operation of a general learning or memory factor.

So far, the most convincing evidence in favor of a general strategic factor and consistently high intertask correlations stems from a study by Cavanaugh and Borkowski (1980). The authors tested kindergarten children, 1st-, 3rd-, and 5th-graders by using three different memory tasks (i.e., cognitive cuing, free sort, alphabet search), and assessed the degree of consistency across the three tasks by computing intercorrelations among measures of study strategy, recall, and clustering during recall. A significant developmental improvement was found for almost all sets of intercorrelation with strategy measures showing particularly high intertask correlations in 1st-, 3rd-, and 5th-graders. Although these results seem to be very encouraging, it should be noted that only laboratory type tasks were used in the studies by Kail (1979) and Cavanaugh and Borkowski (1980).

Though these investigations on developmental aspects of memory differences produced an impressive body of interesting data, from a developmental point of view these studies suffer from some essential shortcomings. First, given the frequent criticism that laboratory studies have little relevance for understanding learning and memory processes as they occur in everyday life, we obviously need analysis of intertask consistency for memory tasks that differ with regard to structure, content, and the degree of ecological validity. Second, as the age range for subjects included in the studies is rather restricted, almost nothing is known about the consistency of memory performances over the life span.

In the following short-term longitudinal study, an attempt was made to reconsider the question of universal versus task-specific lines of memory development by enhancing the range of chronological ages included, by using a field-experimental approach to overcome problems related to small sample sizes, and by including memory tasks that differed with regard to content and structure, as well as to the degree of ecological validity.

The study focused on the problem of universal lines of memory development, that is, high intertask consistencies, can be demonstrated across the life-span when rather artificial, laboratory-type tasks as well as more natural, everyday memory tasks are simultaneously considered. A two-step procedure was chosen to test this assumption. First, interrelations among the different indicators were analyzed separately for each age group. As mentioned earlier, this has been the typical procedure to assess intertask consistencies. Given the predominantly low intercorrelations found in most of the previous studies, a second step of analysis was added that used a more liberal criterion of intertask consistency: Subjects were grouped into one of three categories according to their achievement (high, middle, low), separately for each task and age group. It was argued that universal lines of memory development may be claimed if high percentages of stable intertask classification of subjects can be found within each age group.

When the hypotheses of universal lines of memory development were not supported by both the more traditional and the more liberal tests, additional steps of analysis seemed appropriate to clarify the impact of strategy use and metacognition on memory performance in the various tasks. Intertask classifications of the various strategy and metacognition measures using the liberal criterion, already described should provide further information concerning the validity of a "general strategic factor" proposed by Kail 1979). Here again, a negative finding, that is, a lack of intertask consistency would justify the decision to concentrate on the analysis of task-specific lines of memory development. With negative cases, a final step of analysis should focus on the explanation of age-related changes in memory performance separately for each memory task by using measures of memory capacity, strategy use, and metamemory as covariates or possible explanatory concepts. This could give us a first estimate of the relative impact of memory capacity, strategy use, and metamemorial knowledge on performance in laboratory-type versus everyday memory tasks. More specifically, this kind of analysis could provide us with information concerning the degree of ecological validity involved in the laboratory-type tasks used in the present study.

METHOD

Our short-term longitudinal study was originally designed for different purposes (i.e., the analysis of the interaction among metacognition, attributional style, and self-instruction across the life span). Only those tasks and procedures relevant to the topic of universal versus task-specific lines of memory development are described below.

Samples: Two different samples were available for data analysis. The children sample consisted of 106 3rd-graders, 236 5th-graders, and 236 7th-graders. A total number of 124 adults and elderly people aged 50- to 84-years also participated in the study. This sample was subdivided into two age groups using the mean (63 years) as a classification criterion.

MATERIAL AND PROCEDURE

Memory Capacity

A digit-span task was used to assess memory capacity in children as well as adults. Subjects were instructed that the goal of the task was to assess one's own memory for telephone numbers. The procedure itself was similar to that used by Wechsler in his intelligence tests (the WISC and the WAIS).

Dependent measures: The maximum number of digits remembered in the correct serial order served as a measure of memory performance in this task for both children and adults.

Sort-recall Tasks

(a) Sort-recall task using nonclusterable stimuli: A total number of 24 word cards were used as stimuli. Words were selected in a way that made it very difficult to cluster or organize them in a meaningful way. Identical stimuli lists were used for children and adults. The children were given metal boards and asked to put the items on the boards. They were instructed to remember as many items as possible, and were free to move the stimulus cards on the board and do whatever they thought helpful for remembering the items. After a short study period, the boards were removed and subjects had to estimate how many items they could remember. Next, subjects had to recall the items. After that, they were asked again to estimate how many items they probably could remember in a similar, future task. The procedure for adults was slightly different in that no metal boards were used and the recall estimation tests were taken at different time points: The first estimate had to be given after a short word inspection period but before learning, whereas the second estimate followed the study and learning period immediately before recall.

Dependent measures: The number of items correctly recalled was used as a measure of memory performance. In addition, the absolute value of the second estimate divided by recall was taken as a measure of procedural metamemory. That is, accuracy of recall prediction was regarded as a measure of subjects' memory monitoring ability.

(b) Sort-recall task using taxonomically clusterable stimuli: Here, different stimulus lists were used for children and adults. The procedure was identical to that described above. Children were provided with 24 word cards with 6 items per category that could be categorized into four categories (animals, body parts, names, fruit), whereas adults were given 24 word cards that could be categorized into four subgroups of animals (birds, insects, exotic animals, and fishes).

Dependent measures: see above. In addition, clustering during study (i.e., sorting behavior) and clustering during recall were assessed by using the ARC-measure developed by Roenker, Thompson, and Brown (1971). Both measures were assumed to be indicators of strategy use.

(c) Sort-recall task using episodically clusterable stimuli (for adults only): A second clusterable list was constructed for the adult sample. Again, the subjects were given 24 word cards that could be categorized according to four episodes or actions (these were "writing a letter," "eating in a restaurant," "cleaning up a room," and "dressing").

Dependent measures: see above.

Everyday memory tasks (stories)

(a) Story about a soccer game: Different stories were constructed for children and adults. The story developed for the child sample consisted of 32 sentences and described a soccer game. It was constructed in a way that text comprehension was difficult for novices but relatively easy for experts. That is, the text required the reader to make several inferences in order to completely understand what was going on.

Children were told that they first had to listen to the story very carefully. After an (audio-taped) presentation of the story, subjects were given the story in a written format. They had another 5 minutes to read the story. After that, they were asked to underline those 10 sentences that they thought to be most important in order to understand the story. Next, a questionnaire was given assessing subjects' memory for details of the story as well as their correct inferences, and their awareness of contradictions or inconsistencies embedded in the text. Finally, they were presented with a quiz assessing their domain-specific knowledge concerning soccer.

Dependent measures: The number of details correctly remembered, the number of correct inferences, and the number of contradictions detected in the story were used as measures of memory performance. The importance-rating procedure (i.e., underlining of important sentences) was used as an indicator of strategy use. Further, the number of questions correctly answered on quiz procedure was taken as an indicator of domain-specific knowledge.

(b) Texts about a political topic: The adults were given six very difficult short texts with unfamiliar contents, addressing the United States Presidential Election campaign of 1980. After an intensive study period and repeated recall, subjects were presented with a 35-item questionnaire assessing their memory for details of the texts as well as their feeling-of-knowing judgments: The latter required a decision about whether the questions could be answered given the information provided by the texts; in fact, several questions could not be answered relying only on textual information.

Dependent measures: A sum score was computed for all those items of the questionnaire that dealt with informations given in the six texts. This score was the criterion for memory performance. The accuracy with which the subjects classified the items as answerable or not was regarded as an indicator of actualized metamemory. A sentence selection task (subjects had to indicate which sentences they thought to be most essential for the reproduction of the text) was used as a measure of strategic study behavior.

Metamemory

Different measures of metamemory were used for children and adults. (a) Metamemory assessment in children: Children's declarative metamemory was assessed using a comprehensive questionnaire including more than 40 items. The contents covered by the questionnaire included memory for prose, strategy knowledge concerning sort-recall tasks, and memory problems occurring in everyday life situations. Some of the items were taken from the Kreutzer, Leonard, & Flavell (1975) metamemory interview, but most of them were self-constructed. In addition, subjects were shown a sequence of slides that presented two children (a blue and a red one) who were instructed to do some shopping. The two models differed extremly with regard to the efficiency they demonstrated when doing the errands. Immediately after the slide series, subjects were given a questionnaire addressing their knowledge about efficient memory behavior in the shopping situation.

Dependent measures: The two components of declarative metamemory used in this study consisted of a sum score derived from the more general metamemory interview, and a sum score representing children's knowledge about memory in everyday life situations (i.e., the shopping situation). Procedural metamemory was assessed by the recall prediction measures used in the sort-recall task described earlier.

(b) Metamemory assessment in adults: Adults' declarative metamemory was assessed by using three self-constructed questionnaires. In a first questionnaire, we assessed subjects' knowledge concerning learning of numbers by asking for an evaluation of six different strategies that could be used for that purpose. In a second questionnaire, subjects were asked to indicate which strategies (out of a total of fourteen) seemed best suited to learn a list of isolated words. In a third questionnaire, they were asked to evaluate which strategies (out of fourteen) were best suited to learn and remember text materials. The rank-ordering of strategy efficacy used was based on the literature and further confirmed by an independent expert rating.

Dependent measures: The three different sum scores derived from the three metamemory measures were used as indicators of the quality of declarative metamemory knowledge in elderly adults. In addition, three measures assessing accuracy of recall estimates for the nonclusterable, taxonomically clusterable, and episodically clusterable word lists described above were used as indicators of procedural metamemory. Furthermore, knowledge about the availability of required information, that is, the feeling-of-knowing judgments, were regarded as a measure of memory monitoring.

RESULTS

1. The development of different aspects of memory performance across the life-span.   Means and standard deviations for all memory performance measures (separately for each age group) are given in Table 15.1. With regard to the child sample, highly significant age differences were found for all measures included. With regard to four of the six performance measures included in the analysis, all age groups differed from each other, whereas for the remaining two measures (i.e., memory span and episodic memory for texts) the 3rd-graders recalled significantly less than the older age groups who did not differ from each other. On the other hand, significant differences between the two elderly adult samples could only be detected for two measures (i.e., recall for the nonclusterable word list and recall for the episodically clusterable list, which was always superior for the younger of the two age groups). Although it should be emphasized that the data stem from cross-sectional analyses, a quasi-longitudinal view across the life span (although leaving out most of the age range of adolescence and adulthood) seems particularly interesting for the memory span task and the sort-recall task using nonclusterable words because these two tasks were directly comparable for all age groups. From Table 15.1, it seems that there is no difference between 7th graders' and adults' average memory span. On the other

TABLE 15.1
Means and Standard Deviations (in Parentheses) for the Memory Performance
Measures, Separately for Children and Adults

| | Age Groups | | | | |
| | Children | | | Elderly Adults | |
Measures	3rd Grades	5th Grades	7th Grades	$\bar{x}_a \leq 63$	$\bar{x}_a > 63$
Memory Span	$5.10^{B,a}$ (1.18)	5.33^{B} (1.10)	6.10^{A} (1.12)	6.10 (1.05)	6.02 (1.14)
Recall Nonclusterable List	7.65^{C} (2.76)	12.32^{B} (3.94)	13.68^{A} (4.29)	14.54^{*b} (4.23)	12.43 (4.53)
Recall Clusterable List	10.41^{C} (3.91)	15.54^{B} (4.18)	17.42^{A} (4.44)	18.30 (3.85)	17.36 (3.47)
Recall Episodic Clusterable List				19.85* (3.99)	16.65 (4.56)
Text Inferences	1.44^{C} (1.30)	4.00^{B} (2.06)	4.58^{A} (2.20)		
Text Episodic Memory	2.06^{B} (0.61)	2.43^{A} (0.68)	2.54^{A} (0.63)		
Text Contradictions	0.11^{C} (0.32)	0.72^{B} (0.73)	1.03^{A} (0.81)		
Text Questionnaire				10.58 (4.52)	10.21 (4.15)

[a]In each row, different capital letters indicate significant group differences for the child sample (i.e., A>B>C).
[b]Similarly, the asterisk indicates significant group differences for the adult sample.

hand, the younger age group within the sample of elderly adults did outperform 7th-graders with regard to recall for the nonclusterable word list. Interestingly enough, average recall of the older subsample was remarkably lower and, by and large, comparable to that of 5th-graders in this type of task. Because these results are based on a cross-sectional design, they can only give us a hint about the idea, that the ability to manage highly strategic learning in memory tasks is decreasing beyond the age of sixty already.

Means and standard deviations of the strategy and metamemory measures are given in Table 15.2 to complete the pattern of results. The developmental trends found for the memory performance measures were replicated for the strategy use and metamemory measures. With regard to the children, significant increases with age were found for all measures. Planned post-hoc comparisons revealed that most age-related differences occured between 3rd- and 5th-graders. It was only for the general metamemory measure and the importance rating procedure that all age groups differed significantly from each other. On the other hand, no significant differences were found between the two subsamples of elderly adults.

2. Age-related patterns of memory performances.   In a further step of analysis, intertask correlations for the various memory performance measures were computed based on the total child sample. As can be seen from Table 15.3, most of the intercorrelations were relatively small in magnitude, especially when relationships among measures derived from different types of tasks were considered. Although all correlations depicted in Table 15.3 were statistically significant (due to large sample size), only the correlation between the recall measures

TABLE 15.2
Means and Standard Deviations (in Parentheses) for the Strategy Measures, Measures of Metamemory, and Domain-Specific Knowledge, Separately for Children and Elderly Adults

| | Age Groups | | | | |
| | Children | | | Elderly Adults | |
Measures	3rd Graders	5th Graders	7th Graders	$\bar{x}_a \leq 63$	$\bar{x}_a > 63$
Clustering during sorting (RCL)	$0.34^{B,a}$ (0.46)	0.50^A (0.40)	0.55^A (0.48)		
Clustering during recall (RCL)	0.31^B (0.42)	0.55^A (0.45)	0.56^A (0.46)	0.85 (0.24)	0.84 (0.22)
Clustering during recall (ECL)				0.94 (0.10)	0.91 (0.22)
Importance rating/ sentence selection task	2.94^C (1.53)	4.63^B (1.37)	5.61^A (1.46)	6.9 (2.0)	6.3 (1.8)
Accuracy of recall estimate (NCL)	0.30^B (0.32)	0.19^A (0.19)	0.17^A (0.20)	0.35 (0.33)	0.40 (0.47)
Accuracy of recall estimate (RCL)	0.36^B (0.32)	0.25^A (0.22)	0.22^A (0.19)	0.24 (0.39)	0.32 (0.29)
Accuracy of recall (ECL)				0.59 (0.26)	0.45 (0.35)
Feeling -of-knowing judgments				22.81 (3.60)	22.04 (3.35)
General metamemory	12.21^C (2.65)	14.03^B (2.37)	14.78^A (2.21)		
Everyday-life memory knowledge	7.38^B (1.65)	8.07^A (1.74)	8.33^A (1.79)		
Strategy knowledge numbers				3.4 (1.32)	2.8 (1.30)
Strategy knowledge words				3.86 (6.05)	5.05 (5.83)
Strategy knowledge text				11.85 (1.42)	11.54 (1.52)
Domain-specific text knowledge	5.24 (2.07)	7.49 (2.29)	7.90 (2.03)	1.24 (1.15)	1.28 (1.32)

[a]In each row, different capital letters indicate significant group differences for the child sample (i.e., A<B<C).

TABLE 15.3
Intertask Correlations for Memory Performance Measures (Child Sample, N = 578)

Memory Performance Measures	Recall Noncluster- able List 2	Recall Cluster- able List 3	Text Infer- ences 4	Text Episodic Memory 5	Text Contra- dictions 6
1. Memory Span	.24*	.29	.12	.10	.16
2. Recall Non-clusterable List		.66	.30	.19	.34
3. Recall Clusterable List			.29	.25	.41
4. Text Inferences				.36	.44
5. Text Epi-sodic Memory					.40

* All correlations are significant (p<.05)

of the two word lists was numerically high enough to indicate high intertask consistency. When intertask correlations were computed separately for each age group (cf. Table 15.4), magnitude of correlation coefficients decreased for all performance measures. Again, only the correlations between the two sort-recall lists were high enough in magnitude to represent sufficient intertask consistency. Interestingly, no clear developmental trend could be detected across the various memory measures. A different pattern of results was found when intercorrelations among memory performance measures were analyzed for the elderly adult sample. Although the structure of intercorrelations was quite similar to that found for the total child sample (cf. Table 15.5) in that the highest intertask consistency was found for the different sort-recall tasks used, the intercorrelations done for all measures separately for each age group clearly showed a developmental trend (cf. Table 15.6). For almost all measures except for the memory span tasks, more substantial correlations were obtained for the younger subsample of elderly adults, thus indicating a decrease of intertask consistency over the years. It should be noted that intercorrelations obtained for the younger subsample of elderly adults were considerably higher than those calculated for the total sample. Apparently, the assumption of a unitary memory ability or high intertask consistency—even between measures of memory tasks differing in content and structure—could be at least partly confirmed for this specific subsample.

But as this was not true for the remaining age groups, a second step of analysis was entered that focused on a more liberal criterion of intertask consistency. That is, subjects were classified as high (best 25%), medium (50%), or low (lowest 25%) achievers separately for every memory task. As can be seen from Table 15.7, percentages of children and adults consistently classified as

TABLE 15.4
Intertask Correlations for Memory Performance Measures, Separately
for Third Graders (Upper Row), Fifth Graders (Middle Row), and
Seventh Graders (Lower Row)

Memory Performance Measures	Recall Noncluster- able List	Recall Cluster- able List	Text Infer- ences	Text Episodic Memory	Text Contra- dictions
	2	3	4	5	6
1. Memory Span	.01	.26*	-.10	.15	-.13
	.07	.17	.08	.00	.13
	.21*	.15	.07	.02	.01
2. Recall Non- clusterable List		.43*	.01	.06	-.01
		.50*	.17	.07	.17
		.62*	.00	.10	.21*
3. Recall Clusterable List			.01	.13	.09
			.10	.08	.18
			.03	.21*	.34*
4. Text Infer- ences				.18	.13
				.34*	.30*
				.24*	.32*
5. Text Epi- sodic Memory					.31*
					.34*
					.34*

Note: Asterisks denote significant correlations ($p < .05$)

high, medium, or low achievers across various combinations of memory tasks were calculated next. As a result, it was found that, again, intertask consistencies were highest for the sort-recall tasks, irrespective of age. In addition, no developmental trends were detected for the laboratory-type tasks for the children, whereas the proportion of consistent classifications in this age group increased with age for the text measures. Finally, and probably most importantly, the number of consistent classifications in the different age groups dropped considerably when measures from memory tasks differing in contents and structure were combined. Somewhat surprisingly, high percentages of intertask consistency could not be detected even when using a more liberal criterion. Given the fact that there has been some empirical evidence in the literature supporting the hypothesis of a "general strategic factor," similar analyses were conducted for the strategy and the metamemory measures to find out if different patterns of consistency across measures could be detected for these variables. But as can be seen from Table 15.8, decreases in the number of consistently classified subjects similar to those observed for the memory performance measures were found when all strategy measures or all metamemory measures were considered simultaneously. This finding sheds doubt on the assumption that concepts like a "general strategic factor" (Kail, 1979) or subgroups of "metamnemonically sophisticated subjects" (Flavell, 1981) can be empirically identified.

TABLE 15.5
Intertask Correlations for Memory Performance Measures (Adult Sample, N = 124)

Memory Performance Measures	Recall Nonclusterable List 2	Recall Taxon. Clusterable List 3	Recall Episodic Clusterable List 4	Text Questionnaire 5	Text Free Recall 6
1. Memory Span	-.13	.09	-.04	.05	.13
2. Recall Nonclusterable List		.44*	.60*	.27*	.33*
3. Recall Taxon. Clusterable List			.58*	.31*	-.03
4. Recall Episodic Clusterable List				.29*	.28*
5. Text Questionnaire					.29*

Note: Asterisks indicate significant intertask correlations ($p < .05$)

3. The stability of memory performances and metamemory measures. In order to complement these findings based on cross-sectional data, we additionally looked at retest stability information that was available for some of the memory performance, strategy use, and metamemory measures. As can be seen from Table 15.9, the percentage of children consistently classified as high, medium, or low in achievement about 1 year later was quite comparable across

TABLE 15.6
Intertask Correlations for Memory Performance Measures Separately for
the Younger Age Group (Upper Row) and the Older Age Group

Memory Performance Measures	Recall Nonclusterable List 2	Recall Taxon. Clusterable List 3	Recall Episodic Clusterable List 4	Text Questionnaire 5	Text Free Recall 6
1. Memory Span	-.16 -.13	-.02 .15	-.01 .12	-.10 -.05	.17
2. Recall Nonclusterable List		.59* .19	.63* .48*	.25* .30*	.47*
3. Recall Taxon. Clusterable List			.64* .44*	.43* .08	-.05
4. Recall Episodic Clusterable List				.32* .31*	.41*
5. Text Questionnaire					.37*

Note: Asterisks denote significant correlations ($p < .05$)

TABLE 15.7
Percentage of Subjects Consistently Classified at High, Medium, or Low
in Achievement for Various Combinations of Memory Tasks

| | Age Groups | | | |
| | Children | | | Elderly Adults |
Measures	3rd Graders	5th Graders	7th Graders	$\bar{x}_a$ = 63.1
Nonclusterable and taxon. clusterable lists	50	56	64	55
Nonclusterable and episodic clusterable lists				59
Two clusterable lists				45
Word lists and memory span	24	21	24	15
Text inferences and Text episodic memory	39	44	39	{ 14% lower group[a] 28% middle group 5% upper group
Text inferences and Text contradictions	31	44	49	
Text episodic memory and contradictions	19	31	39	
All three text variables	4	17	22	
All text variables and memory span	2	7	7	
All word list variables and all text variables	0	4	7	
All word list variables and all text variables and memory span	0	2	2	{ 7% lower group[a] 51% middle group 13% upper group

[a]We changed the classification criterion in the adult sample because of missing data. A person was classified as "consistent" in the lower, middle, or upper group when she has this position in at least 3 (out of 5) performance measures. Further, this analysis was done for the combined adult sample (N=124; $\bar{x}_{age}$=63.1 years).

the different age groups. It should be noted that the *true* proportion of consistent subjects is probably underestimated because standard error of measurements had not been taken into account. Therefore, the estimates of retest-stability we got from these analyses seemed, by and large, acceptable.

4. The impact of memory related variables on memory performance. Nonetheless, the results of the correlational and classification analyses leads one to assume that a unitary memory function cannot be identified. Therefore, a final step of analysis concentrated on task-specific performance differences among age-groups and the role that measures of memory capacity, memory strategy, and metamemory can play in explaining age-related performance differences. This procedure should be likely to answer the questions if subjects' memory

TABLE 15.8
Percentage of Subjects Consistently Classified as High, Medium, or Low in Achievement
for Various Combinations of Strategy and Metamemory Measures

| Measures | Children | | | Elderly Adults |
	3rd Graders	5th Graders	7th Graders	$\bar{x}_a$ = 63.1
Clustering during sorting and during recall	48	61	67	
Importance rating and clustering during sorting	36	36	36	
Importance rating and clustering during recall	34	36	37	37
Importance rating and all cluster measure	16	21	25	
2 accuracy of recall estimates (NCL + RCL)	40	37	36	35
All three accuracy of recall estimates				0
General metamemory and everyday-life memory knowledge	38	37	37	
2 accuracy of recall estimates and 2 general metamemory measures	8	9	6	
All three accuracy of recall estimates and feeling-of-knowing judgment and strategy knowledge numbers				0% lower group[a] 40% middle group 0% upper group

[a]We changed the classification criterion because of missing data. A person was classified as "consistent" in the lower, middle, or upper group when she kept this position in at least 3 (out of 5) metamemory measures. Further, this analysis was done for the combined adult sample (N=124).

capacity, strategy knowledge, strategy use, and domain specific knowledge have a different impact on their performance in different memory tasks.

A series of ANCOVAs was run in order to assess the relative impact of each covariate on age-related differences in memory performance as well as the combined, simultaneous effect of all covariates on age-related memory improvement. Table 15.10 gives an overview of results obtained for the child sample. The age effects on performance differences (F-values) obtained for a series of ANCOVAs are given in the upper row of the table.

For all covariates listed below, the reduced F-value for grade effect caused by their inclusion into the equation is given first, followed by F-values (in parentheses) indicating their importance for the dependent memory measure in question. A comparison of the first and the last row gives a first impression of the combined impact of all covariates on age-related changes in memory performance: that is, the last row shows the attenuated effect (F-value) of grade on memory performance.

With regard to the two recall measures for clusterable and nonclusterable items, the drop in age-effects caused by the combined inclusion of all relevant covariates is remarkable, although the attenuated F-values still remain significant. This finding indicates that the covariates included cannot account for all age-related changes in memory performance. When the separate effects of the covariates are considered, it appears that all of them are comparably high for the nonclusterable list, but that the two strategy variables, that is, clustering during sorting and clustering during recall, had by far the most substantial effect on recall for clusterable lists. It should be noted however, that—with the exception of the memory monitoring measure (accuracy of recall estimate)—indicators of memory capacity as well as indicators of general metamemory had also significant effects on the memory performance measure.

Results are even more impressive when the three text variables are considered. Here, the impact of combined covariates was substituted for all memory performance measures, as can be seen from the dramatically decreased grade effect on performance. In the case of episodic text memory, the simultaneous inclusion of all covariates resulted in a complete elimination of age-related effects. Here, the importance of preexisting domain-specific knowledge, that is, experience with the soccer game, was mainly responsible for the impressive result. This covariate did contribute most to the prediction of performance for all three dependent text measures. But here again, also indicators of strategy use and general metamemory had significant impact on memory for text, whereas the measure of memory capacity proved to be meaningless with regard to this dependent variable.

A similar series of analyses was also done for the elderly adult sample (cf.

TABLE 15.9
Percentage of Subjects Consistently Classified as High, Medium, or Low in Achievement for Selected Memory Tasks Applied Twice Within the Period of One Year (N = 315; Short-Term Longitudinal Study)

Measures	Grades		
	3rd-/4th-Graders	5th-/6th-Graders	7th-/8th-Graders
General metamemory	48	45	49
Importance rating	47	45	40
Recall NCL	55	57	56
Recall RCL	52	42	57
Memory span	50	51	41
Accuracy NCL	42	39	43
Accuracy RCL	30	36	34
Clustering during recall	41	31	61
Clustering during sorting	45	43	41

TABLE 15.10
Results (F-Values) of a Series of ANCOVAs Computed to Assess the Effects of
Different Covariates on Age-Related Changes in Children's
Memory Performance

Effect of Grade and Covariates	Dependent Measures				
	Recall Nonclusterable List	Recall Clusterable List	Text Inferences	Text Episodic Memory	Text Contradictions
Grade	88.27	100.08	91.51	20.55	62.42
Memory Span	73.19 (9.28)*	79.54 (18.53)*	86.19 (0.08)	17.73 (0.63)	53.95 (0.74)
Clustering during sorting		86.75 (85.33)*			
Clustering during Recall		85.79 (132.43)*			
Accuracy of Recall estimate (NCL)	77.36 (10.35)*				
Accuracy of Recall estimate (RCL)		92.64 (0.96)*			
Importance Rating			33.21 (54.02)*	4.59 (21.43)*	20.13 (34.34)
Domain-specific knowledge			34.60 (231.31)*	4.40 (61.08)*	25.52 (107.47)*
General metamemory	64.50 (9.86)*	63.38 (23.40)*			
Everyday-life memory knowledge	77.62 (15.45)*	87.03 (29.47)*	84.60 (2.39)*	17.53 (5.86)*	55.50 (6.63)*
Simultaneous inclusion of all relevant covariates	41.94	41.67	18.41	0.03	7.79

Numbers in parentheses indicate F-values for the covariates in question.

Table 15.11). Of course, as the age group effect on memory performance was relatively small for most dependent measures considered in the analysis, no strong covariate effects could be expected for this sample. Not surprisingly, the simultaneous inclusion of all covariates resulted in nonsignificant attenuated age effects on all dependent measures. Again, memory span did not show any important influences on memory performance in the sort-recall tasks and the text measure used. The most substantial effects were obtained for the memory monitoring measure (feeling-of-knowing judgments) and the domain-specific knowledge measure used to predict performance in the memory for prose task. The significant impact of domain-specific knowledge was somewhat surprising because of the generally low level of preexisting knowledge in most elderly subjects. Obviously, already small differences in domain-specific knowledge proved sufficient to significantly influence recall.

GENERAL DISCUSSION

In our view, the results of the present study do add some information to the issue of unitary versus task-specific lines of memory development. First of all, the analysis of intertask correlations yielded different findings for children and elderly adults. Intertask correlations were generally low for the three child samples

TABLE 15.11
Results (F-Values) of a Series of ANCOVAs Computed to Assess the Effects of Different Covariates on Age-Related Changes in Elderly Adult's Memory Performance

Effect of Grand and Covariates	Dependent Measures			
	Recall Noncluster-able List	Recall Taxon. Clusterable List	Recall Episodic Cluster-able List	Text Question-naire
Age Group	7.07*	1.79	11.29*	0.19
Memory Span	7.59 (2.54)	1.65 (0.24)	11.13 (0.34)	0.21 (0.18)
Clustering during Recall (RCL)	3.85 (0.91)	1.61* (9.48)		
Clustering during Recall			10.58 (1.33)	
Accuracy of Recall estimate (NCL)	2.57 (12.72)*			
Accuracy of Recall estimate (RCL)		1.69 (2.35)		
Accuracy of Recall estimate (ECL)			0.86 (0.00)	
Sentence Selection Task				0.25 (7.17)*
Feeling-of-Knowing Judgments				0.05 (48.78)*
Strategy Knowledge Words	7.93 (9.15)*	1.71 (1.96)	13.29 (2.66)	
Strategy Knowledge Texts				0.55 (0.89)
Domain-specific Knowledge				0.31 (17.31)*
Simultaneous inclusion of all relevant co-variates	1.98	1.91	1.39	0.25

Numbers in parentheses indicate F-values for the covariates in question.

and no developmental trends could be detected. This was particularly true for comparisons among tasks differing with regard to content and structure, that is, for comparisons among laboratory-type and everyday memory tasks. Hence, these findings correspond well with those obtained in the old correlational studies summarized earlier and those reported by Stevenson et al. (1968). The pattern of results found for the two subsamples of elderly adults differed from that for the child sample in that remarkably higher intertask correlations were obtained, particularly when the younger subgroup was considered. Thus it appears that generally higher intraindividual consistencies with regard to performance in various memory tasks can be assumed for this age group. Unfortunately, the fact that we do not yet have any comparable information available concerning intraindividual consistencies in memory performance for subjects aged between 15 and 50 years, there is no possibility to infer life-long developmental trends from the data presented in this study.

When the more liberal criterion was used, the expected improvement, that is, substantially high percentages of subjects showing high intertask consistency, was not supported by the data. Although the absolute number of subjects classified as consistent may have been underestimated due to the fact that no attempt was made to take standard error of measurement into account, the results seem to replicate the findings obtained by intertask correlations. Again, no evidence for the existence of a unitary memory function could be found. It should be noted, however, that the laboratory-type memory tasks and everyday memory task used in this study differed with regard to several aspects. Theoretically, it should be possible to construct tasks representing different degrees of ecological validity that could be more similar concerning task structure and contents. Probably, the inclusion of such a set of tasks would lead to more positive results, that is, higher intertask consistency.

As a consequence, the last step of analysis focused on the explanation of age group differences, separately for each memory task. The findings are particularly interesting with regard to the child sample: Effects of age on the various memory performance measures could be remarkably reduced when covariates like memory capacity, strategy use, and metamemory were taken into account. The substantial effect of domain-specific knowledge on performance in the task assessing memory for prose underlines the theoretical and practical importance of preexisting knowledge structures. Probably, the major difference between laboratory type-tasks and memory problems occurring in everyday-life situations lies in the fact that domain-specific knowledge plays an important role in the latter but not in the former situation. As far as we can judge, it is quite unclear from the literature how domain-specific knowledge is activated in children and if it is used differently in different age groups. This seems to be an interesting question for future research.

Another implication of the present findings for future research in memory concerns the problem that all-too-few different memory tasks have been used in traditional experimental studies. This has been partly due to the fact that the logical analysis of the task structure and the processes involved in its solution has been the main reason for adopting memory tasks, and partly due to the belief that results obtained for one type of task should be also valid for other types of memory tasks. Obviously, the latter assumption is not true. As a consequence, future researchers in memory development are therefore encouraged to include different versions of similar memory tasks in their experimental design (e.g., laboratory-type tasks versus everyday memory tasks with a similar logical task structure) to better control for ecological validity of their findings.

REFERENCES

Anastasi, A. (1932). Further studies on the memory factors. *Archives of Psychology, 20*, No. 142.

Atkinson, R. C., & Shiffrin, R. M. (1968). Human memory: a proposed system and its control processes. In K. W. Spence & J. T. Spence (Eds.), *The psychology of learning and motivation* (Vol. 2). New York: Academic Press.

Balinsky, B. (1941). An analysis of mental factors of various age groups from nine to sixty. *Genetic Psychology Monographs, 23*, 191–234.

Bolton, E. B. (1931). The relation of memory to intelligence. *Journal of Experimental Psychology, 14*, 37–67.

Brown, A. L. (1975). The development of memory: Knowing, knowing about knowing, and knowing how to know. In H. W. Reese (Ed.), *Advances in child development and behavior* (Vol. 10). New York: Academic Press.

Brown, A. L., Bransford, J. D., Ferrara, R. A., & Campione, J. C. (1983). Learning, remembering, and understanding. In J. H. Flavell & E. Markman (Eds.), *Handbook of developmental psychology* (Vol. 3). New York: Wiley.

Burt, C. (1954). The differentiation of intellectual abilities. *British Journal of Educational Psychology, 24*, 76–90.

Campione, J. C., & Brown, A. L. (1977). Memory and metamemory development in educable retarded children. In R. V. Kail & J. W. Hagen (Eds.), *Perspectives on the development of memory and cognition*. Hillsdale, NJ: Lawrence Erlbaum Associates.

Campione, J. C., & Brown, A. L. (1978). Toward a theory of intelligence: contributions from research with retarded children. *Intelligence, 2*, 279–304.

Campione, J. C., Brown, A. L., & Bryant, N. R. (1985). Individual differences in learning and memory. In R. J. Sternberg (Ed.), *Human abilities*. New York: Freeman.

Cavanaugh, J. C., & Borkowski, J. G. (1980). Searching for metamemory-memory connections: A developmental study. *Developmental Psychology, 16*, 441–453.

Chase, W. G., Lyon, D. R., & Ericsson, K. A. (1981). Individual differences in memory span. In M. P. Friedman, J. P. Das, & N. O'Connor (Eds.), *Intelligence and learning*. New York: Plenum.

Cohen, R. L. (1982). Individual differences in short-term memory. In N. R. Ellis (Ed.), *International review of research in mental retardation* (Vol. 11). New York: Academic Press.

Cronbach, L. J. (1957). The two disciplines of scientific psychology. *American Psychologist, 12*, 671–684.

Dempster, F. N. (1981). Memory span: Sources of individual and developmental differences. *Psychological Bulletin, 89*, 63–100.

Ebbinghaus, H. (1885). *Über das Gedächtnis*. Leipzig: Dunker.

Estes, W. K. (1974). Learning theory and intelligence. *American Psychologist, 29*, 740–749.

Flavell, J. H. (1971). What is memory development the development of? *Human development, 14,* 225–286.

Flavell, J. H. (1981). Cognitive monitoring. In P. Dickson (Ed.), *Children's oral communication skills.* New York: Academic Press.

Flavell, J. H., & Wellman, H. M. (1977). Metamemory. In R. V. Kail & J. W. Hagen (Eds.), *Perspectives on the development of memory and cognition.* Hillsdale: Erlbaum.

Friedman, H. (1974). Interrelation of two types of immediate memory in the aged. *Journal of Psychology, 87,* 177–181.

Gagné, R. M. (1967). *Learning and individual differences.* Columbia, OH: Charles E. Merrill.

Garrett, H. E. (1946). A developmental theory of intelligence. *American Psychologist, 1,* 372–378.

Hagen, J. W., Jongeward, R. H., & Kail, R. V. (1975). Cognitive perspectives on the development of memory. In H. W. Reese (Ed.), *Advances in child development and behavior* (Vol. 10). New York: Academic Press.

Humphreys, M. S., Lynch, M. J., Revelle, W., & Hall, J. W. (1983). Individual differences in short-term memory. In R. F. Dillon & R. R. Schmeck (Eds.), *Individual differences in cognition* (Vol. 1). New York: Academic Press.

Hunt, E., Frost, N., & Lunneborg, C. L. (1973). Individual differences in cognition: A new approach to intelligence. In G. Bower (Ed.), *Advances in learning and motivation* (Vol. 7). New York: Academic Press.

Hunt, E., & Lansman, M. (1975). Cognitive theory applied to individual differences. In K. W. Estes (Ed.), *Handbook of learning and cognitive processes* (Vol. 1). Hillsdale, NJ: Lawrence Erlbaum Associates.

Kail, R. V. (1979). Use of strategies and individual differences in children's memory. *Developmental Psychology, 15,* 251–255.

Katzenberger, L. (1964). *Dimensionen des Gedächtnisses.* Unveröffentlichte Dissertation, Universität Würzburg.

Kirby, J. R. (1980). Individual differences and cognitive processes: instructional application and methodological difficulties. In J. R. Kirby & J. B. Biggs (Eds.) *Cognition, development and instruction.* New York: Academic Press.

Kreutzer, M. A., Leonard, C., & Flavell, J. H. (1975). An interview study of children's knowledge about memory. *Monographs of the Society for Research in Child Development, 40,* Serial No. 159.

Lee, A. L. (1925). An experimental study of retention and its relation to intelligence. *Psychological Review Monographs, 34.*

McCall, R. (1977). Challenges to a science of developmental psychology. *Child Development, 48,* 333–344.

Meumann, E. (1907). *Vorlesungen zur Einführung in die experimentelle Pädagogik und ihre psychologischen Grundlagen.* Leipzig: Klinkhardt.

Meumann, E. (1918). *Ökonomie und Technik des Gedächtnisses* (Vol. 1). Leipzig: Klinkhardt.

Perlmutter, M., & Lange, G. (1978). A developmental analysis of recall-recognition distinctions. In P. A. Ornstein (Ed.), *Memory development in children.* Hillsdale, NJ: Lawrence Erlbaum Associates.

Reinert, G. (1970). Comparative factor analytical studies of intelligence throughout the human life-span. In L. R. Goulet & P. B. Baltes (Eds.), *Life-span developmental psychology: Research and theory.* New York: Academic Press.

Roenker, D. L., Thompson, C. P., & Brown, S. (1971). Comparison of measures for the estimation of clustering in free recall. *Psychological Bulletin, 76,* 45–48.

Stevenson, H. W., Hale, G. A., Klein, R. F., & Miller, L. K. (1968). Interrelations and correlates in children's learning and problem solving. *Monographs of the Society for Research in Child Development, 33.*

16 Research on Memory and its Development: Past, Present, and Future

Marion Perlmutter
Institute of Gerontology, University of Michigan

INTRODUCTION

Memory is a phenomenon that has been considered extensively by philosophers, biologists, educators, and psychologists. In psychology, it consistently has been one of the most vital areas of research. This has been true in mainstream experimental psychology (cf. Cofer, 1976; Estes, 1979; Posner, 1978) as well as in child psychology (cf. Brown, Bransford, Ferara, & Campione, 1983; Kail & Hagen, 1977) and gerontology (cf. Craik, 1977; Poon, Fozard, Cermack, Arenberg, & Thompson, 1980). In each of these subfields, there has been a continued and strong interest in understanding the workings and limits of human memory, and in the developmental areas, researchers also have been interested in learning about how memory improves in childhood and deteriorates in old age. It is appropriate, then, to ask, "Why has memory been such a pervasive topic of study?" and "What progress has been made in understanding it?"

In regard to the first question, "Why has memory been such a pervasive topic of study?," several points are relevant. First, remembering is a universal and familiar experience, that intuitively seems extremely useful and important. It allows us to extend ourselves in both time and space, and to conceptualize continuities and discontinuities, both as individuals and as societies. In addition, memory serves as a starting point, as well as a solidifier, of social communication and interpersonal relationships. Thus, memory plays a major role in the way we negotiate our physical and social worlds. *Memory in its own right*, therefore, has an unchallengeable place of significance.

In addition, memory typically is regarded as an important subcomponent of other, more complex, mental abilities. Thus, for example, memory is assumed to be rudimentary to estimation, comprehension, decision making, inferencing, observational learning, and problem solving. Each of these skills is thought to require additional intellectual abilities, but each also relies very importantly upon basic memory capacities. Thus, *memory as a component* of more complex cognition is also important.

Finally, from a less sympathetic point of view, it can be argued that the study of memory simply has propagated itself. Particularly in the experimental literature on memory, there is evidence of paradigm, rather than problem driven work. In these cases, the method of investigation, rather then the problem of itself, has generated research questions and research problems. Paradigms and techniques became paramount, and the phenomenon of interest seems almost to have lost its significance. How much of the psychological research on memory has been motivated in this way is unclear. Unfortunately, however, at least some of it seems to have been guided by *paradigm issues relevant to memory research.*

In turning to the second question, "What progress has been made in understanding memory?," recent appraisals by at least two prominent cognitive psychologists are unsympathetic. Tulving (1979) wrote:

> Countless scholars, sages, and scientists have devoted their lifetimes to the study of the mind in its many manifestations, and they have written countless books and articles about it; but the fruits of their labors have been somewhat less than spectacular. Psychological study of memory, by and large, has shared a similar fate. After over two thousand years of rational speculation and a hundred years of experimental study, we can point to only a few achievements that promise to be of relatively permanent value. (p. 19).

Neisser (1982) also pointed out limitations in the progress that has been made in understanding memory. He wrote:

> In short, the results of a hundred years of the psychological study of memory are somewhat discouraging. We have established firm empirical generalizations, but most of them are so obvious that every ten-year-old knows them anyway. We have made discoveries, but they are only marginally about memory; in many cases we do not know what to do with them, and wear them out with endless experimental variations. We have an intellectually impressive group of theories, but history offers little confidence that they will provide any meaningful insight into natural behavior. (pp. 11–12)

Reluctantly, I come to a somewhat similar appraisal, and like the skeptics before me, I criticize less the soundness of what progress has been made, and point instead to the narrowness of the definition of memory that most often has been adopted by psychologists, and of the limited number of issues that have been addressed. Therefore, in this chapter I consider the concept of memory in a very broad sense, and attempt to stretch our domain of investigation.

First, I provide a brief review of some of the perspectives on memory that have existed in variety of fields over the course of history. In this review, although I am not able to be exhaustive, I do attempt to at least touch on the times in history that memory has been of interest, and to introduce the diversity of perspectives that have been brought to bear on the topic.

Following, I summarize dominant themes in contemporary thinking about memory development, as well as specify the issues and ideas that I believe are emerging as important. I point out that until now, research has been dominated by a concern about the mechanisms and processes of the memory system, and largely has ignored the contents or functions of it. Moreover, I suggest that although recent research has demonstrated that a number of factors relating to environmental context, subject state, and individual differences have considerable impact on memory performance, these factors largely have been underplayed. Instead, the dominant trend in research on memory development has been to search for changes in underlying competencies that characterize universal development. Within this tradition, three forms of knowledge—operative knowledge, epistemic knowledge, and metacognitive knowledge—have been identified as the major contributors to memory development. Over the last decade or two, each of these forms of knowledge has been extensively studied within an experimental–developmental perspective. Considerable progress has been made in advancing understanding of how memory strategies (operative knowledge), domain specific knowledge (epistemic knowledge), and metamemory (metacognitive knowledge) contribute to memory performance on *laboratory tasks,* and to age-related improvements in memory performance. Moreover, it appears that further progress of this sort is likely to continue.

Yet, I shall argue that present understanding of memory is limited by the restrictive focus on only a very special kind of memory, that is, on deliberate memory of symbolic information over short time intervals in extremely sterile situations. Therefore, in the final portion of this paper, I call for a broader conceptualization of memory and provide a preliminary scheme for taxonomizing various kinds of memory that might be worth investigating. I suggest that it may be especially useful for researchers to begin to explicitly deal with nondeliberate, as well as nonconscious, retention and to investigate earnestly the numerous roles of memory in every human functioning.

HISTORICAL PERSPECTIVES ON MEMORY

Early Philosophers

The earliest serious discussions of memory typically are credited to Plato. He expounded a *tabula rasa* theory of memory according to which memories are viewed as analogous to sealed-impressions in wax. In many ways, much current thinking about memory remains rooted in this perspective. For example, virtually all associationist and neo-associationist (e.g., Anderson & Bower, 1974) models of memory fit this view, as do most computer models of memory (e.g., Bobrow & Norman, 1975). The implications of this perspective, as well as alternatives to it, are considered more extensively in later sections.

Plato considered another important aspect of memory that has remained essentially undisputed through time. He articulated two senses of memory. One was referred to as the powers of memory or *retention* and the other as the powers of *recollection* or recall. This distinction remains important today, both in common and scientific uses of the term memory.

For example, Webster's dictionary (1974) describes memory as the ability or power for retaining or retrieving past thoughts, images, ideas, etc. It lists two main definitions. First, referring to the recollectional aspect of the phenomenon, memory is defined as "the power, act, or process of recalling to mind facts previously learned or past experiences." Second, referring to the retentive aspect of the phenomenon, memory is described as "the total of what one remembers."

Experimental psychologists also have assumed a distinction between retentive and recollective aspects of memory. At least since the time that Atkinson and Shiffrin (1968) published their now famous information processing model of memory, researchers have conceptually separated acquisition, retention, and retrieval, and this distinction gained special importance with Tulving and Pearlstone's (1966) empirical demonstration of differences between access and availability of information. In addition, while acquisition and retrieval generally have been regarded as inextricably linked, much research has documented that a variety of variables produce differential effects on retention and recollection.

Aristotle built upon Plato's discussions about memory, preserving the distinction between retention and recollection. He elaborated that *memory* is the consequence of stamping individual perceptions into a receiving surface, and *recollection* is based on the processes of association by contiguity, contrast, and similarity. His discussions of contiguity, contrast, and similarity clearly established the associationist tradition, which has had much influence on both early and contemporary experimental work on memory.

Middle-Age Mnemonicists

Prior to the printed word, memory had a role in human life that probably was even more important than is true in western culture today. In early years, human memory was the only vehicle for carrying individual and communal knowledge through time and through space. For example, Boorstein (1983) writes:

> For millennia personal memory reigned over entertainment and information, over the perpetuation and perfection of crafts, the practice of commerce, and conduct of professions. By memory and in memory the fruits of education were garnered, preserved, and stored. Memory was an awesome faculty which everyone had to cultivate in ways and for reasons we have long since forgotten. In the past five

hundred years we see only pitiful relics of the empire and power of memory. (p. 480)

Even in the Middle Ages, when manuscript books were available, human memory prevailed as the storehouse of knowledge. This situation was only to change when printed books became popularized. The far greater portability, accuracy, and convenience of printed books made them more available and public. In addition, certain characteristics of such books actually aided and expanded human memory capacities. For example, title pages and page numbers made fact retrieval much easier, and subsequent developments in indexing further facilitated human memory. Eventually, it was stated that the only requirement for human memory was "to remember the order of the alphabet" (cf. Boorstin, 1983). This statement, though surely facetious, highlights the differences in the demands placed on human memory that have existed through time.

At least through the middle ages, people relied upon memory much more extensively than contemporaries do. Not surprisingly then, the art and skill of memory was more valued in earlier times, and the expert mnemonicist was much admired. Details of this history have been elaborated by Yates (1966), in his book *The Art of Memory,* which delightfully describes the life of a mnemonicist.

As memory skills were cultivated, pragmatic considerations about memory propagated and a technical jargon was elaborated. This jargon appears to have included a distinction between *natural* and *artificial* memory. Natural memory was considered the memory that all were born with, the memory that could be exercised without training, the memory that was involved in nondeliberate remembering. Artificial memory, on the other hand, was described as the memory that could be developed. It seems most akin to the strategic memory used in intentional remembering of information. Numerous systems and approaches to training *artificial* memory flourished. Most of these seem to have been rooted in the concepts of places of loci and images.

As everyday needs for memory diminished, it is not surprising that previous intrigue with memory skill declined. The change in status of mnemonicists is evident in the following quips, referenced back to the 16th century (cf. Boorstin): "a good memory is generally joined to a weak judgement," and "nothing is more common than a fool with a strong memory." Today, too, no great respect is necessarily afforded to those with outstanding memory abilities. Indeed, quite the contrary; a common caricature is that of the "absent-minded genius."

Thus, it can be seen that the loss of status of memory skill and artificial memory techniques generally have continued through modern times. It is interesting, therefore, that much of the recent work in experimental psychology seems to be focused on artificial memory. For example, numerous pages of recent psychological journals are devoted to mnemonic techniques, such as rehearsal, imagery, elaboration, and organization. Especially in view of the apparent reduction of importance of such techniques, it is somewhat ironic that experimental psychologists have pursued this aspect of memory so extensively.

Early Pedagogues

A focus on artificial memory techniques also pervaded many early discussions of pedagogy. For example, during the 19th century, it typically was assumed that extended *exercise* at memorizing would be beneficial for subsequent memorizing. At that time, memory was viewed much as the apparatus of an athlete. The generalized value of practice and activity was not questioned.

Near the turn of the 20th century, however, this view of memory as a faculty that required exercise was attacked. In particular, James (1890) reported little transfer of training in memorizing. He argued that mnemonic techniques were of minimal value in aiding retentive capacity as such. Slowly the aims of school systems changed, and rote memorization, for its own sake, lost vogue.

It is interesting to note similarities as well as differences between recent discussions of the plasticity of mental abilities (e.g., Baltes & Brim, 1984) and earlier pedagogical arguments. Both sets of work emphasize the plausibility of training mental skill. However, it now seems that the generalized effect of exercise assumed by early pedagogues was too simplistic. Training of mental abilities appears quite possible, but thus far, effects of training have been relatively specific. The more elaborated and specific view of training of mental function that is emerging today seems very promising. It has practical implications that are especially valuable for treating elderly individuals who suffer from memory problems and theoretical implications that argue for malleability of the human cognitive system.

Early Biologists

In the late 19th century there was considerable interest in the *disorders* of memory. In particular, within the medical profession, much activity was devoted to gaining an understanding of aphasia and amnesia. Some of the accomplishments that were made at that time were impressive and laid the groundwork for the study of memory diseases that continues today.

For example, at an anatomical level, localized cerebral brain lesions were identified in individuals suffering from aphasia. This demonstration is important, since it proved for the first time that there is a link between physiological and psychological functioning. Other work was focused on amnesia. Here, an important distinction was made between psychogenic and organic instances of the disease. In addition, it was noted that progressive amnesia followed an invariable path from new to old, or unstable to stable memories, while temporary amnesia was characterized by recovery of recollection in the reverse order.

Psychoanalysts

Freud's work also focused on disorders involving memory, although in his domain, memory disturbances were viewed as the cause, rather than the effect, of disease. He is credited with originating psychoanalysis, a technique in which a patient is guided through self-explorations of his or her memory in order to treat psychogenic diseases. Freud's (1905/1938) insight that many psychoemotional disorders are related to memory was important. Moreover, his techniques for delving into memory must be included in any complete account of memory.

Freud believed that the central problems of human life were in their hidden dimensions. He argued that nothing, once formed in mental life, could perish; everything is somehow preserved. He assumed that human frustrations and conflicts arose from memories that are not conscious. He therefore focused on *forgotten* memories. He believed that if the individual, and for that matter the society, could come to know themselves by uncovering the *unconscious* strata of experience, their ills would be cured. Psychoanalysis, of course, was his method for curing individuals. Using this method, he attempted to revive memories. He believed that only after memories could be recognized as such could their effect on emotion, thought, and behavior be dealt with directly.

The major construct that Freud hypothesized to account for the unconscious or hidden dimension of experience was repression. This concept apparently has been widely misunderstood (Erdelyi & Goldberg, 1979). For Freud, it referred to two phenomena (Freud, 1915/1963). First, repression was seen as the blocking of entry into consciousness of threatening or psychologically painful material. As such, it most often is operationalized as a perceptual defense. In addition, repression was seen as the relegation into unconsciousness of material after it has been consciously recognized. As such, it may be operationalized as a mnemonic defense. In either case, repression was seen as an active filtering process. Freud (1915/1963) believed that the process of repression could be understood in terms of the creation of response interference and withdrawal of attention (''cathexis'') from the offending episode. His (Freud, 1899/1956) model of cognition included two selective filters (''censors''), one between the unconscious and the preconscious and the other between the preconscious and the conscious.

An important aspect of Freud's construct of repression was that it did not imply the obliteration of unpleasant or disagreeable events. On the contrary, Freud (1915/1963) believed that unpleasant memories were ever present, even if in an unconscious state. Moreover, although Freud thought it important to recognize that all unconscious memories could be brought to recollection, of greater consequence, perhaps, was his point that all preserved experience, even in the unconscious state, plays a very powerful role in controlling behavior, emotion, and thought. Although this view is not disputed by contemporary experimental psychologists, the implications of the unconscious memory seem largely to be ignored.

Freud's focus on repression was consistent with the focus on forgetting that prevailed in the experimental psychology of memory that was developing around the same time. However, because Freud defined repression as tendentious, and provided conflicting and incomplete arguments for deciding the necessary qualities of material that would be repressed, the concept was, and has been, subject to much criticism (e.g., Cason, 1932; Erdelyi & Goldberg, 1979; Holmes, 1970; Rapaport, 1942). Still, repression, or some repression-like concept, remains basic to one of the few theories of motivated "forgetting."

Early Experimental Psychologists

Ebbinghaus (1885) is credited with carrying out the first scientific experiments or memory, and thus, with laying the foundation for modern experimental research on memory. It was undoubtedly his use of a laboratory based experimental methodology, at least as much as his findings, that have impacted the field. Since the experimental investigation of memory, and indeed, the experimental investigation of all aspects of psychology, postdated experimentation in other fields, its methods were, and still are, very much borrowed from the methods of other sciences, in particular, those of physics and physiology.

Of major importance in Ebbinghaus' *method* was the simplification and isolation of stimulus and response, as well as the proper quantitative treatment of data. His research was framed within an associationist perspective. He developed nonsense syllables that he believed were lacking in both meaning and association to serve as stimuli in his experiments. Then he used himself as subject to investigate the powers of retention and reproduction. In his first study, Ebbinghaus related the number of repetitions required for adequate learning of a list of nonsense syllables to the length of the list itself. Other experiments were designed to investigate the time saved in learning material that had been learned previously, and the number of syllables that were retained as a function of the amount of the time that had elapsed since original learning.

These studies of Ebbinghaus foreshadowed many of the issues that received extensive investigation by more contemporary experimental psychologists. For example, during the 1960s, several hundred experiments were carried out to examine the effects of list length on learning of lists of items, as well as the effects of frequency of presentation, savings in learning, and the causes of forgetting over time.

A number of other issues that have been considered important by more contemporary experimental psychologists also were introduced by early experimenters. For example, Murray (1976) points out that Muller (Muller & Pilzecker, 1900) started work on the role of interference in learning and forgetting that laid the groundwork for modern interference theory. Likewise, he indicates that recent masking studies of very short-term sensory memory were anticipated by 19th century experiments.

Reconstructionists

Although Bartlett (1932) initiated his study of memory in 1913 with thorough familiarity of early experimental work on the topic, he developed a rather different tradition. He wrote:

> I followed his (Ebbinghaus') lead and worked for some time with nonsense material. The result was disappointment and a growing dissatisfaction. . . . The upshot was that I was determined to try to retain the advantages of an experimental method of approach, with relatively controlled situations, and also to keep my study as realistic as possible. . . . Believing, as I do, that psychology in its experimental aspect is a biological science, I have endeavored throughout to adopt a strictly functional point of view. . . . The central problem all the time has been the conditions, and variety of conditions, under which perceiving, imagining, and remembering take place. (pp. 5–6)

Bartlett proposed a reconstructive theory of memory that challenged the view of remembering as the re-excitation of traces. He believed that rather than reactivation of a trace, remembering involves an imaginative construction or reconstruction. He stated that the construction "is built out of the relation of our attitude towards a whole active mass of organized past reactions or experiences, and to a little outstanding detail which commonly appears in image or in language form." For example, he states that only when there is nothing but "low-level mental life, which is cut off from all but a few often repeated environmental stimuli, is rote memory seen."

Bartlett used the term *schema* to refer to the "active organization of past reactions or experiences" which he believed molded the impressions of all incoming impulses and also produced reproductive memory. All experiences were believed to be incorporated into the schema. Moreover, in schematic form, the past was seen as operating *en masse,* although there was a caveat here, since the last constituents added to the schema were thought to carry a predominance of influence.

Barlett acknowledged that in remembering one has the impression of the domination of a particular past event. That is, in the experience of remembering, it seems as though a part of the schema that is remote in time takes a leading edge. According to Bartlett's theory, when an organism is stimulated, the stimulus becomes a cue that sets up a series of reactions which are carried out in a fixed temporal order and result in perception. In addition, however, the stimulus becomes a cue to a portion of the schemata of past responses that is most relevant to the needs of the moment. This cue leads to the impression of memory. Barlett suggested that this experience is accounted for by an "organism's acquisition of the capacity to turn around upon its own schemata and construct them afresh." Unfortunately, as even Bartlett admitted, these notions were left quite vague.

The idea that memory involves the turning around upon one's own schemata is also seen in Piaget's (1973) writings about evocative memory. Piaget was a genetic epistemologist whose orientation was constructivism, and whose main interests were the nature and development of intelligence. Memory, like all cognitive functions (e.g., perception, imagery, memory), was assumed to depend upon intelligence. As such, for Piaget, the main quality of memory that was interesting was the way in which it illuminated the operations of intelligence.

Nevertheless, Piaget's constructivist views led to some useful discussions about the nature of memory. He distinguished recall and recognition memory, suggesting that recognition is a primitive process found even in lower vertebrates. It occurs in the presence of an object and consists of perceiving the object as something that has been perceived in the past. In other words, recognition, is (Piaget & Inhelder, 1973) "a double utilization of that figurative mechanism which we designate as perception" (p. 13). It requires only a match between current perceptual activity and prior perceptual activity.

On the other hand, Piaget viewed recall, or evocative memory, to be specific to higher primates or man. It involves the impression, in the absence of a model, that an object or event has been experienced or perceived at a prior moment in time. Recall is said (Piaget & Inhelder, 1973) to "involve the use of a memory image, that is, a figurative cum semiotic mechanism or a purely semiotic mechanism" (p. 13). Since no external stimulus is available during recall, memory must rely on symbolic representation.

This distinction between recall and recognition may be summarized in terms of Piaget's view that perceptual schemata are the instruments of recognition, whereas nonperceptual schemata, or internalized images, are the instruments of recall. This difference accounts for Piaget's observation that recognition is present during the first months of life, but that recall is not evidenced before about 1-year-of-age. According to Piaget (1968), because "recognition can rely on perception and sensorimotor schemes alone, while evocation requires mental imagery or language, that is, some form of symbolic function" (p. 11), the young infant would not be expected to exhibit recall. The young infant, equipped with perceptual schemata, is capable of recognition. However, only at about 1-year-of-age when the child develops symbolic functions (i.e., mental imagery and language) does he or she become capable of recall. For Piaget then, a major cognitive developmental accomplishment, that is, the growth of symbolic functions, is reflected in an important mnemonic feat, the emergence of recall.

Bartlett and Piaget's additions of notions such as schema and construction draw from an *organismic* world view that requires *wholistic* analysis. This perspective represents quite a significant departure from earlier views of memory that tended to be more *mechanistic* and could, therefore, be comfortable with the *reductionistic* mode of analysis that has been pervasive in science (Overton & Reese, 1973). It might be added, however, that despite seemingly radical differences in the assumptions inherent in mechanistic and organic models, the two perspectives most often have been blurred in research concerning memory. In addition, while the pendulum of contemporary conceptualizations of memory seems to be swaying toward the organismic model, the methodologies used in research still seem to be rooted in the mechanistic tradition.

Dialecticians

The *dialectic* world view involves still other assumptions about humans. In particular, it views the human as an ever changing being in an ever changing environment. Although the implications of this alternative may be profound, in psychological research, the adoption of such a perspective seems mainly to result in a difference in focus. Some of the points of particular emphasis of the dialectic approach, for example, the issues emphasized in work carried out by Soviet psychologists, are worth noting. It might be indicated, also, that there seems to be a perceptible shift towards this focus in contemporary western psychology (e.g., Meadows, 1983).

Within the traditional conception of the mechanistic, and to a lesser extent, organismic world views, a knower is conceived of as an isolated individual knowing the world apart from its social context. Consciousness is separate from the external social world. Indeed, consciousness permits one to contemplate, rather than to simply act on the world. Knowledge comes from deduction of stimuli impinging upon the knower from the external world and is assessed for adequacy relevant to some formal truth system. The individual may be justifiably studied in isolation.

On the other hand, within the dialectic conception, the knower is assumed to develop knowledge inextricably in and with a social context. Thought may be pragmatic as much as logical, and it continually gets transformed. Knowing, in general, and memory, in particular, must be viewed within the social, rather than individual, context. Both the form and function of knowledge are social entities. It would be inappropriate, therefore, to investigate the individual devoid of his or her social context.

Contemporary Experimental Psychology

Early contemporary experimental research on memory was dominated by questions drawn from the associationist tradition, as previously established by Ebbinghaus (1885). During its first few decades, this research was referred to as the study of verbal learning. Subjects were required to engage in rote learning of lists of words or nonsense syllables. Cofer (1976) summarized the major questions addressed as follows:

> How is the acquisition of lists affected by features of the learning methods and materials used? What are economical ways of learning lists? What processes underlie list learning and what is their status? What governs transfer of learning from one task to another? How may forgetting be explained? (p. 330)

Since it was assumed that general laws of behavior existed, the use of lists of nonsense syllables, or of lists of simple words was considered a reasonable, indeed an ideal, situation for investigating learning and memory. The laws of behavior that were established were assumed to generalize to more complex situations. In the past decade or two, however, the credibility of this assumption has been seriously questioned. Thus, summarizing the first century of experimental research on memory, Cofer (1976) wrote: There have been innumerable investigations, but the problems that have been studied were derived from a conception of human memory that no longer seems tenable.

In more recent experimental research on memory there are noticeable changes in emphases, as well as changes in procedures. Much of the current research is framed, at least in a loose way, within an information-processing perspective. Often the computer is used as a metaphor for the human cognitive system. Memory is conceptualized as the transfer of information within an information-processing system. Very generally, retention is thought to involve acquisition and storage of information. Subsequent recollection is thought to involve retrieval of retained information. A data base is assumed to be established from information that has been acquired and stored. It may be recollected through recall or recognition.

Sometimes relatively explicit task analyses are made of the paradigms used to assess memory. This technique involves hypothesizing various component memory processes to account for performance. Then research is carried out to experimentally manipulate factors that may affect each process differentially. An understanding of the workings of the memory system is assumed to be gained by noting the limiting and affecting circumstances of its functioning.

In more recent research on memory, materials used in experiments are more likely to be meaningful, for example, words, sentences. or prose material are typically used. In addition, investigators are much more likely to examine the learning of material presented only once. There also has been new interest in such issues as organization and coding processes. Furthermore, the role of preexisting knowledge on memory is now recognized as important.

These changes often have been described as a shift from the study of *learning* to the study of *memory*. However, this characterization seems largely to be a misnomer. Learning and memory connote two distinct phenomena. Indeed, the distinction between them is quite analogous to the early distinction that was made between retention and recollection. However, these two phenomena have not been empirically disentangled in *learning* or *memory* experiments, that is, measures that are purported to assess learning are contaminated by memory, and vice-versa.

Another characteristic about memory that has received current attention relates to the degree to which it can be brought under intentional control. In earlier discussions about this issue the terms artificial versus natural memory were used. In more recent discussions terms such as *deliberate* versus *automatic* or *effortful* versus *effortless* (e.g., Hasher & Zacks, 1979; Shiffrin & Schneider, 1977) are used. In all instances, there has been a realization that some degree of memory accompanies all experience, but that this automatic memory can be extended by invoking deliberate techniques. There appear to be some important differences in the nature of each of these types of memory. Thus, each has been pursued separately. In addition, however, the way in which they interact has been recognized as important.

A further principle about memory that has emerged in contemporary experimental psychology seems likely to be of special importance. This principle, which is often referred to as *encoding specificity* (Tulving & Thompson, 1973), articulates the fact that events are remembered in ways that depend on their initial perception and encoding, as well as on the conditions that exist at the time of attempted recollection. The more closely retrieval conditions match encoding conditions, the higher the probability of recollection. Moreover, the aspects of an event that will be recollected are those that were both originally taken note of and subsequently reconsidered. Thus, what will be remembered cannot be determined solely by an externally objective analysis of a stimulus. Rather, the internal subjective experience of the stimulus when initially encountered, as well as the subjective experience of stimuli present during recollection, will be relevant.

Although most experimental research on memory has investigated retention and recollection of specific experiences, contemporary experimental psychology also has recognized a more generalized kind of remembering. For example, Tulving (1972) brought attention to the distinctiveness between specific and general memories. He used the term *episodic memory* to describe retention of specific, personally experienced, and datable events. *Semantic memory,* on the other hand, referred to knowledge of the world that is not necessarily dependent upon one's personal identity or past.

Contemporary Developmental Psychology

In the last 20 or more years, sizeable literatures have emerged on memory of children (see Kail & Hagen, 1977; Ornstein, 1978; Perlmutter, 1985) and older adults (see Craik, 1977; Perlmutter, 1985; Poon et al., 1980). Most of this work draws directly from theories and methods guiding nondevelopmental research on memory. In general, the aim has been to specify the processing changes that account for performance improvements during childhood or performance declines during adulthood.

A fairly consistent pattern has emerged (see Perlmutter, 1985). It emphasizes the malleable, or plastic, character of human memory. Although during childhood, particularly during early infancy, some *memory capacities* may improve perhaps because of biological maturation, most age differences in children's memory performance can be accounted for by their expanding *memory contents.* Thus, children's increasing *knowledge about the world* (i.e., epistemic memory), and in particular, their increasing *knowledge about the workings of the human memory system* (i.e., metamemory), allow them to use their memory systems more effectively. Therefore, young children show the greatest disadvantage on memory tasks that depend most on epistemic or metacognitive knowledge.

Epistemic knowledge in general, and metacognitive knowledge in particular, also have an important role in memory development during adulthood. Although biological deterioration probably diminishes older adults' *memory capacities,* at least to some extent, their accumulated *memory contents* often compensate for this loss. Thus, the older adult shows the least deficit on memory tasks that depend most on the substance, rather than processes, of memory.

Contemporary Biologists

One subfield of contemporary biology, often identified as *neuroscience,* seems to be making great strides in identifying biochemical changes in the brain that accompany memory functioning. The new techniques that are being developed for viewing and analyzing brain activity hold much promise for understanding normal memory as well as pathologies of memory. Several age-related memory dysfunctions seem especially likely to be conquered by such a biological perspective. For example, approximately 15% of the apparent cases of senility now can be diagnosed as reversible brain syndromes that are associated with various treatable toxicities in the brain. Moreover, significant breakthrough in understanding the biology of other memory dysfunctions, such as Alzheimer's disease, seem to be on the horizon.

Another subfield of contemporary biology also seems relevant to conceptualization about memory. That is, recent work or *molecular genetics* has increased our understanding of the retention and transmission of biological information. With the discovery of DNA, and the breaking of the "genetic code," biologists now can specify both the way in which biological information is retained and the way in which it is reproduced. The relevance of understanding retention and reproduction of information at a molecular level, to understanding retention and reproduction of information at a cognitive level, has not yet been pursued, but may be fruitful.

CONTEMPORARY PERSPECTIVES ON MEMORY DEVELOPMENT

Declining Themes

Developmental researchers often have turned to nondevelopmentalists for questions, theories, and methods. This borrowing of modes of inquiry is especially characteristic in the area of memory, perhaps because the experimental tradition has been so active on this topic, and its theories and methods are well developed. As discussed earlier, experimental research on memory typically is traced back to the last century, when Ebbinghaus (1885) investigated memory by adopting the rigorous procedures used by other already established sciences.

Ebbinghaus' approach was rooted in a *mechanistic world view.* Many of the important assumptions underlying this perspective are discussed by Overton and

Reese (1973) and Reese and Overton (1970). In general, strict mechanists view the world as uniform, stable, and fixed; and humans as inherently at rest, organized simply as a reflection of the world around them, and changing only in quantitative ways. Because elementalism is assumed, understanding is pursued through reductionism.

Early associationist models of memory and verbal learning were quite faithful to the mechanistic perspective. Subsequent information processing models are less faithful to it. For example, most current information processing accounts recognize the assumption of uniformity to be untenable (see Estes, 1979), and do not really accept a passive view of this subject. Indeed, many of the chapters in this volume focus on the ways in which task (e.g., Hussey & von Eye, this volume; Knopf, Körkel, Schneider, & Weinert, this volume), context (Ceci, Bronfenbrenner, & Baker, this volume; Ornstein, Baker-Ward, & Naus, this volume; Paris, this volume) and state (Dixon & Hertzog, this volume) affect memory performance.

The *organismic world view* is an alternative perspective (see also Overton & Reese, 1973; Reese & Overton, 1970) that has been prevalent in much work on cognitive development. For example, Piaget's structural view of the development of intelligence fits within the organismic model. General assumptions of this world view include lack of uniformity and change. The human is assumed to be inherently active, constructing a reality that reflects the interaction between his inherent organization and the external world, and characterized by quantitative as well as qualitative change. Because wholism is basic to this perspective, full understanding only is regarded as possible through consideration of the organic whole. As already indicated, most contemporary views of memory adopt some of the assumptions of the organismic perspective, including an appreciation of the active nature of humans, constructed nature of knowledge, and contextual influences on behavior. Nevertheless, the experimental methods that prevail in memory research are rooted in assumptions of uniformity and reductionism.

Although current views of memory have abandoned a strict mechanistic perspective, a full appreciation of the implications of this change in world view has not occurred. For example, although the reality of contextual influence is no longer controversial, their centrality to theory is not yet apparent. Moreover, the methods of the mechanistic view generally have been retained. Further progress requires the development of new methods and analytic techniques that are not rooted in assumptions of reductionism.

Dominant Themes

Three classes of factors now predominate as explanations of memory development. These include operative knowledge, epistemic knowledge, and metacognitive knowledge. *Operative knowledge* includes the operations, procedures, strategies, and skills of memory. Several such operations have received extensive attention in research on memory development. These include rehearsal, organization, and imagery. There presently is a lack of agreement about the importance of intentional, conscious control of these processes (see Paris, this volume; Pressley, Forrest-Pressley, & Elliott-Faust, this volume); however, there is a shared view that age-related improvements in memory performance are related to increased mnemonic processing skills (see Denhiere, this volume; Ornstein, Baker-Ward, & Naus, this volume; Wellman, this volume).

Epistemic knowledge refers to the information about the world that accrues through life. It has been found that memory about things that one has a great deal of world knowledge about is better than one's memory information that is not so easily related to what is already known. Similarly, it has been found that the increasing world knowledge base that accrues during development accounts for some of the age-related improvement in memory performance that is observed. Still, many details remain to be understood concerning the ways in which general knowledge supports specific memory.

Metacognitive knowledge refers to the knowledge that one has about the workings of the cognitive system. This knowledge has been found to increase through childhood, and appears also to contribute to the improved memory performance that is observed with age. Of considerable interest now is the extent to which training of metamemory knowledge can improve memory performance (see Borkowski, Milstead, & Hale, this volume; Büchel, this volume; Pressley, Forrest-Pressley, & Elliott-Faust, this volume). In particular, much current attention is focused on assessing the value of training specific and generalized (transferable) improvements in memory.

It might be noted that each of these factors that contribute to age-related improvements in memory performance, that is, operative knowledge, epistemic knowledge, and metacognitive knowledge, actually are themselves contents of memory. Thus, it is the internal retention of the past that facilitates remembering in the future. The "experience of remembering" occurs as present environmental information interacts with cognitively generated information about the past and reaches some threshold of familiarity. To the degree that cognitive constructions may draw upon enriched remnants of the past, remembering will be more likely. On the other hand, to the degree that only a limited store of the past is available, for example, in the young child, the experience of remembering may be more dependent upon supports from the environment. Indeed, some of the research reported in this volume is consistent with this view. For example, Ornstein's research illustrates the importance of salience of conceptual features of stimuli for promoting good memory in early childhood, and Paris (this volume) and Verdonik (this volume) suggest that social support may be important for early memory as well.

Emerging Themes

Several classes of factors are now gaining attention in considerations of memory development. In particular, *environmental context* factors increasingly are being recognized as important in early memory development (see Ornstein, Baker-Ward, & Naus, this volume; Paris, this volume; Verdonik, this volume), and *subject state* factors are beginning to be seen as important in memory aging (see Dixon & Hertzog, this volume). In addition, several investigators now see a need to include an *individual difference* component in formulations of memory development (see Hussy & von Eye, this volume; Knopf et al., this volume).

Environmental context and subject state factors have been accepted as relevant to memory performance at least since the time that Jenkins (1974) proposed his tetrahedral framework for formulating and interpreting memory research. In this framework, *task materials,* and *subject* factors were recognized as having an important influence on memory performance. Because the relevance of one's world to materials used in memory studies has been found to have a major effect on performance, investigators tend to be sensitive to the ecological validity of materials that are used. Task structure, including environmental context, also is known to affect memory performance, as it contributes to the acquisition and retrieval operations that subjects engage in. Similarly, memory performance is known to vary as a function of subject state, for example, with physical status (e.g., health, restedness, hunger, and alertness), emotional status (e.g., anxiety, depression), and self-efficacy. Yet, memory researchers have not adequately incorporated these last two factors into their theories or investigations.

Figure 16.1 represents an attempt to portray an analytic framework that is necessitated by the acceptance of *environmental context, subject state, developmental level,* and *individual differences* as important factors in memory performance. The figure is meant to illustrate the data points that are potentially available for investigating memory. The population of individuals who might be assumed to contribute a unique individual retention capacity trait is shown within each cell. Developmental levels are portrayed along the y-axis, environmental context along the x-axis, and potential transient subject states are shown along the z-axis. Performance data from each subject in a memory experiment is assumed to reflect their memory capacity (I), developmental level (D), and state (S), as well as task factors (T).

Inherent within this framework is the view that stable individual differences, transient subject states, developmental levels, and environmental contexts all contribute important, systematic, and discoverable variance to performance. While in the past, much of the variance that is attributable to stable individual differences and transient subject states has been regulated to the status of error, this practice no longer seems warranted. Although it is not yet clear what the relative contribution of each factor is, there already is evidence to indicate that all are nontrivial. Thus, just as it is acknowledged to be unreasonable to generalize across developmental levels, it probably is unreasonable to generalize across environmental contexts and subject states, and perhaps across individuals as well.

Although the above statement would not seem to be especially controversial,

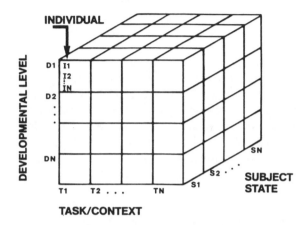

FIG. 16.1. Framework for considering memory performance data.

its implications seem underappreciated. In particular, because the range of environmental contexts and subject states that have been investigated in research on memory is so limited, the assumed importance of the variables that are now considered to be central to memory performance and memory development probably is distorted, and other important factors probably have been neglected.

Figure 16.2 shows hypothetical data that might be generated by individuals, or age groups, in the populations of memory experiments that could be derived from the framework shown in Figure 16.1. Across the range of environmental contexts and subject states, a range of performances would be observed. The maximum and minimum levels of performances shown in the figure are consistent with three generalizations that may be derived from research on memory development. First, both minimum and maximum performance levels tend to increase during childhood. Second, minimum, but probably not maximum, performance seems to decrease during later adulthood. Finally, the difference between minimum and maximum performance seems to be greater in early childhood and later adulthood than in later childhood and early adulthood.

Figure 16.3 attempts to illustrate the way each of the factors included in the framework presented in Figure 16.1 may contribute to memory performance across development. First, a stable individual *retention capacity trait* is shown. This factor is assumed to account for relatively little of the variance in memory performance data gathered from a group of subjects (see the work of Hussy & von Eye, this volume, as well as Knopf et al., this volume). However, across the life span, it is likely that each individual will contribute some relatively stable variance associated with their general memory capacity or memory trait. A clearer estimation of the actual importance of this individual retention trait to memory performance could be derived from longitudinal data in which individuals are assessed in a broad range of environmental contexts and subject states.

Developmental mnemonic skill level is shown as a relatively important factor that contributes to increases in memory performance across childhood and re-

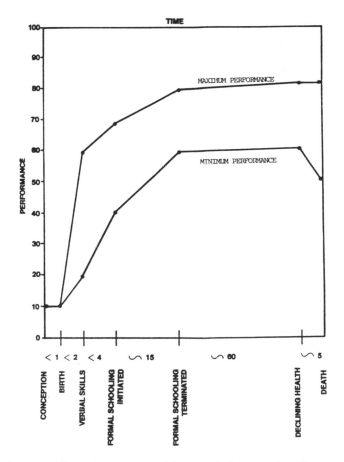

FIG. 16.2. Minimal and maximal hypothetical levels of performance across the life span.

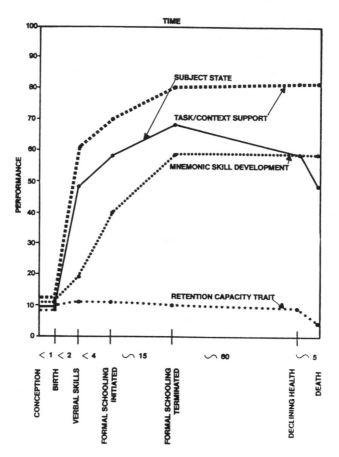

FIG. 16.3.   Hypothesized contribution of retention capacity, skill level, task support, and state to memory performance across the life span.

mains relatively stable in its contribution to memory performance across most of adulthood. It is assumed to reflect the age-related change in mnemonic competence that derives from age changes in operative knowledge, epistemic knowledge, metacognitive knowledge, and perhaps other, as yet undiscovered, factors. The pattern of age change that is illustrated draws from the considerable research available on age differences in memory performance on laboratory tasks. Actually, the relative contribution of developmental mnemonic skill level to memory performance is difficult to portray with confidence. Although developmental mnemonic skill level has been assumed to be quite important, the range of performance that has been observed on different tasks within developmental levels, and even within individual subjects, suggests that the contribution of underlying skill may be less important than has been assumed. If level of mnemonic skill played a major role in memory performance, a consistent pattern of performance across environmental contexts and subject states would be expected for any group of subjects at a particular skill level. Such consistency has not been the role. Moreover, the range of performances that have been observed within age groups, and the lack of intraindividual consistency that has been observed within individuals, is especially impressive, since it derives from assessments that have been made within a relatively narrow range of environmental contexts and subject states.

The top curve in Fig. 16.3 refers to the maximal performance that is derived from a maximally supportive *environmental context*. The range of performance improvement derived from environmental support seems, in many ways, analogous to Vygotsky's notion of a zone of proximal development. It should be noted, however, that some zone of additional performance potential is present throughout the lifespan, although it may be particularly large during early childhood. It is difficult, given research presently available, to estimate the possible contribution of environmental support to memory performance. It is suggested here that its contribution probably has been underestimated. Moreover, even if available research accurately represents the contribution of environmental context, it is argued that the implications of this contribution has been inadequately appreciated, and therefore, that the contribution of mnemonic skill development to memory performance generally has been overemphasized.

The final curve in Figure 16.3 represents the hypothesized influence of factors related to *subject state*. It is included to capture the fluctuation in performance that is accounted for by physical status, mood, self-efficacy, and other state variables. Since there has been relatively little research on how these factors affect memory performance, it presently is difficult to estimate their contribution. However, as is illustrated in the figure, it appears that subject state may be particularly important in later adulthood. At that time, low state valences can contribute to considerable depressions of performance.

SUGGESTIONS FOR FUTURE DIRECTIONS

There still is a need for research to further our understanding of the ways in which operative knowledge, epistemic knowledge, and metacognitive knowledge contribute to memory competence and age-related improvements in memory performance. While the past 2 decades of research in this area have radically changed our views of the child's developing competencies, and provided many details about age differences in the cognitive processing that children engage in when faced with laboratory memory tasks, additional questions remain. Similarly, there is much to be learned about the ways in which environmental context and subject status contribute to memory. Less data concerning these factors are available, although there is at least some suggestion that they mediate developmental skill in interesting ways. In this domain, the focus on contextual factors are both determinants of performance and guides for development is encouraging and seems likely to pay off in the years ahead.

All of these directions are likely to be fruitful, and would add to our understanding of memory and its development. Nevertheless, a decade or two of such research would, it seems to me, still leave us with a relatively impoverished view of memory and its development. It would, for example, add little to our understanding of the ways in which memory is a vehicle for carrying individual and societal knowledge through time and space, or of the implications of these functions of memory. Likewise, for the most part, it would leave us with no greater appreciation of the ways in which memory serves, or fails to serve, our negotiations with the physical and social world.

Since the generality of experimental findings can no longer be assumed to carry across environmental context or subject state, the range of situations investigated needs to be greatly expanded. In particular, it would be wise to choose contexts and states that are most similar to situations of importance. While this goal reportedly has been directing much of the current research, I believe a close scrutiny of the literature brings this belief into question. For example, many investigators have moved to the study of memory for texts, rather than word lists. Text memory is easily seen as having importance in our educated, technologically sophisticated society. On the other hand, list memory, although perhaps having some real world analogue (e.g., remembering a grocery list), is less plausibly important. But are the texts that are used in memory investigations characteristic of the professional and entertainment texts that typically occupy us? Are the situations in which memory investigations are carried out representative of the rich and distracting contexts in which most reading occurs? Are the subjects participating in memory studies at states of arousal, levels of involvement, or feelings of self-efficacy that are comparable to that in which they carry out most of their reading? None of these questions can be answered affirmatively. The representatives of text materials is perhaps most easy to evaluate. Early investigations had been criticized on this account, and more recent work appears somewhat improved. However, the materials used in text memory studies are still open to criticism. Since only brief, self-contained passages are used in most research, it is impossible to develop complicated threads of understanding that are common in lengthier prose. The appropriateness of environmental contexts and subject states that characterize most text memory studies has been largely ignored. Because reading generally is motivated by particular professional or recreational goals, and it tends to occur in distracting environments, this neglect probably has led to an inaccurate understanding of natural text memory.

Moreover, much is remembered about things we are not even entirely aware of encountering, and many interesting memory phenomena actually involve remembering at a nonconscious level. Thus, for example, the background conversation being held by colleagues in an adjacent office may prove to be more memorable than the deliberately reviewed manuscript to which one is attending, or the evaluation of the manuscript may unknowingly affect the attitude conveyed, but not content, of future interactions with the author. None of these types of experiences have received much attention in research on memory. Perhaps such effort would enrich our view of deliberately recollected memory for deliberately recorded information. More importantly, it would contribute to understanding of additional types of memory that may have even greater functional significance than that of the memory phenomena that have captured so much contemporary attention.

TAXONOMY OF MEMORY PHENOMENA

A variety of schemes could be developed to characterize the diversity of memory phenomena that exist. One is offered here, not so much with zeal for its particulars, but rather as a catalyst for expansion in thinking about memory. Its formulation focuses on three dimensions that are inherent in virtually all definitions of memory, from Plato and Aristotle, to Ebbinghaus (1884) and Tulving (1979), and even to Webster (1974). That is, that memory involves the *recording* and *recollecting* of *information*. The distinctions that can be made within each of these dimensions are numerous. I have attempted to keep them to a minimum, specifying only the most obvious categories.

The taxonomy is shown in Fig. 16.4. Six *types of information* have been indicated. These include physical, behavioral, emotional, imaginal, verbal, and conceptual information. The last three categories (imaginal, verbal, and conceptual) involve the types of representational information that have been the focus of most psychological research on memory. Although noncognitive psychologists have been interested in behavior and emotion, theoretical and empirical work on memory largely has excluded these categories. This limitation of focus seems unfortunate.

The two other dimensions incorporated in the taxonomy concern the *modes in which information are recorded* and *the modes in which information are recollected*. In both receptive and reproductive memory, the degree of awareness or consciousness of the information may differ in important ways. Thus, for example, a rememberer may be totally unaware of some information that is nevertheless recorded and retained, may be aware though not directly focused on the information, or may be intentionally attentive to the information. Similarly, recollection may occur without awareness, with awareness though not deliberateness, or with intentional focus.

Physical information often is recorded and retained without awareness, and its recollection generally is directly observable. Thus, for example, one may speak of the earth's memory of glacial movement or volcanic eruption, an automobile's memory of an accident or simonizing, a sheep's memory of its branding or

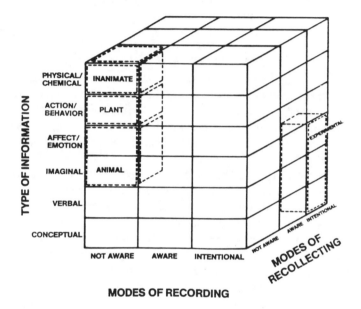

FIG. 16.4.   Taxonomy of memory situations.

sheering, or a human's memory of exposure to sun or suturing during surgery. An event, or series of events, has irreversibly changed these objects. The earth, automobile, sheep, and human continue to exist, but only in forms that are physically altered by their experience. Memory is evidenced as a physical change in the object with no awareness required at time of record or recollection. Thus, even inanimate objects may possess physical memory.

Actions or behavior may be recorded and recollected by animate, but not inanimate entities. Thus, living organisms show changes in their activities that are related to their experiences. For example, even in lower organisms, memory may be seen in the form of habituation of some actions, and preparedness or expectancy for others. Similarly, in humans, certain biological functions develop a rhythm that may be viewed as behavioral memory. Such readying of activity does not necessarily occur at a level of awareness, but may only be brought to consciousness when disrupted, for example, when sleep and eating rhythms are disrupted by jet-lag. Such behavioral memory might be reviewed as an adaptive biological phenomenon. In this sense, the memory, or record of experience, does not exist as change in the physical nature of the object, but rather as a change in the activity of the organism. Such changes usually appear to have functional payoff for the organism.

Affective information also may be recorded and recollected without awareness, although this type of information is only within the realm of animal, not plant or nonliving experience. This form of memory is sometimes directly observable, but particularly in mature humans, it is likely that it often escapes observation. While this affect memory is central to the concerns of clinicians, it virtually has been ignored by experimental researchers of memory.

Representational (imaginal, verbal, conceptual) memory is not directly observable, but rather, it usually must be inferred from introspection or behavior. Much of our knowledge about representational memory therefore is restricted to the situations in which recollection is intentional. As such, it requires a self-reflective process of consciousness that probably is only available to mature humans. The degree to which our dogma about memory is a reflection of this self-reflective process, rather than an accurate portrayal of recording and reproduction of information, is unknown. However, it may be worth considering the usefulness of some well worked out, noncognitive, conceptions of memory, for example, genetic models.

CONCLUSIONS

In this paper I have indicated that considerable progress has been made in understanding certain kinds of memory and its development. In particular, much is now known about memory processing that is involved in deliberate retention of representational information over short time intervals in controlled, nondistracting situations. Moreover, real progress is evident in understanding the ways in which age-related increases in operative, epistemic, and metacognitive knowledge contribute to age-related improvements in memory performance in laboratory memory tasks. It is noted, too, that new and important insights about the influences on memory of environmental context and subject states appear to be on the horizon.

Nevertheless, a number of limitations in current approaches were noted. In particular, it was argued that a true appreciation of the implications of the nonuniversal character of memory has not yet occurred. While most researchers accept a model of memory that predicts important variance associated with environmental context and subject state, they have continued to investigate situations that control context and state in ways that are likely to limit, if not distort, our understanding of memory. In addition, although an organismic, or even dialectic world view generally has been adopted, most investigators still rely upon methodological and analytic techniques that have been developed within a mechanistic world view. These methods are rooted in assumptions of reductionism, and therefore, they may be inadequate for capturing important wholistic phenomena that are now assumed.

I have suggested that if future research efforts continue to be focused solely on the memory phenomena and memory situations that have predominated until now, our understanding of memory will remain impoverished. Therefore, I have included a brief review of inquiry about memory in earlier times, and have offered a taxonomic scheme for considering the diversity of memory phenomena. Each of these was provided as a stimulus for broader conceptualization about memory. I argued that such a broadening of thinking is called for, and specially suggested that future research should explicitly deal with nondeliberate, as well as nonconscious, retention, and researchers should investigate in earnest the numerous roles memory plays in everyday human functioning.

REFERENCES

Anderson, J. R., & Bower, G. H. (1974). A propositional theory of recognition memory. *Memory and Cognition, 2,* 406–412.

Atkinson, R. C., & Shiffrin, R. M. (1968). Human memory: A proposed system and its control processes. In K. W. Spence & J. T. Spence (Eds.), *The Psychology of Learning and Motivation* (Vol. 2). New York: Academic Press.

Baltes, P. B., & Brim, O. G. (Eds.). (1984). *Life-span development and behavior* (Vol. 6). New York: Academic Press.

Bartlett, F. C. (1932). *Remembering: A study in experimental and social psychology.* Cambridge, England: Cambridge University Press.

Bobrow, D. G., & Norman, D. A. (1975). Some principles of memory schemata. In D. G. Bobrow & A. Collins (Eds.), *Representation and understanding: Studies in cognitive science.* New York: Academic Press.

Boorstin, D. J. (1983). *Discovers.* New York: Random House.

Brown, A. L., Bransford, J. D., Ferrara, R. A., & Campione, J. C. (1983). Learning, remembering, and understanding. In P. H. Mussen (Ed.), *Handbook of child psychology* (Vol. 3, edited by J. H. Flavell and E. M. Markman). New York: Wiley.

Cason, H. (1932). The learning and retention of pleasant and unpleasant activities. *Archives of Psychology* (No. 134).

Cofer, C. N. (1976). *The structure of human memory.* San Francisco: Freeman.

Craik, F. I. M. (1977). Age differences in human memory. In J. E. Birren & K. W. Schaie (Eds.), *Handbook of the psychology of aging.* New York: Van Nostrand Reinhold.

Ebbinghaus, H. E. (1885/1964). *Memory: A contribution to experimental psychology.* New York: Dover.

Erdelyi, M. H., & Goldberg, B. (1979). Let's not sweep repression under the rug: Towards a cognitive psychology of repression. In J. F. Kihlstrom & F. J. Evans (Eds.), *Functional disorders of memory.* Hillsdale, NJ: Lawrence Erlbaum Associates.

Estes, W. K. (1979). On the descriptive and explanatory functions of theories of memory. In L-G Nilsson (Ed.), *Perspectives on memory research: Essays in honour of Uppsala University's 500th Anniversary.* Hillsdale, NJ: Lawrence Erlbaum Associates.

Freud, S. (1899/1956). Screen memories. In S. Strackey (ed.), *Collected papers of Sigmund Freud* (Vol. 5). London: Hogarth Press, (1899; republished 1956).

Freud, S. (1905/1938). Three contributions to the theory of sex. In A. A. Brill (Ed.), *The basic writings of Sigmund Freud.* New York: Random House, 1905; republished 1938).

Freud, S. (1915/1963). [The unconscious.] (C. M. Baines, trans.) In P. Rieff (Ed.), *Freud: General psychological theory.* New York: Collier.

Hasher, L., & Zacks, R. T. (1979). Automatic and effortful processes in memory. *Journal of Exoerimental Psychology: General, 108,* 356–388.

Holmes, D. S. (1970). Differential change in affective intensity and the forgetting of unpleasant personal experiences. *Journal of Personality and Social Psychology, 15,* 234–239.

James, W. (1890). *The principles of psychology* (Vol. 1). New York: Holt.

Jenkins, J. J. (1974). Remember that old theory of memory? Well, forget it! *American Psychologist, 29,* 785–795.

Kail, R. V., & Hagen, J. W. (1977). *Perspective on the development of memory and cognition.* Hillsdale, NJ: Lawrence Erlbaum Associates.

Meadows, S. (1983). *Developing thinking: Approach to children's cognitive development.* New York: Methuen.

Muller, G. S., & Pilzecker, A. (1900). Experimentelle Beiträge zur Lehre vom Gedächtnis. *Z. Psycholog., Ergänzungsband, 1,* 1–300.

Murray, D. J. (1976). Research on human memory in the nineteenth century. *Canadian Journal of Psychology, 30,* 201–220.

Neisser, V. (1982). Memory: What are the important questions. In V. Neisser (Ed.), *Memory observed: Remembering in Natural Contexts.* San Francisco, CA: W. H. Freeman.

Ornstein, P. A. (1978). *Memory development in children.* Hillsdale, NJ: Lawrence Erlbaum Associates.

Overton, W. F., & Reese, H. W. (1973). Models of development: Methodological implications. In J. R. Nesselroade & H. W. Reese (Eds.), *Life-span Developmental Psychology: Methodological Issues.* New York: Academic Press.

Perlmutter, M. (1985). Memory development across the lifespan. In P. B. Baltes, D. Featherman, & R. Lerner (Eds.), *Life span development and behavior* (Vol. 7). New York: Academic Press.

Piaget, J. (1968). *On the development of memory and identity.* Worcester, MA: Clark University Press.

Piaget, J. (1973). *The child and reality.* New York: Grossman.

Piaget, J., & Inhelder, B. (1973). *Memory and intelligence.* New York: Basic Books.

Poon, L. W., Fozard, J. L., Cermak, L. S., Arenberg, D., & Thompson, L. W. (1980). *New Direction in Memory and Aging.* Hillsdale, NJ: Lawrence Erlbaum Associates.

Posner, M. T. (1978). *Chronometric Explorations of Mind.* Hillsdale, NJ: Lawrence Erlbaum Associates.

Rapaport, D. (1942). *Emotions and Memory.* Baltimore, MD: Williams & Wilkins.

Reese, H. W., & Overton, W. F. (1970). Models of development and theories of development. In L. R. Goulet & P. B. Baltes (Eds.), *Life-span Developmental Psychology: Theory and Research.* New York: Associated Press.

Shiffrin, R. M., & Schneider, W. (1977). Controlled and automatic human information processing. II. Perceptual learning automatic attending, and a general theory. *Psychological Review, 84,* 127–190.

Tulving, E. (1972). Episodic and semantic memory. In E. Tulving & W. Donaldson (Eds.), *Organization of memory.* New York: Academic Press.

Tulving, E. (1979). Memory research: What kind of progress. In L-G Nilsson (Ed.), *Perspectives on memory research: Essays in honor of Uppsala University's 500th anniversary.* Hillsdale, NJ: Lawrence Erlbaum Associates.

Tulving, E., & Pearlstone, Z. (1966). Availability versus accessibility of information in memory for words. *Journal of Verbal Learning and Verbal Behavior, 5,* 381–391.

Tulving, E., & Thompson, D. M. (1973). Encoding specifity and retrieval processes in episodic memory. *Psychological Review, 80,* 352–373.

Webster's new world dictionary, 2nd college edition (1974). New York: William Collins & World Publishing Co.

Yates, F. A. (1966). *The art of memory.* Middlesex, England: Penguin.

17 Epilogue

F. E. Weinert
Max Planck Institute for Psychological Research, Munich

The sixteen chapters in this volume document that the field of memory development is active and still expanding. Although the bibliography comprises but a fragment of the relevant publications, it nonetheless reflects the range and variety of studies that have addressed this topic over the past 25 years. One may ask why so many developmental psychologists have concentrated their attention on describing and explaining memory performance across the life span. Marion Perlmutter (this volume) has given several answers to this question. One reason is the obvious importance of memory to the individual, for social communication, and especially for the way individuals use and remember past experiences. More generally, memory has been a pervasive topic of study because of its role as a component of the individual cognitive functions needed to deal with the problems of everyday life, and needed to achieve life goals, goals which differ greatly among individuals and may change radically over the life course (Dixon & Hertzog, this volume).

It may be that so many researchers have been attracted to the study of memory development because this topic has in recent years awakened great interest among the general public as well as within the scientific community. There was a time when, in relation to intellectual abilities, memory was held to be a more humble mental faculty and extraordinary feats of memory were more the object of ironical quips than admired. Today, however, rich knowledge, intelligent learning, and proficient memory are rated highly. Presumably one reason for this is the constant increase in the amount of information that people must encode, process, and store. This reappraisal of the role of memory may also stem from the demands formal education makes in childhood and youth, and from the increasingly demanding tasks of life-long learning. For many people, therefore, poor memory is a serious problem. Empirical findings from studies conducted across different countries indicate that although poor memory is certainly a predicament for elderly adults, it is not limited to them.

Although pills, popular books, and training programs are enjoying a boom, most of these offers are ineffective at improving memory, and some of them are not even good placebos. Partly as a result of this trend, public opinion has come to expect that memory research will provide the solutions to practical problems.

Such expectations are consonant with the hopes (and promises) of many researchers. Their assumption is that adequate theoretical explanations of the functioning of human memory will also yield information that could be applied to improving memory performance. A number of recent studies have demonstrated that training in the effective use of mnemonic strategies does actually improve memory performance (Pressley et al., this volume), although not as effectively as expected (Büchel, this volume).

Thus, study of the structures, processes, and functioning of the memory system continues to be a fundamental endeavor of cognitive psychology in the expectation that the findings will advance theoretical ideas and produce practical benefits. The study of memory development plays a significant role in this endeavor. Systematic observation of the ways in which changes in cognitive resources across the life span affect different types of memory performance is likely to encompass a greater range of phenomena than can be obtained in laboratory investigations with adult subjects. In addition, cross-cultural comparisons and training studies allow the investigation of the plasticity of human memory systems. Such studies have the particular value of providing a basis on which instructional treatments and teaching demands can be adjusted to the developmental levels achieved by the learners.

Considering the volume of theoretical and experimental work in memory development during the past decades, it is at first glance surprising that the results of current research receive such disparate evaluations in the different chapters of this volume. Whereas some of the contributors note that significant progress has been made in our understanding of memory development (e.g., Borkowski et al., Pressley et al.), others tend to be more skeptical and critical. Thus Perlmutter (this volume) emphasizes that "present understanding of memory is limited by the restrictive focus on only a very special kind of memory, that is on deliberate memory of symbolic information over short time intervals in extremely sterile situations." Similar deficits are noted by Paris, Ceci et al., Verdonik, and Dixon and Hertzog. In general, although these critiques do not deny that progress has been made within a number of research paradigms, they point to the narrow scope of current definitions of memory development and current methodological approaches. It is worthwhile to examine the progress and shortcomings a little more closely. To this end, I first discuss the highlights of current research on memory development, then attempt to clarify what memory research in developmental psychology really studies, and finally, draw some conclusions concerning the directions that future research should take.

SOME HIGHLIGHTS OF PRESENT RESEARCH IN MEMORY DEVELOPMENT

To specify the merits of present memory research in a developmental perspective, it is useful to take as a basis of comparison two different but similar reference systems. One is the research situation as it was some 30 or 40 years ago. Then, there was only limited concern with the development of learning and memory, and the theoretical value of the few empirical studies was considered less than spectacular by Munn (1946) in his integrative review. Learning and memory performance were held to be based on abilities that grow during childhood reach a relatively constant plateau in young and middle adulthood, and then decline. Such a pattern was explained in terms of a universal maturation–degeneration hypothesis: "The organism provides the framework of mechanisms within which learning occurs and by which learning bounds are set. Maturation and degeneration probably change this framework in many, now unknown ways which subtly affect the role of learning" (McGeoch & Irion, 1952, p. 550).

A similar conception is found in the second reference system, in intuitive theories about memory development. Here, memory is conceived as a more or less uniform set of separable abilities (Jäger & Sitarek, 1985), which change consistently over the life course and which reveal stable interindividual differences.

In relation to the state of research some 30 years ago and in comparison with the intuitive theories, current scientific knowledge about memory development appears highly elaborate.

Modern research programs started with the assumption that improvement on a wide range of memory skills during childhood can be attributed to increasingly intelligent and thereby more efficient forms of encoding, recoding, and decoding of information. This thesis was postulated by William James at the turn of the century: "All improvements of memory consist in better thinking" (1890, p.XII).

In this volume, Hussy and von Eye are guided by a similar orientation. They tested the hypothesis that age-related differences in memory performance across a wide age range, from 8 to 60 years, do not indicate changes in memory capabilities but in concept-formation ability: "As expected, there are age differences in both memory performance and concept-forming performance. . . . The model suggests, that age is only related to concept-forming performance but not to memory performance . . . the model supports the notion of a causal relationship between concept forming and memory" (Hussy & von Eye, this volume). This result is in principle consistent with theoretical conceptions as disparate as those postulated by Piaget and Inhelder (1973), Ericsson (1985), Chi (this volume), Denhière (this volume) or by Perlmutter (this volume). The differences among these concepts relate to the question of what it is that develops when the level of intelligent encoding, storing, and retrieving changes. Perlmutter (this volume) emphasizes the role of knowledge accessibility for understanding and remembering information. She distinguishes operative, metacognitive, and epistemic forms of knowledge, and in so doing, combines the three most important perspectives of current memory development research. These perspectives are represented at three different parts of this volume.

Many studies of memory development took as their starting point the hypothesis that age-related improvements in memory performance in childhood are associated with changes in strategy use. This assumption has been impressively supported. Pressley et al. (this volume) define strategies "as composed of cognitive operations over and above the processes that are a natural consequence of carrying out a task, ranging from one such operation to a sequence of interdependent operations. Strategies achieve cognitive purposes (e.g., comprehending, memorizing) and are potentially conscious and controllable activities." With age, children not only acquire more and more effective memory strategies (e.g., rehearsal, grouping, elaboration, etc.) but may become more active, flexible, and automatic in the application of available strategies thus requiring increasingly less mental effort (Ornstein et al., this volume). This holds true also for retrieval strategies available to the learner (trace strategies and call-up strategies) which can be used selectively, contingent upon task demands, even by 10-year-olds (Flammer & Lüthi, this volume).

For a long time the emergence of deliberate memory strategies was held to be correlated with formal education, and preschoolers were believed to lack strategy use for learning and for retrieval situations. Wellman, among others, has shown that this assumption is not generally valid. On the contrary: "Memory activities in young children are strategic and mnemonic, memory strategies are rich and frequently employed, and they exert an important influence on relevant, age-related improvements in memory performance" (Wellman, this volume).

The assumption that even preschoolers are able to employ strategies does not, of course, suggest that the mnemonics employed by younger and older children are equivalent. Experimental evidence shows that with age there occurs a shift to more and more complex, flexible, and task-tailored strategies. This development is due to two related factors: Different strategies are acquired and automatized at different ages, and knowledge concerning the specific conditions and goals to which the strategies can be applied and adapted must be acquired.

The declarative knowledge and executive skills involved in memory performance have been subsumed under the term metamemory (Flavell, 1971). In recent years the concept of metamemory has held as much fascination for many researchers as it has caused confusion. What are the factors underlying such a mixed effect?

Many uses of the term metamemory in the 1970s were grounded on a very simple functional schema. The use of appropriate strategies facilitates the performance of most memory tasks, therefore the quality of memory performance is contingent on two preconditions: availability of appropriate strategies, and (meta-)knowledge about conditions under which such strategies can be used most effectively. A large number of empirical studies have been conducted to test the validity of the following predictions drawn from this simplified assumption: (a) When the individual has suitable strategies available, the correlation between indicators of metamemory and performance on complex memory tasks will be high; (b) The correlational pattern between the use of available strategies, and memory performance will be closer the higher the level of metamemory development; (c) It is possible to compensate for a lack of metamemorial knowledge and to increase the correlational relationship between strategic behavior and memory performance by training in metamemory strategies or by appropriate instructions concerning the effectiveness of memory strategies for the solution of specific tasks.

Although the empirical correlations found between metamemory and memory performance have on the average been higher and theoretically more consistent than many of the critics claimed (Schneider, 1985), this failed to counteract the disappointment felt by many concerning the limited explanatory and predictive value of metamemorial variables.

For many researchers this dissatisfaction did not lead to attempts to provide a clear definition of the concept of metamemory, or to undertake analyses of the mechanisms by which metamemorial knowledge influences memory performance. Rather, it led to a strong extension of the meaning of the metamemory concept. An initially uniform class of declarative metaknowledge was changed into a multidimensional concept. Thus, for instance, Borkowski et al. (this volume) distinguish the following components: specific strategy knowledge, relational strategy knowledge, general strategy knowledge, and metamemory acquisition procedures. Nor is that the end of the list: In addition to declarative metaknowledge, procedural meta-skills, such as monitoring, planning, and checking have also been considered (Brown, 1978). Besides domain-unspecific metaknowledge, domain-specific metacompetences have also been identified (Chi, 1987) and finally the concept has been used not only to characterize knowledge in the narrower sense of the term but also to describe beliefs, expectations, attitudes and perceptions. For example, Dixon and Hertzog (this volume) define metamemory as "knowledge and beliefs about the functioning, development, limitations, and capacities of (a) one's own memory, and (b) the human memory system." In adopting this functionalist perspective, authors appear to assume that the relationship between metamemory and memory is a multifaceted one, so that divergent correlational relationships may be expected when differing indicators of metamemory and memory performance are used.

The similar proliferation of meanings for what is called "metacognition" recently brought Siegler and Kotovski (1986) to ask the provocative question: "Is metacognition the 1980s equivalent of g?" They go on to note: "Ability to learn, to generalize, to go beyond the information given, and to use strategies flexibly and appropriately are all attributes of that venerable construct. How exactly does metacognition differ? Metacognition also has encountered a number of difficulties in the area in which it has received the greatest study—cognitive development. Empirical relations between measures of metacognitive knowledge and performance have frequently not been found when expected. . . . Even when such relations do appear, it often is unclear exactly how metacognition influenced performance. Beyond this no one knows how well the various mental operations that are said to constitute metacognition correlate with each other. In other words, we have no measure of construct validity, despite the construct having been used quite widely for a full decade" (p. 428f).

Supposing that this criticism is justified at least in part and it also may be applied to metamemory, the question arises why so many investigators still continue to use the concepts of metamemory and metacognition. Several chapters of this volume attempt to answer this question (Borkowski et al., Pressley et al., Dixon & Hertzog). The arguments presented demonstrate that memory development is not only based on the acquisition and automatic employment of domain-specific knowledge and of specific strategies, but that above and beyond this, more-or-less generalized competencies develop, competencies which interact with the individual's state of knowledge about her or his own actions in given situations (Weinert, 1986). There is no uniform definition for such knowledge because it includes a number of divergent components. These components range from declarative, procedural, and tacit knowledge to metacognitive sensibility in relation to task demands and awareness of memory behavior. It is on the basis of such knowledge, and beliefs, attitudes and expectations associated with it, that coping with variable task demands need not rely only on trial and error or on empirical generalizations from successful performance. In this sense, the metamemory concept describes a knowledge system that enables effective use of mental resources when coping with varying demands of learning and memory tasks. Although metamemory is a "fuzzy" concept it will continue to be a fruitful variable in memory development research. Moreover, the close relation between this kind of self-related knowledge and motivational variables suggests that future research on metamemory should give more emphasis to it as a kind of intuitive theory that people have about their own memory system and the actions related to memory (Dixon & Hertzog, this volume).

The one-track focus of memory development research on the use of memory strategies in the 1960s and 1970s was broadened only during the last decade. The newer theoretical positions emphasize the role of content knowledge for the acquisition, storage, and retrieval of related information: In a specific content domain, available knowledge is the best predictor of knowledge acquisition. A common appreciation of this fact now appears in the literature, but the knowledge base is not regarded as standing in contrast to the role of strategies in memory development (Ornstein et al., this volume; Borkowski et al., this volume). Wellman (this volume) emphasizes: "Knowledge base explanations of memory development are complements rather than contrasts to strategy acquisition explanations."

The role of the knowledge base for learning and memorizing was first analyzed in studies that contrasted the performance of experts and novices in a specific domain (Chi, 1978; Körkel, 1987). These experiments demonstrated that age-related performance differences could be compensated for and in part even reversed when younger subjects were the experts and older subjects were novices in a specific domain (e.g., chess or soccer). Such comparisons of experts and novices, however, are but the first step in developmental studies of the knowledge base, children, in contrast to adults, are "universal novices" (Carey, 1985). Several chapters in this volume (Nelson & Hudson; Chi; Denhiere) provide a broader and deeper analysis of the role of the knowledge base. As evident from these studies, it is the better organization of knowledge rather than its sheer amount that is of major importance for processing relevant new information.

For younger children, in particular, the mental representation of routine events appears to play a central role in the mastery of age-typical memory tasks. These knowledge structures are termed scripts. "Scripts, like other schemas, organize information about the world and provide top-down structures that automatically guide comprehension and action within situations to which a schema representation applies" (Nelson & Hudson, this volume). During childhood the developmental trend is toward a flexible use of schemas, increasingly more and more complex scripts are acquired, and other types of general knowledge structures are generated. The world knowledge of younger children is organized in the form of "micro worlds" (or encapsulated knowledge structures); it is "contextually bound, that is, it can only be accessed in one context and not another. What this means, essentially, is that it was stored under one set of context and thus it can only be retrieved under the same set of context" (Chi, this volume). In the course of cognitive development the knowledge base not only expands, but is subject to more or less radical restructuring (Carey, 1985) and with this, a more flexible, less contextually bound access to stored knowledge in variable learning and retrieval situations becomes available. In this process, content-unspecific strategies and more formal principles to organize knowledge, e.g., taxonomic organizations become increasingly important.

The ongoing systematic study of the relational network between knowledge base, strategy use, and metamemory illustrates how memory development paradigms that were pursued in isolation in recent years are being integrated into a consistent research program (Nelson & Hudson, this volume; Ornstein et al., this volume).

WHAT IS MEMORY RESEARCH IN DEVELOPMENTAL PSYCHOLOGY THE RESEARCH OF?

Modern developmental memory research did not start with systematic observation of children's and adults' learning and memory behavior in their everyday world, but was concentrated on experimental studies conducted in psychological laboratories. The focus of these studies was primarily on the acquisition and impact of memory strategies on recall performance. This emphasis fixed the research program within one frame of reference: Children of various age-groups intentionally learned more or less structured material and were instructed to recall it as exactly as possible after a short retention interval. The paradigm was thus characterized by restricted learning and recall situations.

Even though it has been emphasized time and again that memorizing telephone numbers or lists of names, learning new words, or memorizing facts are real life activities as well, such claims have disregarded the peripheral nature of these "real world phenomena." Analysis of this research paradigm in terms of its ecological validity affords very few positive results.

Of course, external validity criteria do not always require that experimental designs be aligned with real life situations. Mook (1983) has pointed this out with some emphasis: "Ultimately, what makes research findings of interest is that they help us in understanding everyday life. That understanding, however, comes from theory or analysis of the mechanism; it is not a matter of generalizing the findings themselves. . . The validity of these generalizations is tested by their success at predictions and has nothing to do with the naturalness, representativeness or even non-creativity of the investigation on which they rest" (p. 386).

Yet in general, traditional developmental memory research has not even satisfied the theory-related criterion underscored by Mook. The biased selection of memory tasks (e.g., word lists) as predictors and as performance criteria obscured this deficiency. The tendency to underestimate the importance of the individual knowledge base for acquisition of new knowledge is both typical for and indicative of this class of approaches. "For the same reasons that the fish will be the last to discover water, developmental psychologists until recently devoted almost no attention to changes in children's knowledge of specific content. Such changes are so omnipresent that they seemed uninviting targets for study" (Siegler & Richards, 1982, p. 93).

In recent years content-specific knowledge has been incorporated into many research programs; this move has not only introduced a new variable into the analysis of memory development but has had the effect of creating a new paradigm. Instead of research focusing on the more exceptional conditions concerning the mastery of deliberate memory tasks (as for instance, intentionally learned word lists), memory is now analyzed with greater intensity as a "by-product" of comprehending information.

This alternative perspective has drawn attention to a number of other deficits that are highlighted in various chapters of this volume. The recommendations and expectations concerning future research appear to be based on the assumption that a better understanding of the functions that memory serves in human behavior and action will also allow a more adequate analysis of how memory processes function and develop (Dixon & Hertzog, this volume). Important to the development of this new paradigm is overcoming a purely cognitivistic view of memory performance and memory development that presumes that differences and changes in the memory system can be explained, as consequences of more or less effective information processing, independent from context. In contrast, Paris, Ceci et al., Verdonik, and Dixon and Hertzog (all this volume) emphasize on the influence of motivational, emotional and social factors on memory. Paris (this volume) has summarized this approach in four points: "First, remembering is often directed to achieve specific purposes that are embedded in other activities that serve larger functions for the individual. . . . Second, there are extrinsic and intrinsic consequences for remembering. . . . Anticipation of memory outcomes and consequences can lead to different strategic behavior depending on the values and expectations that are associated with the task. Third, everyday memory demands usually afford alternatives. One can choose to use one strategy rather than another, to try with more or less effort, or to avoid the situation entirely. Fourth, common tasks include environmental supports for performance such as physical cues, external models or standards, and periodic feedback, instruction, and encouragement from other people."

The impact of social context on memory development, only too often neglected in current research, is discussed in detail by Verdonik (this volume). Verdonik emphasizes the role of social memory processes, which emerge from communication between participants in social interaction, and which are the precondition for better social communication. He notes that individuals develop shared knowledge and shared meaning in social contexts on the basis of such social communication. In their chapter, Ceci et al. (this volume) give a systematic analysis of the interdependence of memory processes and social contexts and posit an ecological model of human memory. They demonstrate the utility of the model in investigation of both retrospective and prospective memory.

The present state of research can be summarized, with emphasis on the critical issues. In current memory development research,

• the use of memory strategies and the availability of domain-specific knowledge are often studied in isolation from each other and with totally neglecting motivational and social factors;

- intentional learning dominates over incidental learning;
- the acquisition and recall of verbal materials predominate, whereas non-verbal contents and representations are considered only rarely;
- short-term recognition and recall are emphasized whereas long-term memory and the multiple modes of human memorizing are rarely studied;
- research is primarily conducted under experimental conditions, with systematic observation of memory processes and performance in real life situations as exceptions;
- similar to developmental psychology in general, memory research has concentrated efforts on universal changes in memory processes and performance, and has largely neglected intra- and interindividual differences.

Examination of recent research on memory development justifies the conclusion that the efforts devoted to this area have produced results that are empirically rich and theoretically relevant. It also reveals, however, that only a very small portion of the phenomena of human memory and memory development has been studied thus restricting the generalizability of the research findings.

SOME PERSPECTIVES OF RESEARCH IN MEMORY DEVELOPMENT

One criterion for evaluating the state of a research area is whether there is a positive correlation between the increase in significant knowledge and new research questions. This volume contains much evidence showing that memory development research meets this requirement. In this section some current and future research trends are discussed in terms of a very simple classification: universal changes and individual differences in memory development.

The concept of *universal changes* has been addressed in two senses in developmental psychology. In the first sense, the concept refers to general laws governing behavioral change. Change is defined as resulting from the emergence of a set of necessary and sufficient external conditions. The other sense is that universal changes are subject to species-specific laws of human development, which apply to all individuals, largely in ways that are relatively unrelated to the individual's specific life history. In contrast to both, the concept of *individual differences* refers to quantitative and qualitative variations in the patterns, sequences, and causes of human behavior across the life span.

In view of the conceptual ambivalence of universal change, it is easy to understand why Cronbach (1957) in his classification of psychological research paradigms classed developmental psychology with the differential disciplines (and thus as a nonexperimental field) even though the study of individual differences in developmental psychology always was subordinate to research on universal change. The dominant focus on universal change stems from the major legacy from theory, genetic epistomology, and experimental research, and perhaps is also rooted in the Galilean belief implicitly held by many researchers that the study of universals is a little bit *more scientific* than the analysis of individual differences.

Most developmentalists would probably agree with the cautionary note voiced by Maratsos (1983) about the study of language acquisition: "Individual variations should not be allowed to overshadow the important general uniformities that are found and the important general acquisitional processes that necessarily underlie all children's acquisitions" (p. 776). And about as many would doubt Jensen's (1966) contrary claim: "Practically all of the subject matter of experimental psychology is, of course, eventually going to have to be reworked from the standpoint of individual differences" (p. 139).

Universal Changes in Memory Development

When analyzing memory development under extremely divergent environmental conditions in cross-cultural studies, one is particularly struck by the similarity among changes in memory performance and underlying cognitive processes (Wagner, 1981). This applies especially to memory development in childhood and in early adolescence. Moreover, the consistencies registered primarily involve the formal levels and features of representation of stored knowledge and the associated possibilities and limitations of the acquisition and retrieval of information rather than the contents of memory. This volume contains many examples of such similar developmental sequences.

The theoretical models developed concerning ontogenetic changes in memory are almost exclusively based on cross-sectional studies in which only a small number of learning and memory tasks were considered. Typical developmental functions are constructed from only a few developmental differences, and these are ultimately regarded as valid descriptions of memory changes in the individual. An almost inevitable consequence of this procedure is that many of the current models of memory development appear to be idealized. That is, "the traditional research strategy of comparing average, isolated memory performances with average performance-related memory processes in two or more age groups supports a tendency to overestimate the universality, intraindividual homogeneity, and interindividual consistency of developmental sequences. Thus, according to this approach, memory development is viewed as a regular rule-bound sequence of changes in cognitive competencies and related memory skills. Typically, deviations from this typical sequence have been ignored. If not ignored, they have been either treated as error variance or interpreted as individual acceleration or retardation, compared to the prototypical developmental sequence" (Schneider & Weinert, 1987, p. 31).

To overcome the shortcomings of idealized models of universal memory changes, a necessary first step is to supplement the comparative analysis of subject samples from different age groups by (a) studies that incorporate a wider range of different tasks, memory contents, and performance indicators (Knopf et al., this volume); (b) investigations that analyze differences and changes in memory performance within the frame of a broadly defined system of cognitive competences (Hussy & von Eye, this volume); (c) efforts to address not only memory performance but also memory development in the context of variations in personal beliefs, motives, and expectations (Paris, this volume); (d) approaches that seek to capture memory functioning within the context of social and cultural demands and opportunities (Verdonik, this volume); (e) longitudinal studies, which can test the implicit assumption that memory performance is subject to linear changes. Such a methodological approach is also needed because it will clarify the issue of the necessary, compensational, and sufficient prerequisites for changes in the memory system.

Individual Differences in Memory Development

To investigate variation in structure, process, and performance of the memory system across the life span, two points must be recognized. Intraindividual differences relate to variations in performance and competence across different tasks or at various measurement points within an individual. Knopf et al. (this volume) have demonstrated great intraindividual variance in memory performance of both children and older adults. Within this same perspective, Dixon and Hertzog (this volume) and Ceci et al. (this volume) urge that intraindividual variations in memory receive more attention: "There is a need for memory researchers to address the issues of *intra*individual variations and challenge the implicit 'trait-like' assumption about memory" (Ceci et al.). Furthermore, to achieve a better clarification of the stability of intraindividual differences over longer time periods, a systemic combination of cross-sectional, longitudinal, and training studies is needed. There is no other way to analyze the interrelationships among the acquisition of domain specific knowledge and skills, the associated transfer effects, and the more general changes in cognitive competencies that characterize memory development. The learning of skills and the acquisition of knowledge under controlled conditions are particularly significant in this context because more stable and more general cognitive differences are likely to manifest themselves in the periods of acquisition compared with periods in which stored knowledge is used to solve problems. Thus, if only the relations between differences in the individual knowledge base and domain-specific memory performance are considered, intraindividual knowledge differences are then confounded with a given state of knowledge at a given time, the past opportunities to learn and acquire such knowledge, and individual aptitudes to make use of such opportunities.

The problem of the variable relationships between developmental level and further acquisition processes is even more serious in the analysis of interindividual differences in memory development. When the performance differences of same-age individuals are compared at one time point, then the effects of the availability of special memory skills, more general cognitive developmental level, and last but not least, the role of "trait-like" memory capacities are seriously confounded. The relationships among stable basic characteristics of the individual cognitive system (e.g., speed of processing, total working memory capacity, acquisition capacity, retention capacity, accessibility of long-term memory), and the knowledge base available over an individual's life history is at present not clear. Whether the acquisition of exceptional memory skills and exceptional memory performance is generally possible across the life span (Ericsson, 1985), or whether fundamental differences in memory capacity are not modifiable by learning experiences (Wundt, 1920) is again an open question. Estes' (1982) appraisal of the current state of research is correspondingly skeptical concerning the resolution to this issue:

> Presumably, individual differences in the structural aspects of memory (referring to aspects that are independent of experience and that impose limits on the capacity and efficiency of operations of the system) would be set by individual anatomical and physiological characteristics innately determined to some major extent. Control processes refer to aspects of the system that do result from training and individual experience and are presumably under voluntary control—for example, the use of mnemonic strategies. . . . Because both structural and control processes must be implicated in every test used to assess memory or memory abilities, it follows that all of the results on individual differences . . . must have utilized measures of abilities in which structural and control processes are confounded. Consequently, no conclusion can be drawn from that body of work regarding individual differences in aspects of memory that should be relatively persistent over time. (p. 205)

It is unlikely that a method that will disentangle this confounding of individual differences in stable memory capacities and acquired memory skills will be developed in the near future. Research can, rather, set itself the more realistic goal of studying the changes of human memory in varying contexts to capture and distinguish between ephemeral and stable individual differences. Very recently some progress has been made in this direction (Dillon & Schmeck, 1983; Resnick & Neches, 1984; Weinert, Schneider & Knopf, 1988). One of the essential preconditions for such progress is that the weaknesses of each particular sampling paradigm (cross-sectional, longitudinal, and training studies) are partly compensated for by systematic combination of different approaches. This is especially the case when one wants to move beyond description and explanation of particular memory change phenomena to achieve a comprehensive understanding of universal changes and individual differences of the human memory system across the life span.

REFERENCES

Brown, A. L. (1978). Knowing when, where, and how to remember: A problem of metacognition. In R. Glaser (Ed.), *Advances in instructional psychology* (Vol. 1). Hillsdale, NJ: Lawrence Erlbaum Associates.

Carey, S. (1985). *Conceptual change in childhood.* Cambridge, MA: MIT Press.

Chi, M. T. H. (1978). Knowledge structure and memory development. In R. Siegler (Ed.), *Children's thinking: What develops?* Hillsdale, NJ: Lawrence Erlbaum Associates.

Chi, M. T. H. (1987). Domain-specific knowledge and metacognition. In F. E. Weinert & R. H. Kluwe (Eds.), *Metacognition, motivation, and learning.* Hillsdale, NJ: Lawrence Erlbaum Associates.

Cronbach, L. J. (1957). The two disciplines of scientific psvchology. *American Psychologist, 12,* 671–684.

Dillon, R. F., & Schmeck, R. R. (Eds.). (1983). *Individual differences in cognition* (Vol. 1). New York: Academic Press.

Ericsson, K. A. (1985). Memory skill. *Canadian Journal of Psychology, 39,* 188–231.

Estes, W. K. (1982). Learning, memory, and intelligence. In R. J. Sternberg (Ed.), *Handbook of Human Intelligence.* Cambridge, England: Cambridge University Press.

Flavell, J. H. (1971). First discussant comments: What is memory development the development of? *Human Development, 14,* 272–278.

Jäger, A. O., & Sitarek, E. (1985). *Implizite Fähigkeitskonzepte in der Kognition von Laien.* Unpublished manuscript, Institut für Psychologie der FU Berlin.

James, W. (1890). *The principles of psychology* (Vol. 1). New York: Dover.

Jensen, A. R. (1966). Individual differences in concept learning. In H. J. Klausmeier & C. W. Harris (Eds.), *Analysis of concept learning* (pp. 139–154). New York: Academic Press.

Körkel, J. (1987). *Die Entwicklung von Gedächtnis- und Metagedächtnisleistungen in Abhängigkeit von bereichsspezifischen Vorkenntnissen.* Frankfurt: Peter Lang.

Maratsos, M. (1983). Some current issues in the study of the acquisition of grammar. In J. H. Flavell & E. M. Markman (Eds.), *Handbook of child psychology: Cognitive development* (Vol. 3). New York: Wiley.

McGeoch, J. A., & Irion, A. L. (1952). *The psychology of human learning. 2nd ed.,* New York: Longmans, Green.

Mook, D. A. (1983). In defense of external invalidity. *American Psychologist, 38,* 379–387.

Munn, N. L. (1946). Learning in children. In L. Carmichael (Ed.), *Manual of child psychology.* New York: Wiley.

Piaget, J., & Inhelder, B. (1973). *Memory and intelligence.* New York: Basic Books.

Resnick, L. B., & Neches, R. (1984). Factors affecting individual differences in learning ability. In R. J. Sternberg (Ed.), *Advances in the psychology of human intelligence* (Vol. 2). Hillsdale, NJ: Lawrence Erlbaum Associates.

Schneider, W. (1985). Developmental trends in the metamemory-memory behavior relationship: An integrative review. In D. L. Forrest-Pressley, G. E. MacKinnon, & T. G. Waller (Eds.), *Cognition, metacognition, and human performance* (Vol. 1). New York: Academic Press.

Schneider, W., & Weinert, F. E. (1987). *Memory development: Universal changes and individual differences.* Unpublished manuscript, MPI für psychologische Forschung, München.

Siegler, R. S. & Kotovsky, K. (1986). Two levels of giftedness: Shall ever the twain meet? In R. J. Sternberg & J. E. Davidson (Eds.), *Conceptions of giftedness.* Cambridge, England: Cambridge University Press.

Siegler, R., & Richards, D. D. (1982). The development of intelligence. In R. J. Sternberg (Ed.), *Handbook of human intelligence.* Cambridge, England: Cambridge University Press.

Wagner, D. A. (1981). Culture and memory development. In H. C. Triandis & A. Heron (Eds.), *Handbook of cross-cultural psychology* (Vol. 4). Boston: Allyn & Bacon.

Weinert, F. E. (1986). Developmental variations of memory performance and memory-related knowledge across the life span. In A. B. Sørensen, F. E. Weinert, & L. R. Sherrod (Eds.), *Human development and the life course: Multidisciplinary perspectives.* Hillsdale, NJ: Lawrence Erlbaum Associates.

Weinert, F. E., Schneider, W., & Knopf, M. (1988). Individual differences in memory development across the life span. In P. B. Baltes, D. L. Featherman, & R. M. Lerner (Eds.), *Life-span development and behavior* (Vol. 8). Hillsdale, NJ: Lawrence Erlbaum Associates.

Wundt, W. (1920). *Erlebtes und Erinnertes.* Leipzig: Kröner.

Author Index

Subject Index

A

ability, 316
access, lack of, 169–170
activation, in a memory network, 59–61
affect memory, 377
age-effect, 200–204, 210
Alzheimer's disease, 366
amnesia, 358
animism
  children's misconception, 173–186
  implicit understanding by children, 175, 179
  taxonomy of, 175
anxiety, and memory performance, 229, 249, 251–252
aphasia, 358
applied psychology, 131
artificial intelligence, 195
attribution
  and metamemory, 89–91, 95–97, 114, 230
  paradigm, 184
  training, 85–87, 90, 115–116
attributional
  beliefs, and general strategy knowledge, 84–87
  processes, assessment, 94–95
autobiographic memory, 157, 161, 163–165
  role of verbal rehearsal, 163–164
automatic processes, 13, 35, 58, 364

automatization, 37–39, 305–306
availability heuristic, 234

B

behavioral memory, 376–377
blocked recall, 223

C

calibration strategy, 246–248, 250–252
call-up strategy, 53–58, 61, 63–68, 384
causal attributions, 90, 95, 114
central processing unit (CPU), 277–278, 282, 284, 290
certainty effect, 234
CIP, cf. complex information processing, structural and processual model
cloze test, 110
cognitions, contextual constraints on, 253
cognitive operator, 277–278, 280, 282, 290
cognitive psychology, 32, 52, 148, 195, 382
cognitive structures, in text comprehension and memorization, 199
cognitive tempo, as predictor of memory performance, 78, 84
coherent structure, 182–183